AF608593

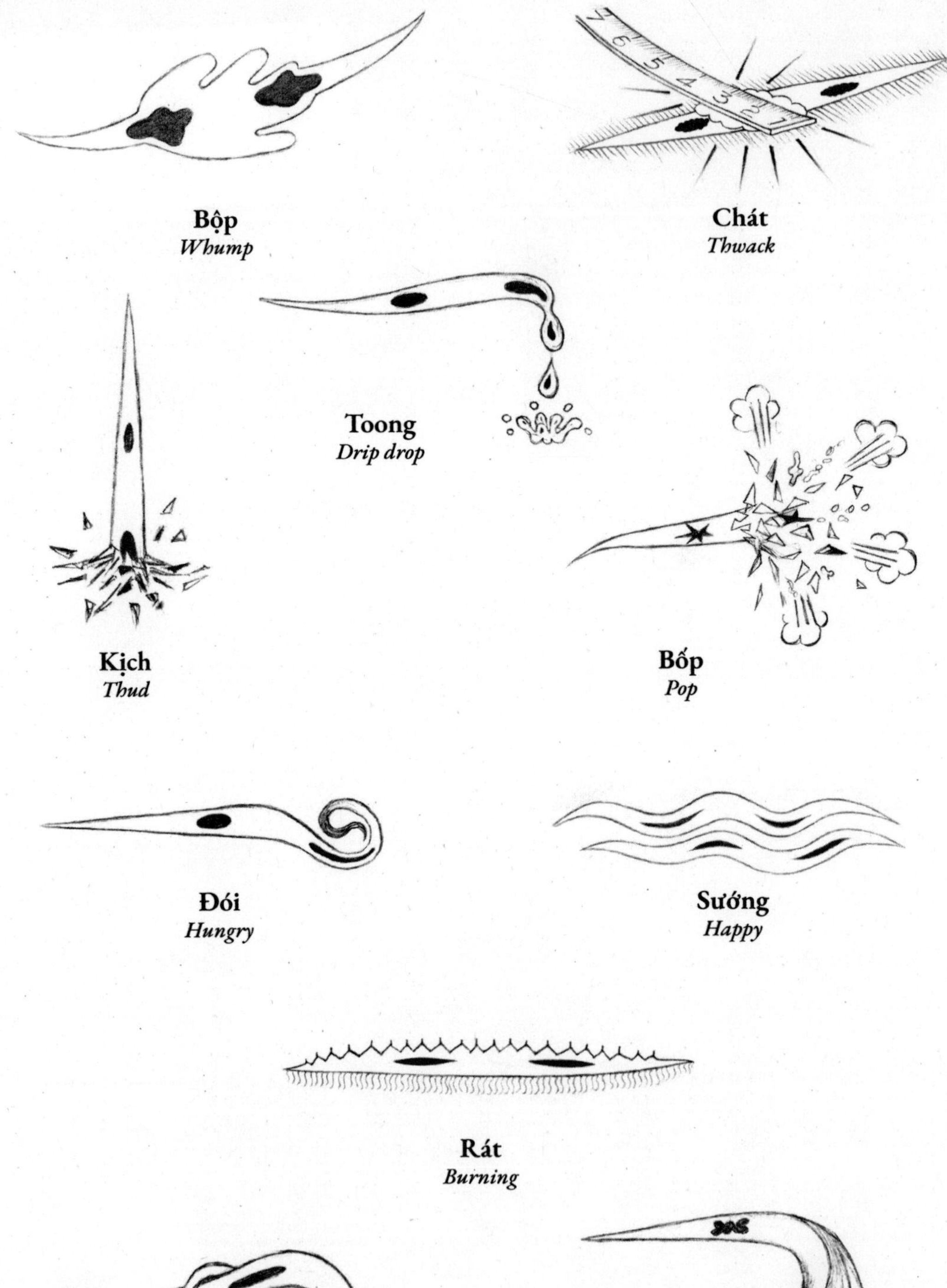

Lạnh
Cold

Tê
Numb

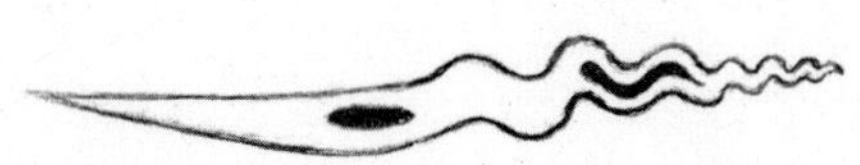

Sợ
Fear

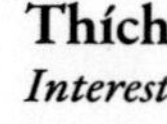

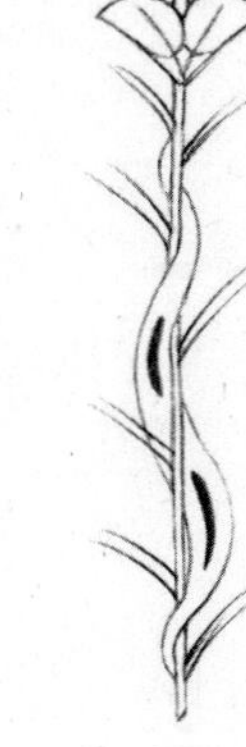

Thích
Interest

Ngượng
Embarrassment

Buồn
Sadness

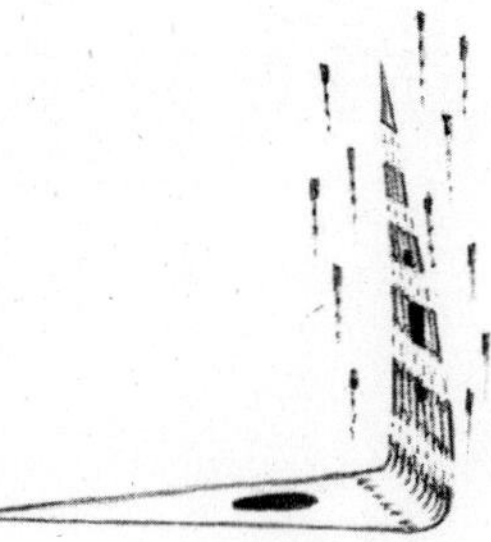

Mê
Infatuation

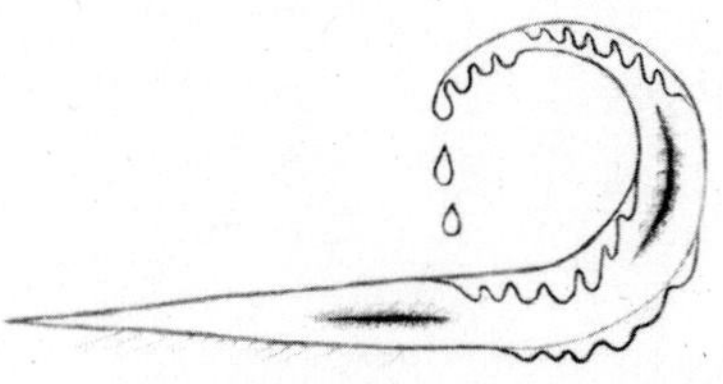

Chua
Sour

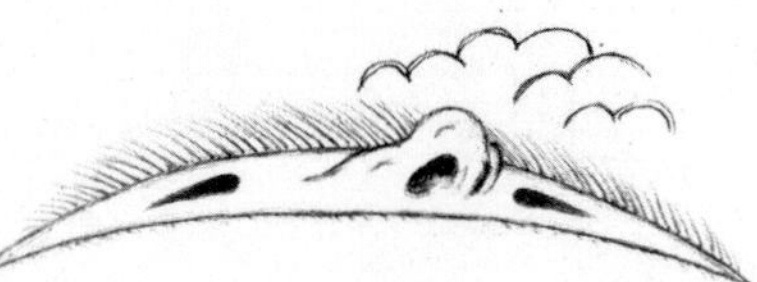

Nồng
Pungent

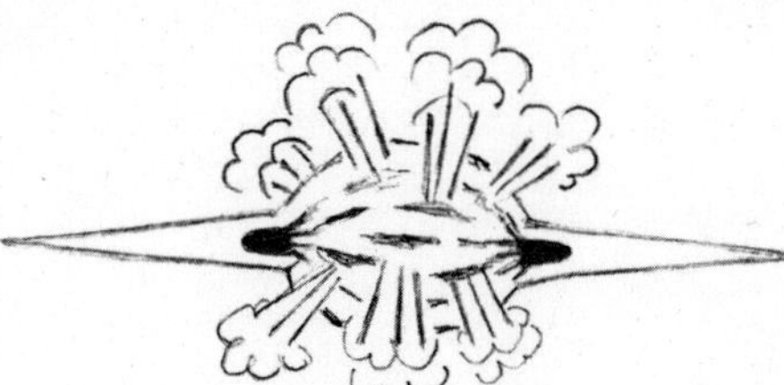

Cay
Hot spicy

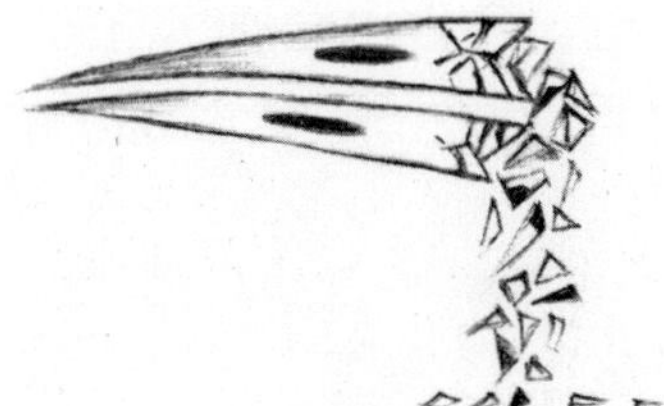

Mặn
Salty

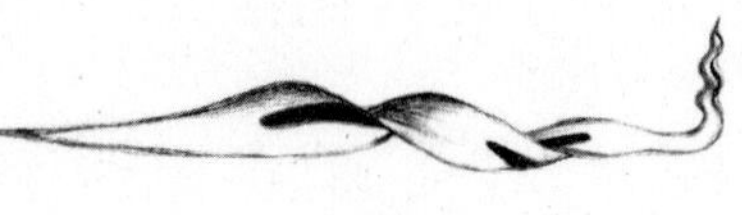

Chát
Tannic

Bộp, chát, toong, kịch, bốp
Đói, sướng, rát, lạnh, tê
Sợ, thích, ngượng, buồn, mê
Chua, nồng, cay, mặn, chát.

* Trần Lương wrote this poem as a self-reflective statement on his work and life. The poem is shared here in its original Vietnamese language for two reasons. First, translating the poem's meaning into English would be difficult due to the complexity of the language and its nuances. Second, preserving the poem's sonic effects, which are closely tied to its meaning, is best achieved by maintaining its original language. To convey the poem's meaning to non-Vietnamese speakers, Trần Lương has created a set of drawings.

The poem is a combination of single words that represent emotional states experienced by the artist, expressed as typical sounds. The poem's structure consists of four sentences, each presented as a single line containing five words. This five-word poetry structure, known as "thơ năm chữ" in Vietnamese, is one of the most common and familiar poetic forms in Vietnam. In this form, each line is composed of five words that are carefully coordinated in terms of rhyme and rhythm. This structure creates a sense of intimacy and ease of reading, making it particularly suitable for children's poetry.

Basic word translation

Onomatopoeia:

Bộp: The word bộp can be translated to "thud" in English (though not exactly). It's the sound of something hollow or filled with liquid falling and hitting the ground, like the sound of a coconut falling.

Chát: The sound of two hard objects hitting each other.

Toong: The sound of water droplets falling continuously can be described as "drip-drip" or "plink-plink" in English. These words mimic the sound of water intermittently hitting a surface.

Kịch: The word kịch in Vietnamese describes the sound of a fairly heavy and hard object hitting another heavy object or hitting a hard surface.

Bốp: The sound bốp in Vietnamese can be translated to "smack" or "thwack" in English. It describes the sound of a slap hitting a face, or a light bulb exploding.

Adjective:	Noun:	Adjective:
Đói: hungry	Sợ: fear	Chua: sour
Sướng: happy	Thích: interest	Nồng: pungent
Rát: burning	Ngượng: embarrassment	Cay: hot spicy
Lạnh: cold	Buồn: sadness	Mặn: salty
Tê: numb	Mê: infatuation	Chát: tannic

TRẦN LƯƠNG

Tầm Tã

CONCEIVED BY Biljana Ciric

SOAKED IN THE LONG RAIN

TABLE OF CONTENTS

PREFACE

NORA RAZIAN
Deputy Director and Head of Exhibitions and Programmes
Art Jameel

An accomplished artist working for over three decades, it is difficult to pin Trần Lương's practice to discrete categories; his is a career that flows freely and simultaneously between artist, curator, activist, mentor, director, architect and forest maker. What is evident across his many roles is his singular commitment to furthering both the place of art within Vietnam's ever changing social and political reality, as well as fostering an understanding of the role and responsibility of the artist within that context.

From his lyrical paintings drawing on memories of a childhood spent on the move and hiding from US bombs in the Vietnamese countryside, to his high energy single-man performances implicating audience members in their enactment, Trần Lương's multifaceted outputs span a wide range. His influential roles in setting up Nhà Sàn studio in the 1990s and organizing *Lim Dim*, Vietnam's first performance arts festival in 2004, demonstrate that his work is deeply embedded in and receptive to transformations in Vietnamese society. He is distinct in his ability and desire to push the role of the artist, as he so elegantly articulates in his interview with curator Biljana Ciric: "I don't separate between curating, organising events and my own work; for me, everything is one. Whatever I do is not for my own reputation but for everyone."

Trần Lương's commitment to art – and the practice of art – as an instigator of social relations and an agent of positive change, resonates deeply with the work of Art Jameel across exhibition making, research, learning and community engagement. As an institution whose geographic home extends through the Middle East and South/Southeast Asia, Art Jameel is committed to supporting exhibition making and scholarship around artists working within these geographies, whose legacy and impact on their communities and on art histories has yet to be fully recognised. We are honored that the Jameel Arts Centre in Dubai is hosting Trần Lương's first ever retrospective exhibition, celebrating his remarkable practice and significant legacy, and supporting new scholarship on his work through this publication – with the exhibition then touring in 2025-2026 to the Govett Brewster Gallery in New Plymouth, Aotearoa New Zealand, the Art Gallery of Western Australia in Perth, Australia and the Art Museum of the Guangzhou Academy of Fine Arts, Guangzhou, China.

The Art Jameel team has worked hand in hand with Lương and Biljana to bring this exhibition together, with a special thanks going to Giacomo Pietro Lamborizio, Zahra Mansoor, Naseef Ismail and Dina Al Khatib. We are thankful to Biljana Ciric for bringing Trần Lương's work to our attention and for her meticulous research and deep care in putting this exhibition and publication together. We are also deeply thankful to Trần Lương for his trust and for sharing so much of his work and life with us.

ZARA STANHOPE, Ringatohu / Director
and SIMON GENNARD, Ringahāpai Kaitakatū Tāreitanga me ngā Kohikohinga Hōu / Assistant Curator Contemporary Art and Collection
Govett-Brewster Art Gallery

Tầm Tã is notable as the first solo presentation of Trần Lương's work in Aotearoa New Zealand. When curator Biljana Ciric approached gallery curator Simon Gennard with her exhibition concept in early 2023, we agreed that there were multiple strategic reasons for presenting Lương's work to audiences in Aotearoa New Zealand.

Over his career Lương has been a constant provocateur and a leader. The first is only possible in Vietnam under the guise of a profession that can avoid appearing demonstrably oppositional – such as an artist – and even then, requires a person who can carefully navigate the complex web of state institutions and processes. Lương has this capability. The context of Communist Vietnam is infused in and informs his life practice not only as an artist but also as a mentor, curator, teacher, and founder of influential organisations in his country. It is a fact that his context is responsible for his unique work, and a reality that his practice is little known outside his country and parts of Southeast Asia.

At the Govett-Brewster Art Gallery | Len Lye Centre we are excited to host this project for the wealth of its offering. As part of the Gang of Five who graduated from the conservative École des Beaux-Arts, Hà Nội and began showing art several years before the commencement of Đổi-Mới, Lương alongside the other members of the group created a shift in the understanding of contemporary art in Vietnam. Subsequently casting aside painting as his primary medium, Lương took the surrounding environment and the perspectives he bought to it as the components for art making, tending towards socially conscious initiatives. His skill in enabling others to, often inadvertently, find themselves participants in performative or relational works and being confronted perhaps by previously unthought cultural tensions, are amongst the types of purposeful outcomes activated by Lương's collective engagements.

Zara Stanhope's first encounter with Lương's art was during a research visit to Vietnam around 2004, in a memorable introduction to his paintings at Suzanne Lecht's

Art Vietnam gallery in Hà Nội. However, it was not until later research visits that they had the chance to meet, when Lương would typically invite her to his home and connect her with other artists. Building community through contemporary art and facilitating engagement with new ways of thinking about the world we share, are key principles for us at the Govett-Brewster, sensibilities that the artist shares.

As this exhibition and publication demonstrate, Lương has been instrumental in the development of the very possibility of critically engaged, radically inclined artistic practice within post-Đổi-Mới Vietnam. The projects together track Tran Lương's early painterly experimentation and his direct engagement with varied communities who more often find themselves spoken on behalf of, or else excluded entirely, within sites of exhibition-making in urban centres. The project also considers Trần Lương's methods of institution-building within a state system which places heavy restrictions on the social and political claims artists are safe to make, and the modes of expression through which actions are articulated. The artist continues to influence and support generations of artists living in Vietnam, insisting on the critical possibilities of practice and participation, and affirming the role artists can play in metabolising complex political, historical and economic realities, and imagining the arrangement of social life anew.

The Govett-Brewster Art Gallery has, since its founding in 1970, sought to provide conditions within which artists and communities can share radical propositions, opening room for dialogue that would enable us to rethink the everyday conditions we inhabit. The Govett-Brewster is situated upon the lands of Ngāti Te Whiti hapū (sub-tribe), of Te Atiawa iwi (tribe). The gallery sits under the shadow of the ancestral mountain Taranaki, within a wider region which has, since the 1860s been witness to the widespread confiscation of indigenous Māori lands through violent means by New Zealand's colonial government, followed by the development of an extractive economy heavily dependent firstly on intensive dairy-based agriculture, and more recently, energy production – most notably natural gas. Situated with Te Moana nui-a Kiwa (the Pacific) the region is also home to growing diasporic communities from many contexts, including Southeast Asia. It is from these local conditions that our priorities for exhibition-making and programming depart.

The ambitions of the Govett-Brewster have always been twofold: to seek to be attentive to local histories of place, accountable to and reflective of those who have called this place home for generations, as well as to be connective to broader contexts – the region known as the Asia-Pacific and more globally – seeking opportunities for artists as individual practitioners, organisers, conduits, or at times antagonists and always in relationship, be it culturally, conceptually or historically. This exhibition offers audiences an opportunity to engage with the work of an artist whose influence within Vietnamese culture is profound and wide ranging, as well as it opens the possibility of finding routes to consider points of commonality and solidarity from within two historically distinct contexts – Aotearoa and Vietnam. Finally, the exhibition enables us to build on networks for experimentation and collaborative relationships between artists, communities and institutions across the Asia-Pacific region, at times in parallel, and at times in opposition to Aotearoa's historical diplomatic and cultural outlook towards the centres of power in the northern hemisphere. We are heartfelt in our thanks to Trần Lương for expressing as an artist what a democratic, inquiring and respectful life could look like, Biljana Ciric for her curatorial rigour and the generosity and tenacity she has brought to this collaboration, and the institutional partners who enabled the realisation of the exhibition and publication.

RACHEL CIESLA
Lead Creative, Simon Lee Foundation Institute of Contemporary Asian Art
The Art Gallery of Western Australia

The Art Gallery of Western Australia in Boorloo (Perth) is delighted to partner with Jameel Arts Centre, Dubai; Govett-Brewster Art Gallery, New Plymouth; and the Art Museum of Guang Zhou Academy of Fine Arts to present the first retrospective of Trần Lương, and to co-publish this accompanying book.

Trần Lương is one of the boldest artists working today. He is widely recognised for his critically significant contributions to the development of contemporary art in Vietnam in terms of subject matter, production methods, conceptual frameworks and resistance to State censorship.

The exhibition at AGWA provides Australian audiences with an expansive overview of Trần's practice over the past three decades, showcasing his critical focus on environmental issues alongside an ongoing engagement with class struggles and public life.

The diversity of aesthetic forms and the breadth of social and political engagement that comprise Trần's practice are reflected in this exhibition and publication. They span his early ecologically minded expressionistic paintings and works on paper made before 1997 and involvement in the experimental artist group, Gang of Five, through to his video installations and community-based performances of the 2000s, his pivotal role in the creation of alternative spaces for contemporary art and ongoing support of community development projects across Vietnam.

By making use of the participatory and discursive strategies of community-based art that include acts of connectivity, collectivity and shared resistance – experiences in which 'we-are-(all)-in-this-together-but-we-are-not-one-and-the-same' – his artistic career troubles the categories of artist, curator, activist and educator at a time when singular positions are becoming increasingly entrenched.[1]

Like the artist himself, this show embraces the specificity and the complexity of Vietnam and the wider Asian region, thereby grounding its politics and its contribution to one of the most urgent themes in contemporary culture – the climate

1. Rosi Braidotti, *Posthuman Knowledge* (Cambridge: Polity Press, 2019), 54.

crisis, in the multiple perspectives embodied by the many art spaces, networks and communities of which Trần is a part.

I would like to thank the curator of this exhibition, Biljana Ciric, for developing such a gently powerful presentation of Trần Lương's work. It is one that helps us to understand the importance of Trần's artistic practice across the different social, political and cultural contexts of Australia and Southeast Asia.

Thank you, Trần Lương, for sharing your life's work with AGWA; your exhibition is profoundly resonant most especially as it does not cultivate despair but points towards the building of new worlds, together.

CHEN XIAOYANG
Doctor of Anthropology
Executive Deputy Director of Art Museum, Guangzhou Academy of Fine Arts

At the end of 2019, just a month before the onset of the pandemic, the Art Museum of the Guangzhou Academy of Fine Arts announced plans for the *Trans-Southeast Asia Triennial* program. Based on our understanding of the history and contemporary reality of this region, as well as our vision for innovative museum practices, our aim was to engage in a dialogue and foster exhibition exchanges with this complex region. Embracing a fluid and decentralized curatorial approach, we opted for "trans" rather than "pan" to convey the concept of "fan" in Chinese. Our goal was to promote constructive dialogue within an inclusive view of art history, facilitating a dispassionate framework for cross-cultural communication and deepening conversation and interaction between the many neighbours in the region. Unfortunately, our plans for field trips throughout Southeast Asia were thwarted by international travel restrictions during the pandemic. Consequently, we pivoted to a collaborative approach, enlisting the expertise of several seasoned curators specialising in contemporary Southeast Asian art, and Biljana Ciric was the first curator with whom we partnered to realise our vision.

The first phase of Biljana's curatorial work was the presentation of two thematic exhibitions in Guangzhou in March 2021, centred around the theme of *Repetition as a Gesture Towards Deep Listening*. This project aimed to prompt a reconsideration of how we perceive and engage with the production of knowledge through exhibitions during periods of pandemic and social separation, by revisiting important exhibitions and public moments relevant to the local context through the lens of repetition.

Within this framework, we revisited the *Spirit of Friendship* exhibition, originally organised by the Factory Contemporary Arts Center in Ho Chi Minh City in 2017. This exhibition reviewed the artistic practices of 25 important contemporary art groups working in Vietnam during the period from 1975 to 2020, following the end of the U.S.-Vietnam War and the reunification of North and South

Vietnam. These diverse art collectives, operating outside the official cultural systems in both the North and the South of the country, relied on friendship and mutual support among artists and groups. Through their creative expressions, exhibitions and various forms of gathering and discussion, they constantly reflected on and responded to the realities and historical issues arising from Vietnam's tumultuous social change process, which had been shaped by many years of war.

The second phase of Biljana's project involved curating a solo exhibition of works by Trần Lương, an artist who has been the heart and soul of Vietnamese contemporary art. Unfortunately, we had to postpone this exhibition for various reasons. However, this delay gave us a chance to gain further insight into the profound thoughts and motivations underpinning Trần Lương's multifaceted practices as an artist, curator and the "godfather" of Vietnamese contemporary art.

Vietnam and China have comparable structures and mechanisms in developing contemporary art. Following the Government of Vietnam's reform and opening in 1986, Vietnamese society underwent a social transformation and economic take-off. Against this background, and much like China's 1985 New Wave Art Movement, Vietnamese contemporary artists began to leave the Academy of Fine Arts and National Art Association system. Instead, they sought to address the root of the problem by reflecting on the Soviet model of the academy system and the even earlier colonial French Academy of Fine Arts knowledge system. This led them to explore new artistic outlets, often challenging irrational taboos in societal and artistic mechanisms.

One notable example is the artist group Gang of Five, established in 1983, of which Trần Lương was a member. Gang of Five became known for questioning customs as a means to express diverse viewpoints. Challenging unreasonable rules and established social norms through artistic expressions and actions has become a significant feature of Trần Lương's artistic practice.

In his critique and reflection on irrational mechanisms, Trần Lương never stops exploring his practice as a means of expressing views and attitudes. In Vietnam, where infrastructure for contemporary art is lacking, he organises and curates art exhibitions for many artist collectives, while also supporting young artists by helping them to showcase their work to a broader audience. He has even extended his work beyond the confines of the art world, engaging with various communities in broader social contexts.

Trần Lương brings a deep understanding of the essence of contemporary art and an open-minded approach to his socially engaged art practice. Through this engagement, he has gained deeper insights into real Vietnamese society and the contemporary world and has taken part in actions to promote community development and social change.

Trần Lương's artistic career and body of work have profoundly touched and inspired us, offering us an in-depth understanding of both the developments and the predicaments of contemporary art in Vietnam. We hope that this touring solo exhibition will allow more researchers and audiences interested in the multifaceted development of global contemporary art, the opportunity to engage with his work, grasp its significance and derive diverse inspiration and reflections from his practice.

TRẦN LƯƠNG'S PERFORMANCE OF COMPLICIT RESISTANCE: LOCATING ITS INNOVATIONS IN VIETNAMESE AND SOUTHEAST ASIAN CONTEMPORARY ART AND PARTICIPATIVE PRACTICE HISTORY.

by Iola Lenzi

A figure covered from head-to-toe with rice, sifts coal dust through his fingers in a provincial mining community. The same man orchestrates collective teeth-brushing on the banks of Phnom Penh's Tonle Sap River. The artist exposes his bare torso to a barrage of lashes administered by a scarf-wielding audience member. This is the sensory-enriching, viewer-empowering performance practice of Hà Nội artist-curator Trần Lương (b. 1960).

In this study, Trần Lương's performances *Steam Rice Man* (2001), *Moving Forwards and Backwards* (2006) and *Welts* (2007) are analysed and compared to determine their aesthetic-conceptual mechanics and how these intersect with public space. Their pioneering traits are underlined, showing how the three pieces are located in, and expand Southeast Asian and Vietnamese performance and contemporary art. Providing context for Trần Lương's creative explorations, relevant aspects of Southeast Asian contemporary art history are evoked, followed by a snapshot of Vietnam's emerging contemporary scene of the 1990s where Trần Lương rose to prominence. Against this backdrop, the paper locates Trần Lương's expressive breakthroughs in Vietnamese and regional art history.

PERFORMATIVITY AND PERFORMANCE: CENTRALITY TO EARLY SOUTHEAST ASIAN CONTEMPORARY ART

Researchers have lamented the absence of a comprehensive, pan-Southeast Asian study of performance art beyond existing essays focusing on selected artists or practices in specific regional locales.[1] Nevertheless, foregoing a compartmentalised study of media and genre to scrutinise Southeast Asian contemporary art holistically, the beginnings of regional contemporary art in the 1970s reveal artworks of disciplinary integration, including performative components. In these pieces, form, sign and unscripted audience performative action are conjoined. Indeed,

1. For more on this dearth, see: Eva Bentcheva, Annie Jael Kwan, Roger Nelson, "Editorial Introduction: Pathways of Performativity in Contemporary Art of Southeast Asia," *Southeast of Now: Directions in Contemporary and Modern Art in Asia*, 6, no. 1 (March 2022): 3-9. For texts spotlighting specific locales and artists see: Clara Ling Boon Ing and Sarena Abdullah, "Socially Responsive Performance Art: The History and Context of Selected Performance Art in Malaysia," *Wacana Seni Journal of Arts Discourse 22* (September 2023): 1–16; Nora A. Taylor, "Sedimented Acts: Performing History and Historicizing Performance in Vietnam, Myanmar and Singapore," *Southeast of Now: Directions in Contemporary and Modern Art in Asia*, Vol.6, 1 (March 2022): 13-31; Wee W.-L., "Body and Communication: the 'ordinary' art of Tang Da Wu," *Theatre Research International* 42, no. 3 (2018): 286-306; Roger Nelson, "Performance is contemporary: Performance and its documentation in visual art in Cambodia," *Udaya, Journal of Khmer Studies* 12 (2014): 95-143, among others. Also: Steven Tonkin, *Political Acts-Pioneers of Performance Art in Southeast Asia* (Melbourne: Victoria Art Centre Trust, 2017).

performativity – whereby members of the public penetrate a piece's semantic-formal structure with critical agency by producing something or doing something over time – emerges as an early and distinctive feature of contemporary Southeast Asian art linked with social awareness, emblematic of the region's contemporary turn in the 1970s.[2]

An early example of performative art soliciting audience involvement was produced by FX Harsono (b. 1949), a founding member of the Indonesian artist group Gerakan Seni Rupa Baru (GSRB, the New Art Movement).[3] Despite being a small avant-garde tackling Indonesian social tensions, in contrast to institutionally-endorsed non-political decorative painting, GSRB and core members FX Harsono and Jim Supangkat changed Indonesian art history with conceptual, socially-critical aesthetics – today identified as contemporary art. Harsono's 1977 piece *Apa yang anda lakukan jika krupuk ini adalah pistol beneran?* (What Would You Do If These Crackers Were Real Pistols?) was an ephemeral piece that was destroyed long ago. When Harsono described it to me in 2012, I was struck by how its mechanics are comparable to those of more recent Southeast Asian contemporary art: socially-meaningful iconography; incongruity of aesthetics and materials in relation to theme; and a title-question intended to mobilise viewers. The work aligns form and concept to activate intercession around the violence of Indonesian life under military dictatorship. Beyond 1970s Indonesia, the piece, with its inexhaustible iterations, continues to resonate with viewers today, affirming its conceptual underpinnings.[4]

The artistically polished, audience-inviting rice-cracker gun installation embodies the aesthetic-conceptual critical DNA of Southeast Asian contemporary art, as it has been surveyed in increasing detail since the 1990s.[5] Relevant to Trần Lương's works, is the rice-cracker gun installation's capacity to engage viewers inside and outside institutional walls without curatorial explanation and to form a new work with each viewer's intervention.

From the 1970s to the 1990s, Southeast Asian contemporary art languages, characterised by socially-engaged conceptual approaches, were but a tiny fraction of regional production dominated by mainstream art. Yet, even as artists were unaware of each other, selected pieces reveal comparable strategies for enlisting audiences on sensitive societal topics.[6] The inclusion of new expressions such as 'performativity' served multiple purposes, particularly in navigating Southeast Asian illiberal contexts. Firstly, they were effective at bridging the artwork/viewer separation,

2. Iola Lenzi, "Conceptual Strategies in Southeast Asian Art: a local narrative," in *Concept Context Contestation: Art and the collective in Southeast Asia*, Lenzi ed. (Bangkok: Bangkok Art and Culture Centre, 2014), 10-25.

3. GSRB Manifesto, see Jessica Lack, *Why Are We 'Artists'?: 100 World Art Manifestos* (London: Penguin, 2017), 243-244; for a detailed discussion of Harsono's *Apa yang anda* Lenzi, "Conceptual Strategies in Southeast Asia: a local strategy", 12.

4. The piece's steel molds and hundreds of cracker-pistols were remade for *Concept Context Contestation: Art and the collective in Southeast Asia*, BACC & Goethe, 2013-2019. The piece, curated in different forms in five Southeast Asian cities, 2013-2019, worked effectively in each.

5. Tatehata, Guillermo, Supangkat et al., *Asian Modernism: Diverse Development in Indonesia, the Philippines, and Thailand* (Tokyo: Japan Foundation Asia Centre, 1995); Apinan Poshyananda et al., *Contemporary Art in Asia Traditions/Tensions* (New York: Asia Society Galleries, 1996); Caroline Turner ed., *Art and Social Change–Contemporary Art in Asia and the Pacific* (Canberra: Pandanus Books/ANU, 2005); Iola Lenzi ed. *Negotiating Home History and Nation–two decades of contemporary art in Southeast Asia 1991-2011* (Singapore: SAM, 2011); Lenzi, "Conceptual Strategies", 2014; Asia Pacific Triennials of Contemporary Art texts, from 1993; Fukuoka Asian Art Triennale texts, from 1999.

facilitating audience immersion in otherwise proscribed social debates that the works referred to. This immersion in socially-questioning pieces helped deflect censorship by diluting responsibility for provocative ideas among participants. Finally, performance art's inherent ambiguity and lack of material form made it difficult to patrol and censor.

Performativity, detected in the 1970s, was joined by performance, whereby artists used their bodies and movement as expressive elements. In 1980s Singapore, pluri-disciplinary events were staged in private galleries by artists, such as Cheo Chai-Hiang (b. 1946) and the trio S. Chandrasekaran (b. 1959), Goh Ee Choo (b. 1962) and Salleh Japar (b. 1962), whose *Trimurti* comprised installation and body-action. Other Singapore artists took performance into urban zones, notably the Art Commandos, a short-lived group of visual artists, musicians and dancers helmed in 1988 by Vincent Leow (b. 1961). However, performance art (as opposed to spontaneous public-space dance or theatrical spectacle) was introduced by multimedia artist Tang Da Wu (b. 1943), whose body-action works, in public or institutional spaces, probed social topics. With Amanda Heng (b. 1951), Koh Nguang How (b. 1963) and others, Tang formed The Artists Village (TAV), a still-thriving collective whose members were early proponents of performance art characterised by its use of space, time, movement and audience awareness; attributes shared with performance art in wider contexts, as described by RoseLee Goldberg in 1998. However, beyond these generic traits, The Artists Village (TAV) and other Southeast Asian performance were contextually-responsive, as discussed below.[7] Unsurprisingly, a close study of works has revealed that performativity and performance in some cases emerged in Southeast Asia in response to specific contextual needs.[8] Tang's social performances, particularly those in public spaces, had the potential to galvanise ordinary peoples' critical response. His piece *Life Boat* (1989), referencing stateless Vietnamese boat people and refugee issues more broadly, was performed unauthorised on a pedestrian shopping street in central Singapore.[9] In the 1990s and 2000s, other Singapore-based artists, some from TAV, produced socially-themed performance. Among them, Vincent Leow (b. 1961), Lee Wen (1957-2019), Amanda Heng (b. 1951), Josef Ng (b. 1972), Zai Kuning (b. 1964), Juliana Yasin (1970-2014), Kai Lam (b. 1974) and Jeremy Hiah (b. 1972), used their bodies as moving spectacle and/or actioning objects. Josef Ng's New Year's eve 1993/1994 performance *Brother Cane*, flagged draconian police treatment of Singapore's gay community and

6. Iola Lenzi, *Power, Politics and the Street: contemporary art in Southeast Asia after 1970* (London: Lund Humphries, 2024).

7. RoseLee Goldberg, *Performance: Live Art Since the 60s* (New York: Thames & Hudson, 1998); Kwok Kian Woon, Wee W.-L. et al, *The Artists Village 20 Years On* (Singapore: SAM, 2009); Koh Nguang How and Iola Lenzi, "The Artists Village and the birth of contemporary art in Singapore," in *Concept Context Contestation: Art and the Collective in Southeast Asia*, Iola Lenzi ed. (Bangkok: BACC, 2014), 190-191.

8. Lenzi, "Conceptual Strategies," 2014.

9. Lenzi, "Conceptual"; Iola Lenzi, *Stealing Public Space: How Southeast Asian Contemporary Art Co-opts the City and Other Collective Sites*, (Singapore: The Substation, 2020), 11.

spawned a public decency scandal and court case. As a result, performance in Singapore was suspended for a decade, and was stringently monitored thereafter.

In early 1990s Thailand, Chumpon Apisuk (b. 1948), Paisan Plienbangchang (1961-2015), Vasan Sitthiket (b. 1957), and Jittima Pholsawek (1959-2023), among others, produced socially-incisive performance. Some took their works into Bangkok streets, for instance, Vasan's 1993 *Top Boot on my Head*[10] and Manit Sriwanichpoom's 1997 shopping-cart performances, *Pink Man Begins*. Chumpon, wearing curator and organiser hats, founded Southeast Asia's first international performance festival *Asiatopia* in 1998. In Indonesia, Heri Dono (b. 1960) merged wayang (traditional Javanese narrative puppetry integrating classical stories and commentary on contemporary life), fiery vernacular references to animist culture, and body-action in public space to create *Kuda Binal* (1992), a chaotic nocturnal performance enlisting workers from the community.[11] Arahmaiani Feisal (b. 1961) and Iwan Wijono (b. 1971) also harnessed performance to articulate critical ideas about Indonesian life. Arahmaiani's 1996 *Handle Without Care* at the *2nd Asia Pacific Triennial of Contemporary Art (APT2)* is among the pieces from this period that have become iconic. Many of the performance practitioners mentioned above are self-declared activist–artists, highlighting the connection between performance art and social activism in Southeast Asia, which has yet to be more thoroughly explored.

Southeast Asia's contemporary turn revolved around new aesthetic-conceptual modes, often driven by a social function that engaged viewers through the erosion of the conventional separation between artwork and audience, a notion posited by the Western art academy and reinforced by dominant international high-modern art precepts of the past century. Performance was intrinsic to this regional turn, serving as a familiar, but potentially coded language of resistance, especially compelling for artists working in tightly controlled conditions. The familiarity derived from the performance genre's premodern history within regional, multidisciplinary, traditional and secular entertainment, as well as sacred ritual practices presented in communal spaces – which were still somewhat pervasive – provided contemporary performance art basic legibility.[12] Moreover, even in its traditional form, regional secular performative practice could be employed to challenge authority, with the form's inherent ephemerality affording the performer protection.[13]

The versatility of performance and performativity

10. Bae Myungli, Seng Yu Jin, Suzuki Katsuo, eds. *Awakenings: Art and Society in Asia–1960s-1990s* (Singapore: NGS, 2019), plate 87, p.193.

11. See Elly Kent, Virginia Hooker, Caroline Turner eds., *Living Art-Indonesian Artists Engage Politics, Society and History* (Canberra: ANU Press, 2023), 85-88.

12. Anthony Reid, *Southeast Asia in the Age of Commerce 1450-1860*, vol.1 (Chiangmai: Silkworm Books, 1988), 202-203; 210.

13. Tony Day and Sarah Weiss, "Performance in Southeast Asian History," in *Routledge Handbook of Southeast Asian History*, Norman Owen ed. (London/NY: Routledge, 2014), 300.

cannot be understated, a point raised by Jittima Pholsawek (referenced above), one of Thailand's experimental performance artists who organised feminist *Womanifesto* exhibitions in the 1990s. In 2018, Jittima underlined the fluidity of performance when she called an object-installation performative.[14] Southeast Asian performance, when analysed over decades, reveals itself as well-suited to forming cryptic yet socially trenchant conversations that are intelligible to broad audiences.

Where, then, do Vietnamese art and Trần Lương's community performances fit into this expressive, regional metamorphosis? As elsewhere in Southeast Asia, in Vietnam the contemporary turn and social-political realities, are intertwined.

14. Pongpan Suriyapat, Interview with Jittima "Len" Pholsawek *On Curating* Issue 41/June 2019, Centres/ Peripheries – Complex Constellations Notes on Curating, https://www.on-curating.org/issue-41-reader/interview-with-jittima-len-pholsawek.html.

VIETNAMESE ARTWORLD CONTEXTS: THE MAINSTREAM AND THE MARGINS

In 1986, following policy decisions taken at the Communist Party's 6th National Congress, Vietnam radically changed economic direction, abandoning its centrally planned economy for a socialist-oriented market system. These reforms, known as *Đổi Mới* (renovation), brought sudden and sweeping shifts that, while improving citizen prosperity, irreversibly altered Vietnamese social and cultural life. By 1995, trade sanctions and travel embargos that had long kept the country closed to Western Bloc goods and visitors were lifted, and consumer products, businessmen and international popular culture flowed in.

Preceding this opening, in the 1980s, a few painters were already experimenting outside mandatory socialist realism, exploring abstraction and expressionism forbidden in the North for decades due to the imperialist associations of such styles. Trần Lương recounts his and a few of his classmates' interest in working outside socialist realism in the 1980s, while academic Natalia Kraevskaia (based in Vietnam since 1983 and cofounder of the Hà Nội art space/gallery Salon Natasha) recalls sporadic early-1980s underground exhibitions of non-authorised paintings, organised in private homes in Hà Nội.[15] Evidence of pre-*Đổi Mới* permissiveness appears in the form of an exhibition catalogue produced when the Vietnam Visual Artists Association (now Vietnam Fine Arts Association) organised a 1984 Bùi Xuân Phái (1924-1988) solo exhibition including cityscapes and portraits. Phai, who had been excluded from official culture by the regime for having joined the *Nhân Văn-Giai Phẩm* movement which pressed

15. Natalia Kraevskaia, personal communication with the author, December 15, 2015.

for greater intellectual and cultural freedom in the 1950s, did not produce socialist realist painting, and thus had not had a formal show in decades.[16] Phái's paintings were not avant-garde, but his 1984 Hà Nội exhibition signalled loosening cultural rules.

Đổi Mới, which catalysed Vietnam's 1990s global integration, provided painters access to the international art market and caused Hà Nội's art arena to grow. However, a small minority of artists, spurning a return to established styles, cultivated fresh expressive idioms to contend with the complicated times, as Vietnam opened to the world and to capitalism – nearly overnight.[17]

Art historiographies examining late-20th century Vietnamese art predominantly focus on mainstream painting of the 1990s, or what art historian Nora Taylor calls the "standard classification."[18] These historiographies note the decade's limited expressive evolution, which authors explain is due to Vietnam's semi-closed status and stringent cultural control.[19] These accounts, which posit that Vietnamese contemporary art emerged after 2000 when practitioners gained access to world art via the internet or travel, have ignored the alternative art of the 1990s that was sprouting on the margins of the mainstream. A 2019 article acknowledged two vanguard Hà Nội artists of the 1990s (unnamed, but inferred via brief descriptions of their work), but they are deemed innovative only within Vietnam, their production viewed as non-contemporary since it was not aligned with contemporaneous New York conceptual art, which these Hà Nội practitioners did not know.[20]

But do creators need foreign models to innovate? And how is contemporary art defined? Decades ago, other art historians, myself included, analysed selected practices in Hà Nội in the 1990s as early Vietnamese contemporary art – part of Southeast Asian contemporary art – framed by scholarship in the 1990s and later, that recognised regional contemporary art modes since the 1970s.[21] This production is also part of global contemporary art as articulated by Terry Smith.[22] Typically, it is minority vanguards, as opposed to mainstream figures that drive expressive evolution. Corroborating this, a clutch of iconoclasts from Hà Nội were included in Asia-Pacific and European contemporary art exhibitions during the 1990s, indicating a sea change that curators and critics detected ahead of art historians.[23]

Thus, Vietnam's late 20th century art arena devolved into distinct channels as a handful of Hà Nội artists diverged from the conventional portrayal of floaty women and rural

16. Bùi Xuân Phái's 1984 Hà Nội solo *Triển Lãm Tác Phẩm Hội Họa của Họa Sĩ Bùi Xuân Phái* (Hà Nội: Hội nghệ sĩ tạo hình Việt Nam, 1984) [Paintings exhibition of Bùi Xuân Phái] Dec 22, 1984–Jan 22, 1985.

17. Iola Lenzi, "Early contemporary art in Vietnam: Đổi Mới shift as spur of innovation in globalizing 1990s-Hanoi," *Russian Journal of Vietnamese Studies* 6, no.1 (2022): 77-78.

18. Nora A. Taylor, *Painters in Hanoi, An Ethnography of Vietnamese Art*, Sec. Ed. (Singapore: NUS Press, 2009), "Preface" xvi, where the author specifies her book's 1990s purview as mainstream art, which she labels art of "the standard classification."

19. Nora A. Taylor, "What is Đổi Mới in Art?" (2011-2012) on Southeast Asia Digital Library, Northern Illinois University URL: https://sea.lib.niu.edu/seadl/whatisdoimoi ; Bùi Thị Thanh Mai, "Nghiên Cứu Xác Định Thời Gian Và Đặc Điểm: Mỹ Thuật Hậu Đổi Mới" [Periodisation & traits of post-renovation fine art], *Nghiên cứu Mỹ thuật* [Fine Arts Studies], 6-19. Both texts assert the marginal evolution of 1990s Vietnamese art, with the authors proposing contemporary art's emergence post-2000.

20. Nora A. Taylor and Pamela Corey, "Đổi Mới and the Globalization of Vietnamese Art," *Journal of Vietnamese Studies*, v.14, 1 (2019): 1-34, specifically page 25.

21. Lenzi, *Negotiating Home History and Nation*, SAM, 2011; Lenzi, "Conceptual Strategies: a local Narrative", BACC, 2014; Đào Mai Trang ed., *12 Contemporary artists*

idylls in standard classification painting, opting instead for multimedia works and innovative graphic forms. Among those dissatisfied with standard painting, Trần Lương stands out. After inventing semi-abstract pictorial codes in the mid-1990s, Lương began rethinking the larger circulation of and inclusive access to contemporary art in Vietnam. His conjuring of connections between art's democratic reception in ordinary communities likely drove the innovative, community-including performative modes that he began to materialise in the wake of his co-founding of Nhà Sàn Studio, discussed below. The split of Vietnam's artworld into distinct and sometimes intersecting camps – the mainstream and the margins – persists today.

of Vietnam (Hà Nội: Thế Giới Publishers, 2010) proposes a preliminary Vietnamese contemporary canon, including Trần Lương and others producing non-mainstream art before 2000; Bùi Như Hương and Phạm Trung, *Vietnamese Contemporary Art 1990-2010* (Hà Nội: Knowledge Publishing House, 2012).

22. Terry Smith, *Contemporary Art World Currents* (Upper Saddle River: Prentice Hall, 2011), 8; 82.

23. Notably in APT, the Fukuoka Asian Art Triennale, and in various European and Asia-Pacific curated exhibitions after 1995.

SEEDS OF INNOVATION: TRẦN LƯƠNG ARTIST-CURATOR

From the eclectic 1990s Vietnamese art scene sprang Gang of Five. Formed by five painter friends who had been active individually since the 1980s, art historian Phan Cẩm Thượng credits the group with connecting Vietnamese art with the world in the early 1990s.[24] After 1995, when the mainstream and vanguard artworlds were developing concurrently in Hà Nội, Gang of Five member Trần Lương played a crucial role in shaping the evolving contemporary art scene, when, in 1998, he and painter and antique specialist Nguyễn Mạnh Đức founded the independent, artist-run space Nhà Sàn Studio. Also known as Nhà Sàn Đức, the space was established in Đức's home, a walled, ethnic house on stilts in Vĩnh Phúc street, in the Hà Nội suburban district of Ba Đình.

Post-millennium, Nhà Sàn garnered a reputation as a venue for Vietnamese and Southeast Asian performance art as well as other multidisciplinary forms, with its events often organised and collaboratively curated by Trần Lương. International from the beginning, these events frequently included regional participants such as Singapore's Jason Lim (b. 1966), Malaysian Sharon Chin (b. 1980) and Burmese Moe Satt (b. 1983), among others. Early local Nhà Sàn habitués were Nguyễn Xuân Sơn, Lê Vũ (b. 1972), Nguyễn Trí Mạnh (b. 1970), Vũ Thuỵ, Hoàng Dương Cầm (b. 1974) and Nguyễn Minh Phước (b. 1973). Others involved in the space post-1999 were Nguyễn Quang Huy (b. 1971), Nguyễn Minh Thành (b. 1971), Nguyễn Văn Cường (b. 1972), Nguyễn Mạnh Hùng (b. 1976), Phạm Ngọc Dương (b. 1976) and Trương Tân (b. 1963) who shuttled between Paris and Hà Nội. Experimental musician/composer Trần Kim Ngọc was also present.

24. Phan Cẩm Thượng, "Artists in the Renovation Period", in *Be Open' 30 Years of Fine Art after doi moi (1986-2016)* (Hà Nội: Thế Giới Publishers, 2016), 184.

Trần Lương was a driving force from 1998 onwards and into the new century, as Nhà Sàn became more established. Testing alternative idioms, notably installation, while concurrently organising events, Lương's interests permeated Nhà Sàn and shaped its collaborative framework. As the Studio operated both "underground" – within a family home, insulated from official oversight – and offering a kind of art-home to a small but engaged community, Trần Lương adeptly catered to audience experience in ways artists seldom do. This melding of art and exhibition practice possibly provided the kernel of his breakthroughs in community performance. Certainly, Nhà Sàn's relatively generous physical space, its protective walls and private-public hybridity, attracted risk-taking artists, who were also viewers. All were welcome, an openness fostering the mixing of disciplines, graphics, objects, movement and sound. Early-career artists of the day attest to the contribution that this freedom made to their creative evolution.[25] Equally significantly, Trần Lương's push for contemporary art as part of social progress, unrelated to Vietnam's booming art market, infused Nhà Sàn. Despite considerable changes over its 25 year history, the collective ethos instigated by Nguyễn Mạnh Đức and Trần Lương in the late 1990s persists to this day at Nhà Sàn Collective.[26] To provide basic seed funding for the project, Trần Lương petitioned his American philanthropist friends, hitching his personal artistic vision to his practical efforts to grow Nhà Sàn as an inclusive community. By 2003, Nhà Sàn was hosting international performance festivals supported by masters such as Seiji Shimoda.

A locus of creative freedom, improvisation and audience involvement – features exceptional in illiberal Southeast Asia – early Nhà Sàn both embodied and informed Trần Lương's innovative practice of community-engaged performance, which took shape in 2001. The unusual merging of these elements, resulting in new expressive modes, may be attributed to the unique nature of Nhà Sàn – a space that is both private yet inclusive of its audience – as well as Trần Lương's commitment to art for social progress. Whatever the motivations, Trần Lương's organisational responsibilities morphed into a curatorial role by both necessity and inclination. He learned his curatorial craft on the job at a time when in Southeast Asia, professional curators barely existed. Trần Lương was not alone in bridging art-making and curation. Figures like Apinan Poshyananda and Oscar Ho were both artists before transitioning into curating. While Mella Jaarsma, Jason Lim, Arahmaiani, Yee I-Lann,

25. Nguyễn Mạnh Hùng, personal communication with the author, November 9, 2021.

26. "Introduce," Nha San Collective, https://nhasan.org/introduces

Jeremy Hiah, Moe Satt, Vuth Lyno and others, similar to Trần Lương, wear both artist and curator hats. However, arguably Trần Lương stands out among his peers for his mining of curatorial principles to expand the scope of performance expressions.

By 2000, Trần Lương was not only curating at the grassroots level at Nhà Sàn, but also in a more official frame, serving as first Director of Hà Nội Contemporary Art Center (HCAC), which was founded in the same year. His appointment affirmed a tentative institutional openness to contemporary art in Vietnam, a realm that was still considered alien in official cultural circles at the time. While it is certain that artist-curators bring creative flair and fluency to curating, what does curating bring to individual artistic practice? In Trần Lương's case, how did his collaborative work with Nhà Sàn, along with his HCAC duties, influence his personal production? A primary concern of all curators is how to engage diverse audiences, given that audiences are not monoliths. Curators of group exhibitions face greater complications as they orchestrate works by various artists with distinct goals into a cohesive body capable of engaging a plurality of viewers. In Southeast Asia, where art museums and the institutional presentation of art are relatively recent colonial imports, are highly codified and do not cater to all strata of society, how do curators account for viewers? In politically controlled environments, where cultural venues are monitored for dissent, how does one bypass the authorities in order to offer unmediated access to an ordinary public? Did Trần Lương's curatorial style spur his collegial, inclusive performance practice of the 2000s? Or, did Trần Lương inject his own community focus into Nhà Sàn and HCAC? Causality is difficult to ascertain, but Trần Lương's rule-defiant performances, with their aesthetics and structure revolving around people, choice, inclusivity and agency, suggest a blurring between his personal creative interests, and Nhà Sàn's vanguard, turn-of-the-millennium collectivist curatorial ethos that he was so influential in forming.

Notably, more than two decades after establishing Nhà Sàn, in 2020, Trần Lương co-founded the non-profit, Center for Art Patronage and Development, known as APD, in Hà Nội, serving as its first and current Director.[27] The APD Center, with its library, artist residencies, educational events, and research and archival exhibitions, among other activities, embodies Trần Lương's unwavering commitment to art as driver of social progress, a position that was already visible in his initiatives at Nhà Sàn in the late 1990s. Philosophically, it

27. "Organization," APD, https://apd.org.vn/en/uncategorized-en/officers-and-trustees/

is this attitude that underpins Trần Lương's distinctive 21st century community-centric performance practice.

MẠO KHÊ COAL MINE PROJECT, 2001

In October 2001, combining curatorial leadership and his own art practice, Trần Lương instigated community-based art making, including performance, within the context of his *Mạo Khê Coal Mine Project*. The project, supported by the Vietnam Fine Arts Association, and referenced in detail in this volume by Phoebe Scott,[28] involved Trần Lương leading an artist research field trip to experience coal mining life in Mạo Khê, a village outside Hà Nội. As Trần Lương was the Director of HCAC in 2001, the trip received an "official" stamp, ensuring that the Mạo Khê Coal Mine Factory provided artists with meals and lodgings. This degree of homestay support was significant, arguably contributing to Trần Lương's innovative expansion of performance practice in Vietnam.

28. Phoebe Scott, "Residues of the Past, Trần Lươngs's 2001 Collaborative Projects" In *Tầm Tã:, Soaked in the Long Rain*, ed. Biljana Ciric (Milan: Mousse, 2024), 55-63.

The sponsorship reflected the meshing of art and life fostered by such field trips – a practice habitual in socialist Vietnam's art school curricula. Urban students and painting teachers were regularly dispatched to worker communities in order to immerse themselves more realistically in life there. The artistic outcome – socialist realist painting celebrating the backbone of Vietnamese society: laborers, soldiers, and farmers – was de rigueur in communist North Vietnam (the Democratic Republic of Vietnam) from the 1950s. This tradition continued in reunified Vietnam (the Socialist Republic of Vietnam) after 1975, furthering the nation's socialist mission. Notably, later-generation Vietnamese performance artists Bùi Công Khánh (b. 1972) and Ly Hoàng Ly (b. 1975), who attended art school in Sài Gòn, also recall such ideologically inspired field trips. Socialist realism was practised well into the 1990s, although as mentioned above, some artists ignored the style. The Mạo Khê trip's motivation and process were truthfully described to the authorities. But with Trần Lương as leader, the trip yielded artistic outcomes that, with historical hindsight, must be highlighted as innovative expansions of Vietnamese contemporary art in its form, reception and circulation.

The artists spent a day deep down a coal shaft, walking through kilometres of dark underground tunnels in the oppressive air, thick with coal-dust. Trần Lương filmed the expedition, and nearly a quarter century later recalls its discomfort, riskiness and the collegiality spurred by the shared experience of fear.[29] Normally, post-shaft visit, the painters would have returned to Hà Nội where, in the privacy of their studios, far from the miner community, they would have depicted the mining life that they had witnessed. But this is not what happened. Instead, the urban artists spent over two weeks in the village, producing a collective mural on a long concrete wall, graffiti on buildings, and talking and drinking with community members with whom they forged bonds due to sharing dormitory and canteen facilities.[30]

Trần Lương had subverted the standard field trip: the Mạo Khê Project's expressive result, which was free and organic, did *not* consist of realist depictions of miners living harsh lives. Such images were not destined for the miners themselves but rather for others, designed to prompt a celebration of Vietnam's heroic workers and their contribution to the nation. In socialist realist images, and similarly in romantic portraits, miners are subject-cues, without agency. Rather, led by Trần Lương, the artist trip engendered alternative ways of communicating the realities of miners' lives on site, *within* the community, as the lives of the villagers and the artists converged.

The mural, occupying public space, eroded the typical artwork/audience separation found in institutional settings. However, it was Trần Lương's performance *Steam Rice Man* on October 19th, that saw community members transcend their role as passive, mute subjects. This performance metaphorically invited them to join a conversation elliptically referencing social questions that concerned all Vietnamese people, particularly regarding the position of workers in a globalising Vietnam that appeared to be moving away from its egalitarian, collectivist principles. By presenting his body crusted with rice as the artwork-theatre of action, and sifting black coal dust meditatively through his fingers, Trần Lương conflated the vulnerability of his nearly naked body with public accessibility and the trust he had built with the audience through the lived intimacy of co-habitation over weeks. The piece's conceptual method was linked to Trần Lương's choice of steamed rice and his endurance over long hours, to form a sensorial, durational work that simmered with a low-voltage tension, engaging viewers in its ongoing and open debate. The rice-coal juxtaposition was sophisticated in its play on incongruity, but also legible to non-art savvy community members for whom rice and coal represented connected sustenance and livelihood for both family and nation. Ultimately, by deploying aesthetics and materials as conceptual clues in ways typical of Southeast

29. Trần Lương, personal communication with the author, December 15, 2023, Hà Nội.

30. Per the performance documentation the original 11 were: Trần Lương with Lê Hồng Thái, Lê Quảng Hà, Nguyễn Trí Mạnh, Hà Trí Hiếu, Phạm Ngọc Minh, Đinh Quân, Đào Anh Khánh, Lê Vũ, Nguyễn Bảo Toàn, and Đinh Công Đạt. In the project's final days, intrigued by what they were hearing about Mạo Khê and its novelty, cultural figure Dương Tường, along with other Hà Nội artists visited the site, with Đặng Xuân Hoà joining the mural production.

31. Lenzi, "Conceptual Strategies," 2014.

32. Veronika Radulovic, personal communication with author, February 2, 2024.

Asian conceptual-aesthetic idioms,[31] miner-viewers, if not directly participating in the work, integrated Steam Rice Man's exchange about the evolving place of rural and industrial labour in capitalist-leaning, 21st century Vietnam. The villagers and their lives were not objectified elements of artists' paintings, but rather infiltrated the art as thoughtful respondents. The piece's formal construction, deliberate use of materials as symbolic code, extensive duration and public setting contributed to its democratic reach.

Community-located performance was not unprecedented in Vietnam: Trương Tân and Nguyễn Quang Huy's 1996 Mộc Châu village performance *Water Buffalo* had also grappled with labour. In this work, Huy drove Trương Tân as a farm beast in Mộc Châu village square, signalling the disturbing rural/urban divide and more general social inequalities in reform-era Vietnam. But Huy and Trương Tân's performance was ad hoc, improvised on site as the artists travelled around the countryside with friends.[32] This differed from Trần Lương's Steam Rice Man, which was cultivated within the community itself, where artists had befriended miners over weeks through communal living, eating, and drinking. Moreover, the durational form of Steam Rice Man metaphorically included Mao Khe community members by establishing both familiarity and a metaphoric conversation over many hours as Trần Lương's performance subtly answered its audience. Unlike performance-as-spectacle, it eroded the divide between viewer and artwork. Anticipating performance works to come, in Steam Rice Man Trần Lương innovatively deployed his body as a site of open and collective discourse, inviting ordinary audiences in.

Deconstructing Steam Rice Man into its formal, conceptual, and circulatory components, and unpicking its mechanics, reveals Trần Lương's ability to maintain aesthetic and sensorial seduction, while simultaneously exploiting them both to transform the performance from a self-contained spectacle into an inclusive forum. Audiences, neither passive spectators nor subjects, claim agency in questions about collective life, thereby manifesting democratic affirmation. Steam Rice Man embodies aesthetic-conceptual play, compelling via the talismanic power of the body. It garners viewer interest and involvement through incongruous associations: first through the materials rice and coal, which heighten tension thanks to the black/white aesthetic contrast; secondly, through the use of rice, normally ingested into the body – here outside the body, its calories left unused. While Steam Rice Man does not solicit physical audience interference, it paves the way for community-integrating methods to come. The novelty of the form was such that Hà Nội literary figure Dương Tường (1932-2023), a supporter of the Gang of Five painters, drove from Hà Nội to Mạo Khê for the performance event.[33]

33. As reported by Trần Lương, personal communication with the author, February 14, 2024.

TRẦN LƯƠNG ARTIST-CURATOR OUTSIDE INSTITUTIONAL WALLS

The new millennium appeared to herald Vietnam's tentative institutional acceptance of contemporary art *forms* – as opposed to contemporary art's critical drive, which was still out of bounds. But this "mainstreaming" did not translate as carte blanche for artists and curators, and if anything, more care was needed when conceptualising projects outside institutional walls, since contemporary art was now on the officials' radar.

In 2003, Trần Lương quit HCAC, resigning his directorship in protest "against government corruption in the administration of arts funding."[34] As HCAC Director, Trần Lương was not spared the demands of reporting activities and ensuring presented art complied with state regulations – an environment inevitably restrictive of creative freedom. The Centre, like all registered spaces, lacked independence, unlike Nhà Sàn. Resigning his post freed Trần Lương from the control of his HCAC bureaucratic minders and permitted him to curate two large Hà Nội exhibitions using non-conformist strategies. While some may speculate that Trần Lương's artistic path shifted due to his leaving HCAC, it may be more accurate to suggest that the creative path he had embarked upon at Nhà Sàn in 1998 was instrumental in forcing his resignation. Whether this career change was result or instigator, Trần Lương curated two major exhibitions that would further his skills and curatorial credentials.

34. "Tran Luong," Guggenheim Museum. Accessed April 29, 2024. https://www.guggenheim.org/artwork/artist/tran-luong

Of the two shows, 2003's *Green Red & Yellow* held at Goethe Institut, Hà Nội, was the better known and was revisited in 2023 with a documentary and archival exhibition at APD Center, as discussed earlier.[35] Goethe Institut Hà Nội, which opened in December 1997, was a unique art space in Hà Nội due to its special status which shielded it from the need to obtain Vietnamese government permissions for its events, including art exhibitions – a privileged status which was lost in 2012. By 2003, the Institut had thrived, and its programming expanded, leading Goethe to secure larger premises for its activities. *Green Red & Yellow*,

35. *Green Red & Yellow* artists: Nguyễn Quỳnh Chi, Nguyễn Văn Cường, Phạm Ngọc Dương, Lê Quang Đỉnh, Nguyễn Mạnh Hùng, Nguyễn Quang Huy, Trần Lương, Nguyễn Trí Mạnh, Nguyễn Minh Phước, Nguyễn Quân, Veronika Radulovic, Brian Ring, Nguyễn Minh Thành, Vũ Thụy, Trương Tân, Lê Vũ.

situated in the un-renovated building that had been recently acquired to house the expanding Institut, marked Goethe's transition to the larger premises, which opened in 2004 after refurbishment.[36]

The other 2003 exhibition, *Fairytale Soup (Súp Cổ Tích)*, which occurred a few months before *Green Red & Yellow* and celebrated 30 years of UK-Vietnamese diplomatic relations, was supported by the British Council.[37] This 15-artist show, installed in the garden of the Hà Nội Opera House, presented multi-media, sound, and kinetic works, including 15 TV sets screening video art – two by Trần Lương, and 13 by other artists. Water tanks, bubbles, and smoke were also present in the Opera House grounds, which, being park-like and open in busy, central Hà Nội, were accessible to socially mixed crowds who would not necessarily have entered an art museum or other cultural institution. Unfortunately, *Fairytale Soup* was closed by the authorities within days. However, by integrating the physical fabric of the city, the show was designed for democratic encounter and exchange, continuing what Trần Lương had initiated with *Steam Rice Man*. Indeed, this encroachment into public space, characteristic of contemporary Southeast Asian art, constituted a covert challenge to the status quo, in what Sandra Kurfürst describes as citizens' negotiation of the current order.[38] In the case of *Fairytale Soup*, Trần Lương's installation permitted art's direct dialogue with ordinary Hanoians, solidifying the foundations of his practice defined by the interconnection of art and community, where aesthetic expression, ideas, and viewer-response circulated symbiotically as one.

Following on from these exhibitions, Trần Lương consolidated his understanding of performance art as an effective means of critically engaging the contemporary condition and for challenging systems that enforce various status quos. In October 2004, in Hà Nội, wearing his curator's hat, Trần Lương conceptualised and organised *Lim Dim* (literally "eyes half-open"), Vietnam's first international performance festival. The festival featured performers from Vietnam, Japan, Singapore, UK and Germany, making it not only the first of its kind in Vietnamese art history in terms of its performance content, but also boundary-pushing for Trần Lương's forging of ties with international institutions.

Lim Dim demonstrated a strong Vietnamese uptake of performance art, an interest nurtured in the experimental haven of Nhà Sàn, among other places. While performance works had been presented by a few Hà Nội artists in the 1990s (Trương Tân, mentioned above, Nguyễn Quang Huy,

36. Veronika Radulovic, personal communication with the author, April 2, 2024.

37. In the publication, the show was called *Legends Retold*, with Trần Lương, Lê Vũ, Phạm Ngọc Dương, Trương Tân, Vũ Thuỵ, Nguyễn Quang Huy, Nguyễn Mạnh Hùng, Nguyễn Minh Phước, Nguyễn Văn Cường, Nguyễn Mạnh Đức, Nguyễn Trí Mạnh, Nguyễn Quỳnh Chi, Nguyễn Xuân Sơn, Vũ Dân Tân & Khuyết danh.

38. Sandra Kurfürst, *Redefining public space in Hanoi: Places, Practices and Meaning* (Zurich/Berlin: LIT, 2012), 89.

and Nguyễn Văn Cường), by the 21st century the genre was increasingly integral to Vietnam's evolving contemporary art repertoire, with Trần Lương its leading proponent. Like their counterparts in Southeast Asia, Vietnamese contemporary practitioners valued performance art for its visceral idiomatic familiarity. Its language, combining body and movement, resonated particularly strongly in Vietnam, due to the continued presence of traditional performance forms such as Chèo opera, Ca Trù singing and other forms that were still alive within the culture. Even Vietnam's urbanites, several generations removed from rural life (as was the Hà Nội elite), kept close ties to their family village, where traditional performance was ubiquitous, secular and sacred.

As elsewhere in Southeast Asia, performance was popular for its ease of practice, democratic access, and minimal cost. However, beyond these practical considerations, performance art was well suited to tightly controlled environments like Vietnam, where public assembly was forbidden. This was because body movement in public space could happen in a flash, without warning, then cease – leaving no incriminating evidence, even if witnessed by a large group. Performance art did not require institutional framing, which it bypassed, making it perfectly suited to grappling with power, a topic impossible to broach in official venues. Finally, in its form as body action, performance could evoke discomfort in viewers through violence, and from there, spawn resistance in ways images might not. Expressively charged in its complex fusion of body, space, audience and time, performance artworks cryptically left the public to determine their significance, thereby diluting the risk for the artist.

MOVING FORWARDS AND BACKWARDS, 2006

In 2006, Trần Lương led another field trip outside Hà Nội involving Vietnamese artists from both the North and South of the country.[39] The group made its way to Sài Gòn by train and then crossed Vietnam's south-western border into Cambodia by road, travelling as tourists, without official Vietnamese permissions. The project was supported by the Asian Culture Council (ACC), New York, attesting to Trần Lương's international network dating back to his foreign residencies in the early 1990s. These residencies were rare for Vietnamese artists at the time, as those venturing overseas required official exit permissions, without which returning to Vietnam was difficult. The 2006 initiative, formally

39. With Trần Lương, Lê Vũ, Nguyễn Minh Phước, Nguyễn Quang Huy, Trương Tân, Nguyễn Minh Thành, Nguyễn Thuý Hằng, Nguyễn Trí Mạnh, and Vũ Thuỵ.

titled *Hà Nội–Phnom Penh Arts Exchange Program*, was co-organised by Trần Lương and Phnom Penh's Reyum Institute of Arts & Culture, an NGO for Cambodian cultural outreach and research – an early force for 1990s Cambodian arts regeneration – founded by art historians Ly Daravuth and Ingrid Muan.

Whereas the 2001 coal mine excursion was pedagogical in nature, the 2006 trip aimed to materialise a conceptually-structured plan devised by Trần Lương as a written art project proposal backed by ACC.[40] The artwork's articulation was intrinsic to its site: Cambodia. *Steam Rice Man* opened critical discourses on meanings of labour in a globalising Vietnam, whereas *Moving Forwards and Backwards* wrestled critically with Vietnamese modern political history and cross-border conflicts that continued to shape lives in both Cambodia and Vietnam.

40. An earlier, thwarted iteration of the project involved Vietnam-China relations and overcoming historical animosities between the two nations via art. Trần Lương, personal communication with the author, November, 2008.

In Phnom Penh, the Hanoians stationed themselves on Tonle Sap River promenade, a popular park-come-pedestrian thoroughfare in the city centre. This choice of location ensured a socially diverse audience, including couples, students, food-hawkers, children, flower-sellers, tourists and beggars. There, from late-afternoon until nightfall, they distributed toothbrushes, toothpaste and water to Cambodians and others to join in a collective tooth-brushing action. No explanations were given, the assumption being that those joining would decode the work as they performed it, which many did.

The piece embodies Trần Lương's conceptualisation of a performance that through mundane, repetitive gestures, group involvement, incongruity and context, cues the complicated and often conflictual historical relationship between Vietnam and Cambodia. Rather than making definitive statements, the piece addressed these histories as questions, fostering an openness manifested through the neutrality of Vietnamese and Cambodians brushing their teeth together as equals. In this way, they symbolically cleansed their antagonisms through group play, cultivating a sense of collegiality, without winners or losers.

Similar to *Steam Rice Man*'s reliance on rice and coal as ubiquitous, meaning-laden images, Trần Lương chose aesthetic prompts for his Cambodian piece to maximise both formal and critical impact. Tooth brushing – a universal action typically conducted in the intimacy of the bathroom and usually in the morning – was transferred from the private to the public setting, taking place in the late-afternoon. This shift embodied semantic-aesthetic incongruity, driving viewer engagement. Moreover, tooth brushing prevented coherent speech, as this foamy impediment to verbal communication heightened the expressive power of the shared, communal 'language' of performative tooth brushing. Additionally, when participants were asked for the camera, to identify their country of origin, the foam muffled their responses, effacing national difference and, by extension, subverting the nationalism (Vietnamese, or otherwise) that is frequently used to drive xenophobia, aggression and war.

Without making explicit declarations, the piece offered the means of transcending old narratives to forge new ones, with each viewer-performer a potential change-maker. Unlike Lee Wen's *Yellow Man*, Josef Ng's *Brother Cane*, and Trương Tân and Nguyễn Quang Huy's *Water Buffalo*, where artists produce the action, Trần Lương's *Moving Forwards and Backwards* cedes this central position. Here, both artists and audiences are equally responsible for production, transmission and critical thinking. The piece's design, in alliance with physical public space – referenced earlier as the hijacking of public space serving as a kind of low-key contestation of authority, or even a form of political agency[41] – and the intellectual public space of history, ensures a critical response from viewers, as each is empowered to recall the past and action the future. The piece expands performance art in Vietnam and Southeast Asia in its democratic insistence on individual involvement in and responsibility for shaping reality. It also innovates in its back and forth juggling of perspectives, as the performance includes Vietnamese and Cambodians, as well as other passers-by. This inclusion of diverse perspectives necessarily bridges different positions, facilitated by the conceptually-underpinned expressive mechanics of the piece.

41. Kurfurst, "Redefining," 2012, 89.

Like other conceptual Southeast Asian contemporary artworks, *Moving Forwards and Backwards* is transferable to different cultures, times and geographies. The piece was performed the following year by Trần Lương in Beijing's Tiananmen Square, albeit without audience participation, with the intention of contending with Sino-Vietnamese historical connections. It could easily work in other settings, there is no shortage of antagonism-creating vexed histories that could be critically engaged and grappled with artistically via Trần Lương's work.

The 2006 Phnom Penh community piece, photographed by Vũ Thuỵ and filmed by Nguyễn Quang Huy and Nguyễn Trí Mạnh, became the 2009 video *Moving Forwards and Backwards*, which was shown in exhibitions in both Singapore and Kuala Lumpur, including SAM's *Negotiating Home History and Nation* in 2011, captivating audiences even with little knowledge of Vietnam-Cambodia relations.[42] Outside its original locus of production, the piece embodies Trần Lương's performance practice as a new form whereby artist and audiences share action, and therefore the power to think and perhaps shape new worlds.

42. Shown September – November 2009 in *Intersection Vietnam: new art from North and South*, VWFA Singapore & Kuala Lumpur; in 2011, at Singapore Art Museum, in *Negotiating Home History and Nation - Two Decades of Contemporary Art in Southeast Asia 1991-2011*.

WELTS, 2007

In 2007, a year after Phnom Penh, Trần Lương conceptualised *Welts* (sometimes referenced as *Red Scarf*) for a performance event in October 2007 at Beijing's 798 Art District. *Welts* is better known than the previously examined works due to its live performance, with over a dozen variations in different locales since 2007 (although it has only been performed once to date in Vietnam). Well-documented in both photo and video, like *Moving Forwards and Backwards*, it was recognised as a seminal Southeast Asian artwork through its inclusion (with three documentary variations screened) in SAM's 2011 *Negotiating Home History and Nation* exhibition, which revolved around artistic grappling with the state, power and history as a means of probing contemporary conditions. However, where the toothbrush performance staged collegial play, Welts introduces violence and the pairing of opposed protagonists, artist + audience, to produce a dramatic tension absent in Trần Lương's earlier performances.

In *Steam Rice Man*, and *Moving Forwards and Backwards* it is the incongruity of rice-as-body-cladding in a semi-public venue, and group tooth brushing mid-afternoon in a public space, that catch the audience's attention, and in the case of *Moving Forwards and Backwards*, the option to join in. *Welts*, however, engages through sensuality, focusing on stealth and the fascination of the body as an aesthetic field, with incongruity emerging later as the flimsy scarf causes injury.

Trần Lương begins the work by playing with the scarf, tossing it in the air and catching it, a kind of teasing dance. Then, he demonstrates the scarf's function as he whip-cracks it through the air at high speed, producing a dry, snapping sound. Only then, without a word, does he proffer the scarf to a viewer, removing his t-shirt to bare his torso, thereby bringing the performance action, and the audience's role, into focus. Trần Lương thus offers his body as an object for viewers to whip. But this is no ordinary textile, rather it is a red scarf worn by socialist schoolchildren (communist youth known as 'pioneers'), which is still ubiquitous in state schools for children aged 10 and older in Vietnam. Whereas neutral rice and tooth brushing acquire critical meanings once integrated into Trần Lương's performances, the red scarf's connection with socialism, group ideological belonging, and state-controlled education, indicates Welts' political slant, particularly in Vietnamese and Chinese communist contexts, hence *Welts*' appeal in China. Yet the piece conveys no explicit message, and like *Steam Rice Man* and *Moving Forwards and Backwards*, is presented without verbal or textual information. Instead, *Welts* imparts agency to viewers who come forward to brandish the scarf, while the artist – deliberately vulnerable – receives his lashes in silence. As audiences observe or perform this action, they contemplate power imbalances and their consequences as the welts accrue on the artist's back, while those doing the whipping consider their capacity to continue or cease inflicting violence. Although participants control the action, in practice, it lasts no more than 40 minutes, as art festival organisers encourage audiences to move from one performance to the next.

Just as rice serves as an aesthetic-semantic prompt in *Steam Rice Man*, and intimate tooth brushing transferred to public space serves as an aesthetic-semantic prompt in *Moving Forwards and Backwards*, the red scarf in *Welts* plays a crucial aesthetic and meaning-charged activating role, a clue that provides access to viewers of all social strata, whether familiar with art or not. In communist Vietnam and China, the red scarf indicates allegiance to socialism, so *Welts* may be a provocative critique of the system and its conformity-imposing violence. But beyond those environments, *Welts* is constructed as a conversation about power – a public space belonging to all, a struggle for control and choice. The artist holds the scarf, then relinquishes it, then opts for passive non-resistance vis-à-vis the whipper. Who is in charge? The piece is no simplistic binary, the subject-perpetrator duo embody a co-dependent intimacy, even if inimical. This back and forth alteration of perspective as the artist authorises the assailant, alternating from actor to subject-victim, underlines the fragility of power, the potential for reversal and resistance. *Welts* is atemporal, corroborating the translatability of Southeast Asian artworks that evoke viewer responses in various settings.

However, while live performances of *Welts* translate beyond their initial environment, filmed or photographed documentation of these actions may not convey the live performance's immediate, sizzling tension and brutality, which are gripping and present. Therefore, in 2012 Trần Lương created a new work by producing a three-channel video installation *Lập Lòe* (blink, flicker) that rethinks *Welts* outside its original context where the red scarf has cultural-political meaning, and outside its original performative nature. Shown at the Guggenheim Museum, New York, in the exhibition *No Country: Contemporary Art in South and Southeast Asia* (2013), *Lập Lòe* uses stylisation and a three-screen deployment of a trio of image-symbols – a blue sky; a flicking, floating red scarf; a static, blemished torso – to task viewers with cerebrally connecting images, power and violence. Whether *Lập Lòe* translates better than *Welts* to global audiences is uncertain, but its video medium ensures worldwide access.

BEYOND SPECTACLE: TRẦN LƯƠNG'S PERFORMANCE AESTHETICS OF INCLUSIVITY

The works examined in this study show Trần Lương grappling with his Vietnamese context to devise new aesthetic-conceptual methods for the expansion of performance art. Negotiating complex contemporary tensions such as the position of manual labour and labourers in capitalist-leaning, yet still socialist Vietnam; thorny transnational histories of war, invasion and migration, seen differently by peoples across borders; and power and the state, Trần Lương shapes performance for community engagement. In these pieces, more or less cryptic in their exploration of social topics, viewers are self-directed actors and interlocutors, rather than mere accessories or subjects of the artwork. By offering his pieces about collective stresses to the collective, the artist realises new performance forms of potent inclusivity structured around simple actions.

In addition to the expressive power of body or bodies, space is a central material and political component of these works. The democratic ethos of these performances is heightened by their utilising of public areas where people of all types circulate – the Tonle Sap River Promenade in Phnom Penh, or village grounds and communal buildings in Mạo Khê. When situated in public zones, artworks can be read as harbouring political implications. Indeed, in illiberal settings, the works' encroachment into state-controlled locations can be seen as a tussling with authority. Engaging in a discourse about commerce and urbanism, urbanist Mandy Thomas noted state-citizen frictions in Hà Nội's public areas, which she identified as Arendtian public space, as viable for the cultivation of public and political concerns.[43]

Public intellectual space is also co-opted for semantic depth: contentious histories in *Moving Forwards and Backwards*, citizens' relationship with power in *Welts*, and the state's attitude to labour in *Steam Rice Man*. By embedding history and politics (theoretically belonging to all but controlled by few) in the performances discussed in this study, the artist presents these to community members as theirs. Yet, there is nothing didactic about these works: with their artistic command, and manifesting close attention to conceptual design and profound respect for audiences – possibly resulting from Trần Lương's curatorial mission – they do not treat viewers as pedagogical subjects, but instead as audience-collaborators. This is achieved through involvement over time, as the durational nature of the performances forge intimacy that spurs viewer immersion and individual critical response.

However novel Trần Lương's performance idiom is, it retains aesthetic properties: the immediate and universally intuitive sensuality of the body in Welts and Steam Rice Man – the former violent, the latter low-voltage but durationally tense; or the playful, time-evolving group teeth-brushing dance in Moving Forwards and Backwards, with participants entering and exiting as they wish, while the day ebbs from afternoon into sunset and then into night. Material and haptic engagement play a part too, with rice, coal and the red scarf. The pieces mobilise viewers visually as much as conceptually, differing from organised projects of the participative, dialogical type analysed by Grant Kester.[44] Via performance form and structure that he conceptualises and authors, Trần Lương draws plural audiences into ownership of action and narrative, whether the interceding crowd of Welts, the tooth brushers in Phnom Penh, or viewers in silent communion with Trần Lương performing Steam Rice Man.

As mentioned earlier, performance art in 1990s Southeast Asia predominantly featured sole actors. When viewer-participants were involved, as in Amanda Heng's *Let's Chat* (1996) and Mella Jaarsma's *PribumiPribumi* (1998), they were typically corralled into an artistic storyline. The performance works of Trần Lương discussed here are distinctive within Southeast Asian performance art as they facilitate back and forth conversations between artist and audiences, with unscripted, open-ended critical outcomes, making participants active or engaged observers. Designed for presentation outside

43. Kurfürst, "Redefining," 2012; Mandy Thomas, "Out of Control: Emergent Cultural Landscapes and Political Change in Urban Vietnam," *Urban Studies* 39, no.9 (2002): 1616; 1622, referencing Hannah Arendt, Thomas attributes a political dimension to Hà Nội's contestation of space. See also Mandy Thomas, "Public spaces/public disgraces: Crowds and the state in contemporary Vietnam," *SOJOURN Journal of Social Issues in Southeast Asia* 16, no.2 (2001): 306.

44. Grant H. Kester, *Conversation Pieces: Community and Communication in Modern art* (Berkely: University of California Press, 2004), 2-8.

institutional walls, these works reflect an interest in general audiences as Trần Lương juggles viewpoints, demonstrating a multi-perspective approach that takes into account the public and attests to curatorial care, potentially coaxing viewers into roles concerned with society.

While the pieces discussed here initially enlist Vietnamese audiences, their iconic imagery, sensorially-compelling gestures, and use of conceptually-underpinned aesthetics for cryptic communication, enable them to transcend the local. Outside their original production contexts, Trần Lương's works embody a form accessible to viewers of various social strata and cultures, whether familiar with art or not, merging activating empowerment, agency creation, politics and aesthetics in ways that theorists such as Claire Bishop see as integral to contemporary art, sometimes missing in Bourriaud's relational aesthetics.[45]

45. Claire Bishop, "Antagonism and Relational Aesthetics," *October*, 110 (Autumn, 2004): 52-53; 58; Nicolas Bourriaud, *L'Esthétique relationelle* (Dijon: Les Presses du Réel, 1998).

Nimbly renewing themselves in time and place, Trần Lương's unscripted, yet tightly conceived performances showcase aesthetic command and critical range, expanding Southeast Asian contemporary art. Vanguard practices around the region have grown from local soil, fertilised by a mix of local and incoming ideas and images from high art, popular and vernacular culture. These artworks, creations of necessity, combine formal virtuosity and conceptual strategies to address unprecedented stresses with unprecedented idioms, producing a Southeast Asian contemporary art at home in the world. Among these idioms are Trần Lương's innovative 21st century performances.

RESIDUES OF THE PAST: TRẦN LƯƠNG'S 2001 COLLABORATIVE PROJECTS

by **Phoebe Scott**

In 2001, Trần Lương instigated two collaborative projects – *Mạo Khê Coal Mine Project* and *On the Banks of the Red River*.[1] Both projects involved groups of artists working together with a community and both were at sites with very specific associations. Looking at the year in terms of the sweep of Trần's career, we could see these works as part of his transition, beginning in 1997, away from the lyrical and semi-abstract paintings he had previously pursued. This was a deliberate stance against the increasing commercialisation of painting in Vietnam, which pushed him toward the experimental and conceptual practices for which he would later become well known.[2] That both of these 2001 works involved an organisational, collective component, and that they both had social justice implications, also anticipated Trần's later roles as *artist-curator* and *artist-activist*. Looking laterally across the region, as Iola Lenzi does elsewhere in this book, this period in Trần's work can also be seen as part of a turn towards socially charged and performative art in the works shared by his peers across Southeast Asia. But writing as a historian of Vietnamese modern art, what was most apparent to me on encountering the documentation of these projects was their interplay with the past: specifically, the past of Vietnamese socialist realism. In a reading of these works against their historical setting, we can see them, not as part of an undifferentiated, globalised condition of contemporaneity, but more as an expression of the contemporary that is deeply intertwined with local art, history and place.

Born in 1960, Trần Lương is one of a generation of Vietnamese artists whose lifetimes bridge very disparate historical experiences: beginning with the "Vietnam" War, 1955-75 (*kháng chiến chống Mỹ* or the "resistance against America" as it was known in north Vietnam); the difficult time of post-war material hardship known as the subsidy period, 1976-86 (*thời bao cấp*); the optimism and uncertainty of the economic and cultural "renovation" of 1986 and beyond (*đổi mới*); and finally, Vietnam's emergence as a "socialist market economy," where the country began to participate in

1. Both works exist today only as documentation footage, compiled from various sources. *Mạo Khê Coal Mine Project* footage was recut in 2015 as a new iteration, which also includes a second-channel component featuring narrative commentary by the original project participants reflecting on the original events. It thus exists as something between documentation, artwork and documentary. *On the Banks of the Red River* was similarly compiled and cut by the Lim Dim studio in 2014, but with no narrative or commentary added. It maintains the raw and uneven quality of the original footage. Trần Lương has explained that both sets of footage are perceived more as records of the works – the site-specific activities and engagements – rather than as works in their own right; author's discussion with Trần Lương, March 15th, 2024. Publicly available versions of the footage can be seen at Art Patronage & Development (APD), "Mạo Khê Coal Mine Project," http://apd.org.vn/2022/08/10/mao-khe-coal-mine-project/. At time of writing, a publicly available version of *On the Banks of the Red River* was being compiled for future release on the APD website.

2. Regarding Trần Lương's earlier work, see *Gang of 5: Chancing Modern*, eds. Lê Thuận Uyên and Suzanne Lecht (Hà Nội:

the international market and world order, while retaining the form of the socialist state. This cohort of artists experienced startling political and cultural change. For an artist like Trần Lương, even though he was increasingly operating in the globalised (or at least regionalised) field of contemporary art by the 1990s, he also had first-hand knowledge of an entirely different form of art system.

During the time of Trần Lương's youth and education – including his training in fine arts at the Hà Nội University of Fine Arts, from which he graduated in 1983 – socialist realism was still the officially dominant style. Although linked to socialist realism as it existed in the USSR, the Vietnamese variant of the style was also quite particular, to the extent that some scholars have even questioned whether "socialist realism" is a meaningful description of it.[3] Lacking the grandeur and academicism of Soviet socialist realism, Vietnamese socialist realism (*chủ nghĩa hiện thực xã hội chủ nghĩa*) was more adaptive: borrowing from folk aesthetics, existing modern styles, and making use of whatever limited materials were available in wartime conditions.[4] Leading members of the Vietnamese Communist Party, like Hồ Chí Minh (1890-1969) and Trường Chinh (1907-1988), specified that artists should focus on the subjects of workers, farmers and soldiers (*công, nông, binh*) and to target their art to this class audience.[5] Even more significant than the aesthetic of socialist realism, however, was the system associated with it. Socialist realism was part of a state-based system of art, in which the private art market was replaced almost entirely with state patronage. Access to art materials, opportunities for exhibition and travel, and professional stipends were all mediated via a quasi-state professional body, the Vietnam Fine Arts Association.[6] It was close to impossible to operate as a professional artist outside of this system, which was dominant from about the 1950s to the mid-1980s in Vietnam's north, and from 1975 to the mid-80s in the south.

Trần Lương recalls that, during his university years, ideological training in the arts was still compulsory, but was in a desultory state; it was a subject that students often skimmed over or slept through.[7] Students also still participated in regular field trips to connect with workers or farmers, a practice first instituted in the 1950s as part of the ideological training of the socialist art system. Even though Trần and other young artists of his generation were collectively moving away from socialist realism, the vestiges of the system remained, and left a residue within certain of Trần's later works. Arguably, *Mạo Khê Coal Mine Project*

Art Vietnam Gallery, 2018) and Nora A. Taylor and Pamela N. Corey, "Đổi Mới and the Globalization of Vietnamese Art," *Journal of Vietnamese Studies* 14, no. :1 (2019), 1-34.

3. See Natalia Kraevskaia and Nora Annesley Taylor, "Moscow's Outreach to Hanoi: Artistic Ties Between the Soviet Union and Vietnam," *Art History*, Vol. 45: issue 5, November 2022.

4. For examples of Vietnamese Socialist Realism, see Bùi Như Hương, Phạm Trung & Nguyễn Văn Chiến, *Mỹ thuật Việt Nam hiện đại* [Modern Vietnamese Art] (Hà Nội: Viện Mỹ thuật and Trường Đại học Mỹ thuật, 2005).

5. For English-language translations of these texts, see *The Modern in Southeast Asian Art: A Reader*, eds. T.K. Sabapathy and Patrick Flores (Singapore: National Gallery Singapore, 2023).

6. Nora Taylor, "Framing the National Spirit: Viewing and Reviewing Painting under the Revolution," in *The Country of Memory: Remaking the Past in Late Socialist Vietnam*, ed. Hue-Tam Ho Tai (Berkeley, Los Angeles and London: University of California Press, 2001), 112-114.

7. Based on the author's discussions with Trần Lương, March 15, 2024 and April 16, 2024. The context and circumstances behind the development of both of the art projects discussed in this essay are also derived from these conversations with Trần Lương, as well as an artist statement about *On the Banks of the Red River*, written by Trần, for one of the work's early exhibitions.

and *On the Banks of the Red River* are both rearticulations of certain key values within socialist realism but undertaken at a critical distance from both the aesthetics of the original style, and the state institutions which supported it.

In October 2001, Trần organised a field trip to the Mạo Khê coal mine in the northern province of Quảng Ninh. One of the major sites for mining in northern Vietnam, it is also part of Vietnamese Communist Party history, as the site of the first Party cell in the Quảng Ninh area. In 2019, it was recognised by the Vietnamese Government as a "national relic."[8] Historically Mạo Khê and other mining sites had also been a place for artist field trips as part of the socialist art system. The ideological basis for such trips – known as *đi sát thực tế* or "going into reality" – was to immerse artists in the lives of the working class, as well as giving them the practical exposure to be able to generate representations of labour in their art. Trần's 2001 Mạo Khê trip followed a similarly immersive logic: the artist group lived at a guest house on the site for two weeks, ate their meals with the miners, went down into the mines, shared recreation and leisure time and made their works directly in the environment of the site. In doing so, the artists were reiterating the practice known as the *ba cùng* ("three togethers") – living, eating and working with the people – initially introduced to artists and intellectuals in the 1950s as a Party-led initiative to promote the mass mobilisation of the working and farming classes in revolutionary activities.[9]

By 2001, this kind of activity had lost its intensely ideological character; yet the footage of the artists and mine workers together still holds a residual charge, suggesting the kind of intimacy and solidarity that the system was historically intended to create. The group at Mạo Khê included artists of Trần Lương's generation, such as painters Hà Trí Hiếu, Đinh Quân, Lê Quảng Hà, Lê Hồng Thái and Phạm Ngọc Minh; and attending for the final two days of the program, Đặng Xuân Hòa, as well as the ceramist Nguyễn Bảo Toàn and performance artist Đào Anh Khánh. Two younger artists who had begun their practice in the 1990s, Nguyễn Trí Mạnh and Lê Vũ, were also among the group. The site-specific works that they produced during the project reflected the general ethos of this group, and the works were very far from the idealised images of workers, farmers and soldiers of the past. Their contributions had individual as well as collective elements, but generally each artist produced their own works within the framework of the project.

In *300 Meters of Murals,* different artists painted on

8. "Mao Khe Coal Mine recognised as national relic," *Quang Ninh Online*, September 11, 2019, https://english.baoquangninh.vn/mao-khe-coal-mine-recognized-as-national-relic-2453926.html

9. On the early development of this practice, see Phoebe Scott, "Forming and Reforming the Artist: Modernity, Agency and the Discourse of Art in North Vietnam, 1925-1954," (PhD. Diss., University of Sydney, 2012), 248-57. On the general ideological developments in north Vietnam in the 1940s-50s, see Kim Ngoc Bao Ninh, *A World Transformed: The Politics of Culture in Revolutionary Vietnam 1945-1965* (Ann Arbor: University of Michigan Press, 2002).

sections of grey, cinderblock wall at the mine site, enlivening and activating the space with various whimsical, semi-abstract images, patterns and slogans [see pages 184-185]. Mạo Khê was also the site for Trần Lương's durational performance, *Steam Rice Man*, where his body was coated with glue and then white rice, which he endured while standing for six hours [see pages 130-131]. The performance was simultaneously a feat of physical stoicism, as well as a meditation on the immense and elemental transfers of energy reflected by the mining process: from body to earth to staple food and back again. As the artist's statement for Steam Rice Man reflected, "how much rice will be eaten in order to make a piece of coal?" We might also wonder whether this form of bodily mortification was also prompted by the exposure to the intense and intimate physicality of mining work itself. Part of the footage of the group's experiences at Mạo Khê showed the extensive washing needed to cleanse the miners' bodies after emerging from the mine's tunnels, coated in black dust. Trần Lương, with his body coated in white rice, formed almost an inverse physical image.

In February 2022, four months after working at the site, the *Mạo Khê Coal Mine Project* was exhibited at the Hà Nội Contemporary Art Centre, where Trần Lương was serving as the director. The exhibited version of the project showed videos and documentation photographs and recreated some of the installation aspects of the project. For instance, the artist Đinh Công Đạt painted graffiti on the façade of the Centre, using the same repeating numerical combinations with which he had also covered certain buildings at Mạo Khê during the site visit [see page 182]. The numbers were not only a form of visual abstraction, but a reference to the digits on metal tags carried by the miners into the tunnels, so that their bodies could be easily identified in the event of an accident. Some of the miners also attended the exhibition, facilitated by an official letter to the Director of the Board of the Mạo Khê mine, who then circulated the invitation to the workers. The mine eventually chartered two buses to bring approximately 70-80 miners to the exhibition space, where they stayed for nearly the whole day of the exhibition opening.

The centrality of the workers as subjects, participants and audience, as well as the process of mutual engagement which led to the project, recall aspects of the art system during the most ideologically driven periods of socialism in Vietnam. However, the final product of the "work" is critically different to what was produced under socialist realism, which was required to be optimistic and galvanising. As a result, the artworks produced almost inevitably idealised the image of the worker and their conditions. By contrast, the footage of *Mạo Khê Coal Mine Project* retains the characteristics of the site as they were directly experienced by the project participants. Danger and hardship are palpably present, as are comradeship and solidarity. By its nuanced reiteration of the practice of *đi sát thực tế*, the project spoke not only about the social conditions of its present but also of the past. In doing so, it also followed another precedent within Vietnamese art history: of artists paying tongue-in-cheek homage to socialist realism while using its framework to their own ends. Thus, the revered modern artist Bùi Xuân Phái (1920-1988), after a period of ideological study and exposure to "reality" at the coal mines of Quảng Ninh in 1968, never produced heroic images of working miners, instead painting subtle, semi-abstract works based on the pattern of striations of earth at the site of the mine.

Vietnamese socialist realism of the 1950s-1970s had tended to focus primarily on the tropes of "the farmer" and "the soldier." This was due to Vietnam's overwhelmingly rural population, as well as the circumstances of war. By the late 1970s-1980s however, the figure of "the worker" was coming to achieve greater prominence. Part of the propaganda to support Vietnam's post-war reconstruction and industrialisation, artists represented workers labouring at construction sites, ports and factories. Thus, in Lê Anh Vân's work *Công nhân lắp máy*, of 1984, the scene shows workers labouring to hoist a gigantic machine, whose overall form we cannot distinguish. The machine appears in the partial form of huge rotors, in the process of being lifted by pulleys and hooks. Painted in a lively, cubistic style somewhat reminiscent of Fernand Léger's machine-age cubism, the figures appear so harmonious with the machine elements that they are almost like its components, working in perfect collaboration. A similar example is Lò An Quang's lacquer painting *Xây trụ cầu Thăng Long* (Constructing the Pylons of Thăng Long Bridge), held in the collection of Vietnam Fine Arts Museum. Here, the figures are stylised and rhythmic, showing teams of workers labouring to construct a bridge over the Red River. The main emphasis of the work is once again on machinery: pipes, pumps, valves, cranes, pulleys and pylons visually dominate the composition. The setting of the Red River itself is obscured, as the focus shifts entirely to the feat of engineering.

It is with these images in mind that we might approach the footage of Trần Lương's project *On the Banks of the*

Red River. Made one month after the Mạo Khê project, in November 2001, the work was born out of Trần's desire to continue to connect his practice more meaningfully with a broader audience, moving art directly into the environment of the working class. The site was the area between the water of the Red River and its reinforced, walled banks; a section of the city that was home to the itinerant workers who had poured into Hà Nội from the provinces in search of work. The area was precarious in every sense of the word. Prone to flooding from the river, the inhabitants would periodically have to seek temporary shelter on the dike wall. As the area was also a dumping ground for broken-down machinery and vehicles, many of its inhabitants worked to sort and process recyclable materials for sale to factories. It was also a site of the shadow economies of desperation, like prostitution and drug trafficking.

At the time, it was very difficult to get permission to create art projects or exhibitions in public sites in Hà Nội (and it continues to be so today). To be able to realise a project of this nature required ingenuity and resourcefulness. By chance, Trần was introduced to a film director who had received permission to make a feature film on the banks of the Red River, a drama about the life of a man from the community of recycling workers. Trần negotiated a trade: the director would allow him to create his own art project at the site by the river, supported by the umbrella of the film company's permit. In exchange, the physical components of the art project could be subsequently used as part of the set design of the film (and in fact, they appeared in the final feature film but in a drastically altered form). By mutual agreement, neither were credited or acknowledged in the others' work, as each project was separately conceived and executed. It was through this arrangement that Trần Lương, along with several artists friends, could come to the site and work throughout a ten-day period, without being constrained by the permit system required for exhibition. While the artwork is credited to Trần Lương due to his conceptualisation and direction of the project, it was also realised with the help of the artists Nguyễn Trí Mạnh, Nguyễn Minh Phước, Lê Vũ, Nguyễn Quỳnh Chi, Nguyễn Quang Đức, Đinh Quân and Doãn Hoàng Lâm, who worked consistently onsite throughout many days, as well as several other artists and friends who came and went from the site intermittently.

In the footage taken of the project, we see the artists working amongst the detritus of the area: rusting machinery and remnants of iron superstructures, discarded cement mixers and trucks, stacks of breeze blocks and rubber tires, intermingled with the flimsy temporary housing made by the residents. The artist group produced site-specific sculptures by meticulously wrapping the abandoned machinery with skeins of white nylon string: the footage shows scenes of their intense concentration and absorption in the task. The string draws attention back to the forms of the discarded pieces – in Trần Lương's words "waking up the material" – elevating them from wastage products perceived only in terms of their possible exchange value to things with an objecthood and history of their own. In reviewing the footage, it is striking the extent to which the site is the reverse of the industrial socialist realist scenes of the 1980s. In those images, the machines appear as towering, invulnerable symbols of optimism, whereas here, they are shown broken, neglected and cast aside. *On the Banks of the Red River* is also far from idealistic in its images of the plight of workers, capturing the hardship of life in this liminal zone. As part of the footage, we see the women on bicycles whose work it is to sort and sell the rubbish, as well as workers transporting machinery, or cartloads of river soil, by buffalo cart. If socialist realism elevated an ideal of "the worker" and Vietnam's industrial development, *On the Banks of the Red River* might be said to critique it. Yet, in certain respects, the project also conforms to certain important principles associated with Vietnamese socialist realism. Workers were not only subjects of the project, but also its intended audience and participants: a key tenet of art in the socialist period.

Once the wrapped structures were complete, the artists strung together little enclosures made with cotton mosquito nets. As night fell, these bright, pristine spots transformed the landscape [see pages 134-135]. For one night, underprivileged children from the SOS Children's Village in Hà Nội were invited to come to the site. Trần had wanted the children to participate in the project, in keeping with its general ethos to democratise the experience of art. As many of the children were the victims of the same cycle of poverty that brought workers to the Red River's banks, they also had a notional connection to the site. To realise their presence in the project, Trần once again drew on a personal connection – a friend who taught performance at the Children's Village – to gain permission for the children to attend, and in return provided transportation, food and agreed to take responsibility for their safety. Inside the mosquito-net enclosures, which the artist intended to act as a form of protective sanctuary for the children, they could choose freely whether to sing, play games or study. Others sang a folk-style song composed by

Trần, which narrated the story of young workers migrating to the city. Some of the children, however, engaged in behaviour that was shocking to audiences in Hà Nội – for instance, deciding to gamble or using profanities – but Trần elected not to censor out this aspect from the final footage. From the ethical point of view of today, we might feel some uneasiness about involving children in a project that was not of their own design and question their level of agency in how they were represented, as well as issues of vulnerability and consent. However, what is undeniable is that the artist's original intention was to de-privilege art, bringing different marginalised social groups together with the art world. Thus, the audience at the "opening" of this unofficial exhibition, to which people found their way via hand-drawn directions to the site, combined artists, art lovers, workers, children and the urban dispossessed.

In situating Trần Lương's 2001 projects within the history of Vietnamese socialist realism, the intention is not to position them as forms of continuity; to do so would undermine the critical perspective potentially offered by the works. Nor is it to suggest that the values of socialist realism were ethically normative, as that would ignore the historical relationship between the style, state control and censorship. Instead, we can consider that exposure to the socialist art system left a residue in terms of its framework and aspirations, which were later critically reactivated by the artists. It is also possible to speculate on the significance of the year 2001, coming 15 years after the initiation of the *đổi mới* policy and the optimism it generated in the cultural sector. While the early post-*đổi mới* years were marked by a creative exuberance and a new embrace of individual expression, by 2001 this impulse was perhaps giving way to the need to undertake a more critical and sobering reflection on the past, made newly possible through the distancing effects of time.

ARTWORKS

Painting | Installation | Performance | Video

NEWSPAPER ILLUSTRATIONS AND BOOKS

Since 1986, Trần Lương has created illustrations for many newspapers and publishing houses including the weekly newspaper Văn Nghệ (Literature and Arts) Weekly Newspaper, the Almanac of Science and Technology publishing house (Nhà Xuất Bản Khoa Học Kỹ Thuật) and Kim Đồng Publishing House (Children Publishing House). He has also illustrated poetry books by invitation from various writers and was commissioned by newspaper editors to illustrate stories on a range of topics. Lương published under his own name or under the name of his sister Văn Cơ, in order to access more commissioned opportunities. Original illustrations were rarely returned to the artist. Besides being a source of income, Lương's illustrations are closely connected to his painting languages, which allowed him to experiment with his own themes through illustrations that were sometimes transformed into larger-scale works. He continues to make illustrations today from time to time when invited.

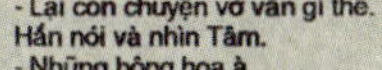

HƯƠNG CÚC DẠI

Truyện ngắn của
TRỊNH ĐÌNH KHÔI

NGÀY ấy, Tâm sống trong túp lều bên bờ sông. Túp lều của mẹ con người lái đò nằm ép vào phía trong lũy tre chắn lũ. Dân làng ít người để mắt tới, mặc dù ngày nào họ cũng qua đò. Chỉ có mấy ông chức dịch thỉnh thoảng đảo qua thu thuế đò hoặc nhìn mặt mẹ con người đàn bà góa nói dăm ba câu bông phèng.

Bằng vào biệt hiệu "Nàng Bân" dân làng đặt cho Tâm, dần dần người ta quên cả cái tên cúng cơm của cô. "Nàng Bân" quanh năm ngồi đan. Cứ ngơi tay chèo ra Tâm lại vớ lấy que đan. Trên tay cô lúc nào cũng có chiếc áo đan dở của khách qua đò. Áo dày, áo mỏng, áo nam, áo nữ đủ loại, nhưng có lẽ nhiều hơn cả là áo con trai. Tâm nổi tiếng khéo tay. Là con gái nhà nghèo nhưng cô xinh đẹp. Bao nhiêu trai làng nhờ Tâm đan áo. Khi nhận áo họ thường buông lời hoa nguyệt, trêu cợt thôi chứ chẳng ai thực lòng. Người ta lấy gì con nhà lái đò nghèo rớt mồng tơi. Tâm nghĩ.

Người già chỉ cản được chuyện vợ chồng chứ làm sao cản được những đêm trăng trai gái. Đám con trai đào thùng đóng cọc, bọn con gái căng dây làm trống. Bên nam bên nữ đối đáp cho đến khi trăng đã xuống ngọn tre mới rõ trống. Tiếng hát, tiếng trống vang vẳng trong đêm khiến làng xóm đỡ hiu quạnh. "Nàng Bân" hát hay nhất hội, tiếng nàng thánh thót :

Trống quân trống quít trống còi
Ta chẳng lấy nó, nó đòi lấy ta...

Đúng là nhiều người muốn lấy Tâm nhưng họ sợ mà nàng cũng chưa định lấy chồng. Tâm còn mẹ già. Ấy thế mà... Một chiều mây đen ùn ùn từ phía đông kéo về, gió lạnh thổi, trời đổ mưa. Những giọt mưa như những mũi tên lao chéo xuống con thuyền. Dân xóm Bãi chạy mưa tụ tập trên điếm canh đê, nhìn con đò khảo nhau.

"Nàng Bân" có chửa. Chửa với ai thì có trời mới biết. Vì nàng là hương của trời, ai chả muốn ngửi. Đám đàn ông cười hô hố, mấy mụ đàn bà nạ dòng lắm mồm lắm miệng cấu chí nhau cười rinh rích rồi kể những chuyện tục tĩu đến nỗi đám con trai mới lớn phát thèm. Mấy ông có chữ bàn luận "Người đẹp nhất làng mà chửa hoang là tại làng mình có miếu mà không thờ". Cái miếu trên núi thờ thần hôn nhân. Mỗi trận mưa rào, trên ngọn núi nước chảy trắng xóa như những dòng sữa xuống cánh đồng. Năm nào cái vú khổng lồ chảy nhiều sữa thì dân no đủ. Năm nào, dòng sữa của nữ thần cạn thì mất mùa đói kém. Cánh thanh niên bảo "Nàng Bân" chửa với thần. Mấy mụ già mắng : thần thánh nào lại làm cái chuyện ấy. Có người cãi "không thế làm sao có thần đồng". Điều này chỉ có "Nàng Bân" mới biết nhưng không ai cạy được răng nàng dù có bị cạo trọc bôi vôi. Huống chi thời bây giờ không ai làm thế. Cái làng nổi tiếng khuôn phép thế mà hoa hậu của làng bỗng trở thành "gái ngoan". Ai cũng tỏ vẻ bất bình. Mẹ Tâm ép buộc thế nào cô cũng không chịu uống thuốc ra thai. "Người ta cười ba tháng chứ ai cười ba năm". Tâm cãi. Một ngày xuân nắng vàng mật ong, cô vừa quấn mấy vòng chão neo con đò vào bờ thì bụng bỗng nhói đau. Nhìn con vật vã bà mẹ thương xót nhưng vui. Người mẹ lưng còng tóc bạc, mặc bộ váy và chằng và đụp, lập cập sửa soạn cho con sinh nở. Bà đặt Tâm nằm ngay ngắn trên chiếc chõng tre rồi pha nước nóng rửa ráy cho cô. Chẳng có dao có kéo, bà sắp sẵn chiếc liềm.

- Cố lên nào con. Đẻ con so đau thế là ít đấy.

Tiếng oe oe... của đứa bé lọt lòng làm căn lều ấm cúng hẳn lên. Một chú thần đồng mặt vuông mắt sáng ra đời. Trời nhá nhem tối, khi bà mẹ bưng cái nồi đất đậy vung bước lật ra vườn thì gặp một người đàn ông đi vào. Chưa nhìn rõ mặt đã nghe tiếng người.

- Thằng cu hay cái đĩ đấy bà ?

- Cám ơn, thằng cu, trông thằng bé khôi ngô lắm.

- Chúc cháu hay ăn chóng lớn.

- Chú vào nhà chơi, tôi về ngay.

Tưởng người đàn ông vào trong nhà, nhưng khi bà mẹ chôn xong nhúm nhau trở về hỏi thì chẳng thấy ai. Hôm sau, khi bà mẹ trở dậy mở cửa liếp che gió đã thấy ai đặt sẵn ngoài cửa một cành dâu uốn cong và ba mũi tên bằng cỏ. Bà lái đò lẩm bẩm một mình : "Quái lạ, ai đã tặng cháu bà cái chí tang bồng hồ thỉ. Thằng bé chắc sẽ nên người".

Đêm đó, bà lão dỗ dành mãi cô con gái mới thú thực. Thế là bà biết cha của đứa cháu là ai, nhưng con gái bà đã không nhận kẻ đó là cha đứa bé từ cái đêm ấy rồi. Cái đêm anh ta sợ đến xanh mắt vì cái tin Tâm đã có thai. Vài ngày sau hắn quất ngựa truy phong. Trước đêm ra thành phố hắn đã tìm gặp Tâm.

- Mai anh đi rồi.

- Sao vội thế.

Tâm run rẩy nhìn hắn rồi lặng lẽ khóc.

- Đừng khóc, nếu không anh về đây.

- Vâng, em không khóc nữa.

Tâm nói vội vã và nuốt những giọt nước mắt.

- Anh đi thật à ?

Tâm hỏi lại sau những phút im lặng.

- Bao giờ anh lại về

- Chắc còn lâu.

- Đừng quên em và con anh nhé !

- Đấy cô lại nói đến con rồi.

Như nhai phải quả đắng, hắn nói thêm.

- Cô phải giấu biệt chuyện này đi, tôi mới dám về làng, không thể để mọi người nhìn tôi là kẻ tồi tệ.

Tâm nuốt những giọt nước mắt. Cô muốn nói với hắn rằng "kẻ bỏ con không dám nhận mới là kẻ tồi tệ" Nhưng Tâm không thốt thành lời. Cô mân mê mãi chiếc khăn vải gói những bông hoa cúc dại trên tay.

- Em có cái này tặng anh.

- Lại còn chuyện vớ vẩn gì thế.

Hắn nói và nhìn Tâm.

- Những bông hoa à.

- Vâng... Hoa cúc dại, thứ hoa mà chúng mình vẫn thích. Tâm đáp với vẻ rầu rĩ.

- Ừ... anh xin.

Giọng bất đắc dĩ của hắn khiến Tâm đau khổ. Hắn uể oải đưa một tay ra nhận. Tâm chờ đợi dù chỉ một lời. Cô nhìn hắn trìu mến đến mức sùng kính. Hắn vẫn dửng dưng. Lòng kiên nhẫn của Tâm không làm hắn xúc động.

- Rồi mẹ con em sẽ sống thế nào.

Tâm nói rồi nấc lên. Cả hai im lặng. Hắn muốn đứng lên nhưng hai bàn tay cô gái vẫn bíu chặt lấy cánh tay hắn.

- Ở lại với em một lát nữa.

Tâm van vỉ. Hắn trừng mắt rít lên :

- Đã bảo không nhắc đến con kia mà...

Tâm chùng lại, giọng cô trở nên lạnh lùng.

- Anh là kẻ có tội.

- Tội gì ?

Hắn cau có nhìn Tâm.

- Tội với con anh.

- Tôi đã nói, tôi không thể lấy cô làm vợ. Rồi mọi người sẽ nhìn tôi như thế nào ?

- Nhìn như thế nào mặc mẹ họ. Anh cút đi. Tôi không nghe anh nói nữa.

Tâm gào lên, nước mắt cô trào ra, hai tay bưng lấy mặt. Khi cô buông tay xuống thì hắn đã quay gót bước những bước dài. Tâm muốn chạy theo nhưng cô bủn rủn ngã vật xuống vạt cỏ. Không biết từ đâu, một người con trai đã đến bế Tâm về túp lều của hai mẹ con. Lúc ấy, mẹ cô đang chèo đò ngoài sông. Anh ta đặt Tâm lên giường rồi sẽ sàng để gói hoa trên gối. Khi cô tỉnh lại, anh đã lặng lẽ bỏ đi. Ai thế ? Lại một người nữa ghé qua đời mình. Tâm thấy sợ.

Sau đêm đó, từ phía thượng nguồn con sông đêm nào Tâm cũng nghe thấy tiếng sáo. Sáo thổi những bài dân ca Tâm thích. Những bài tỏ tình giao duyên trong đêm trống quân. Càng lạ lùng, sáng sáng trên tấm phên che ô cửa sổ, ai đó đã gài sẵn những bông hoa cúc dại. Sau khi sinh nở Tâm khỏe hẳn ra. Đám đàn ông trong làng nhìn cô gái một con gương mặt hồng hào bộ ngực nở nang bằng cái nhìn đầy thèm khát. Dù thế trước mặt mọi người họ vẫn dè bỉu. Tâm thì nghĩ : "Con trai làng này toàn những đồ bỏ đi, họ sợ đủ thứ. Chẳng anh nào đáng mặt làm bố thằng Linh". Sự có mặt của Tâm như thách đố đám đàn ông. Cô chẳng để ý đến ai. Mặc họ lân la tán tỉnh. Chỉ có một người làm cô nghĩ ngợi. Người đàn ông thổi sáo. Bây giờ trong gian lều chỉ còn Tâm và đứa con. Mẹ cô đã qua đời sau một cơn cảm lạnh. Như lời chúc của một người nào đó. Thằng Linh hay ăn chóng lớn. Nó không sài đẹn còi cọc như những đứa trẻ cùng trang lứa. Suốt những tháng ngày nuôi con Tâm không biết đến viên thuốc mặt tròn méo dẹt ra sao. Một đêm Tâm lo mọ ở ngoài sông trở về đã thấy thằng Linh được tắm rửa sạch sẽ đang ngồi gặm bắp ngô nướng.

- Ai cho con ngô.

Tâm Hỏi.

- Cái bác gì ấy.

- Ai tắm rửa cho con.

- Bác ấy không nói tên.

Tâm vừa mừng vừa lo "Ai thế".

- Sao con không giữ bác ấy lại. Lần sau mẹ đi vắng con không được cho ai vào nhà nhé.

- Vâng.

Thằng Linh chỉ vâng lời lúc bấy giờ nhưng rồi đâu lại đóng đấy. Nó vẫn nhận quà và sự chăm sóc của người đàn ông lạ mặt. Thằng bé không dấu mẹ, Tâm cũng chẳng trách mắng con. Cô thấy vui vui. Tâm thương thằng bé thiếu sự chăm bẵm của người cha.

Thằng Linh đã lớn, nó sáng dạ hơn con cái những người trong làng. Lũ bạn học không còn chế giễu nó là "thằng không bố" nữa. Dần dà, nhiều đứa còn nhờ Linh giảng bài cho. Chúng vui vẻ với nhau quên cả chuyện người lớn nói. Túp lều một gian đã thêm hai chái. Vách trát bùn nhào rơm thay cho những cái phên bằng rong tre. Mái lợp lá mía được thay bằng mái rạ vàng thơm. Mảnh vườn sau nhà có sức lực đứa con trai cũng trở nên xanh tốt. Những khóm rong riềng hoàng tinh vươn cao, dây bầu dây bí leo dàn nở hoa vàng rực, góc vườn cây khế, cây ổi gầy guộc nhưng trĩu quả. Mùa hè mít thơm lừng, mùa thu cành hồng trĩu những ngọn đèn ngọn lồng nhỏ xíu.

Nhưng rồi bẵng đi một thời gian Tâm không còn được nghe tiếng sáo, thằng Linh cũng không nhận được quà nữa. Cô không biết người đó ở đâu, không biết bao giờ anh tới. Tâm phải đi tìm anh hay cứ nén lòng chờ. Những đêm trăng sáng, neo con đò vào bến cô lại một mình tha thẩn đi dọc bờ sông về phía có tiếng sáo và hương cúc dại vẫn theo gió về. Vô vọng, có lẽ người ấy đã đi xa. Kỳ này những đoàn tân binh qua đò rất đông. Trong số những gương mặt ấy có ai là anh không. Nghĩ thế, mỗi lần chở một đoàn quân qua sông Tâm thường liếc trộm từng gương mặt. Tất cả đều vui vẻ nhìn cô và tặng những lời hẹn ước. Mỗi đoàn quân qua đò, Tâm lại đứng nhìn cho đến người cuối cùng đi khuất mới quay về. Những ngón tay gầy xanh rờ rẫm từng đường len trên chiếc áo. Hàng chục chuyến đò qua mà chiếc áo vẫn còn đấy. Tâm chợt thấy mình bé nhỏ cô đơn. Gian lều chìm trong đêm tối. Tiếng thở đều đều ấm áp của đứa con khiến cô thấy mình được an ủi. Tâm lặng lẽ nhìn thằng Linh nằm co mình trong chiếc ổ rơm. Ngọn đèn dầu vặn nhỏ bằng hạt đỗ tỏa ra một quầng xanh vẫn nhấp nháy từng đêm từng đêm trong nỗi chờ đợi khắc khoải của người đàn bà.

Chiến tranh thật dài. Nó đã lan đến gian lều của hai mẹ con. Một hôm thằng Linh vừa từ trường về chưa kịp cơm nước gì đã theo đám bạn bè cùng lớp đi đâu không biết. Tối đến nó hí hoáy viết bên bàn học rồi giơ lên trước mặt Tâm một mảnh giấy.

- Mẹ ơi ! Con làm đơn xin đi bộ đội, mẹ có bằng lòng không.

- Tiên sư nhà anh, làm rồi còn hỏi gì mẹ. Tâm mắng yêu con.

- Nhưng chưa đầy mười bảy ai người ta nhận.

- Trai mười bảy bẻ gãy sừng trâu, mẹ chả bảo thế là gì.

Tâm im lặng. Cô còn biết nói gì, thằng bé đã trưởng thành. Tâm cũng qua cái tuổi đã toan về già dăm năm rồi. Cô muốn chợp đi một chốc để ngày mai lấy sức tiễn con nhưng Tâm làm sao ngủ được, cô lại nghĩ đến người ấy. Cái người mà cô chỉ nhìn thấy bóng không nhìn rõ mặt. Tiếng sáo của anh thật réo rắt tha thiết. Anh cứ ngồi lỳ bên bờ sông mặc gió thổi, mặc sương lạnh cho đến lúc trăng tà. Việc ấy chỉ mình Tâm biết. Cô thức dậy im lặng lắng nghe. Đôi lần Tâm len lén đến bên anh. Tiếng sáo bỗng im bặt, anh đứng dậy bước đi không ngoảnh lại. Cái dáng của anh quen quen mà Tâm không nhớ ra. Những đêm Tâm đi với bố thằng Linh thường có một người vẫn đứng nhìn theo.

Có phải người đó không ?

Mỗi lần tiếng sáo im bặt Tâm lại thấy bục thấy tiếc. Cô nghĩ :

Minh họa của TRẦN LƯƠNG

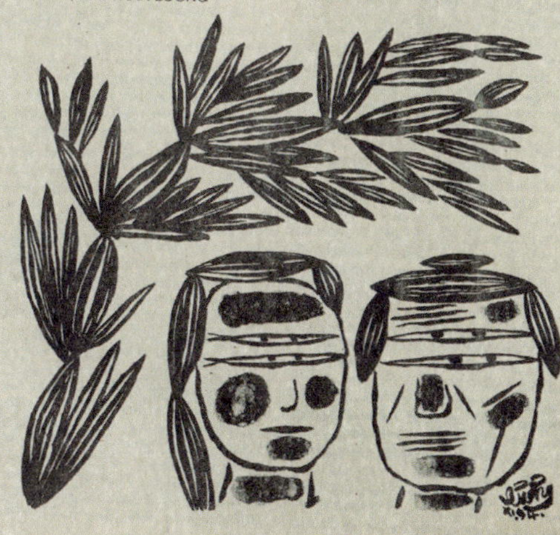

chuyện những vùng đất cao cẳng xa xôi nước biển không bao giờ đuổi tới, chuyện ở đâu đó con chó đẻ ra con dê, cây dừa có chín đọt... Hoặc họ không nói gì cũng được, ca hát cũng được... Nhưng họ phải về, phải sống. Cuối buổi sáng là nhà chức trách xả nước ngọt ở các máy nước công cộng, không kịp chèo ghe đi lấy sẽ không có nước nấu cơm, tắm giặt...

Sáo chỉ còn một mình.

Một mình.

Sáo lết đi bắc xoong cơm lên bếp lửa. Cảm thấy tay áo giở lên còn không nổi. Bụng không đói miệng thì đắng nhưng Sáo phải ăn, để chờ người ta trả lời tại sao chồng nó chết. Đợi chán Sáo lại chèo ghe tới chỗ nhà chức trách thăm chừng, khi thì thấy vài anh say sưa chơi cờ, khi thì thấy một anh ngủ gục bên bàn làm việc kệ ruồi o e trên mép. Hỏi thì họ chưng hửng nói cô còn đợi sự thật nào? Như thể có rất nhiều sự thật nằm nhấp nhổm trong ngăn kéo, và họ đang chọn một cái sự thật hợp với tướng tá xơ rơ, túi áo lép kẹp của Sáo.

Hơi thất vọng, Sáo chèo trong chảo nắng mặn trở về, bỗng nín thở nhìn thấy cái lưng dài nhằng của chồng mình trên mái nhà. Em chồng Sáo mang nó về, cả đôi chân mày rậm. Nó thảng thốt hỏi chị Hai làm gì vậy. Sáo nói chị đâu có làm gì. Trời ơi chị xởn tóc chị xơ cờ kìa.

Em chồng nhìn Sáo như thể kêu Sáo nín đi, như thể Sáo xởn tóc là một cách khóc. Sáo chỉ gượng cười rồi luýnh quýnh đi nấu cơm cho em chồng ăn, bận bịu làm sự sống quay trở lại trong nó. Sáo đã quen sống và làm lụng vì ai đó. Như bà nội Sáo vì thương chồng mà bơi xuống đi cưới hai bà vợ bé cho chồng, như má Sáo vì chuộc chồng khỏi núi nợ ở trường gà mà phải bán hết đất lên ghe sống lênh đênh. Năm mươi chín tuổi, nghe má ao ước "lúc chết được nằm trên đất của mình", Sáo lấy chồng. Lấy người má nó chọn, lý do "thằng đó có tới chục ngoài công đất". Sáo nhìn thấy chồng lần đầu khi anh đang ôm con gà tre đi trên đường, miệng ngậm vung vinh cọng cỏ mần trầu, nó tự hỏi đây sẽ là chồng mình sao? Lễ ăn trầu uống rượu rồi, chồng vỗ mông Sáo, nó lại hỏi đây là chồng mình sao? Hôm cưới nghe chồng phả hơi rượu nóng rực vô vành tai, vẫn hỏi chồng mình đó sao? Nhưng lúc Sáo cài khuy áo lại, ngó cái người đang lật ra ngủ queo đó, nó nghĩ đây là chồng mình. Nghẹn căng ứ mũi.

Má Sáo vui lắm, gói gém mấy lễ, bà mua hai công đất dành để chôn. Nhờ con gái hiếu thảo mà thím đổi đời rồi, má giả đò vu vơ khoe với một khách thương hồ quen, không lâu sau, anh ta cũng lấy con gái nhà giàu dưới chợ.

Nước đuổi vào sâu Châu Thổ, đất - thứ vì nó mà Sáo lấy chồng - trở nên vô nghĩa, như cái tên xóm Rẫy mà còn cái rẫy nào đâu.

Giờ đến cả chồng, Sáo cũng làm mất.

Em chồng rút trong túi xách ra bộ đồ tây mới cáu đặt cạnh đôi dép da mà nó đã mua cho chồng Sáo từ năm trước. Món quà còn nguyên niêm mạc, chồng Sáo chưa đi lần nào, anh nói chờ kiếm có quần áo đẹp mặc cho đúng điệu. Có lần đi chợ gặp em chồng, Sáo kể, nó buột miệng chửi thề: "Má, thằng cha cầu kỳ quá, con nhà lính tính nhà quan...". Giờ thì em chồng im lìm ngồi vuốt mớ đồ của anh nó. Bao giờ chồng nhập thổ, Sáo sẽ chôn chúng theo.

Ngó cái cảnh đợi công lý của Sáo, thằng em chồng cười khảo, con dao bấm trên tay cứ lè lưỡi ra tanh tách, sáng quắc. Nó nói "công lý ở trong tay mình mà, chị Hai..."

Em chồng đi giang hồ từ nhỏ, lưng em giờ đã hai mươi hai cái thẹo, đó là những lần em thực thi công lý hay bị công lý của nhóm giang hồ khác thực thi lên. Không thẹo người ta không biết mình dân giang hồ, em khoe vậy, giống như ở chợ hay gắn chữ văn hóa cho người ta biết là có văn hóa vậy. Em chồng cũng thường khoe công lý của em nhanh hơn, luật của em công bằng, sòng phẳng hơn. Không tin không được, nhiều lần nó tìm lại những món đồ nhà Sáo bị trộm lấy đi, dù chúng đã bị thay hình đổi dạng, bị tháo rã ra bán đầu một nơi mình một nẻo. Nó còn dẫn thằng ăn trộm về biểu: "Xin lỗi anh chị Hai tao, mầy!", và thằng kia cun cút cúi đầu.

Nhưng đó chỉ là thằng trộm nhỏ thó hom hem, giờ em chồng Sáo sẽ đối đầu với một bè rau đông người lắm của. Em chồng đi rồi Sáo nóng ruột bồn chồn quá, như thể chỉ cần vo gạo rồi ôm cái nồi vào bụng, gạo sẽ sôi thành cơm. Mấy bữa sau nghe ở mấy máy nước công cộng người ta hể hả bàn tán, nói xe hơi của nhà Đại Thanh dưới chợ bị đập phá, tụi giang hồ còn đánh thuốc chết mấy con chó, tưới xăng định đốt biệt thự, may mà nhà chức trách tiếp cứu kịp.

Bữa sau nữa, người ta rủ Sáo đi coi một bảo vệ của bè rau bị dìm chết. Sáo không đi, nó không chắc mình sẽ hả hê khi nhìn thi thể đó. Sáo sợ cái bàn lạnh ngắt giữa căn phòng lạnh ngắt, nơi hơi thở một con người bỗng dưng biến mất. Ở đó, biết đâu cũng có con đàn bà gột rửa da thịt chồng bằng nước mắt, mong gọi những hơi thở trở về.

Nhưng buổi tối hôm đó Sáo đã phải xuôi ghe tới văn phòng của nhà chức trách, vì em chồng Sáo. May phước, em chồng không nằm trên bàn mà bị trói gô, khiến cái lưng dài thượt gần như cuốn tròn lại. Sáo thở phào nhẹ nhõm dù hoàn cảnh của thằng em hiện giờ rất cay đắng. Vậy mấy bữa qua Sáo đã bồn chồn lo lắng cho ai? Nó tự hỏi, người mướt mồ hôi lạnh. Ngó vẻ mặt đờ đẫn của Sáo, em chồng cố an ủi mà giọng nói cứ nghiến sít sìn sịt :

- Chị buồn con c. gì, tụi nó bắt tui như bắt cóc bỏ đĩa. Chỉ uổng là tui chưa kịp bẻ cổ thằng Giang.

Câu nói làm Sáo rúm ró. Sáo biết người đàn ông tên Giang đó, lầm lì ít nói, da ngăm đen mắt sâu, hai bàn tay đều chai. Và tóc gội sương gió cứng đến nỗi nếu ai đó để anh ta gối đầu lên đùi, họ sẽ nghe vừa nhột ran vừa đau nhoi nhói. Người đó đã từng hiền lắm, ngập ngừng mãi mới dám nắm bàn tay con gái, nhưng theo lời em chồng Sáo thì giờ anh ta đã đổi thay quay quắt như con cá Sấu Ngư. Sáo muốn đi tìm coi anh ta nhuốm đỏ tới mức nào.

Sáo sẽ đi. Nó quyết định vậy khi nhìn theo em chồng bị người ta đưa đi mất. Nhanh đến nỗi Sáo nhận ra công lý thật ra đâu có già nua hay chậm chạp hay đui mù. Sáo thấy mình vừa mất hết, cả người thân cuối cùng và chút niềm tin cuối cùng. Nhưng cái cảm giác đó thật sự rõ ràng khi nước bắt đầu rút, Sáo đào xuống năm lớp đá, rồi kéo cái thứ đất ngâm lâu bủng beo trong nước đó, đắp lên cho chồng.

Chờ những mầm cỏ Đuôi Mèo lún phún lên xanh, Sáo chèo ghe đến bè rau Đại Thanh. Nhắm mắt thì nó cũng chèo được tới cái chuỗi xanh ngằn ngặt ở ngã ba sông Sắc, chỗ sông Mê cắt qua.

5

Bè đang tuyển người làm. Những nhân công cũ sợ giang hồ đòi công lý nên xin nghỉ quá nửa. Sáo bị xua đuổi ngay khi trờ tới, họ nhận ra vợ của thằng oan gia bứt ngò. Nhưng vì người ta biết Sáo nên nó vẫn cắp cái nón trong nách nấn ná chờ. Hồi lâu có người kêu, cô kia tên gì để tôi ghi hồ sơ ? Ông ta hỏi mà vẻ mặt thảng thốt như không hiểu cái câu vừa rồi sao lại tuôn ra khỏi miệng, như thể đang nghĩ mướn con này chẳng khác nào rước giặc vô nhà, sao ông chủ mình ngu vậy ?

Cũng ngơ ngác, Sáo nói tên mình. Ngay lập tức trên danh nghĩa nó trở thành người của bè rau. Dù Sáo chỉ muốn tới hỏi người đàn ông tên Giang đó có thật đã muốn chồng nó chết không. Sáo nghĩ người đó sẽ im lặng hoặc nói không, vậy đỡ quá. Chối bỏ nghĩa là còn biết sợ hãi. Nhưng con rể của nhà giàu Đại Thanh, người quản lý bè rau mênh mông này, anh ta nói có. Anh ta nhìn thẳng vào Sáo, nói có, nó – đáng – chết...". Anh ta vẫn rám nắng chắc chắn vạm vỡ như năm bảy năm trước, mắt vẫn rười rượi sâu. Mặt anh ta phẳng lặng, giọng cũng đều đặn thản nhiên, mà buốt nhức :

- Em sẽ làm gì tôi ?

Sáo chết trân. Nó không biết. Nó đinh ninh là anh ta sẽ chối bay chối biến và nó cắp nón ra về, an ủi mình đã tìm được sự thật giống như sự thật. Nhưng anh ta thừa nhận, trâng tráo như Sáo không thể làm gì được. Sáo sẽ chạy tới nhờ nhà chức trách đang ngủ gục hay sẽ đòi công lý bằng dao bấm giống như em chồng?

Ngơ ngác, Sáo bỏ đi. Vài ba bận chèo ghe trở lại, cũng chừng ấy lần lủi thủi quay về. Sáo nghĩ chắc tại phải chèo xa mệt mỏi nên sự căm thù hao hụt. Nó quyết định ở lại làm công cho bè rau. Ở đây nó sẽ tích tụ được những cơn giận dữ, đến khi chúng căng chặt, nổ tung thì đường đến căn phòng của tên gian ác

(Xem tiếp trang 21)

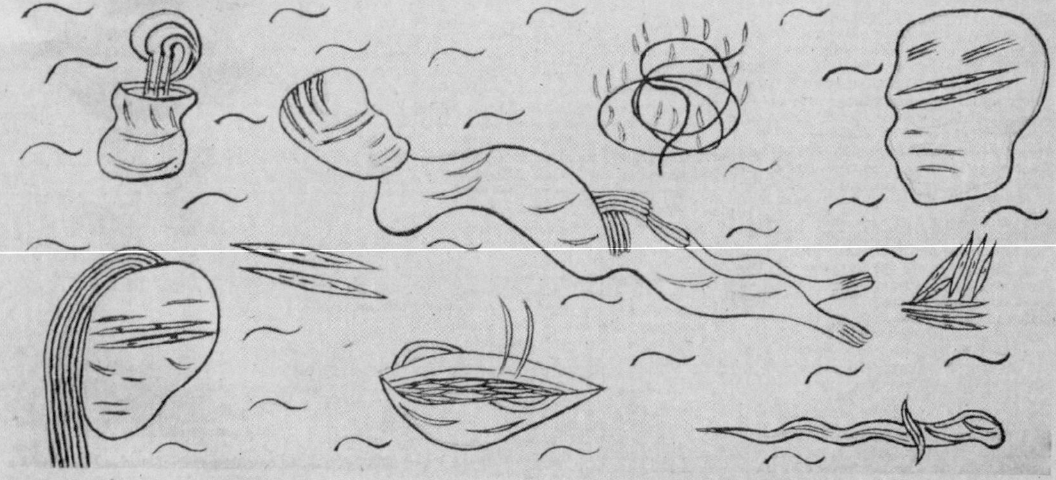

Minh họa của TRẦN LƯƠNG

1,2
Illustration for short story *Hương Cúc Dại* ("The scent of wild daisy"), by Trịnh Đình Khôi, *Văn Nghệ* (Literature and Arts) Newspaper, No.47, p6, published on 19 November, 1994.

4
Illustration sketch for *Văn Nghệ* (Literature and Arts) Newspaper.

3,5
Illustration for short story *Nước như nước mắt* ("Water like tears"), by Nguyễn Ngọc Tư, *Văn Nghệ* (Literature and Arts) Newspaper, No.17 + 18, p5, published on 28 April, 2012.

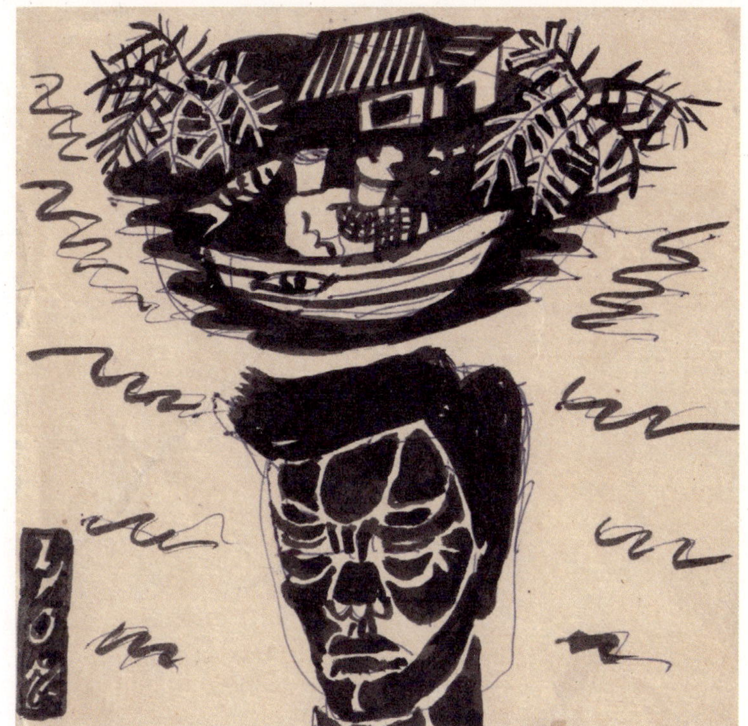

4

5

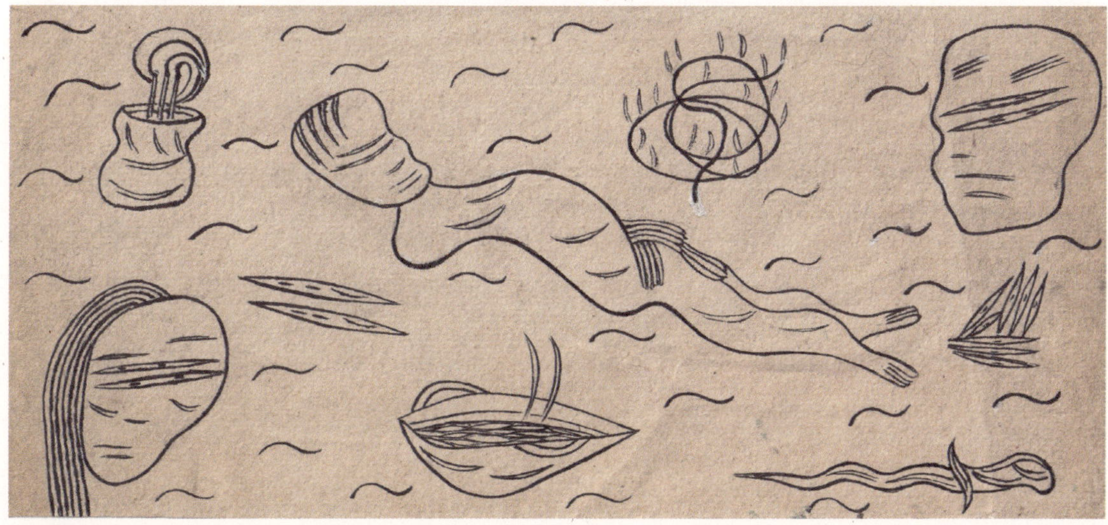

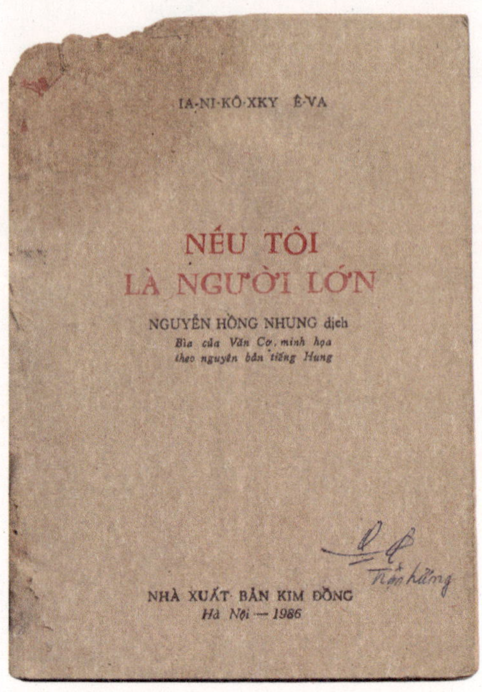

IA-NI-KÔ-XKY Ê-VA

NẾU TÔI
LÀ NGƯỜI LỚN

NGUYÊN HỒNG NHUNG dịch
Bìa của Văn Cơ, minh họa
theo nguyên bản tiếng Hung

NHÀ XUẤT BẢN KIM ĐỒNG
Hà Nội — 1986

"Nếu tôi là người lớn," Vietnamese adaptation of "If I were grown-up" by Janikovszky Éva, 1986, (Hà Nội: Kim Đồng Publishing House).

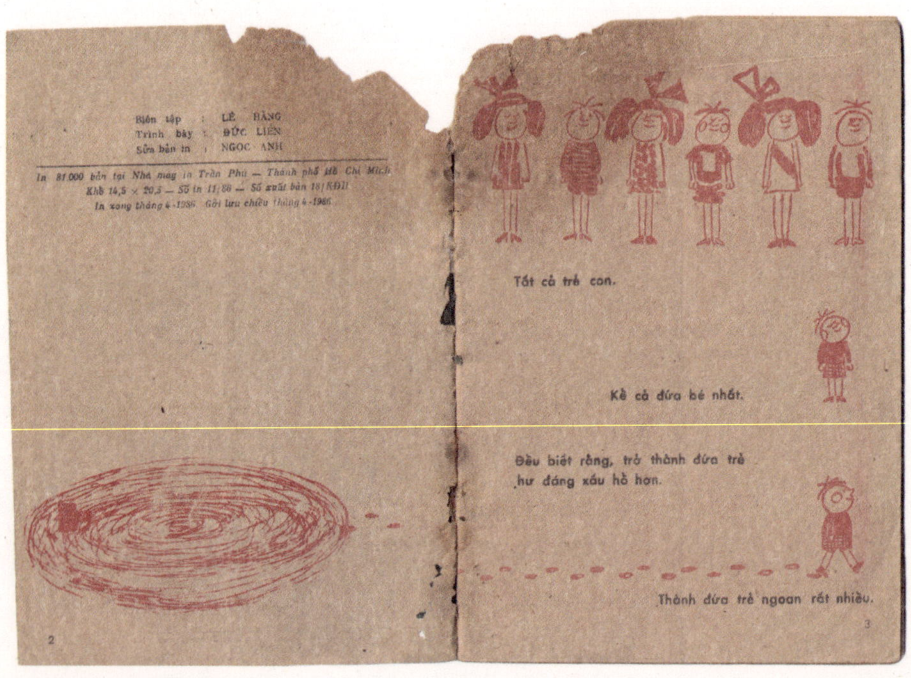

Biên tập : LÊ HẰNG
Trình bày : ĐỨC LIÊN
Sửa bản in : NGỌC ANH

In 81.000 bản tại Nhà máy in Trần Phú — Thành phố Hồ Chí Minh
Khổ 14,5 × 20,5 — Số in 11/86 — Số xuất bản 18/KĐII
In xong tháng 4-1986. Gửi lưu chiểu tháng 4-1986

2

Tất cả trẻ con.

Kể cả đứa bé nhất.

Đều biết rằng, trở thành đứa trẻ hư đáng xấu hổ hơn.

Thành đứa trẻ ngoan rất nhiều.

3

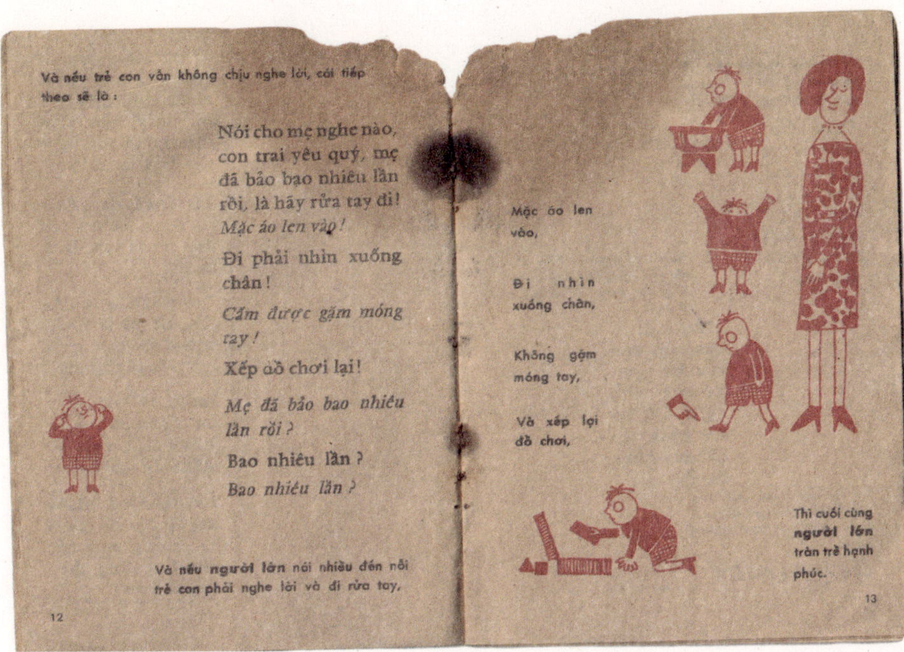
Và nếu trẻ con vẫn không chịu nghe lời, cái tiếp theo sẽ là :
Nói cho mẹ nghe nào, con trai yêu quý, mẹ đã bảo bao nhiêu lần rồi, là hãy rửa tay đi!
Mặc áo len vào!
Đi phải nhìn xuống chân!
Cấm được gặm móng tay!
Xếp đồ chơi lại!
Mẹ đã bảo bao nhiêu lần rồi?
Bao nhiêu lần?
Bao nhiêu lần?
Và nếu người lớn nói nhiều đến nỗi trẻ con phải nghe lời và đi rửa tay,
12
Mặc áo len vào,
Đi nhìn xuống chân,
Không gặm móng tay,
Và xếp lại đồ chơi,
Thì cuối cùng người lớn tràn trề hạnh phúc.
13

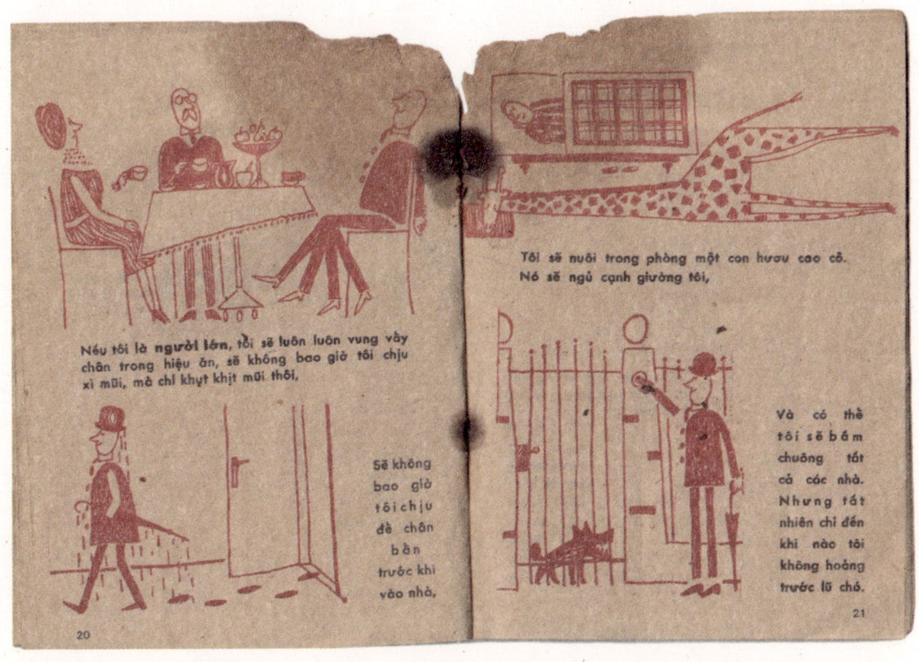
Nếu tôi là người lớn, tôi sẽ luôn luôn vung vẩy chân trong hiệu ăn, sẽ không bao giờ tôi chịu xì mũi, mà chỉ khụt khịt mũi thôi,
Sẽ không bao giờ tôi chịu đè chân bẩn trước khi vào nhà,
20
Tôi sẽ nuôi trong phòng một con hươu cao cổ. Nó sẽ ngủ cạnh giường tôi,
Và có thể tôi sẽ bấm chuông tất cả các nhà. Nhưng tất nhiên chỉ đến khi nào tôi không hoảng trước lũ chó.
21

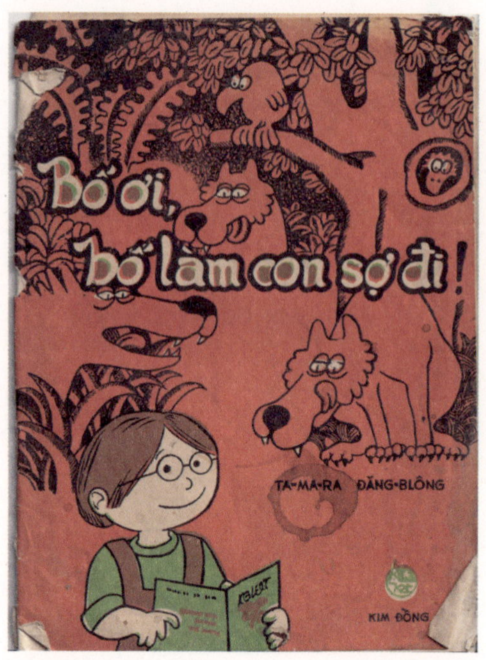

Vietnamese adaptiation of "Papa, fais-moi peur!" by Tamara Danblon, 1989, (Hà Nội: Kim Đồng Publishing House).

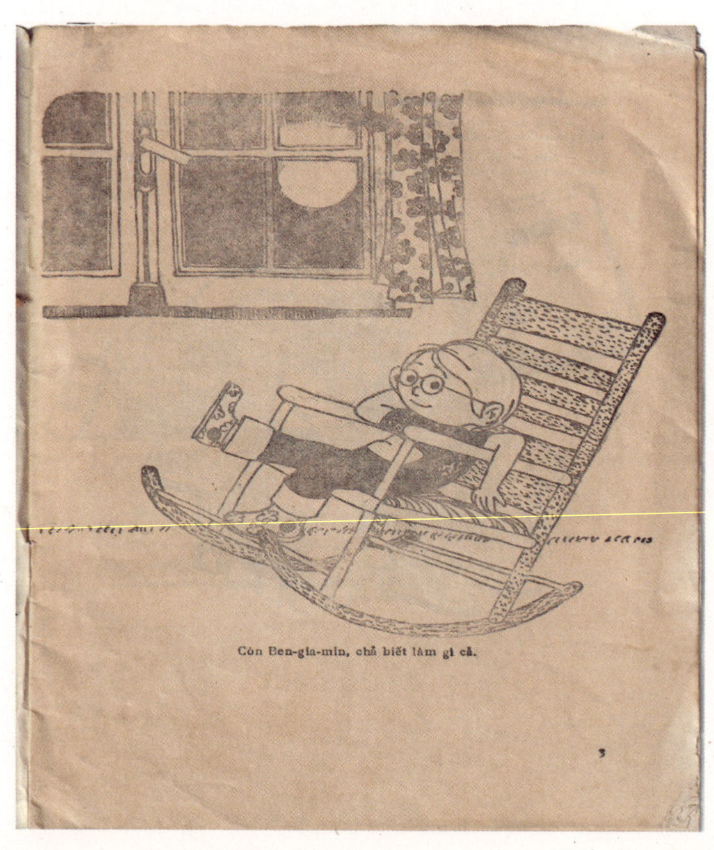

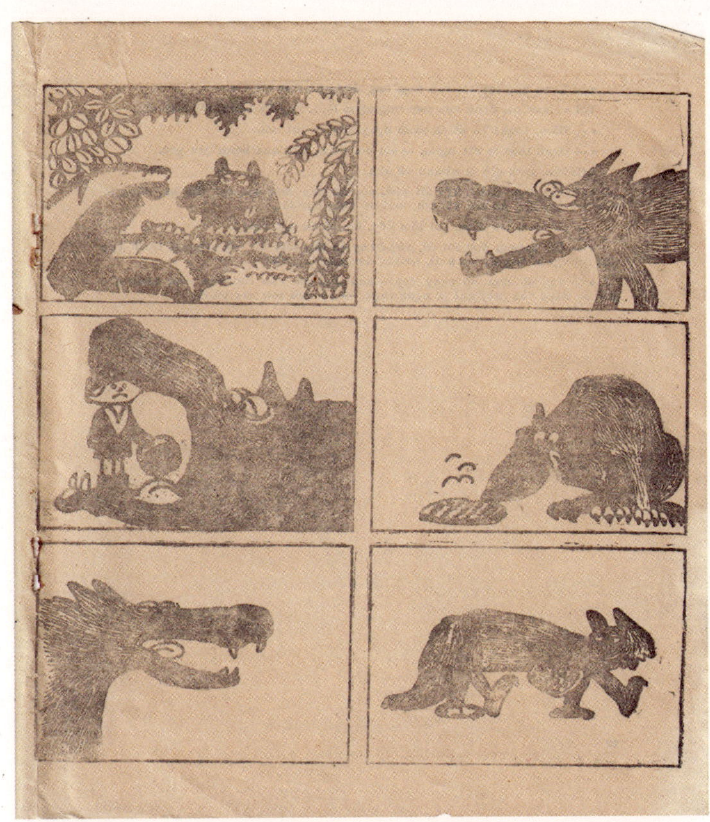

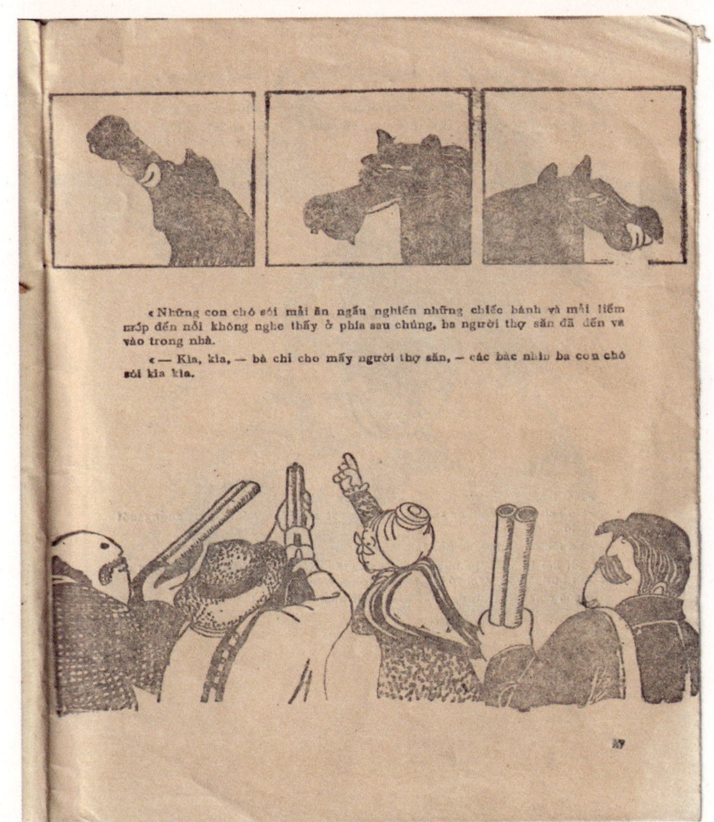

« Những con chó sói mải ăn ngấu nghiến những chiếc bánh và mải liếm mép đến nỗi không nghe thấy ở phía sau chúng, ba người thợ săn đã đến và vào trong nhà.

« — Kia, kia, — bà chỉ cho mấy người thợ săn, — các bác nhìn ba con chó sói kia kia.

CHỬ ĐỒNG TỬ AND TIÊN DUNG

Inspired by a Vietnamese folktale, *Chử Đồng Tử and Tiên Dung* depicts the love story of the poor fisherman Chử Đồng Tử and a royal princess named Tiên Dung. Despite their disparate social backgrounds, the couple makes a bold choice to break free and be together. The story encapsulates the essence of those who defy societal norms, irrespective of their privilege or affluence. The painting depicts the moment of their first encounter, when Princess Tiên Dung took a bath by the river and accidentally saw Chử Đồng Tử hiding under the sand.

The artist felt a personal resonance with this theme, and so took this mythical narrative as a point of departure to reflect on his own experiences growing up in a communist nation. Yearning for change, he navigated through hardships, poverty and stringent regulations, constantly contemplating a means of escape from this structured existence. The painting reflects the artist's transition from figurative work towards abstraction where female and male nude bodies are present within the painting; something that was not a common subject of painting at that time in Vietnam. Within the painting, we also see elements of lotus water plants and the underwater world as an escape passage. This painting, therefore, becomes a visual manifestation of an artistic form of liberation – a transition towards a new life and a portrayal of the yearning for freedom.

1991
Oil on Canvas
H: 124.5 / W: 199 cm

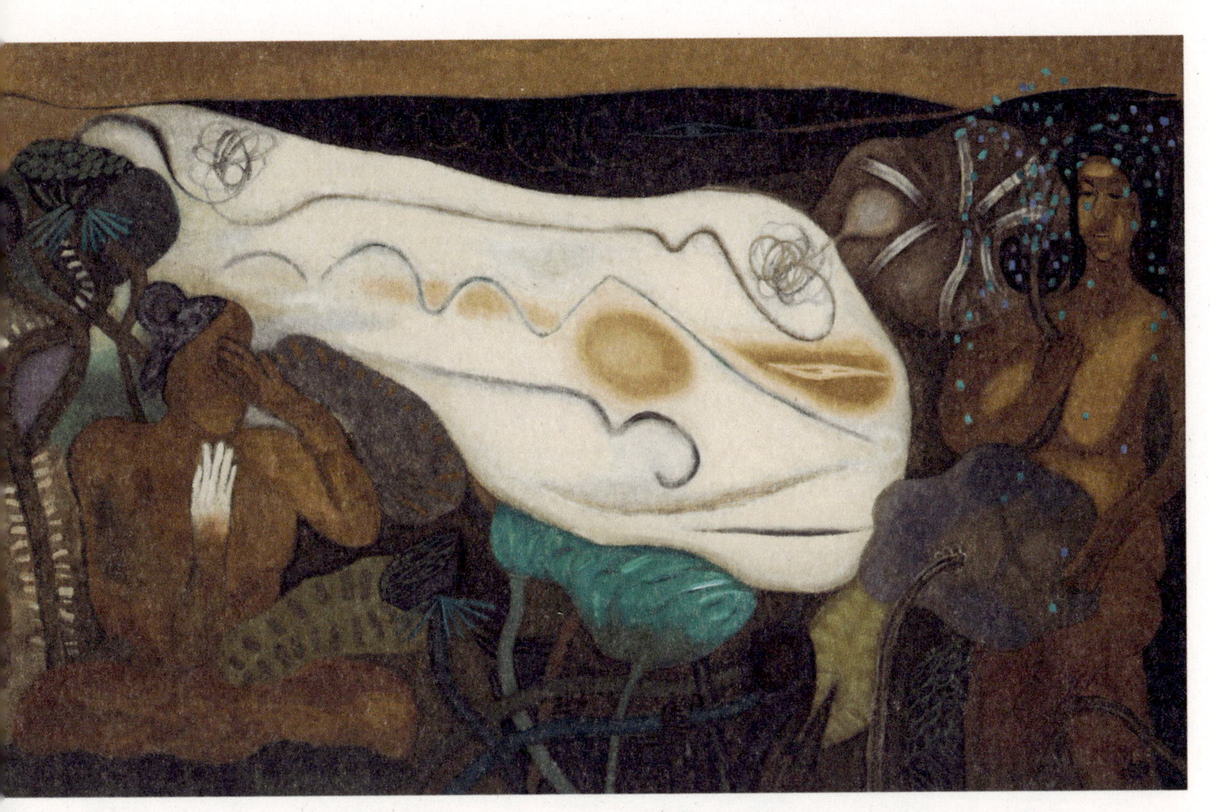

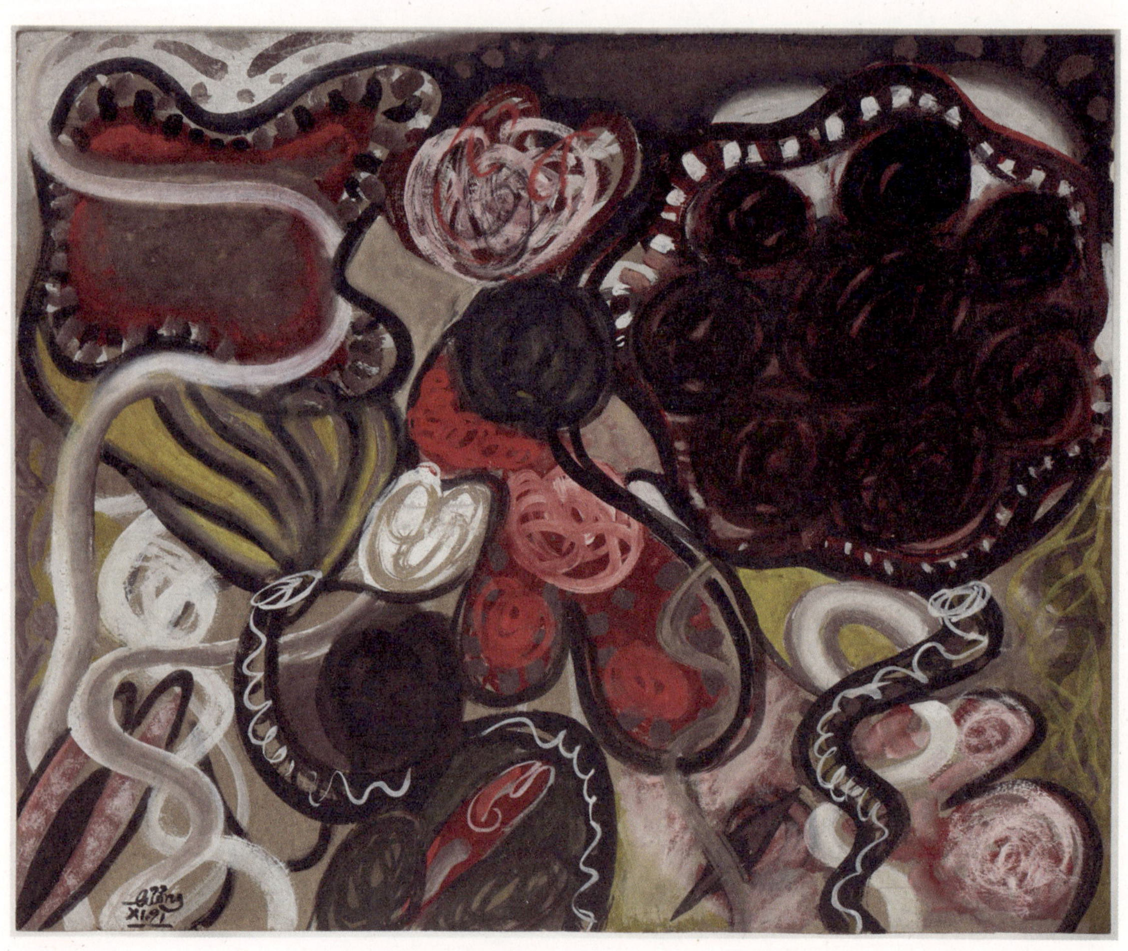

LOTUS 0

1991
Gouache on Cardboard
H: 66.5 / W: 80.5 cm

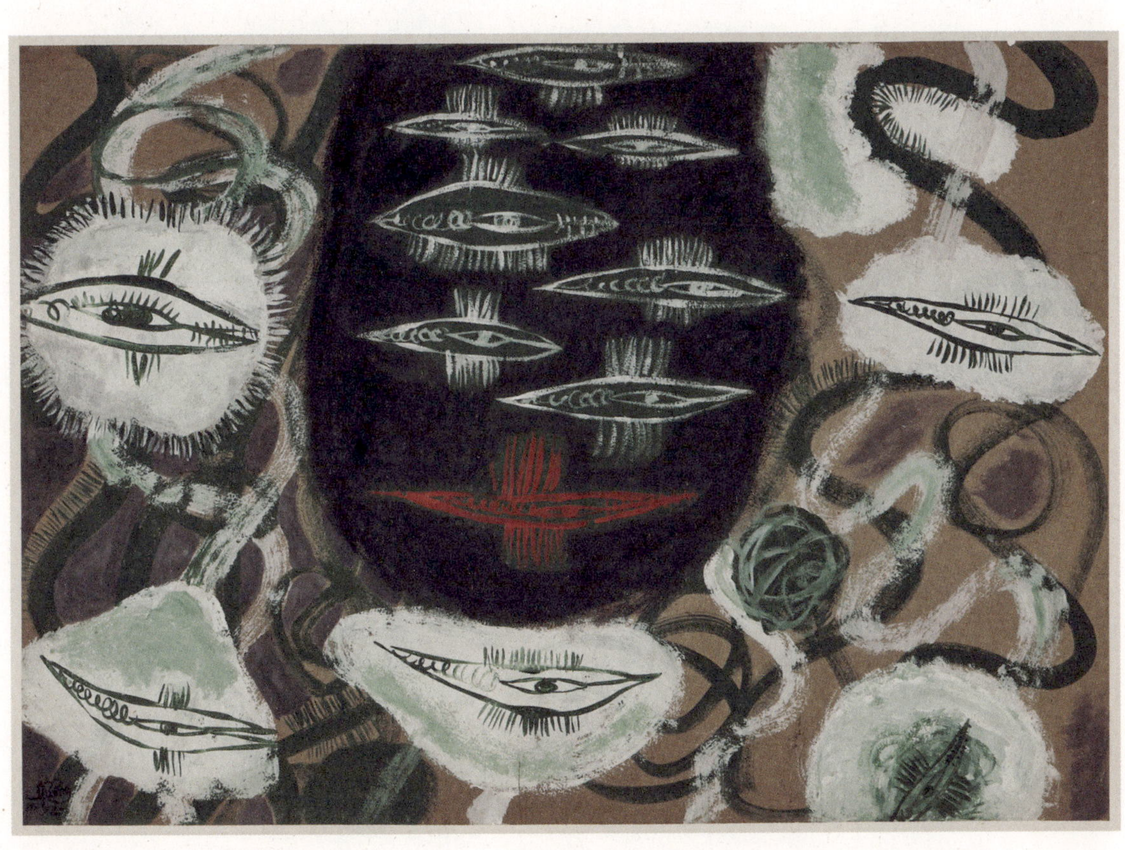

 LOTUS 2

1992
Acrylic on Cardboard
H: 78.5 / W: 108.5 cm

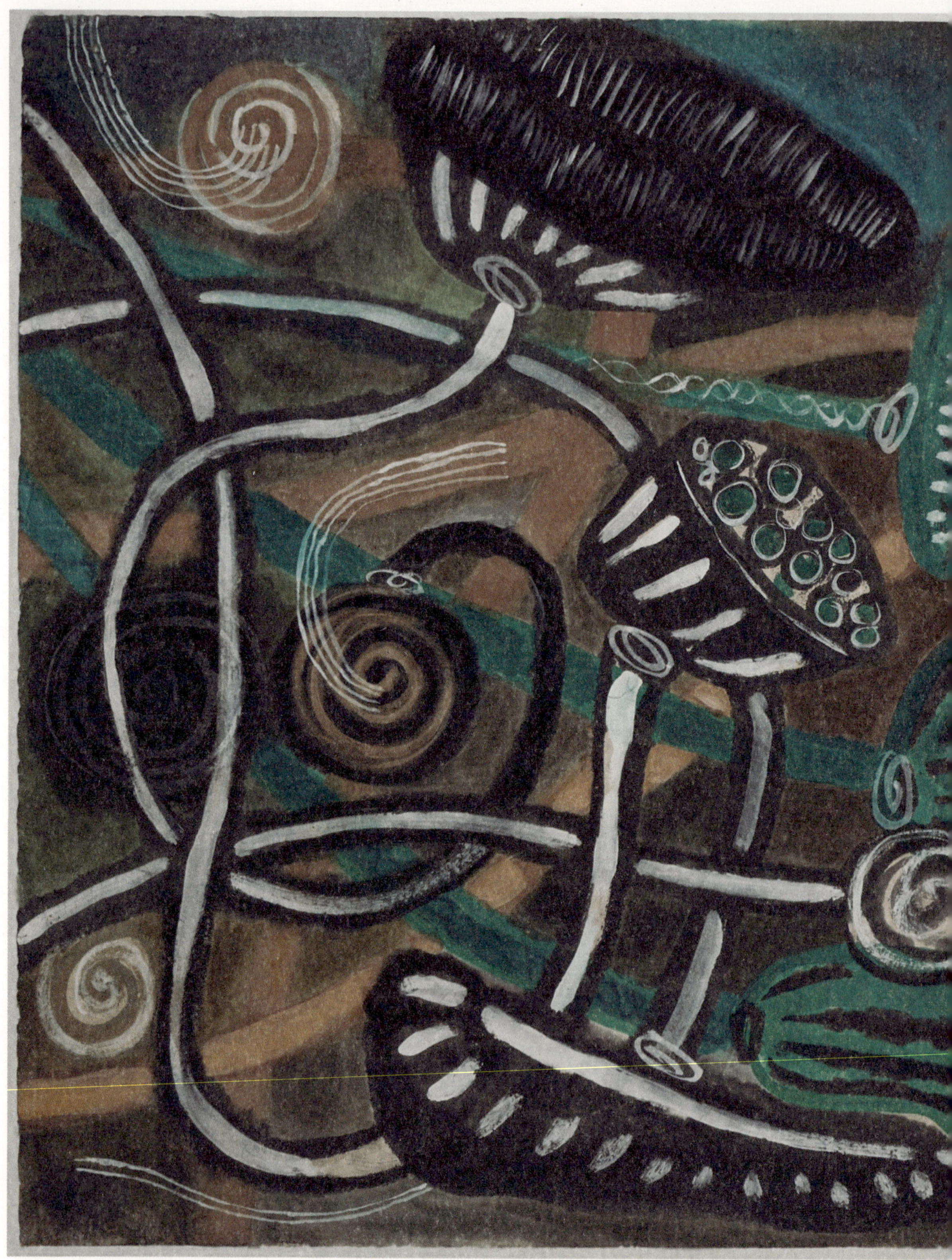

LOVE AFFAIR 2

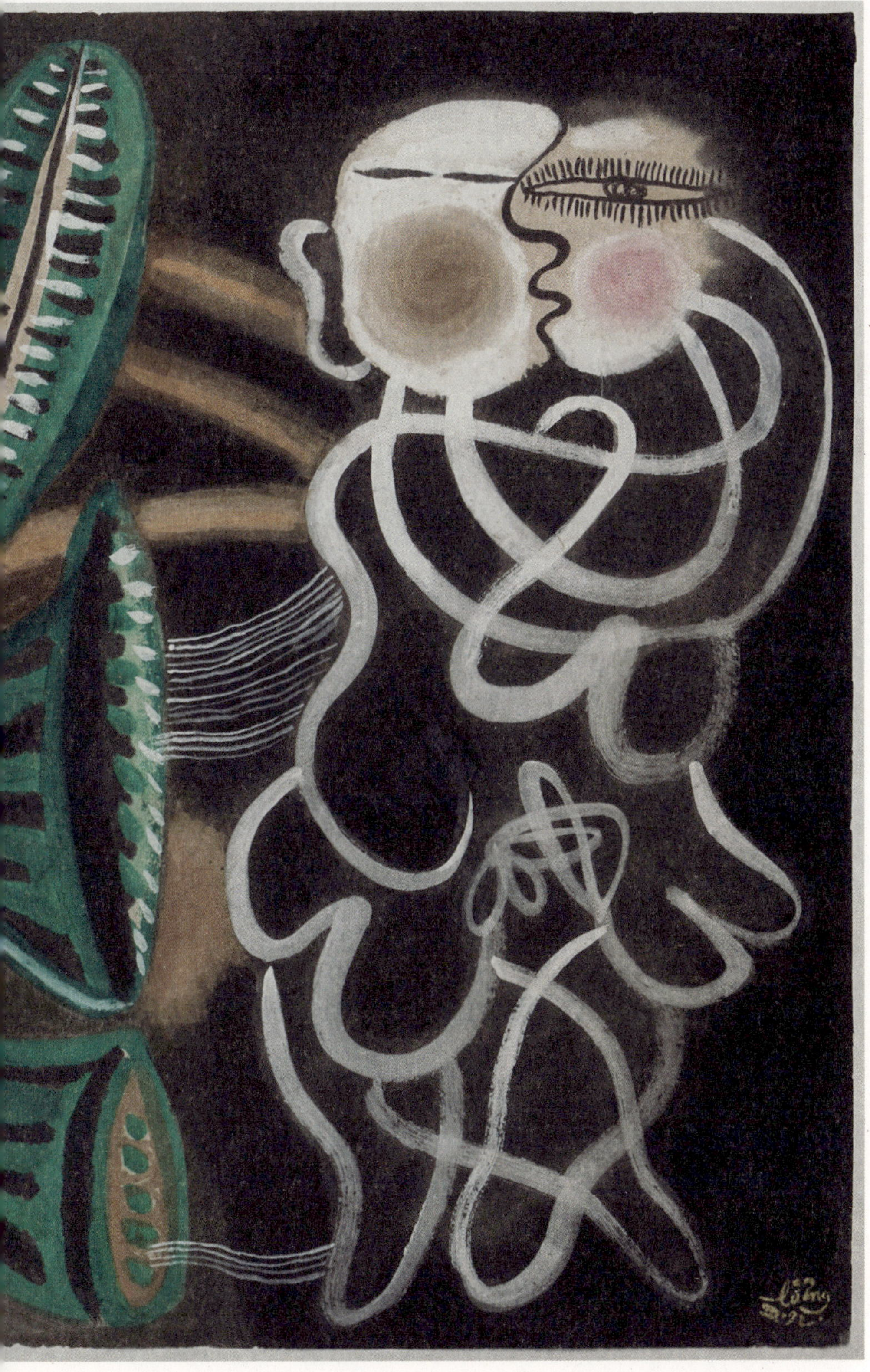

1992 Watercolour and gouache on Dó Paper H: 55.5 / W: 80 cm

UNDER THE WATER

Under the Water draws inspiration from the artist's memories growing up on his own in rural areas during the American bombing of North Vietnam from 1965 to 1972. Away from family and unable to attend school, Lương spent long periods observing life in the water. The underwater world contains many forms of life, both visible and unseen, such as fish, crabs, eels, microorganisms, insects, various types of algae, plants and even mythical creatures from folklore. In the paintings, these critters are transformed and recreated into motifs. The motifs repeat in the paintings, interweaving to create a flat composition, evoking the interconnectedness of human and more-than-human life, proposing water as an archive.

Faintly reflected in the water is a human face, possibly the artist's own. In *Under the Water 18*, we also see Princess Tiên Dung in the process of transforming into another life form under the water as she becomes a water goddess continuing to help humans.

In *Under the Water 1*, the flat symbol of the amoeba appears, signified by the eye shape that will become a landmark of the artist's abstract painting series. The long creature outlined in red with a diamond tail and forked tongue, symbolises Lạc Long Quân, the water dragon and the father of the Viet people in ancient mythology. The painting relates to belief in water worship, closely associated with the spiritual life and river culture of the ancient Vietnamese people who lived in the Red River Delta in Northern Vietnam. The water dragon also represents the people's wish for a good rainy season for rice farming.

Under the Water 1
1992
Watercolour and gouache on Dó Paper
H: 52.4 / W: 65.5 cm

Under the Water 18
1994
Watercolour and gouache on Dó Paper
H: 52.5 / W: 70 cm

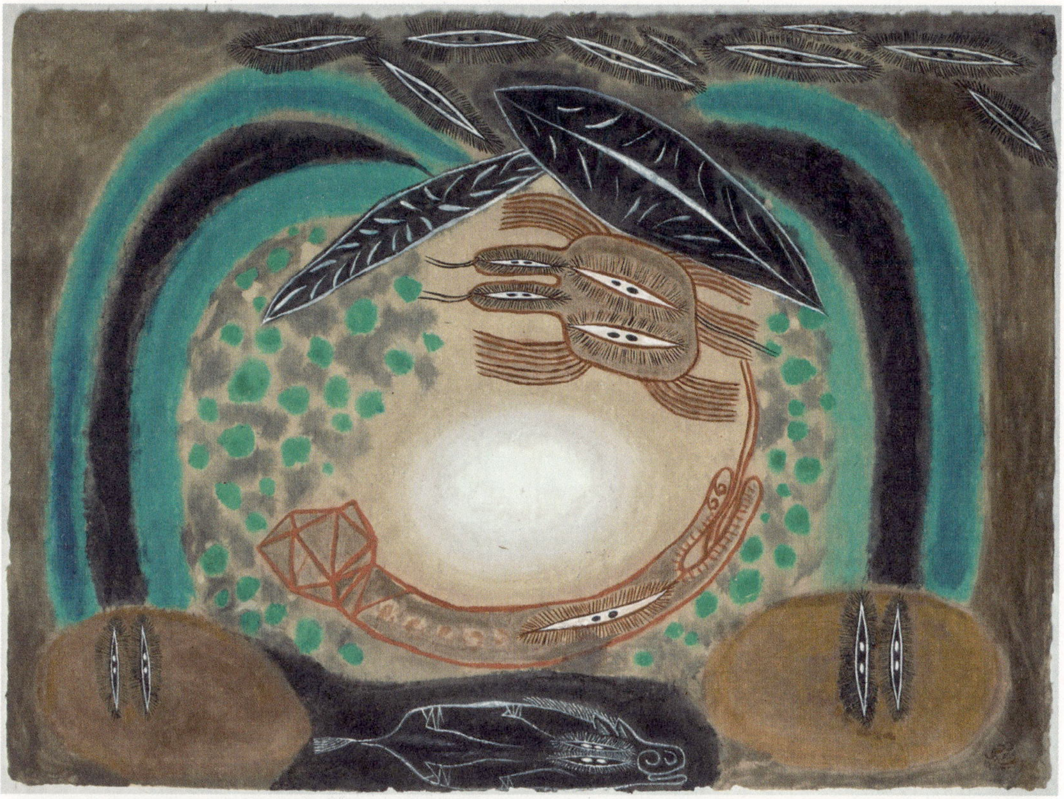

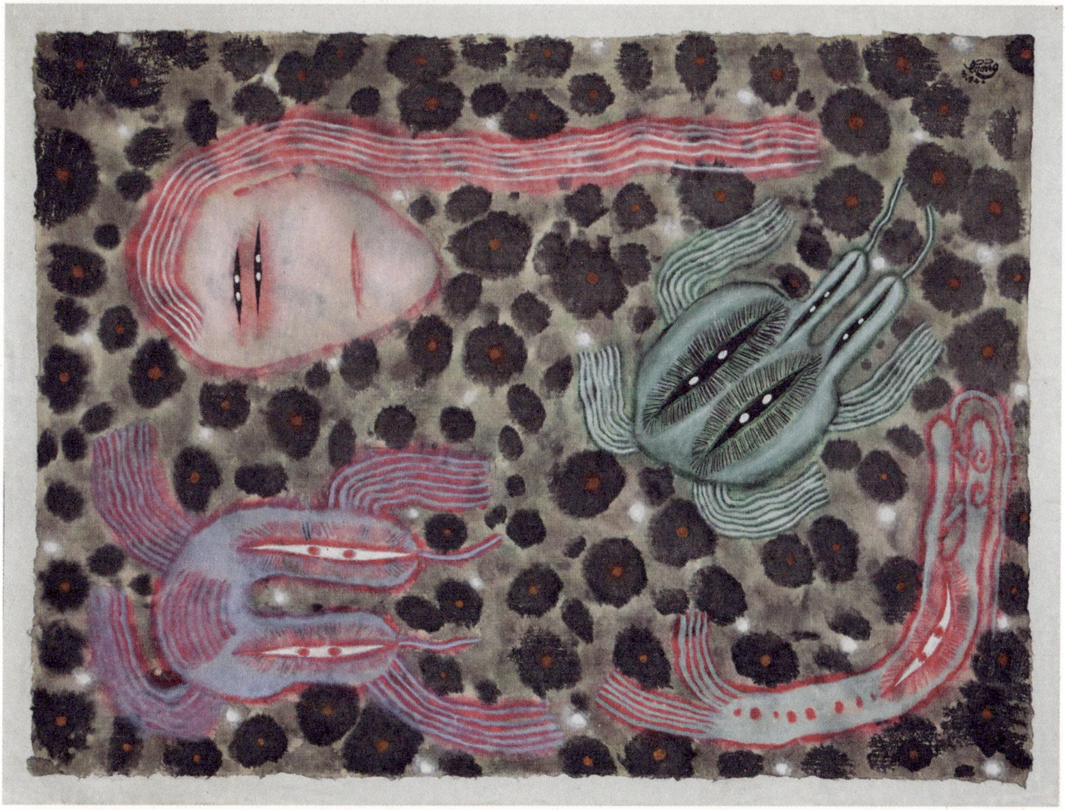

FOOD CHAIN

Food Chain continues to draw inspiration from the underwater world. The central bright circle in the painting takes the form of a pond, a typical feature in a traditional Vietnamese rural village, serving as the domestic water source of the village and a site for communal activities like festivals and ceremonies. Within the pond, images of creatures emerge in succession, forming a circle that begins with small plankton and progresses through to crabs, turtles, eels and finally humans, who are symbolized by a red-coloured head. The artist used carmine red, which according to him, "is an original red, a red that isn't truly red." It evokes the colour of blood in warm-blooded creatures, which in this painting, contrasts somewhat with the muddy brown tones of the underwater world. The painting illustrates how human activity has unbalanced and disrupted the natural cycle of life.

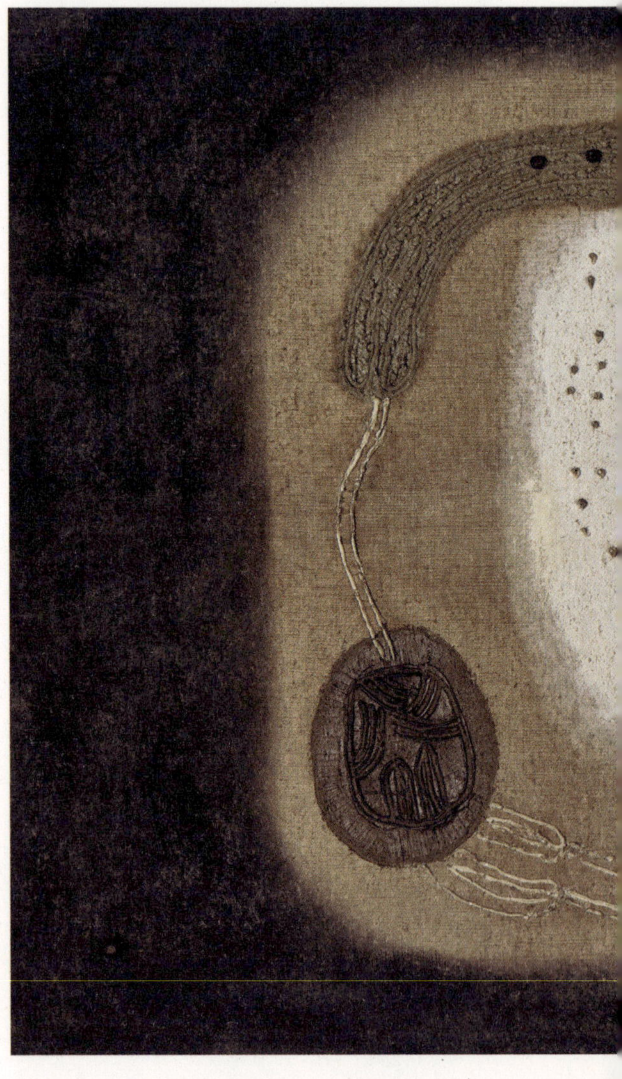

1993
Oil on Canvas
H: 89 / W: 157.8 cm

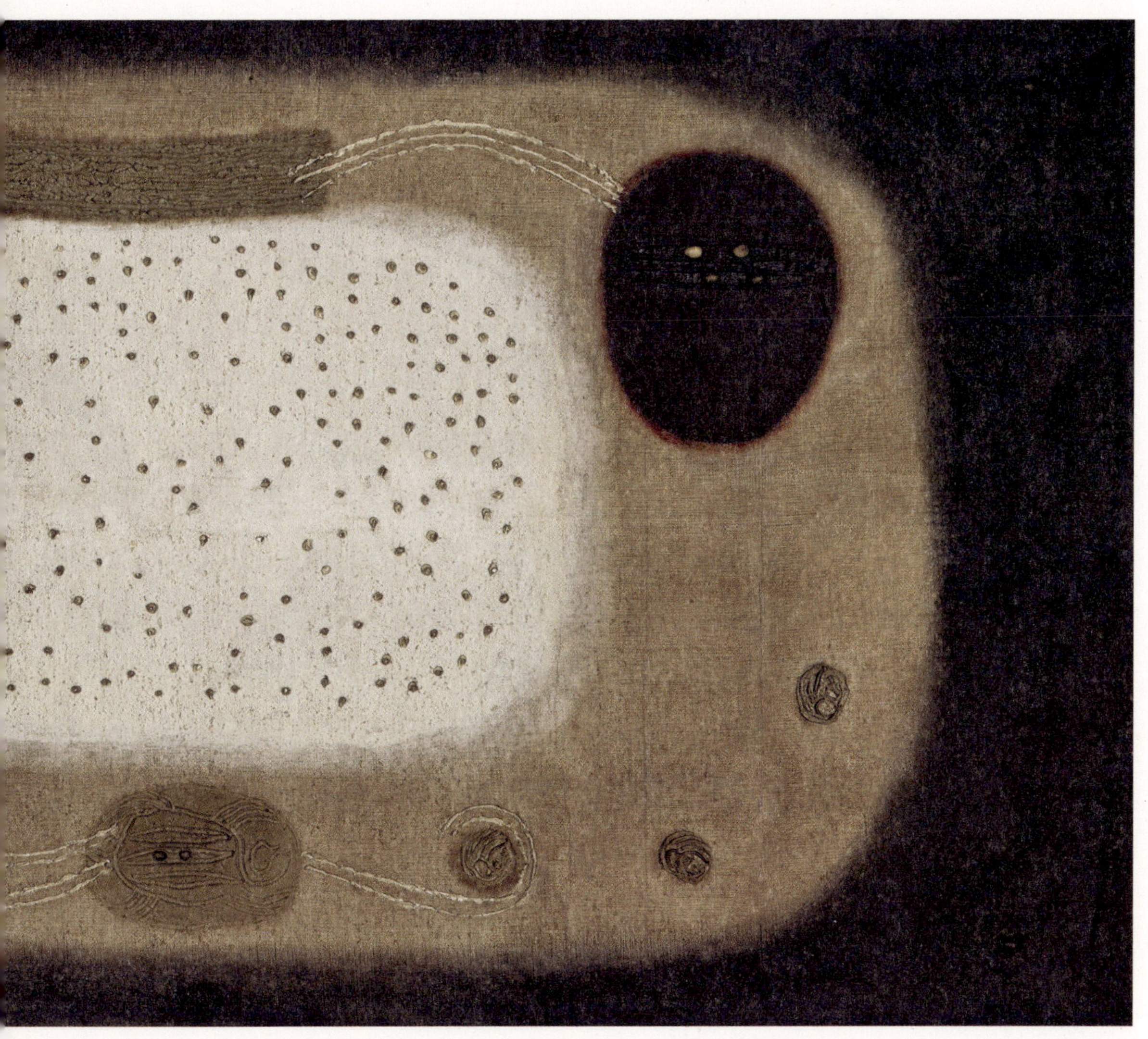

UNDER THE SKY

Under the Sky consists of two oil paintings of the same size, in which the composition of the upper and lower halves depict two contrasting worlds. The dividing line in the middle is a flowing black stream, representing the continuous flow of the universe, with amoeba motifs rushing through. The upper part of the painting abstractly depicts the relationships between living beings using three colour schemes: the green symbolises the world of plants and vegetation; the yellow is the world of animals featuring iconic depictions of the 12 Chinese zodiac signs; and in the middle is the realm of humans.

The lower part of the painting ventures more deeply into the world of human beings with curvy figures representing twisted human body parts and organs. The painting evokes the dynamics of the mundane world where humans are at the centre but lack connection to the more-than-human world.

1994
2 pieces, Oil on Canvas
H: 86.4 / W: 206 cm
H: 82 / W: 204.5 cm

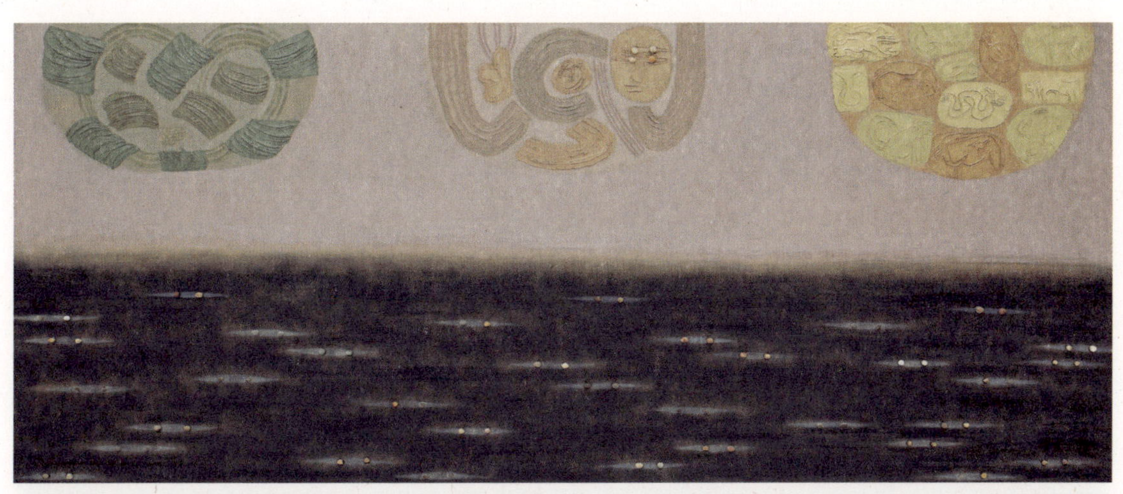

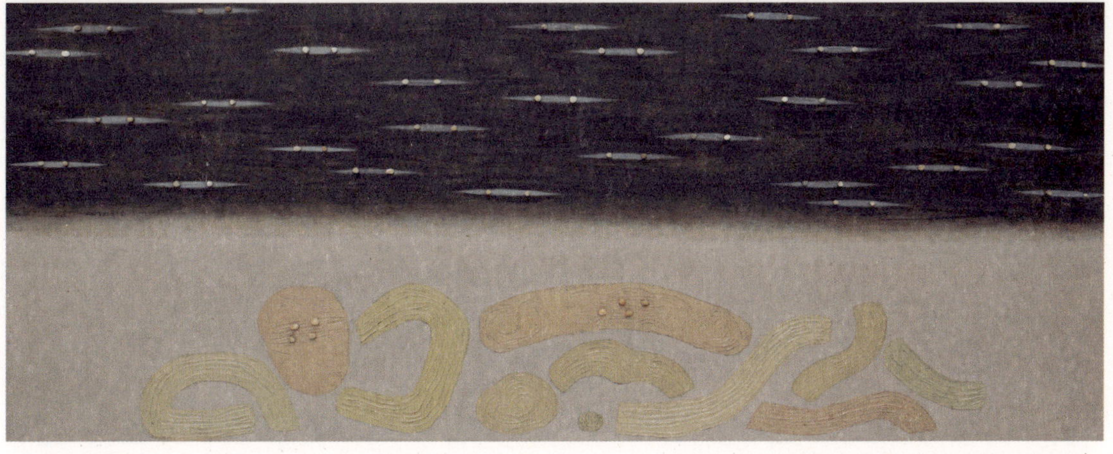

FLOWING SERIES
1991 – 1997

This series uncovers the artist's memories of growing up during the bombing of North Vietnam by American forces from 1965 to 1972. During this period, Lương had to find refuge in a number of villages away from his family, who were in Hà Nội. On his own and unable to attend school, the artist turned to water and the underwater world. The paintings, which were executed on sensitive Xuan or Dó paper, were created in various sizes, often simultaneously. The artist describes the process of making this work as akin to farming, in the sense that the process cannot be rushed and patience is essential due to the materials used.

The paintings suggest an abstract narrative that is interconnected but can also be observed individually. For example, ink black dots in the paintings represent bombs falling, the stillness that follows disaster and the gradual return to calm as the surface becomes quiet again and water covers the devastation. In this series, a key symbol from the artist's 1990s abstract works dominates – the amoeba, which some understand as eyes, aircrafts or humans or more-than-humans floating through the paintings. For the artist, the symbol represents all these interpretations.

The series continued until 1997 when the artist decided to stop painting as a protest and critique of the commercial success of his generation of painters at that time – a success influenced by the free market.

Flowing 25
1996
Watercolour on Dó Paper
H: 63 / W: 81.5 cm

Flowing
1996
Watercolour on Dó Paper
H: 62 / W: 81 cm

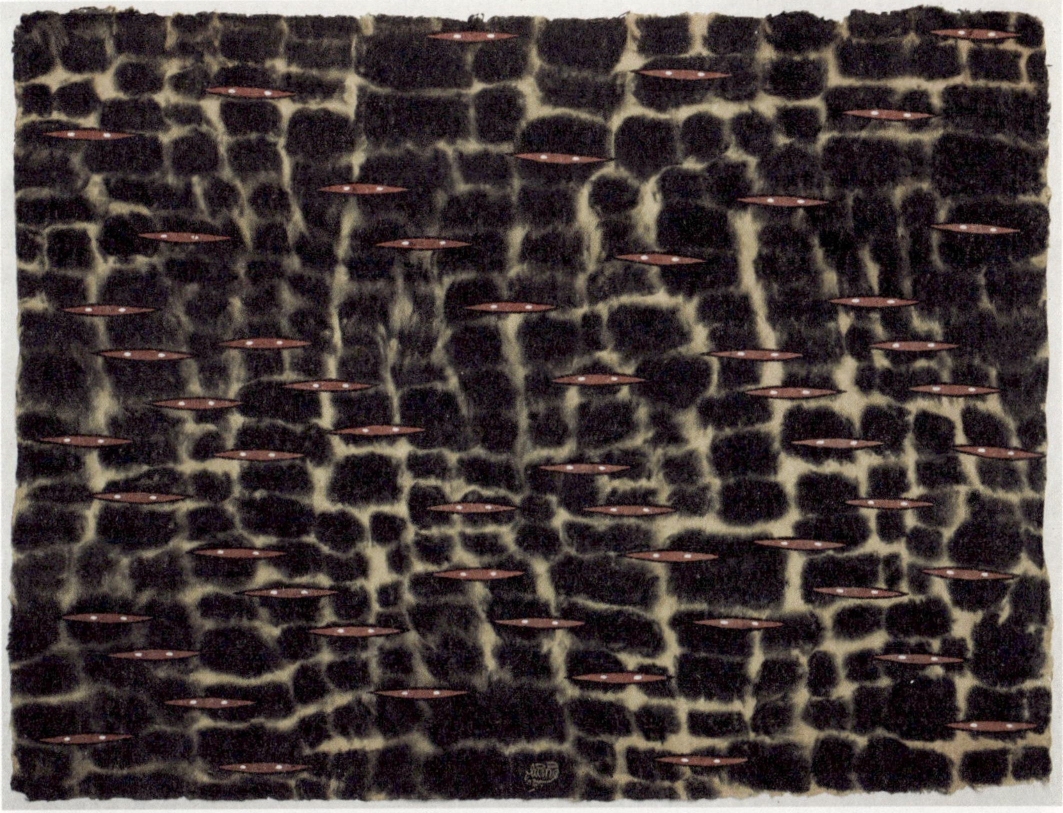

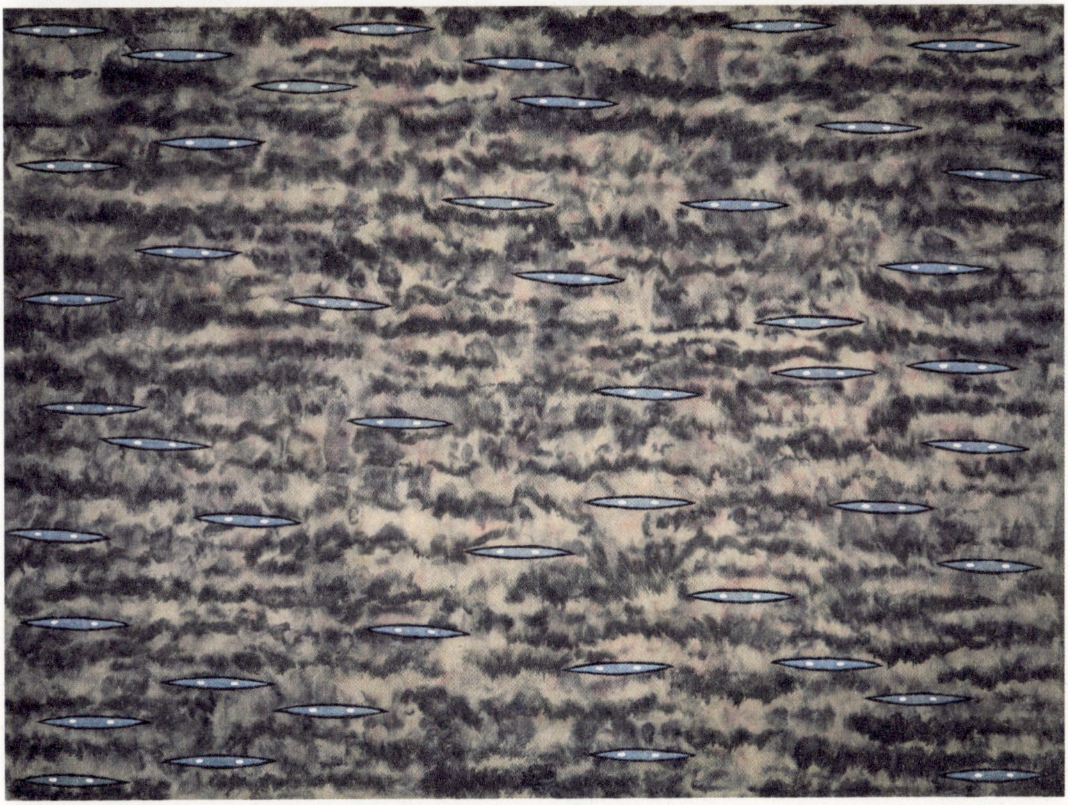

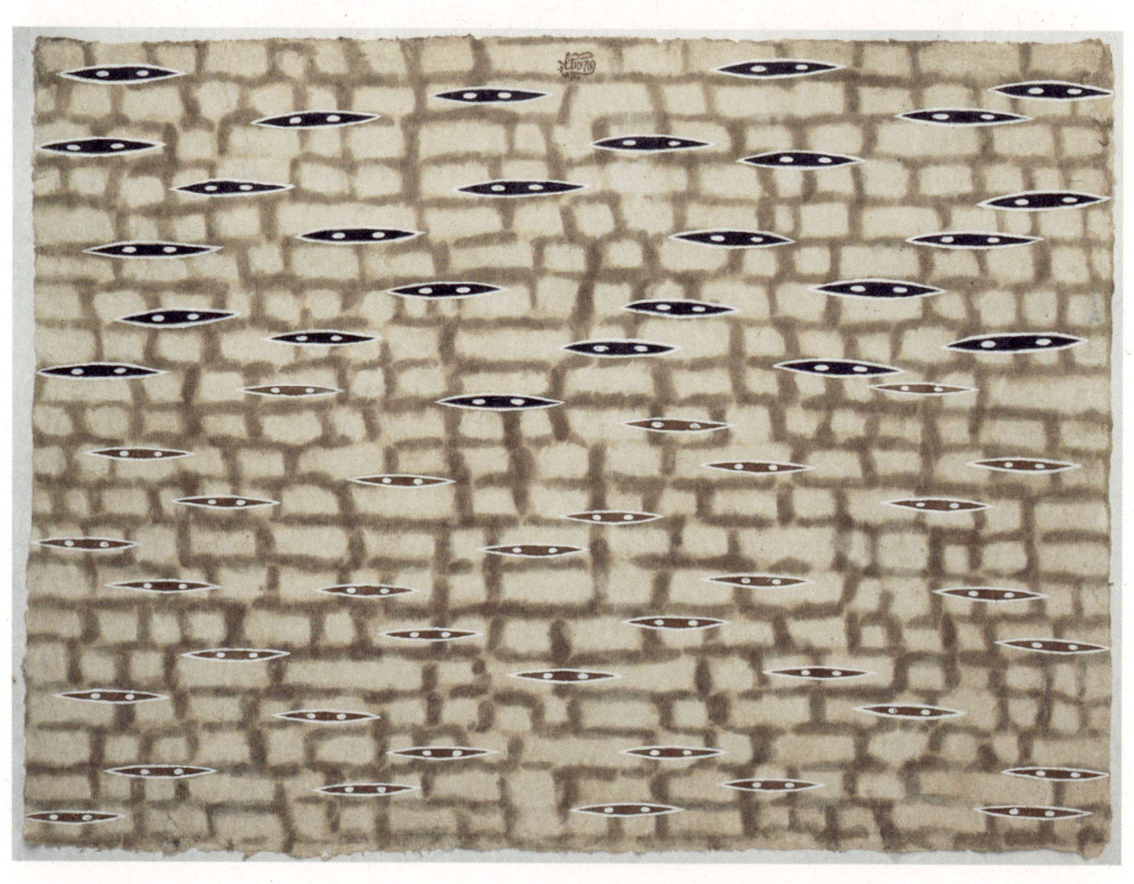

Flowing 27
1996
Watercolour on Dó Paper
H: 62 / W: 81 cm

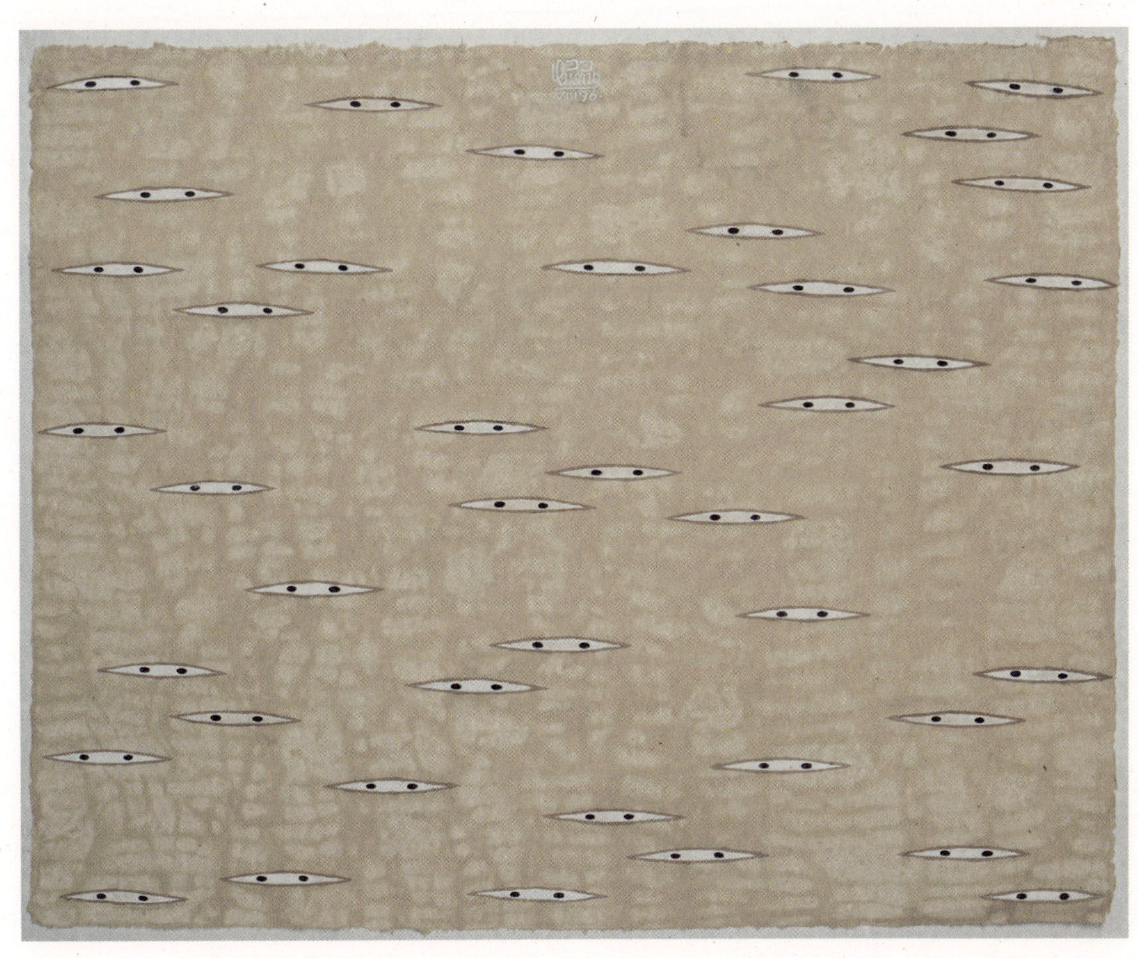

Flowing 31
1996
Watercolour on Dó Paper
H: 58.5 / W: 70.2 cm

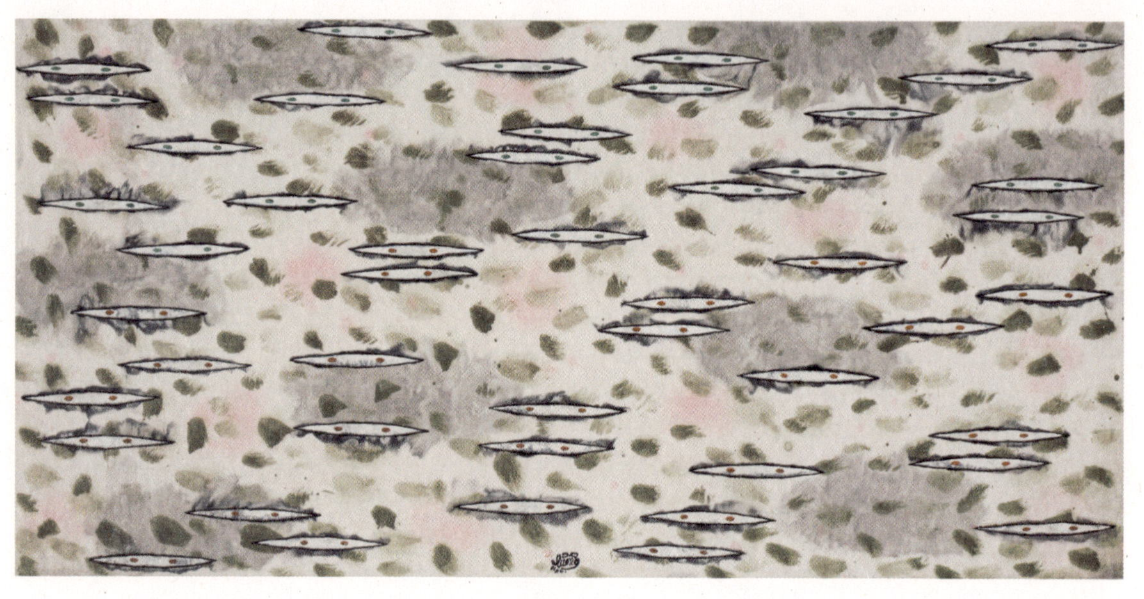

Flowing 0
1996
Watercolour on Xuan Paper
H: 81 / W: 148.8 cm

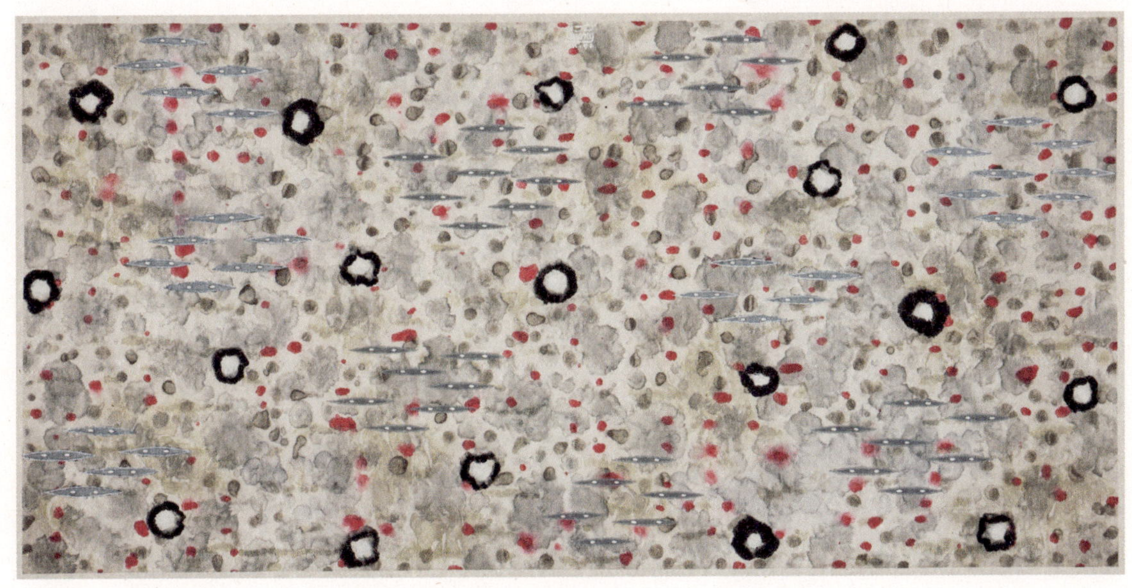

Flowing 33
1996
Watercolour on Xuan Paper
H: 69 / W: 136 cm

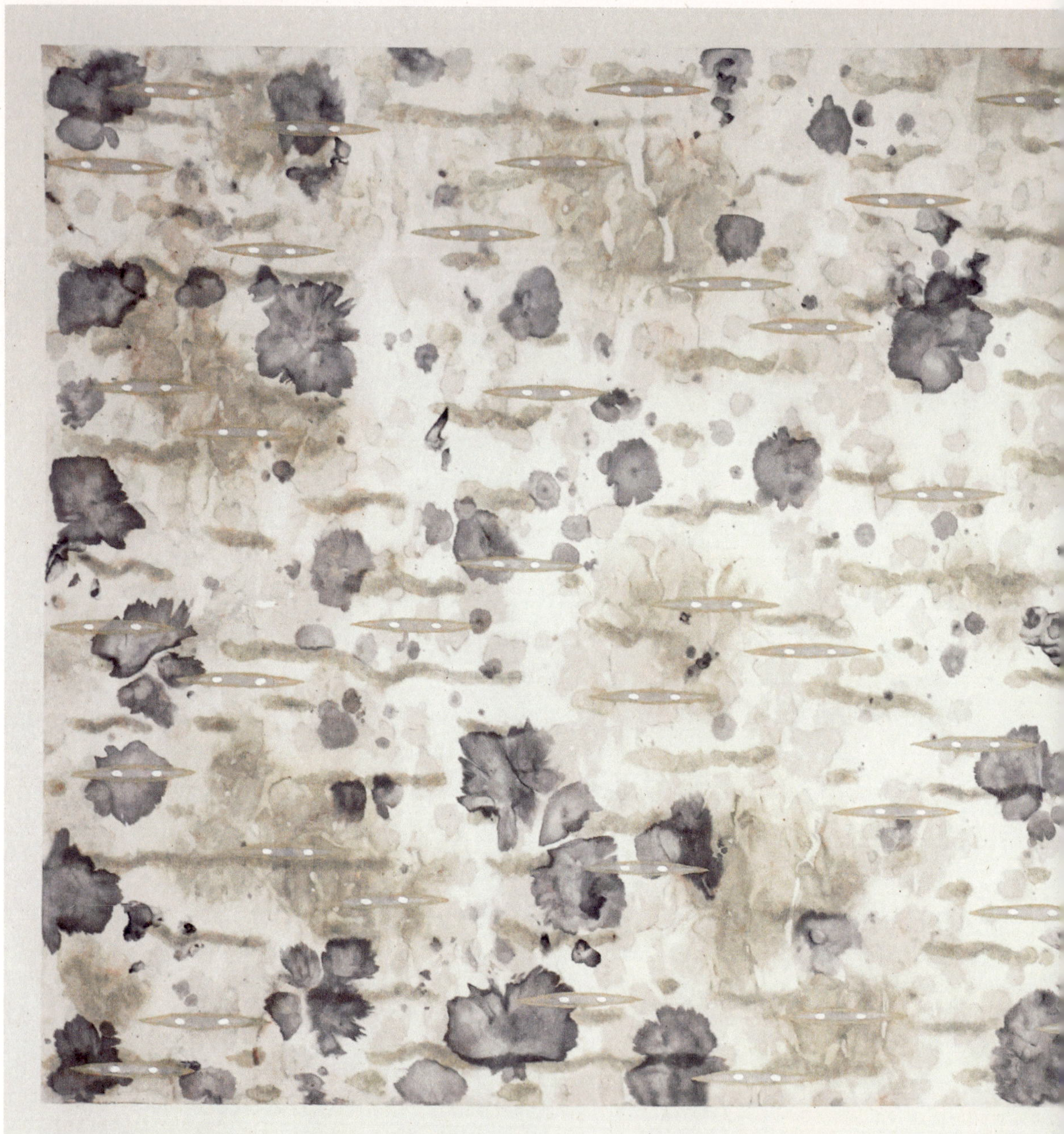

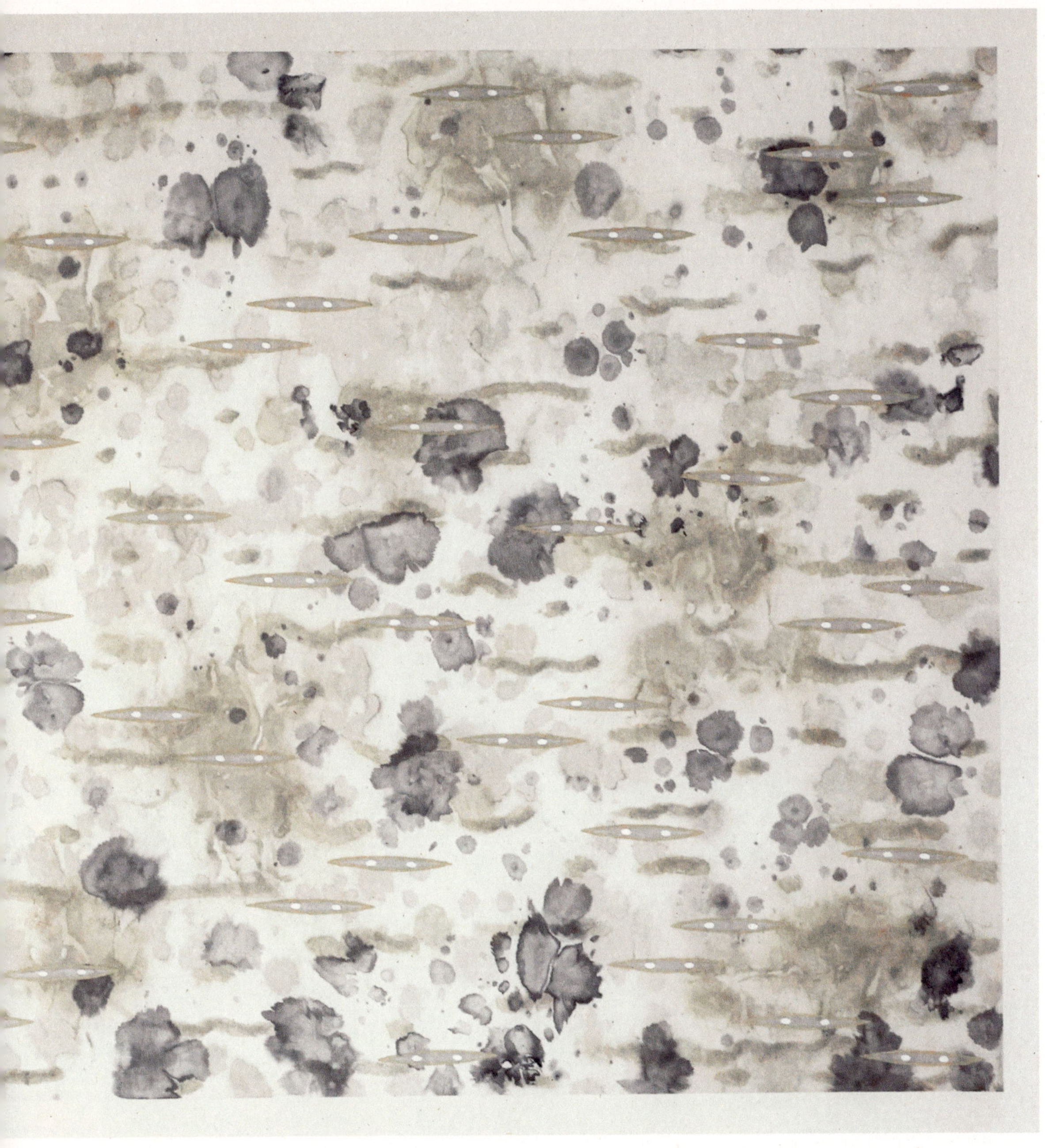

Flowing 4
1996
Watercolour on Xuan Paper
H: 69.5 / W: 137 cm

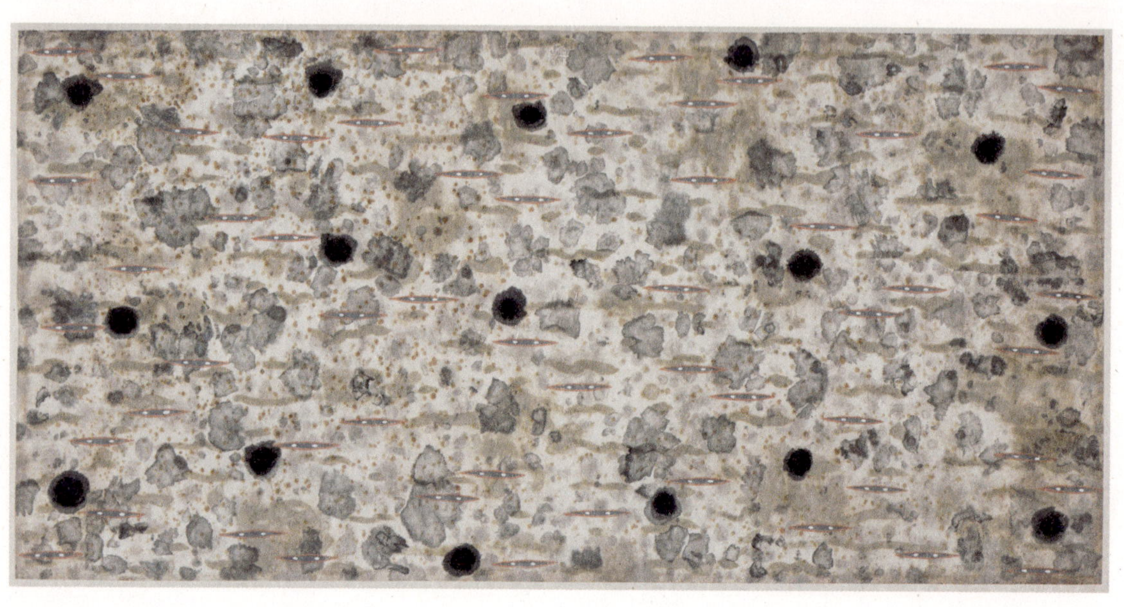

Flowing 37
1997
Watercolour on Xuan Paper
H: 69 / W: 136.5 cm

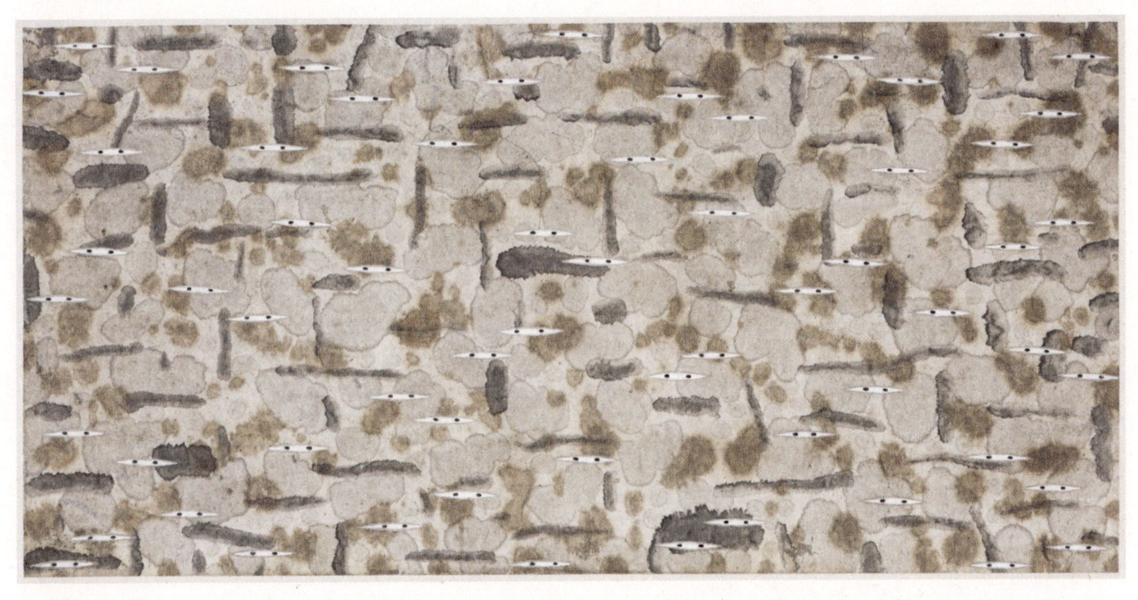

Flowing 38
1997
Watercolour on Xuan Paper
H: 69 / W: 136 cm

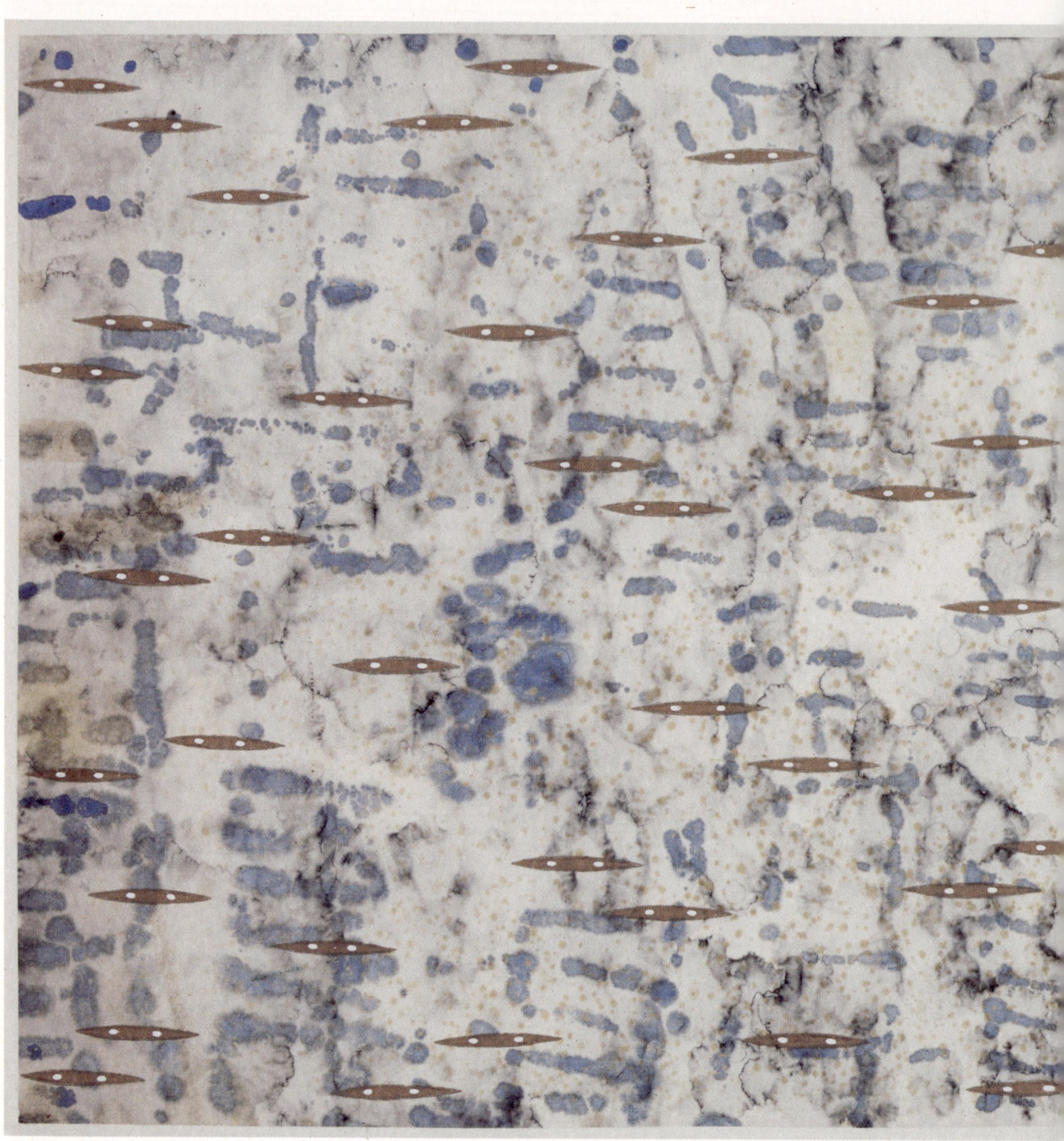

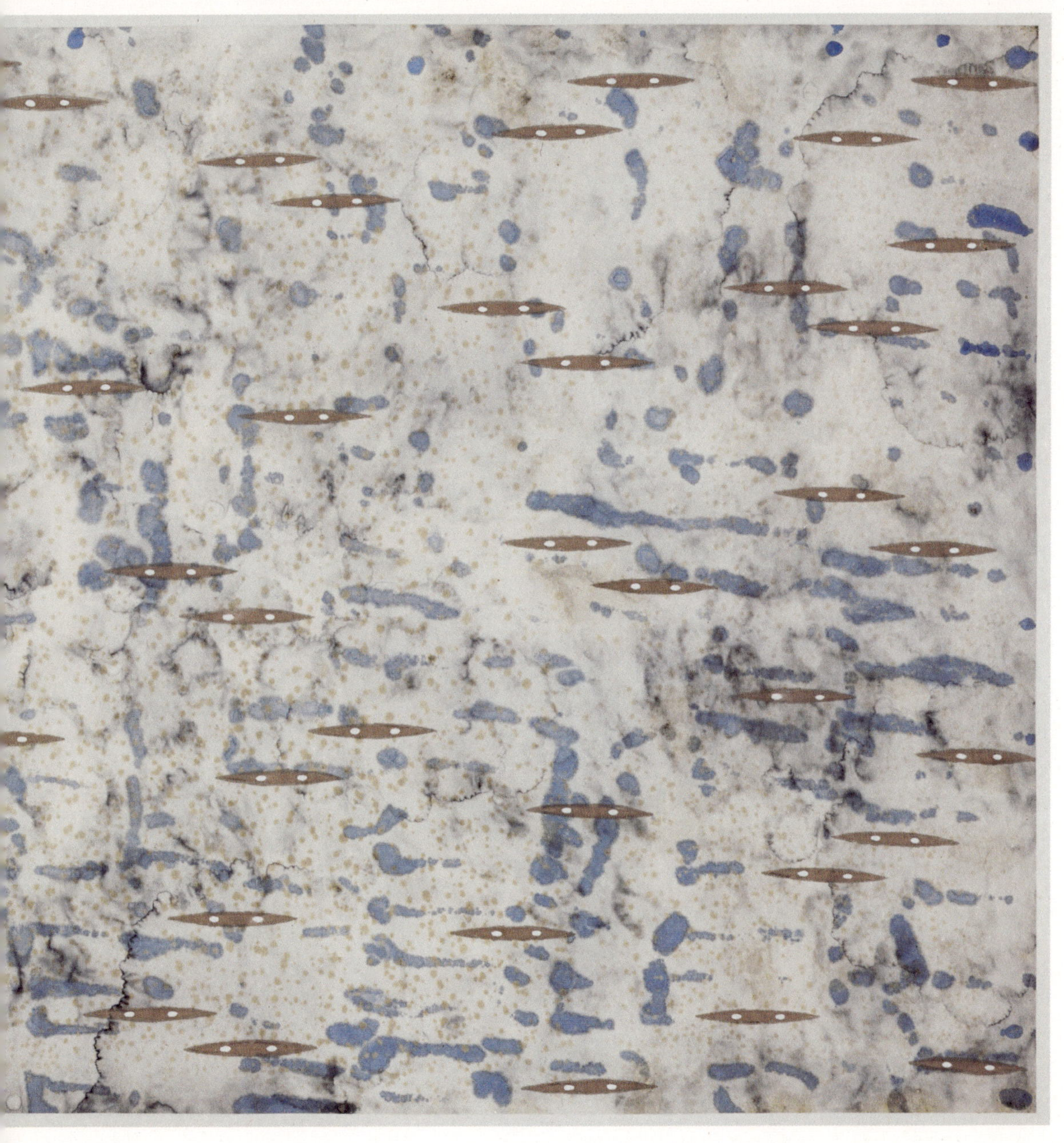

Flowing 40
1997
Watercolour on Xuan Paper
H: 69.5 / W: 136.5 cm

FLOWING - DAY
FLOWING - NIGHT

Flowing-Day and *Flowing-Night* consists of two canvases. The artist repurposed used fishing nets from local fishing villages, incorporating them into the canvas alongside materials such as paper and small pebbles. This experimentation within his practice aimed to create multiple layers of spatial depth within the artwork, challenging established aesthetic norms in the Vietnamese painting community during that period, which was predominantly focused on brushwork and oil painting techniques.

The use of fishing nets references the Vietnamese proverb 'the skynet is endless', similar to the biblical parable describing the kingdom of heaven as a dragnet gathering all types of fish, whether good or bad. The painting's background features consecutive black and white streaks of dry paint, reminiscent of a substantial brick wall, symbolising the artist's experience of suppression whilst living under social repression in Vietnam at that time. On the painting's surface, a motif of swirling amoebae resembling eyes, floats outside the net, inviting one to imagine freedom, independence and resistance against imposed constraints.

1994
Old fishing net, paper, small pebbles, oil on canvas
H: 90.5 / W: 160 cm

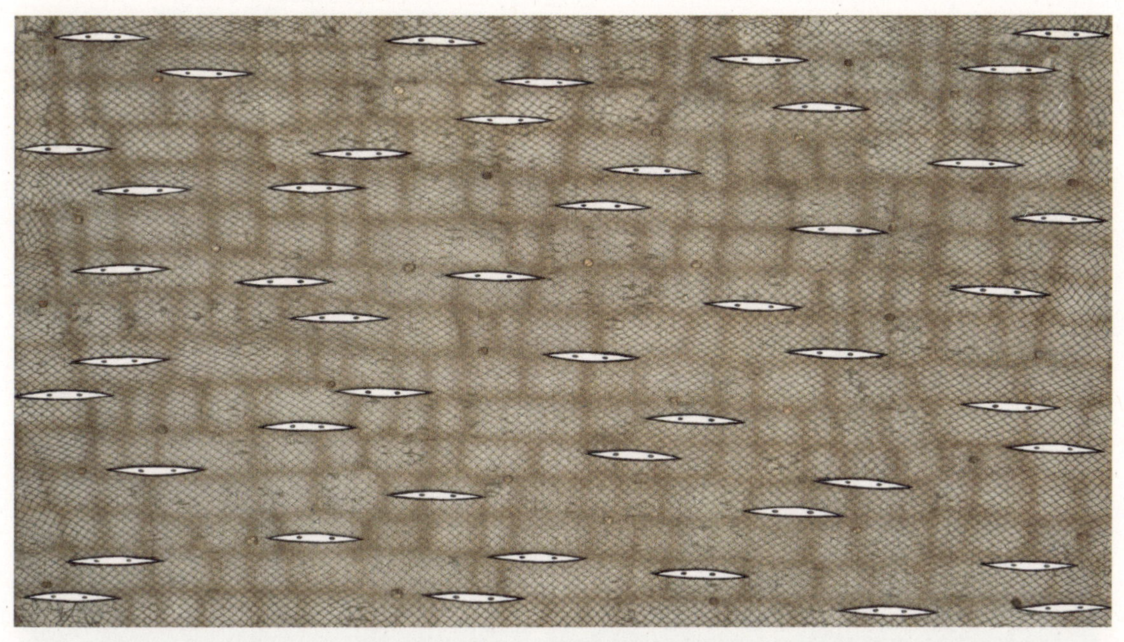

CHẢY – FLOWING
1998

1

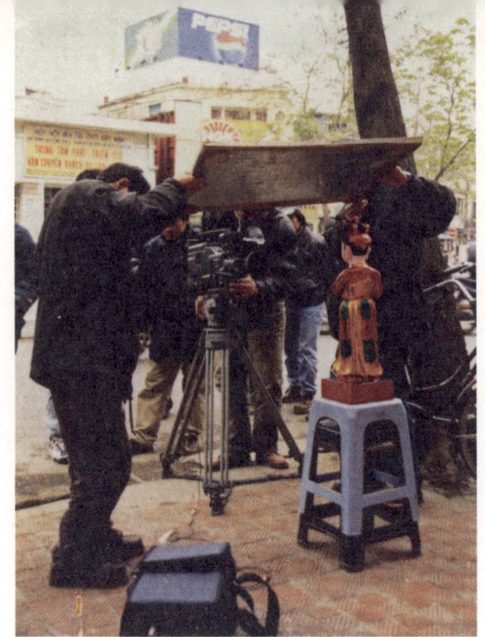

Chảy - Flowing is considered the first video work by a Vietnamese artist. It was filmed around Hà Nội and a countryside suburb near Hà Nội called Phú Cường. The artist filmed the life of the Red River as it passes Hà Nội, intertwining this footage with his painting and other installation-based work, referencing where his work originated and creating an archive of his practice and connection to everyday life. The film takes a journey from the scenery of the countryside to the city, connected through the flow of the Red River. The work depicts the artist's visual diaries containing images of nature that reference his own childhood in villages, his survival during the bombings and the changes brought by the social transition to an open society that followed. The work was combined with his painting and the *Flowing* installations in his solo exhibition *Initial* in 1998.

The presence of the female body in public was also captured by the artist's camera. It reflects a major change in the period after Đổi Mới when, due to new urban lifestyles, women were able to wear tight clothes, showing off their body's curves; something that had been taboo in the old days. For filming purposes, Lương developed a series of interventions in public space with sculptures of deities from the Lên Đồng ritual. Lên Đồng is associated with the lost ancient beliefs of Viet people which praise femininity and non-gender as being closer to God. The sculptures were placed in front of spaces that symbolise the Vietnamese transition after the open-door policy: Catholic churches, one of the earliest five-star hotels, a nude mannequin shop and a Daewoo electronics company showroom, among others. This juxtaposition reflects the complicated layers of culture in Vietnam after decades of changes.

The work was shown internationally for the first time in Fukuoka Triennale in 2002.

2

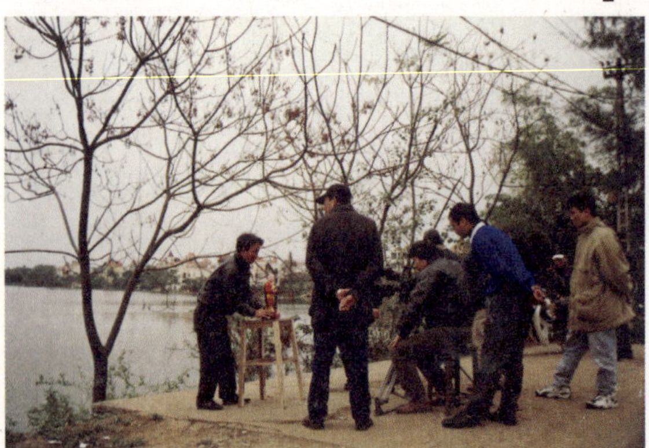

3

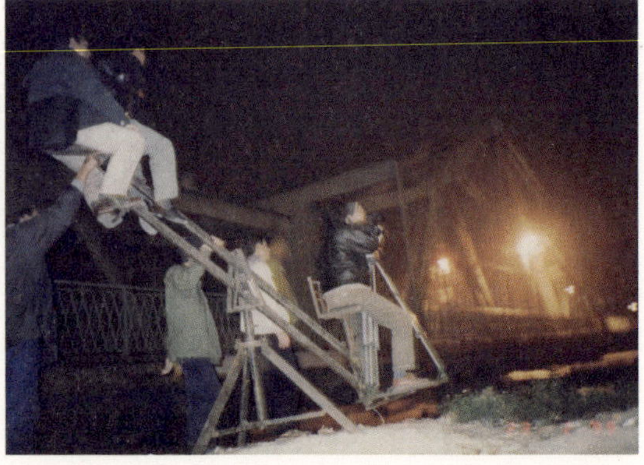

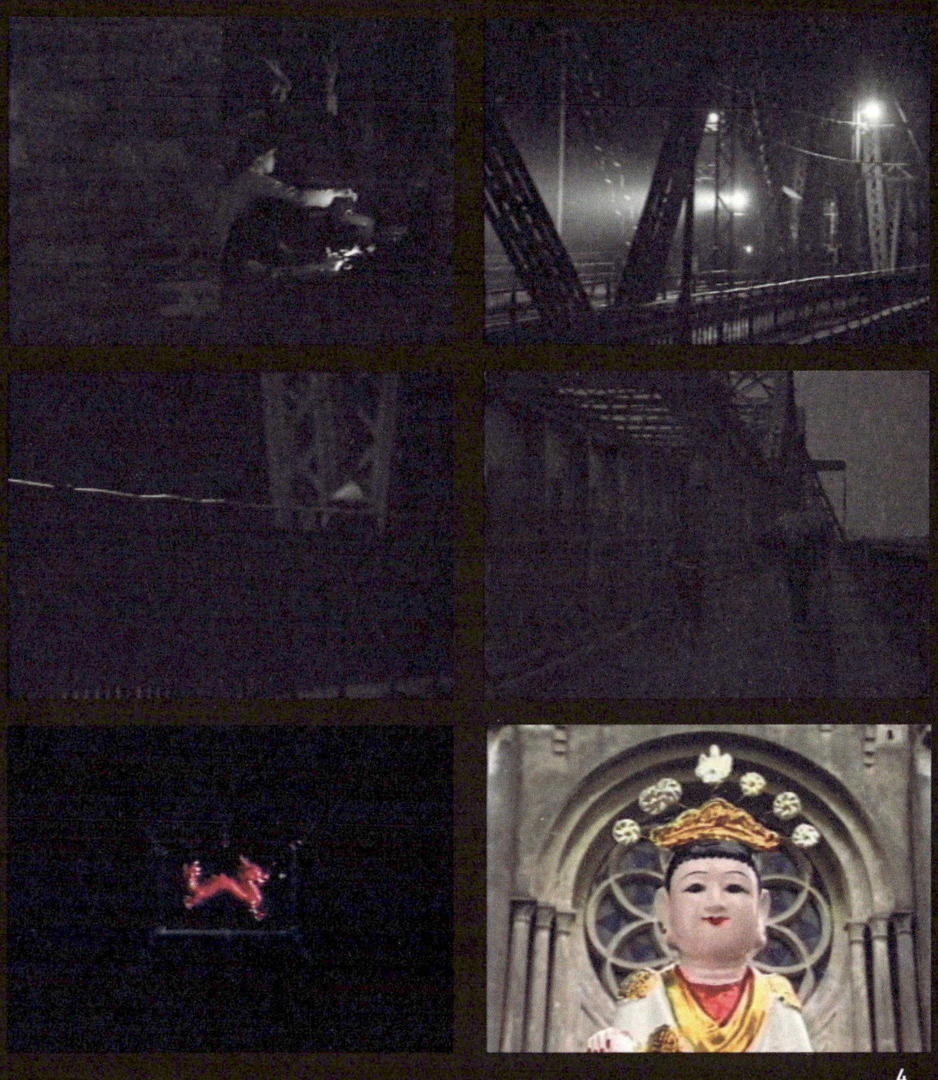

1,2
Behind the scenes, the sculptures of deities from Lên Đồng rituals in public spaces around Hà Nội.

3
The crew film at Long Biên Bridge, a historic structure constructed by the French across the Red River, linking the centre of Hà Nội with its surrounding suburbs.

4
Trần Lương, *Chảy – Flowing*, 1998, single channel video, 11'49".

AN UP-TO-DATE DRAGON

1998
Nhà Sàn Studio

An Up-to-Date Dragon was first featured in the *Initial* exhibition in 1998, marking the opening of Nhà Sàn Studio art space. It consists of a red plastic dragon (a common toy that was made in China and sold in marketplaces) placed in a small glass cage and suspended by eight lengths of chain, representing the eight cardinal directions. The dragon, which carries many historical layers, is frequently employed to promote Vietnamese national identity. In ancient mythology, Lạc Long Quân, the ancestral father of the Viet people, manifests as a water dragon. It later comes to symbolise national power and prosperity during the feudal regime. In the 1990s, following economic reforms, communist leaders pledged to metamorphose the country into a new "Dragon of Asia" – a term used to describe nations undergoing rapid economic transformation and industrialisation.

An Up-to-date Dragon serves as a satirical reinterpretation of the dragon symbol and Vietnam's political conditions during the 1990s. Crafted from cheap plastic in the red hue representing the communist regime, and encased within a glass box as mere decorative trinket, it entirely strips away the power typically associated with authority.

Trần Lương, *An Up-to-Date Dragon*, 1998, installation with plastic toy, glass box, metal chains, hemp fiber, dimensions variable. Installation view at Nhà Sàn Studio.

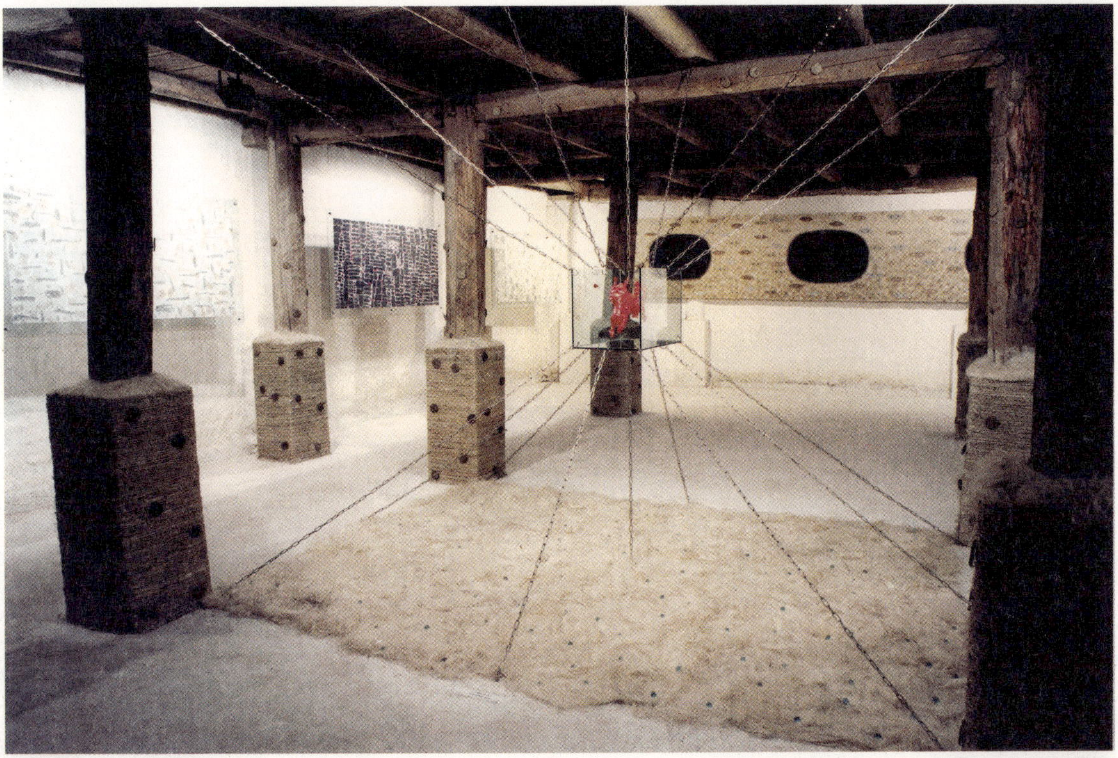

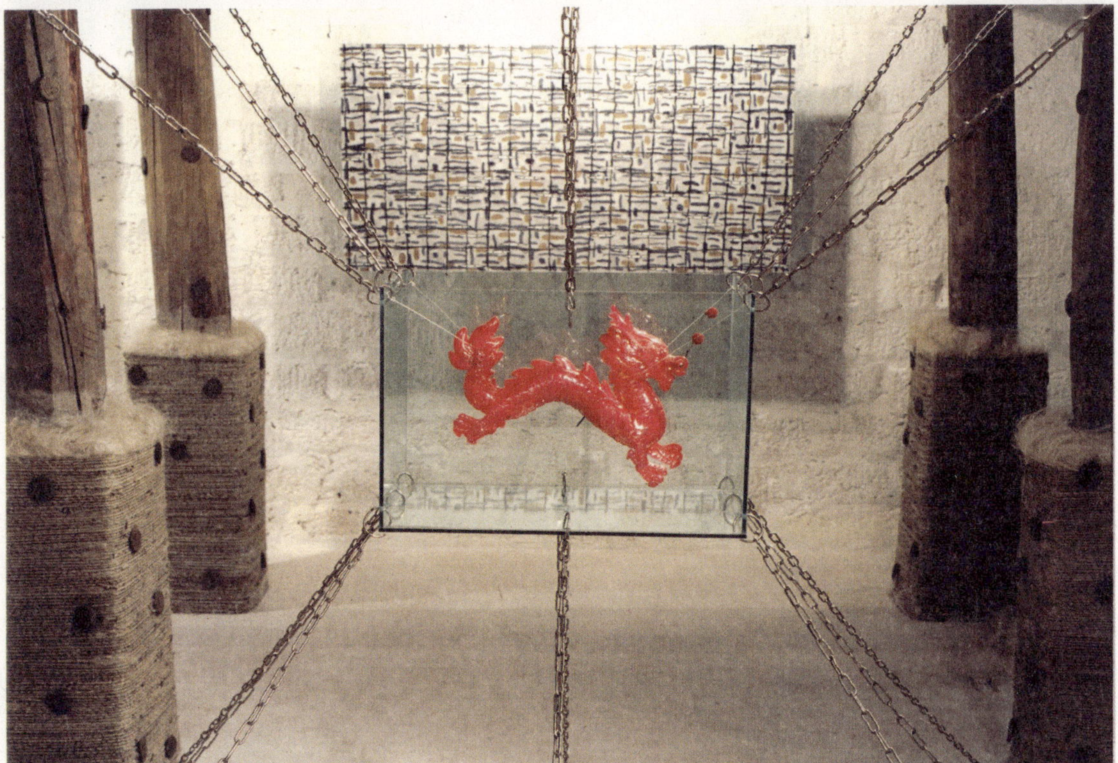

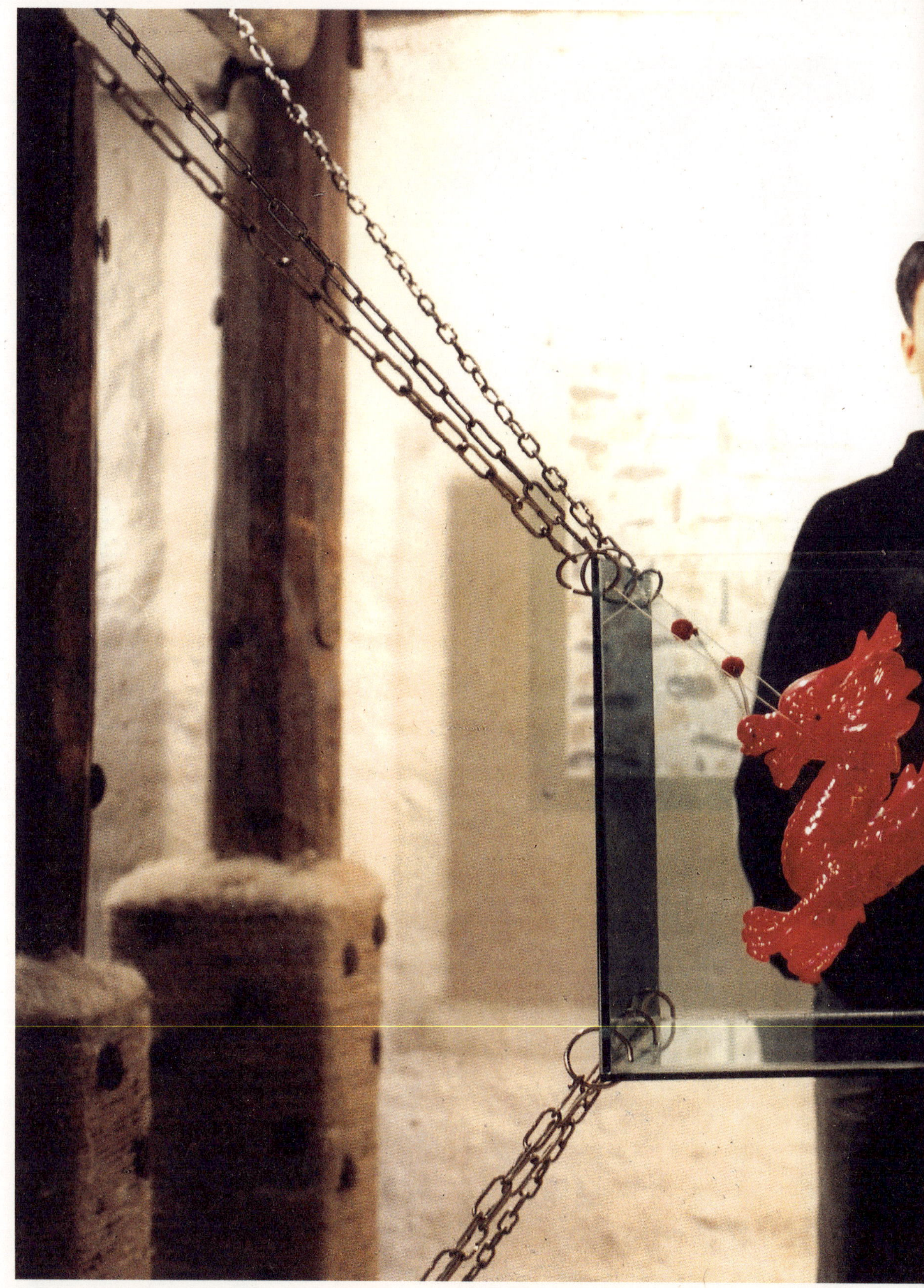

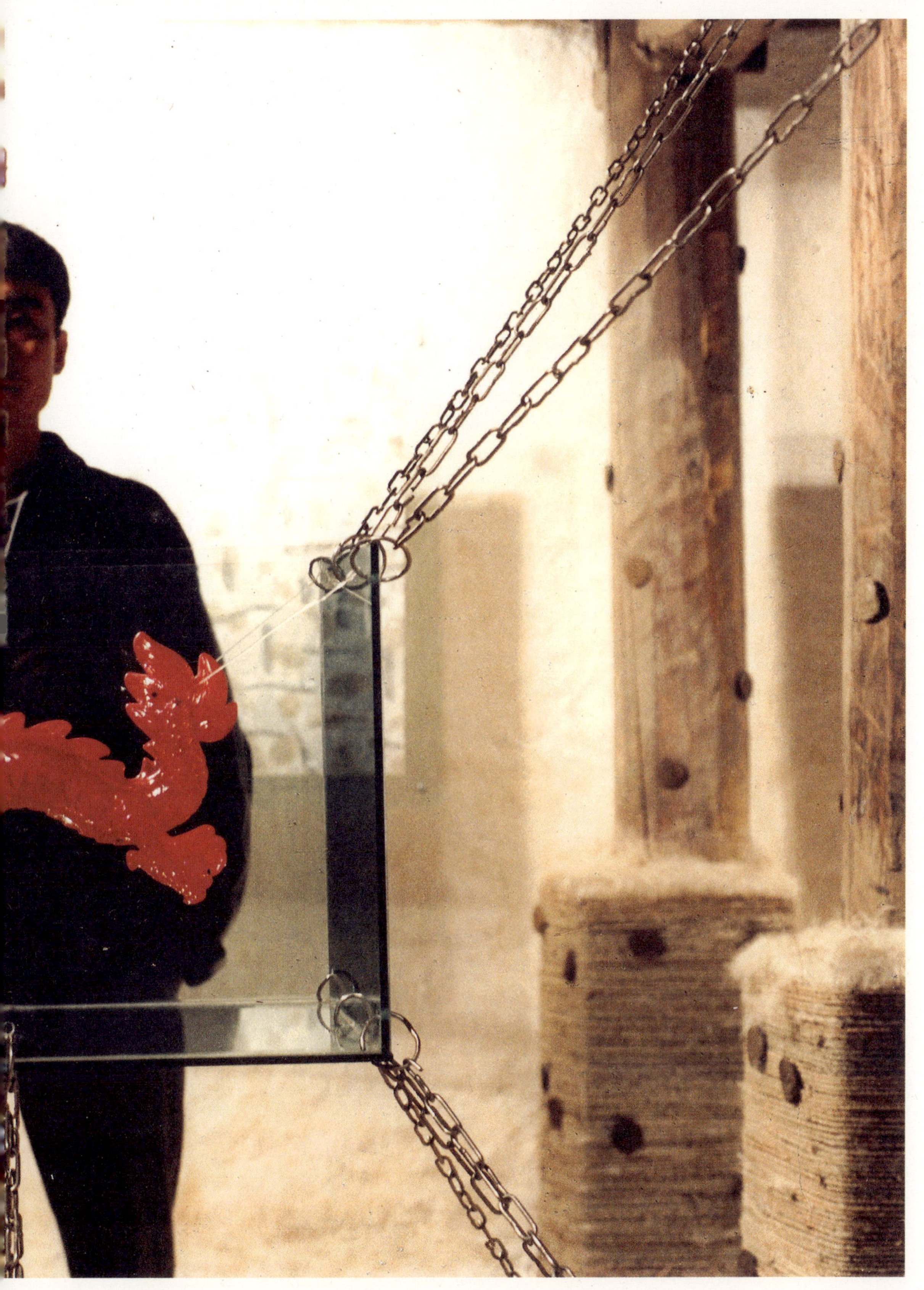

PRACTICE WITH RED CLAY CERAMICS
1999 – 2000

During the 1990s, alongside his installation art practice, Trần Lương frequently visited the pottery villages of Bát Tràng and Phù Lãng. While Bát Tràng specialized in exquisite white porcelain, the village of Phù Lãng focused on crafting large, rough pottery items from red clay, which Lương found intriguing because it provided more room for experimentation. He commissioned craftsmen to produce a collection of cylinder vases, which he then interacted with through violent actions such as striking them with bamboo sticks or binding them with ropes before they were fired. After the firing process, the ceramic vases emerged with contorted, twisted shapes, marked with the visible imprints of the binding ropes, effectively documenting the physical traces the artist had left on them. During the process he failed many times. However, for the artist the results "are similar to how violence interacts with living beings and humans – either succumbing to death or resisting and remaining standing with the scars." This practice was driven by a desire to explore alternative aesthetic outcomes, reflecting the reality of the artist's life without relying on drawings or carving.

Self-portrait, a white ceramic plate piece was shown in the exhibition *Khởi Thuỷ* in l'Atelier Gallery in Hà Nội in 1996. The red clay vases have never been shown.

1

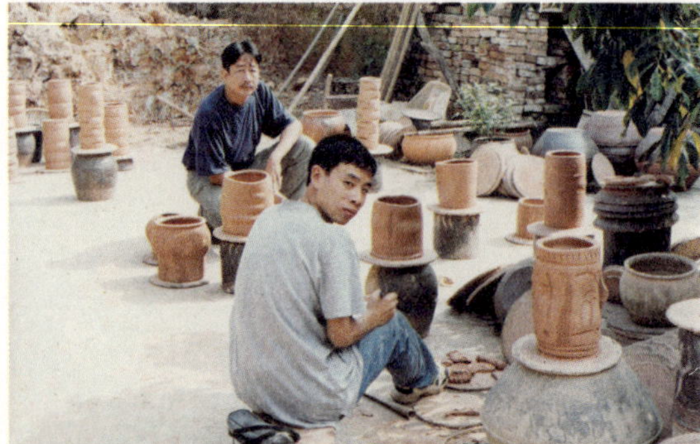

2

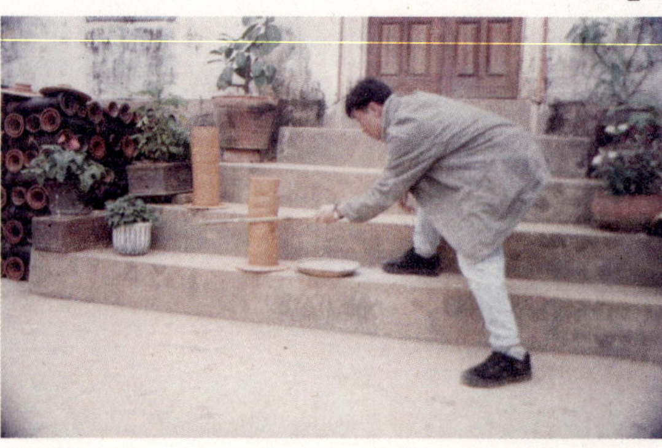

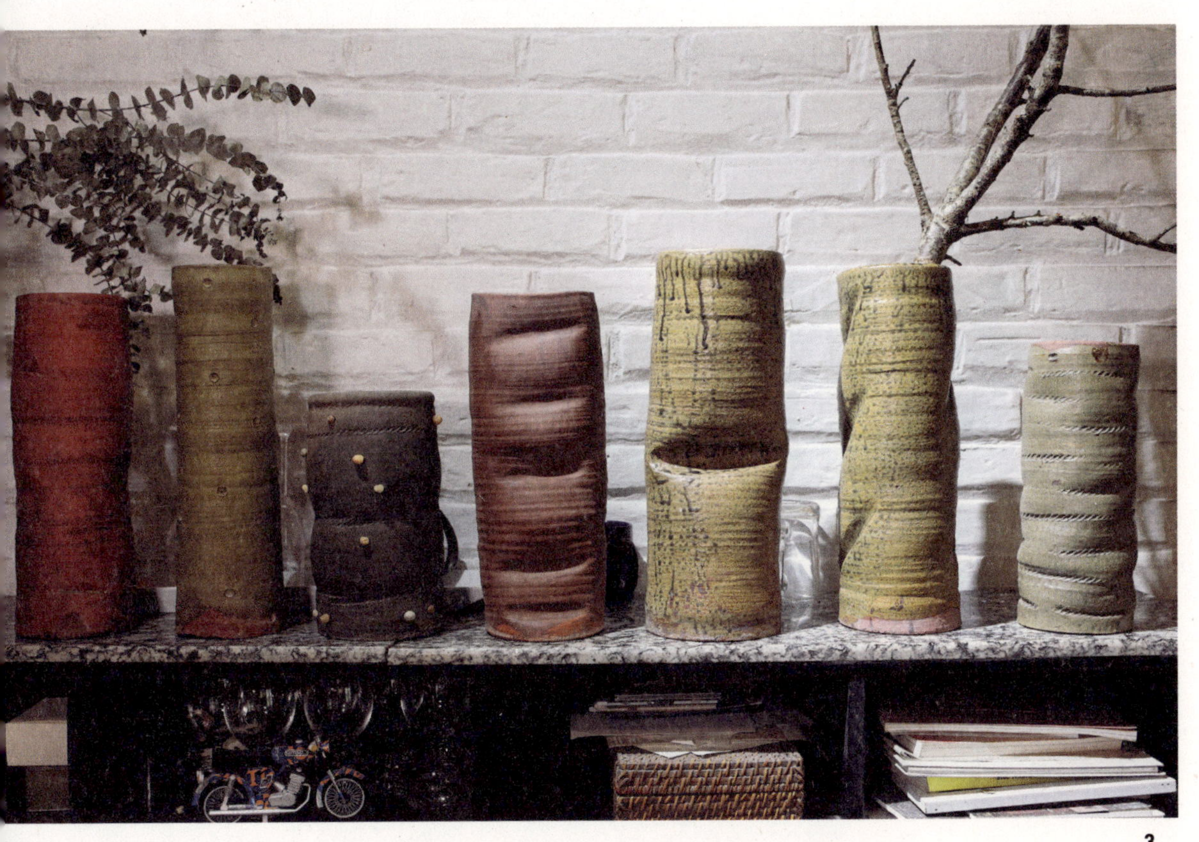

3

1
Trần Lương visits the Phù Lãng pottery vases with a group of artist friends. In the photo, Trần Đỗ Nghĩa (left) and Nguyễn Minh Phước (right) work with the wet red-clay vases.

2
Trần Lương whips the vases with bamboo sticks.

3
Collection of red clay vases in the artist's house.

4
Trần Lương, *Self-portrait*, 1996, Blue glaze on white ceramics, H: 6 / D: 52 cm

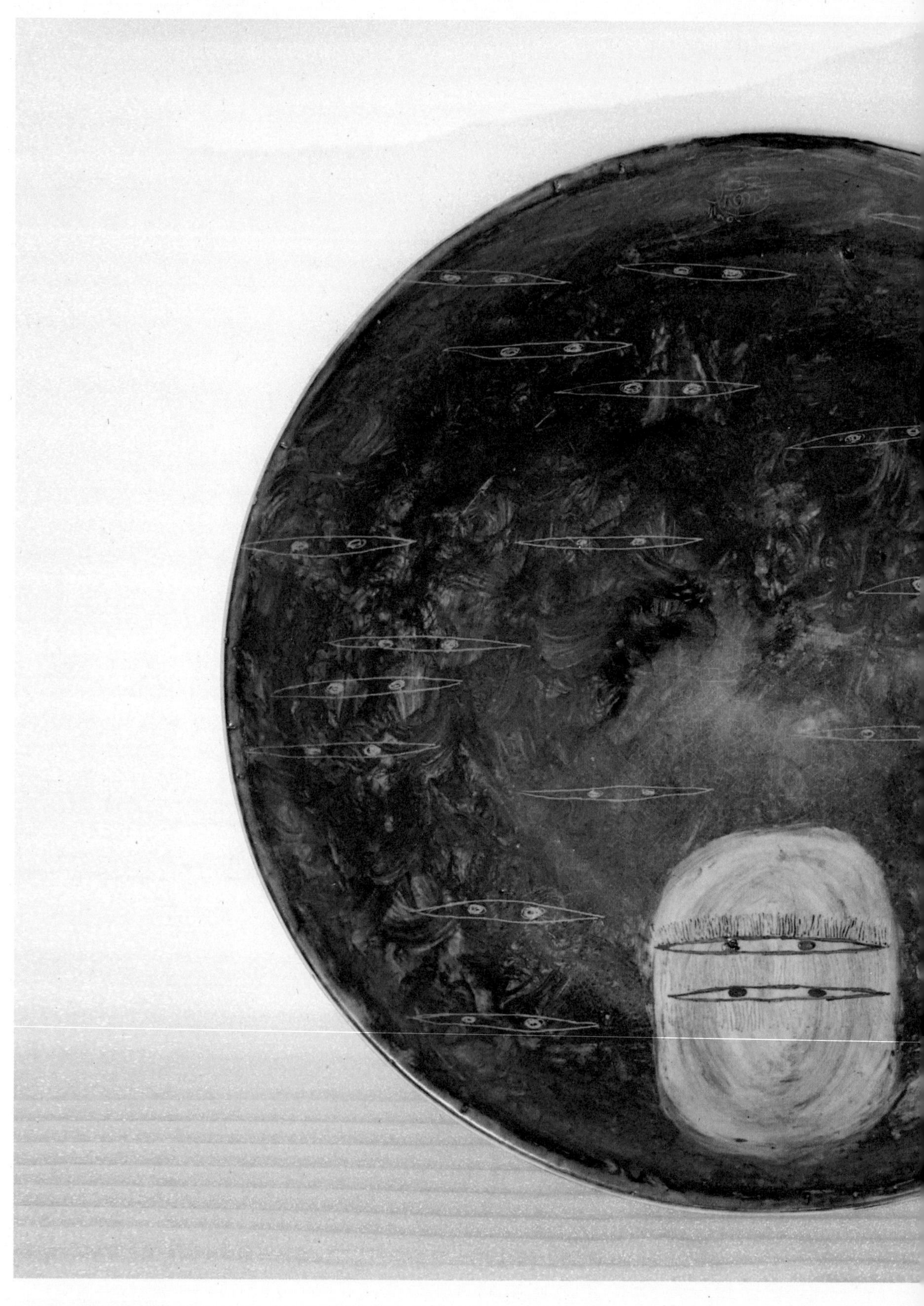

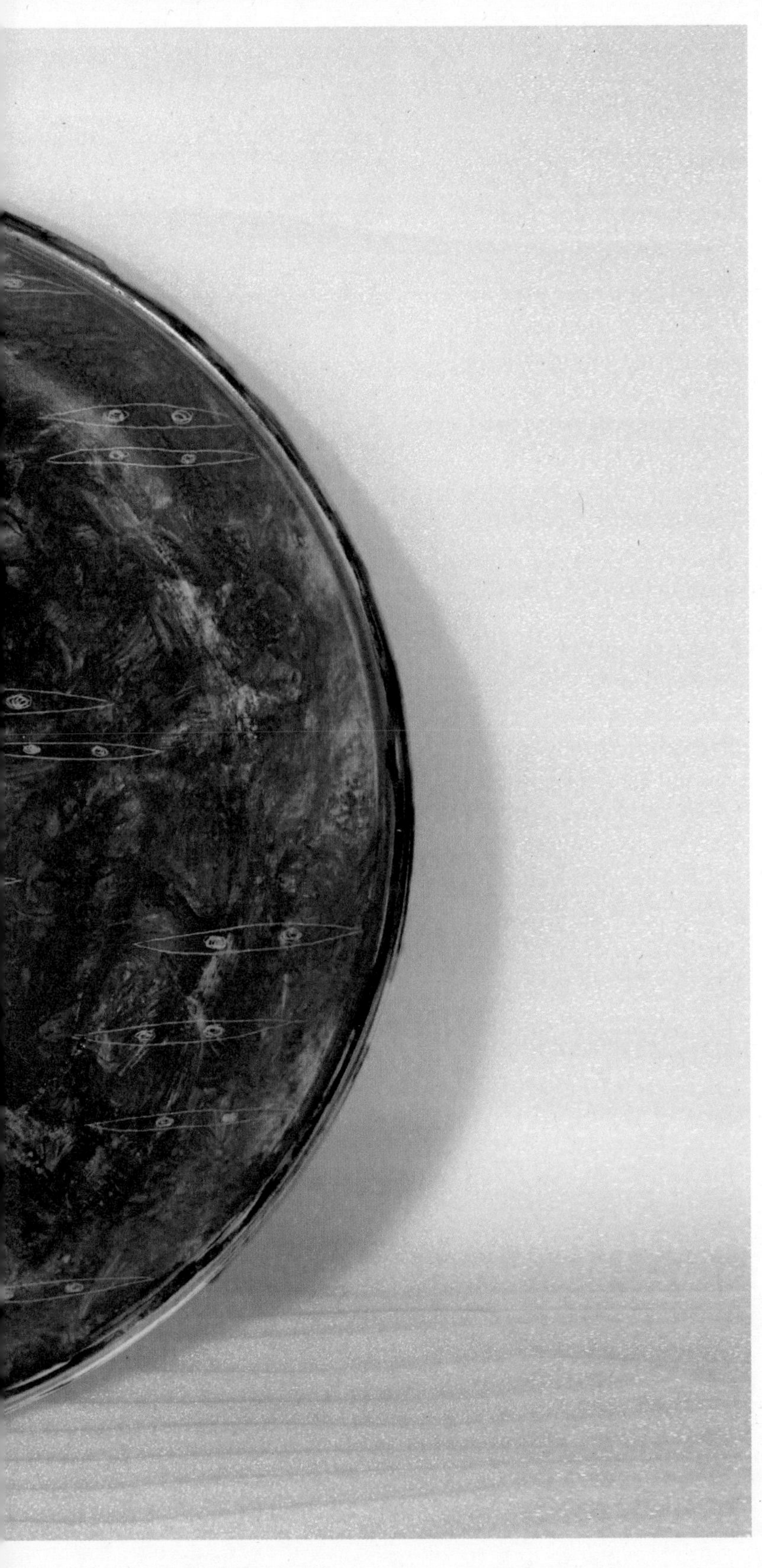

GENERATIONEXT
2000 & 2002

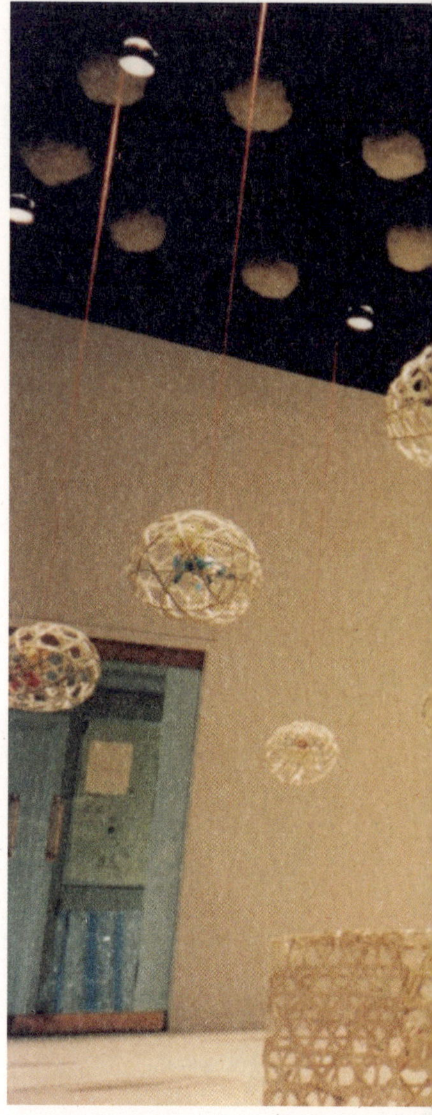

Trần Lương's childhood was populated by handcrafted toys made from natural materials and repurposed scrap metal. In post-1990 Vietnam, traditional toys were swiftly abandoned to make room for industrially manufactured plastic counterparts. Lương collected broken plastic toys from families and pieced them together, giving rise to a diverse ensemble of characters known as *Generationext*. Imagining a new era, the artist conceived of versatile, avant-garde warriors primed for exploration in various spatial contexts. These warriors symbolise the panorama of globalisation, blending multifarious cultures, ethnicities and pop-cultural currents, which advocate both violence and sexual freedom.

The *Generationext* installation has two components: the upper part portrays a forward-looking dimension, featuring the new generation toys suspended within egg-shaped spaceships crafted from woven bamboo baskets. On the floor, the lower part is comprised of bamboo cages containing small drawings, which serve as autobiographical narratives of the artist's childhood memories and those of his generation.

Generationext was first shown at the *Reconsidering Vietnam* exhibition in Richard F. Brush Art Gallery (St. Lawrence University, USA) in 2000. The second version was shown at the Fukuoka Triennale in 2002.

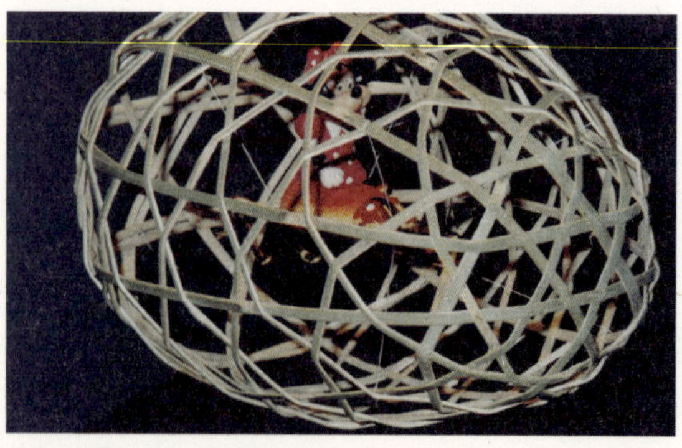

Trần Lương, *Generationext*, 2000, installation with used plastic toys, bamboo cages, drawing on Dó paper. Installation view, St.Lawrence University.

PAGE 112:
Trần Lương, *Generationext*, 2002, installation with used plastic toys, bamboo cages, drawing on Dó paper. Installation view, 2nd Fukuoka Triennale 2002.

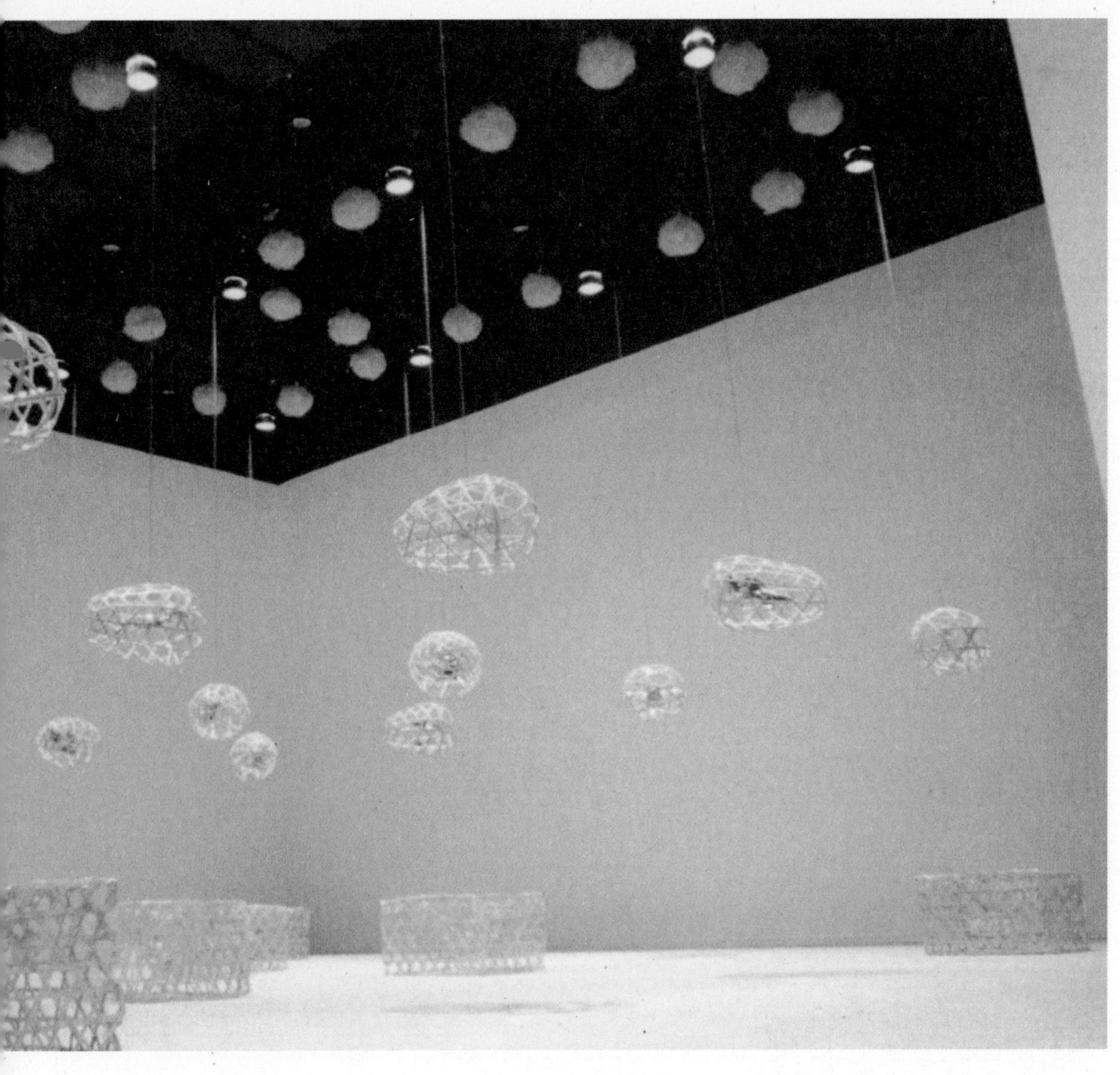

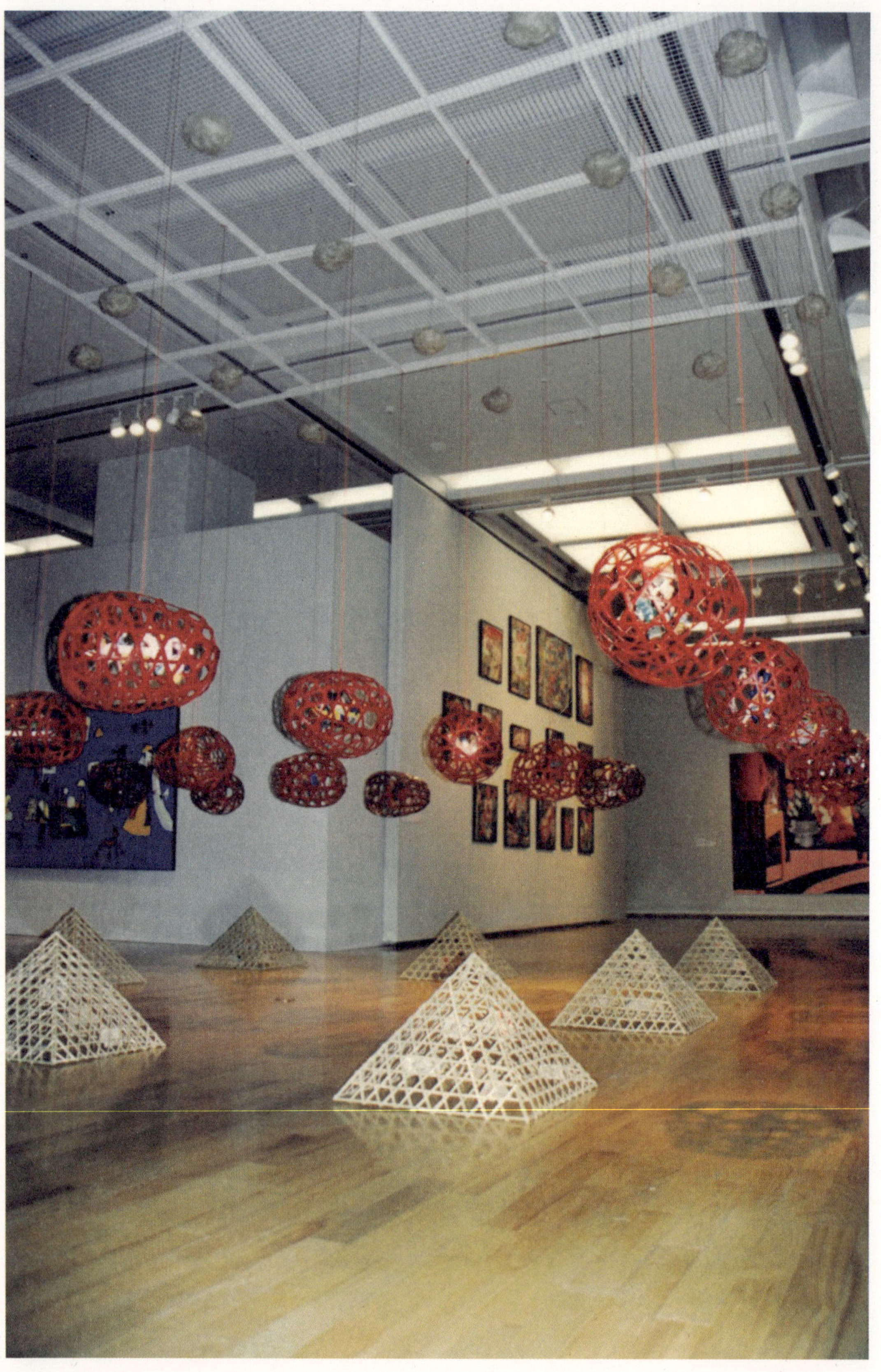

CONVERSATION BETWEEN TRẦN LƯƠNG & BILJANA CIRIC

This conversation took place on two occasions. We initiated the conversation in December 2012 in Hà Nội and continued it in November 2023. It touches on different aspects of Lương's life and practice. Although this book contains texts from various authors reflecting on Lương's practices, engaging in conversation offers the opportunity to read and listen to his voice, observe the way he thinks and hear how he articulates his ideas. This adds an additional layer towards understanding and interpreting his practice. Psychology scholar Svend Brinkmann writes of the knowledge-making potential of conversation, highlighting that our inquiring and interpreting selves are inherently conversational. We are constituted by the numerous relationships we have and have had with other people.[1] Brinkmann also reminds us that the study of the conversational world is a never-ending process.[2] If, as Brinkmann suggests, our conversation and the process of getting to know each other and ourselves is an ongoing process, so too are the encounters that inform Lương's thinking and practising.

1. Svend Brinkmann, "Qualitative Research Between Craftsmanship and McDonaldization," *Qualitative Studies* 3 (2012b): 56–68.

2. Svend Brinkmann, *Qualitative Interviewing, Conversational Knowledge through Interviews,* 2nd edition, (Oxford: Oxford University Press, 2022).

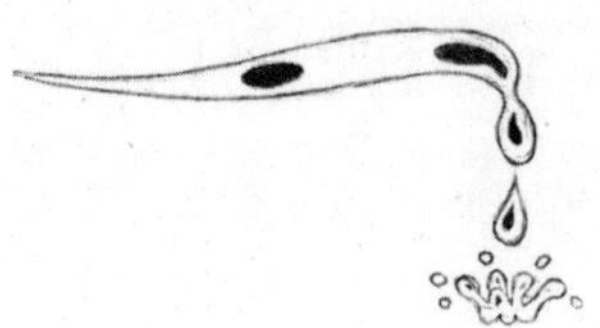

BC: You started with the Gang of Five.

TL: Yes, Gang of Five started gathering in 1983. We were classmates, we were friends. We knew each other even before entering university; we knew each other from high school. We went to the Art Academy together. Three of us went into the art academy, and two went to a more design-oriented art school. At that time, there was no information. We graduated in 1983, and suddenly after graduation, I felt like I was a small boy. This was also a period of transition towards the open-door period (Đổi Mới reforms) that happened in 1986. We started to realise that our education was teaching us only skills, neglecting the mind. During that time, Vietnamese youth were encouraged to go to Eastern Europe to study or to become cheap export labour. Countries like Poland, East Germany, Russia and Czechoslovakia were on the list. We had no support and we felt very lonely. It was just us at that time. We came up with the idea of forming the group because we feared that without it, some of us might give up on doing art.

At the beginning, the group consisted of twelve people, not five. (Alongside the Gang of Five members, there were other friends such as Nguyễn Linh, Võ Tá Hùng, Nguyễn Dũng, Nguyễn Quốc Việt, Nguyễn Trung Phan, Hoàng Văn Quảng.) After forming the group, we decided to present our works at the studio of Phạm Quang Vinh, who was a member of the group. We decided to show the work of one of the members every month in Vinh's studio, which was located in the colonial quarter and had originally been his family's living room. We also held seminars, drank wine and talked about art.

BC: When did activities in the studio start?

TL: They began in 1983, but just three to four months later a few members of the group pulled out because they were no longer interested. They had to work for a living, leaving them with no time to continue with our activities. After one year, only five members remained: Phạm Quang Vinh, Hà Trí Hiếu, Đặng Xuân Hoà, Hồng Việt Dũng and myself. The five of us continued to work together until the group disbanded in 1997.

The last exhibition we did was in 1996 and after that we decided that we would not organise any more exhibitions or events together. The name "Gang of Five" was first used in 1990. Before that, people called us the "Five Young Hà Nội Boys", or something like that.

BC: What kind of work did the group produce?

TL: We worked with oil, gouache and painting on newspaper, as well as watercolour on handmade paper.

BC: Was anyone from an older generation influential on your group?

TL: No, there were no groups before us. Each artist worked individually. There were movements but not groups. There was a movement called the Nhân Văn Giai Phẩm affair in 1956. Nhân Văn translates to "Humanities" and Giai Phẩm to "Masterpieces." It consisted of the most important intellectuals from Vietnam, mainly writers, philosophers, film makers, a few publishers and a few painters. My father, Trần Công, was a member of this group. They followed communism and Ho Chi Minh despite all coming from high-class families. They believed that communism could overthrow colonialism. However, after the war and the communist occupation of the northern part of the country, they were the first to realise that communism and Maoism are very bad. Including my father. They were a movement and they published "Giai Phẩm," which was a very important periodical.

BC: Returning to the activities of the Gang of Five in the 1980s, were they all conducted in that studio space you mentioned?

TL: Yes, we continued exhibiting in that small studio from 1983 to 1990, for seven years. There wasn't really an audience; only relatives, friends and family would come to see our exhibitions. It was just for us. Until 1990, there was no professional art community, no art market, no one to buy the work and no one to support us. Even if we submitted our work to government exhibitions, it would not be accepted.

BC: When did you start to have more public exhibitions?

TL: The first time was in 1990. Around that time, private galleries started appearing and organising shows. We knew a painter friend, Việt Hải, who ran a small government gallery. He agreed to host a Gang of Five exhibition. The gallery was called "7 Hàng Khay Street" (it ceased to exist in 2004). The exhibition was held in July 1990, coinciding with the 100th anniversary of Van Gogh's death. When I see photos from the opening of this exhibition, I can see members of the Nhân Văn Giai Phẩm movement who came to our show as they were excited to see the younger generation.

BC: Why did the group split?

TL: Mainly because of myself and because of the market. At the beginning we all did what we did because we love art, there was no other pragmatic reason. However, as the market emerged, some members started to enjoy material success, becoming best-selling artists in Vietnam. With Vietnam opening its doors, people came to buy cheap works, leading artists to start reproducing their own work. It was the same with the members of our group, they became part of the market. For me, this was a big disappointment. This all happened in 1995/1996. I started to distance myself from the group and the last exhibition we did together was in 1996. So, it was a good lesson for me and for the art community to learn that the free market brings not only vitamins, but also poison.

Coming from a very grassroots farming culture, we were not prepared for the free market. It wasn't easy. The free market is business, after all. So, I decided to quit painting, which was kind of a performance piece, although my paintings are quite different from the works of other friends in the group. I quit painting in 1997. We had only had six years of practice with the free market and so many problems had arisen. I was asking myself why the group died so young. I realised that it had to do with not having professional education. We did things with youthful energy, but that didn't keep us running in the long term. I felt disappointed in myself. I don't consider myself a commercial artist so I told my family and friends that I would stop painting.

BC: When did you start taking on the role of curator and organising exhibitions?

TL: I tried to do some things between 1995 and 1998, but I think that period was more of a transitional phase for me. I was still learning and wasn't really clear on my direction. I increasingly felt that contemporary art could effectively express political and social issues. My opportunity to travel abroad came in late 1992 to early 1993 when I went to Europe – first to the Netherlands and then France. It was during that time that I began questioning why there was a lack of freedom here in Vietnam. Was it because of government pressure or did the local art community not know how to survive? What was the main reason? It took me a few years to understand how I could help the art infrastructure in Vietnam.

By 1996 to 1997, I came to understand that Vietnam lacked the necessary infrastructure to support artists. In the Western art system, artists are surrounded by different professions that serve their needs, such as curators, art historians, writers, art dealers, technicians, engineers, lawyers, fundraisers and many others. Here in Vietnam, we have none of these. Another major issue was funding; there were no non-profits nor non-governmental funding for art, no alternative art spaces to give artists wings. There were many gaps. I was asking myself what I could do, despite my lack of professional training. Should I fund a space where people could gather? For many years, exhibitions in Vietnam were dictated entirely by the authorities. It wasn't possible to introduce any ideas through your curatorial statement, such as exploring artistic relations to the social and local background and environment. I started to learn to raise funds, gather people and learn to negotiate with both sides. It was a long learning process. In 1998, I co-founded Nhà Sàn. I didn't discuss curating with people, I just started doing it.

BC: Were there any other spaces in the 90s?

TL: Yes, but none of them were run by Vietnamese people. Most of what I saw in the West were white cube spaces, but the white cube space did not exist in our lives. We are still very site-specific, very dirty, very local. In the late 1980s to the early 1990s in Vietnam, there were a few galleries engaging in partly experimental activities, such as Natasha Gallery and Mai Gallery. However, they were still basically commercial galleries, displaying and selling mostly paintings and other types of object-based art. They were not open to other activities to promote development, such as talks, discussions, workshops or seminars.

BC: Did you ever discuss your work with your father?

TL: I learned more from him than I learned from school. My childhood was during wartime. It's a long story. Both my grandmother's father and my dad's father were popular teachers, and my maternal grandfather was one of the two people during the French war who bought film equipment and learned to use a camera. He opened his studio Anh Photo, in the centre of Hà Nội, just for himself. Because he didn't have enough money or technical support, his films had no sound. In his films, every five minutes there is a frame with a text comment written by him. I grew up in his house. His name was Nguyễn Văn Vĩnh.

When my mother was 17 years old, my father was forced to work for the cinema department of the Ministry of Culture, after the Nhân Văn Giai Phẩm movement was suppressed in 1957/1958. He got a research job in what was a new department at the time, but they had no equipment so they would requisition from private studios. So, my father went to my grandfather's house around

1957/58 with a group of filmmakers from the government and took all the equipment from my grandfather's family. They took everything. My mother however, looked at my father like a hero because to her he was like a hero bringing freedom to the country. My grandfather was very angry and threatened to kick my mother out of the family if she followed my father, because this man had taken away everything, including his job. However, despite her father's anger, my mother still married my father. They lived in a very small flat. After a year, I was born, and my grandfather allowed my family back into his house. I grew up there, with my grandfather's culture of photography. He had a piano and a violin. Before I learned to read, I started to play piano.

One day, my parents came to me and informed me that I wouldn't be able to continue studying the piano because I needed to go to the countryside, as the Americans were going to bomb us soon. That was in 1965. The following week, they gave me a bag with books, pencils and watercolours and told me that was all I could take. I became a visual artist because of the accident of war; if there hadn't been a war, I might have become a pianist.

At that time, no one believed the bombing would last long, maybe just a few months. I went with a group of children to the countryside. A month later, my parents came to visit me. I stayed in the countryside for nearly eight years, moving to six different places during the bombings in North Vietnam. I was 13 when the bombing finally stopped, which was in early 1973. I officially started going to school when I was 13, so until then, that bag was my constant companion.

BC: What impact did international curators and exhibitions have on the local scene, especially during the 1990s?

TL: They didn't change the scene a lot. The Vietnamese presence at those international events was minor, so connections were not strong. One reason for this is that our scene consists mostly of artists; there are no art historians or writers to contextualise these experiences. Artists take what they can get. Another thing is that when artists travel abroad, they often spend more time shopping or visiting Disneyland than going to museums. We need to have a multifaceted approach that includes perspectives from writers and art historians. Here, artists often feel isolated.

BC: How would you define your role in the Hà Nội art scene?

TL: We are like a village, with village behaviour. Even the director of Goethe once asked me, "You're a good artist, why don't you just do your own work? Why are you doing so many other things?" I don't separate between curating, organising events and my own work; for me, everything is one. Whatever I do is not for my own reputation but for everyone.

*

"...
But, take the traffic police podium placed in the heart of people
Forcing emotional forwards and backwards
Follow the rule of the state road
Can cause a lot of bitterness
in real life
..."

Lê Đạt, "The story of a few people who committed suicide", *Humanities* No 1, 1956.

BC: What were your early performance references?

TL: I started to think about performance during the 1990s while I was travelling abroad. Actually, Yoko Ono's work was one of the first that I saw and that registered in my brain as performance. However, it was Vito Acconci's work that deeply influenced me. I was lucky to have a chance to meet him in New York when I attended a workshop that MoMA organised in 2000. At that time, MoMA was running a series of workshops related to regions that weren't represented in their collection and the one I attended was devoted to East Asia.

That workshop gave me a chance to meet quite a lot of famous artists, including Vito Acconci, who we visited at his Studio in Williamsburg in Brooklyn, where we had an hour-long meeting with him. I remember having a very friendly private talk with him about growing up during the Vietnam War. He heard that I am from Vietnam, and he came to me and said, "I went to demonstrate against the Vietnam War," and we talked. I love his work. I learned performance mainly from his work.

BC: Was the MoMA workshop foundational for your practice?

TL: Yes, both for my performance practice but also for my video works. Thanks to this workshop, I got to see masterpieces like Empire State, the eight-hour long film by Andy Warhol, as well as many other works that were at that time part of the MoMA collection. Robert Storr was curator of painting and drawing at the time and he gave me some insight into many of the works from the collections. I also learned about the shortcomings of MoMA. When Storr showed me a map of MoMA's collection in relation to Asia, I noticed they only had a few pieces from Asian countries, mostly Japan, China, Iran and a few works from Korea. Southeast Asian works didn't exist in their collection. Through those workshops, MoMA slowly started expanding its collection to include works from various regions in Asia.

BC: Before attending the MoMA workshop, there were already some performative elements present in your work. For example, in your first solo exhibition at Nhà Sàn in 1999, you interacted with the installation through performative gestures. In the video *Flowing*, you intervened in public space by placing the sculptures in front of various buildings, indicating an early inclination towards performance.

TL: Sure, I had already started organising performance programs by that time. In 1997, in collaboration with The SIAM Society and Ford Foundation, I co-organised an exchange program between Vietnam and Thailand. We took a big group of artists from Vietnam to travel to Bangkok and produce an exhibition. I also organised a group of artists from Thailand to go to Hà Nội. That was when we met Montien Boonma, a senior Thai artist at that time. So, in that exchange program, back in 1997, there was already a performance piece by Trương Tân. Although I didn't perform on that occasion, I was supporting the other artists; I was more in the role of organiser. I had to learn about performance, and I started to think that performance as a medium fits Vietnamese society and its issues very well. I also started to realise that the body is a material that no one can censor. When returning from travelling abroad, customs normally check which books you bring in, they check paintings, but your body remains uncensored. So, performance is very suitable and convenient as a way for us to raise our voices.

The important thing that the spirit of performance offers is the possibility to transfer your message directly. The dialogue and interactivity that you can establish through performance allows you to share your message directly and get in touch with different social classes. Unlike fancy modern art formats that require specific settings – you need a gallery, you need the lighting, you need a reception – performance can break through all those barriers to give voice to the socio-political issues that directly impact the community you are addressing. Performance can use guerrilla strategies, but with painting that is not possible. In Vietnam, performance was accepted within our artist community, not because we understood performance art conceptually, but because it functioned as a medium through which to respond to our social condition, creating a space for action.

BC: What was your very first performance piece?

TL: I don't know, maybe there were some earlier pieces, but the first complete one was *Steam Rice Man* in 2001. Steam Rice Man is a very academic piece. Not very radical... It departs from the contrast of black and white, you know? I think in this piece you can also sense that my art background is influenced by the European Academy in the way I was thinking about the colours and materials. But at the same time, it was also the reality of the time, the reality of my own childhood growing up in the rice field, in the wetland; of being hungry throughout my whole childhood and youth. Rice for us was a luxury food. During the long years of rice shortages, we had to eat corn and potato all the time. A meal with rice was very rare during wartime. And those living conditions continued until the early '80s. So, Steam Rice Man contains a lot of references from my life.

When the critic and painter Nguyễn Quân saw Steam Rice Man, he didn't understand. I didn't try to explain it to him because I knew that understanding this kind of work takes time. Not only time to research Steam Rice Man and myself, but because it takes time to accept and learn to appreciate the form of this kind of work. For Vietnamese people at that time, it was still early to grasp the form of performance and the form of conceptual image making. Ten years later, around 2011, Nguyễn Quân told me, "I have to say, actually, I love Steam Rice Man. But before, I didn't know it was good." And he is a painter and art critic who studied in Germany. But you see, it's not easy doing things in Vietnam.

The same goes for curating. I have been doing it for a number of years, but I never mentioned that I am curator. I didn't claim it as a kind of job because no one would have understood. I started practising curating in Nhà Sàn in 1998 and every year I organised many shows. I think it was around 2002, four years later, that I started naming myself as a curator and officially writing it. In 2002, I collaborated with Ong Keng Sen from Theater Works in Singapore on the *Windows to Asia* project, which gathered international artists and artists from Asia in the Hà Nội Contemporary Art Center. It was a project that presented many art forms, including music, sound, noise, performing arts and film screenings. Through this project in Hà Nội Contemporary Art Center we started a discussion about the role of the curator. For many people this was brand new; they were asking, *What is the role of the curator?* But I had been doing it for four years by that point, without being able to explain it. You can only show what it is by doing the practical work. We didn't have any theory.

BC: I'd like to talk about aspects of your performance work that are closely related to everyday gestures, such as tooth brushing and washing clothes. Can you talk about how you see them within your work?

TL: Everyday actions already carry their own histories and their own power. I chose these specific daily life actions because they create transparency between individuals, time and the community. They connect through time, through community, through different local contexts and local traditions, because everyone has to do the same thing. These actions contain their own community memory, historical context and personal memory. So, by choosing to work with them, I borrow their inherent power. I try to change their position and the context of the action. For example, I wash clothes, but I wash them on a tree. I brush my teeth, but at different times, not in the morning or at night. I appear in public space during working hours to clean my mouth. By shifting the position of these daily actions, behaviour changes and other issues come up, depending on what I want to communicate.

BC: Let's return to this performance in Phnom Penh.

TL: When I talk to Cambodians and they realise that I'm Vietnamese, there's a change in their attitude. Normally, they're friendly and talk to me in English, but they know... I can see it in their eyes. About 30% of them immediately express gratitude, saying, "Thank you, because if the Vietnamese troops had come even a little bit later, my family and I would have been killed. The Khmer Rouge would have killed us." However, a much larger portion, about 70% of Cambodians, they hate Vietnamese people. They don't say the word "hate," but they say it with their eyes. Suddenly, they become very cold and they don't want to continue talking when I ask them to share a memory of the Khmer Rouge era or the time when the Vietnamese army was stationed in Cambodia. So, in 2006, I changed my method from trying to interview people, to trying to make something together. It turns out that teeth cleaning is actually a successful way to communicate. Teeth cleaning is an everyday action that everyone from the homeless guy to the King has to do. We all do the same.

So, we held a public, collective teeth-cleaning session and at first, you see joy because it's fun. After a while, people start to ask, *why am I doing this?* In Phnom Penh, the participants started asking the Cambodian volunteers, who would reply, "He is from Vietnam, and he wants to talk with us." People don't want to talk with Vietnamese about the past. They don't want to dig up the suffering. Maybe they are afraid? But during that cleaning festival, people started to make room to talk about history. They already feel friendly because of the action of cleaning their teeth together, so the action is working. Cleaning teeth is working.

BC: How did you develop the work, *Welts*?

TL: One day, I saw my son coming home from school with a red scarf around his neck and shoulders. That night, I couldn't sleep. My feelings were a mix of nostalgia and memory. I remember as a young boy fighting with my red scarf because at that time, there were no toys, no entertainment. Boys had to find something to play with and the red scarf turned out to be the most practical and active object to play with. The red scarf was given to all "communist youth" schoolchildren, so everyone had one. As boys we all knew how to play with the red scarf. I can play it for you, so you can see. It's like using a whip. There is a technique to how you whip it when you hit, and it can be very strong and very dangerous. But if you don't know how to use it, it's just floating fabric. I thought the red scarf should have disappeared by the time my son was in school, because I got married very late. But there it was, still there after so many years. Almost forty years later, my son was wearing the same red scarf.

This event with my son was a trigger to start developing a work. Around that time, I was invited by Shu Yang to participate in Dadao Live Art Festival in Beijing. China seemed to me a great place to test the performance.

BC: There is a process in the work where you first engage with the scarf as a proposal to awaken memory.

TL: Yes, I perform a number of actions in order to wake up the history and the memories associated with the red scarf. These actions last for around half an hour, moving from more peaceful gestures towards more violent ones, culminating in the whipping action. The whipping starts very lightly, then becomes really strong. If you whip strongly and do it properly it makes a noise. Then, I hold the scarf and ask the audience who wants to play, who has played like this before? They queue up to play [laughs] and I invite them to play on my body, explaining that as young boys we used to fight each other like this. So now, my body becomes the object for them to interact with and they play. They hit hard. When people are given permission to hurt someone, anger comes up in every single body and they keep doing it. Some people caused me a lot of pain. People carry too much pressure and when they have a chance to hurt someone – officially, with permission – they do it. In the following iterations of the performance, I started to hide my head because I wanted to make the human character less specific, allowing people to hit more freely.

The flow of history has brought a lot of major global changes over the past 70 years. In my work, humans are just like amoeba – similar in their lives and deaths and migrations, regardless of their social class or the knowledge they have gained. Look at COVID-19, or even the wars in Ukraine and Gaza. Sometimes I want to hide away my individual character because when people see my face they start to realise, "Oh, it's a man from Asia...how old is he?" Or even more than that, maybe someone knows that I am an artist. This information can act as a barrier to freely interacting, or to me being turned into a symbol of a whole bunch of people, of shared human pain throughout history. When I cover my head, my body becomes symbolic of an ordinary, unknown human body. A so-called object is reduced to something popular, normal, similar to everything else. But pragmatically, when my face is visible, people will treat me with more care.

BC: I wonder how the work builds up inside of you. You said you wanted to present your body as an object, and then you went even further by hiding your head so that they can't see your facial expressions.

TL: It's very, very exciting. I'm filled with many thoughts and feelings, often very conflicting. If I'm hit hard, I feel happy because it means my work is opening up human relations and waking up histories. But, at the same time, there is also sadness at being physically hurt by people. If we can wake up action and emotion from audiences, then the performance is growing. If we do it to ourselves, the performance can only grow with our own narrative and our own script. When the audience interacts, the work grows in many different possible directions that challenge you as an artist. This really brings a more democratic spirit and spiritual power to contemporary work in society.

BC: Yes, but I'm curious how all these performances inform your work, your body and your mind. How do they manifest within you?

TL: I feel that if I do not get any benefit from performance, then I will not perform. Which means that performance is quite an exciting and mystic world for me. It's different from being a painter or a filmmaker or video maker. Performance engages all the senses, including a sixth sense. A lot of the unconscious or subconscious emerges through performance. I have learned a lot of lessons about how to read the world, how to interpret the world, through performance. Many things might never be realised or understood if we don't do performance.

BC: Why do we see very few installation works from you? Is it because installation wasn't your preferred medium? Or is it that you prefer working with the body? Or maybe it's due to a lack of conditions in Vietnam conducive to producing installations?

TL: Firstly, it's due to a lack of conditions. Installation often occupies public places, which we don't have the right to do in Vietnam, and we didn't have many galleries available. I always preferred site-specific work over the white cube and site-specific work means you have to use public space. At the beginning I made some installations, but since about 2007 I started to be more concerned with environmental issues, which led to always using recycled materials.

Around 2010 I realised that even using recycled materials is not enough. Installation lacks power in comparison with media work or performance.

STEAM RICE MAN
2001

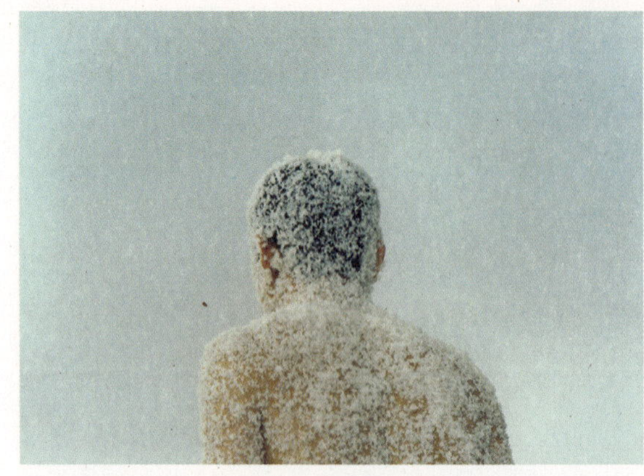

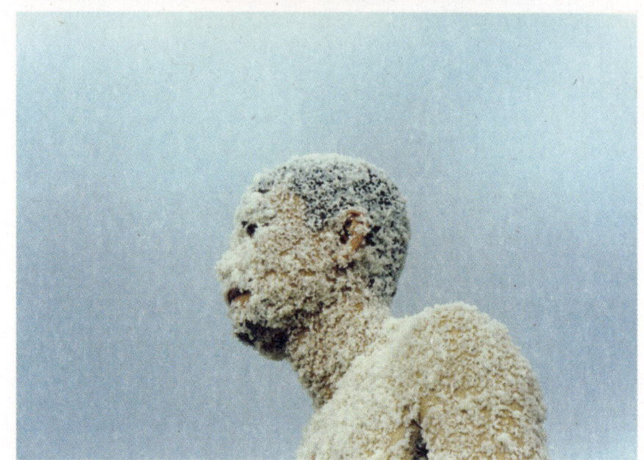

How much rice will be eaten to make
A piece of coal
White and black
Soft, sticky, and hard
Sow a coal seed
It will take a thousand years

- Artist statement, *Steam Rice Man*

Steam Rice Man was a performance developed after the artist spent six hours underground with miners, going as deep as 82 metres below sea level. The work responds to a visual urge for light and something white after so long in the dark.

Trần Lương recalls,

> Before going down into the coal mine tunnels, I had an idea deep in my mind that the hardest life for a man is being a farmer, because I had grown up in the northern countryside of a communist country during the American war. But after coming out of the tunnel and two weeks living with the miners, I realised that the coal miner's life is much harder and more dangerous! The idea came from a flash moment in my brain when I was walking in the long, dark tunnels, to compare farmers/ miners. Rice/coal. White/black. Soft & sticky/shiny & rigid.

The performance was part of the Mạo Khê project that Trần Lương organised in Mao Khe coal mine in Quảng Ninh province [see page 132].

Trần Lương, *Steam Rice Man*, 2001, photo documentation of durational performance. Mạo Khê coal mine factory building, Quảng Ninh, Vietnam.

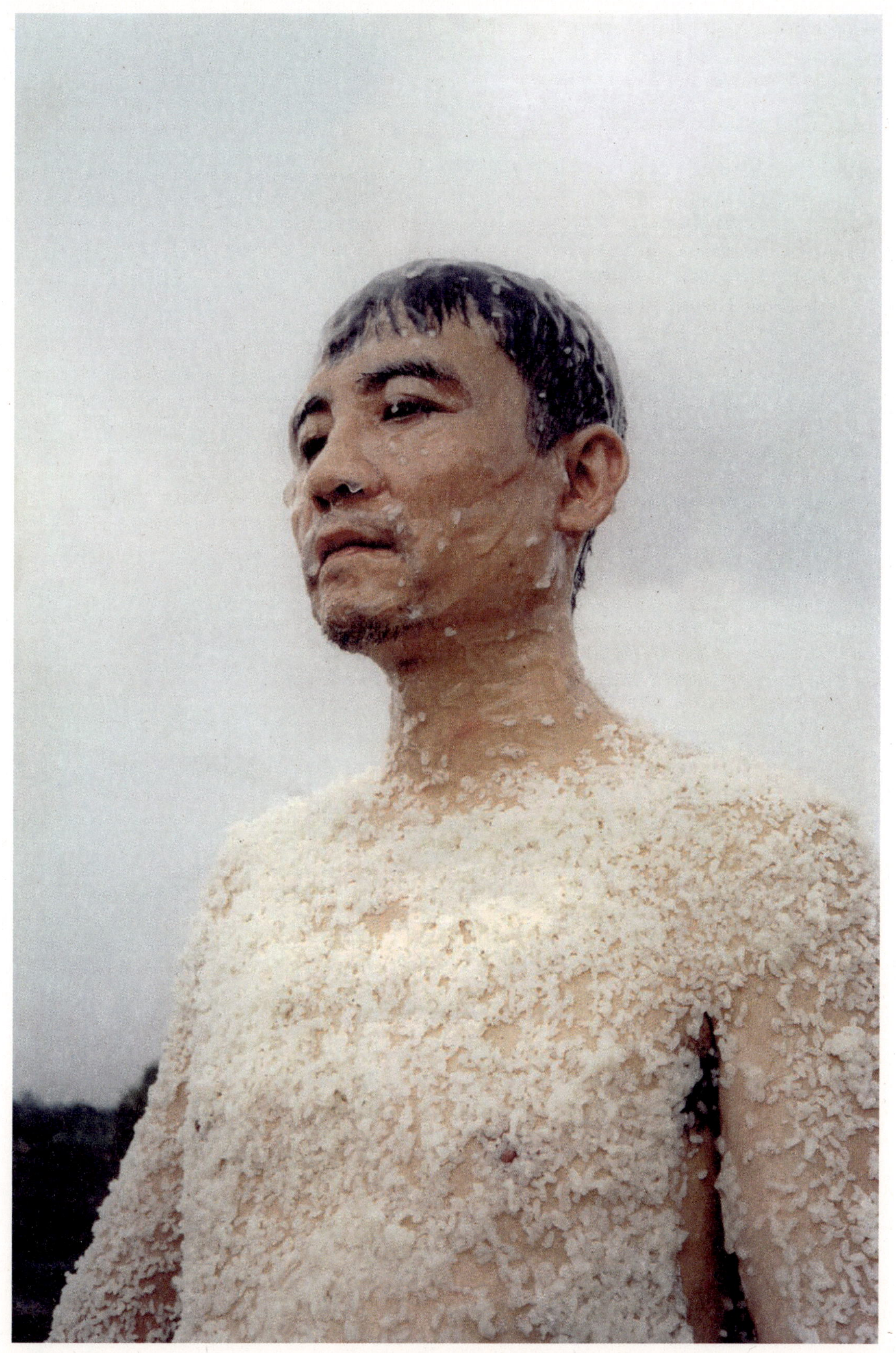

MẠO KHÊ COAL MINE PROJECT

October 2001

For 40 years (from 1954 to 2005) in Vietnam, artist field trips were strictly controlled by the communist government through Vietnam Fine Arts Association and the Ministry of Culture. During the Cold War era and up until the introduction of Đổi Mới in 1986, the government mandated field trips for artists to various remote areas. The purpose was to compel artists to work with farmers and workers, or to produce paintings depicting life in a social realist style, according to governmental guidelines.

In the late 1990s, Trần Lương started looking for opportunities to work with communities on the margins – farmers, the homeless, prostitutes and other workers. These projects are collectively called *Field Trips*. Some of these field trips were with other artists and some were solo trips. To date, Lương has organised the following Field Trips: *Mạo Khê Coal mine Project* (2001), *On the Banks of the Red River* (2001), *Foods of Ground* (1999-2003), *Hà Nội-PhnomPenh Art Exchange Project* (2006), *Blending In* (2004), *Water Droplets* (2005), *Journey of Green Vietnam* (2010-2014) and *Riverscapes IN FLUX* (2011-2013).

In October 2001, Trần Lương organised a two-week field trip to the Mạo Khê coal mine in Quảng Ninh province with 11 artists (Nguyễn Bảo Toàn, Hà Trí Hiếu, Lê Quảng Hà, Lê Hồng Thái, Đinh Quân, Đinh Công Đạt, Đào Anh Khánh, Phạm Ngọc Minh, Lê Vũ, Nguyễn Trí Mạnh, Trần Lương). The trip was mostly self-funded, with the coal mine factory providing meals and accommodation for the artists. The aim was to enable artists to experience being in touch with the lives of coal miners. The invitation that Lương extended to the artists was to live together with the miners but not to create artwork. The artists witnessed and experienced hardship and danger working in the tunnels, which inspired them to create works during their short stay. Works included murals painted on the walls of the mining complex, performances and graffiti-style interventions on the walls of factories, among other interventions.

The two-channel video was re-edited in 2015, commissioned by the National Gallery Singapore. It includes footage from the trip in 2001, capturing moments of the artists and workers living together. This footage was supplemented with interviews conducted in 2015, where participating artists reflected on their experiences.

Trần Lương, *Mạo Khê Coal Mine Project*, two-channel video with sound, 18'41".

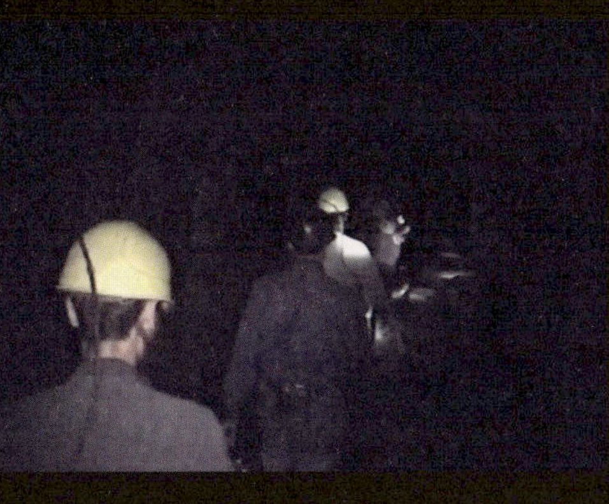

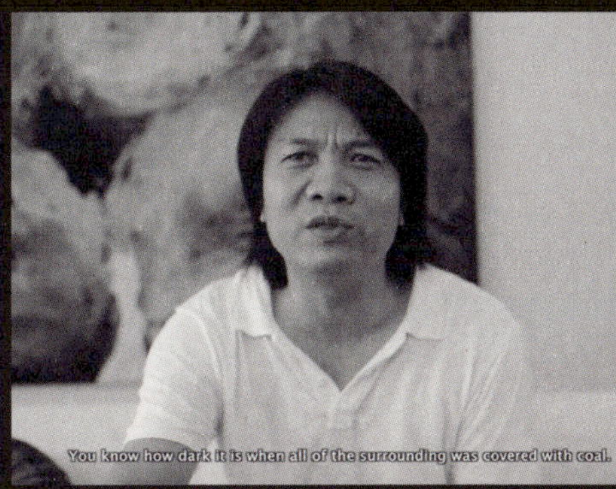
You know how dark it is when all of the surrounding was covered with coal.

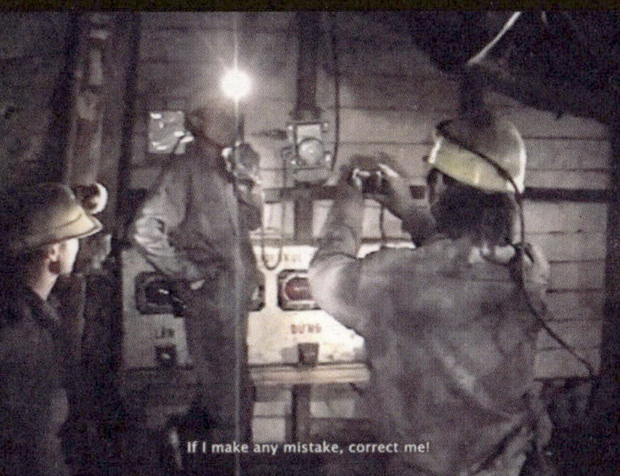
If I make any mistake, correct me!

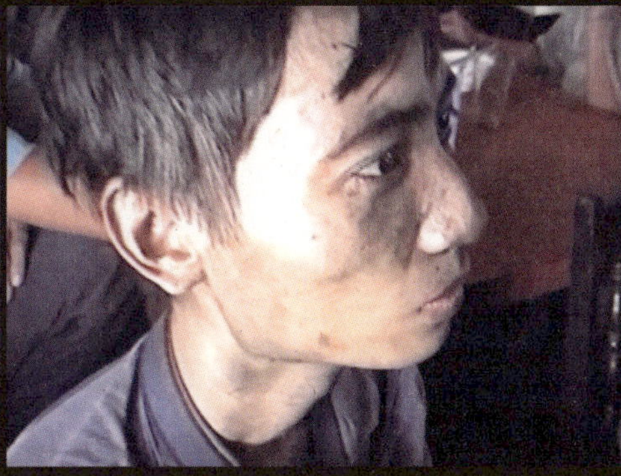

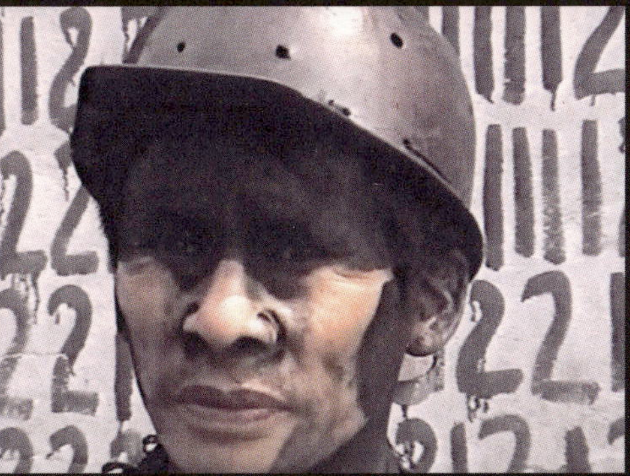

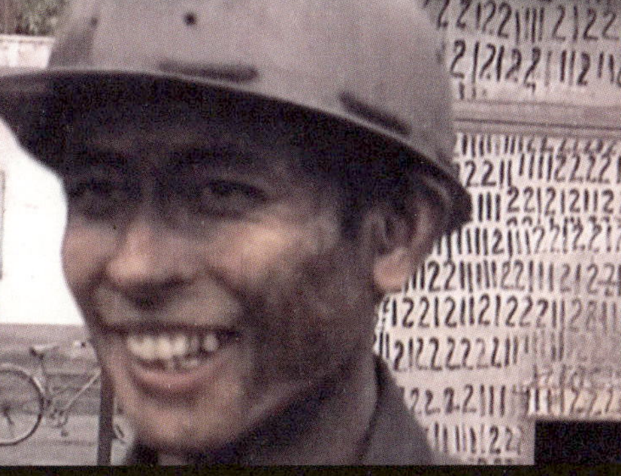

ON THE BANKS OF THE RED RIVER
2001

This artwork was a site-specific installation and performance in the area outside the embankment of the Red River, located in the northern part of Hà Nội. Densely populated with scrap metal and recycling waste, the area serves as the living quarters for poor migrant workers who come to the city to make a living through jobs such as scrap collection, construction work and even involvement in drug trafficking and prostitution. With the help of people living in the area and other artists (Lê Vũ, Nguyễn Minh Phước, Nguyễn Trí Mạnh, Nguyễn Quang Đức, Nguyễn Quỳnh Chi), Trần Lương worked for ten days, using white nylon string to wrap blocks of iron waste, such as trucks, old tramcars, concrete mixers and rubber tires, creating 15 large sculptural clusters scattered throughout the area. In this way, the artist wanted to protect and awaken the history and stories behind these forgotten materials. Between the wrapped iron blocks, ten box-shaped mosquito nets were suspended, illuminated from within.

On the day of the public opening, Trần Lương invited children and caregivers from the S.O.S Village for homeless children to visit the artwork. He also taught them folk songs and children's songs. The children later divided into small groups and played together within the mosquito nets. The youngest group learned to spell, the older group played folk singing games, while the teenage group played card games and engaged in gambling. At the end of the day, the children sang a folk song that had been rewritten by Trần Lương. It recounted stories of changing lifestyles and the blending of rural and urban cultures.

The process of the artwork's construction was participatory. It was on view to the public for one day.

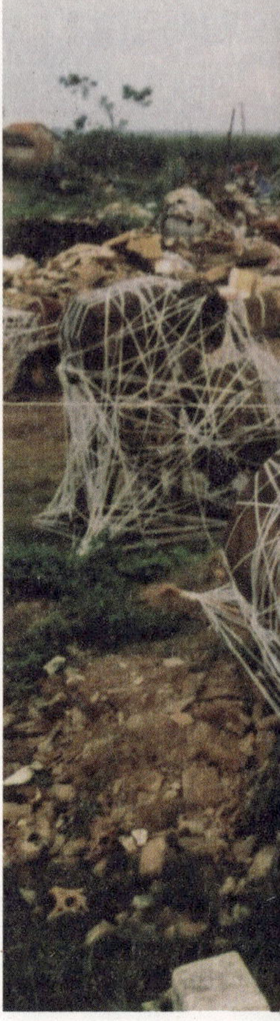

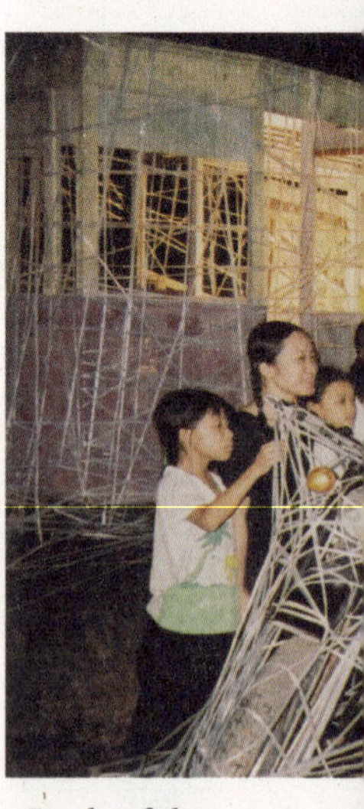

Trần Lương, *On the Banks of the Red River,* 2001, socially engaged project & site-specific installation. Installation view, riverbank, Red River, Hà Nội, Vietnam.

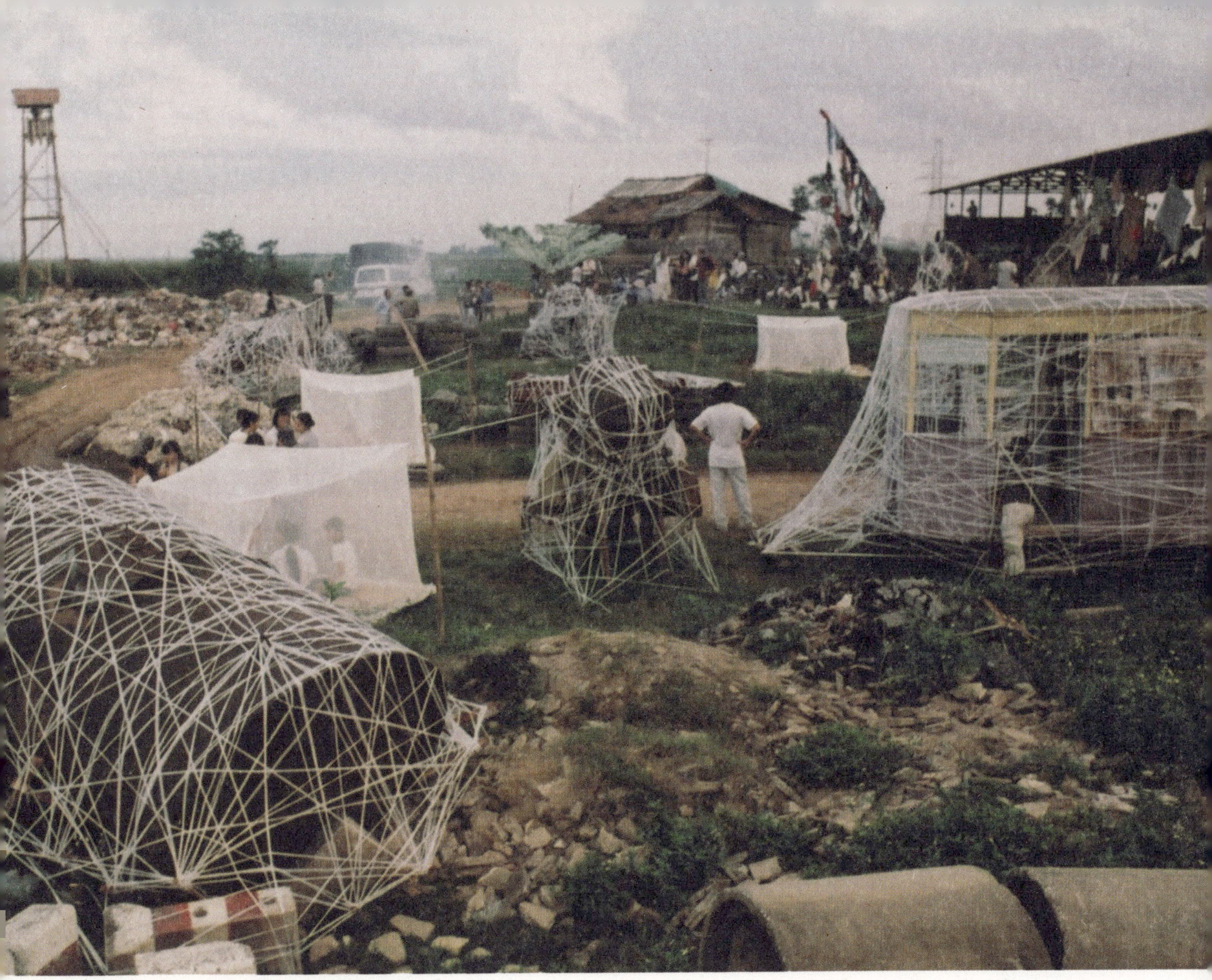

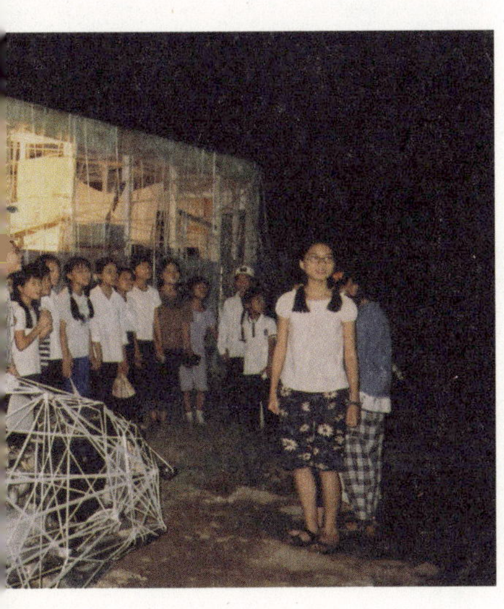

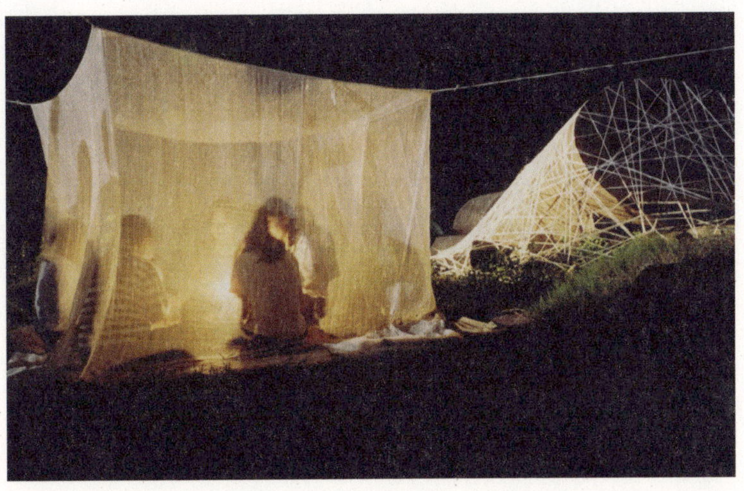

GROPING FOR THE PAST
2002

In 2002, Trần Lương took part in the Civitella Ranieri art residency in Italy. During this period, he discovered that the grounds of Civitella castle had served as a battlefield for the Allies in 1945. The gardeners there often unearthed fragments of bullets and ammunition. This experience triggered memories of his school days when he engaged in community service, often coming across similar remnants of bullets and bombshells from the war in North Vietnam. With the idea of recreating and re-examining history, Lương created a ten-day long durational performance, in which he and his assistant, Nguyễn Minh Phước, collaborated to dig a small pond. The artist threw various items into the pond, including cartridges discovered during the digging, along with several objects brought from Vietnam, such as fragments of ancient sculptures, pieces of bone, fake plastic bomblets and iron rice bowls, among other things. He also borrowed fresh duckweed from the Botanical Museum and Garden at the University of Siena in order to authentically recreate the pond from his childhood. After completing the pond, he ended the performance by immersing himself in the water, searching for objects in the mud and then displaying them on the pond's edge.

In this performance, the pond serves as an intermediary space for storing and reflecting the artist's memories. He views this as a personal experience rather than a performance for the audience, aspiring to revisit his childhood memories, and connect them with both the history and the spiritual aspects of the Civitella castle.

Trần Lương, *Groping for the Past*, 2001, photo documentation of durational performance. Civitella Ranieri Residency Program, Umbria, Italy.

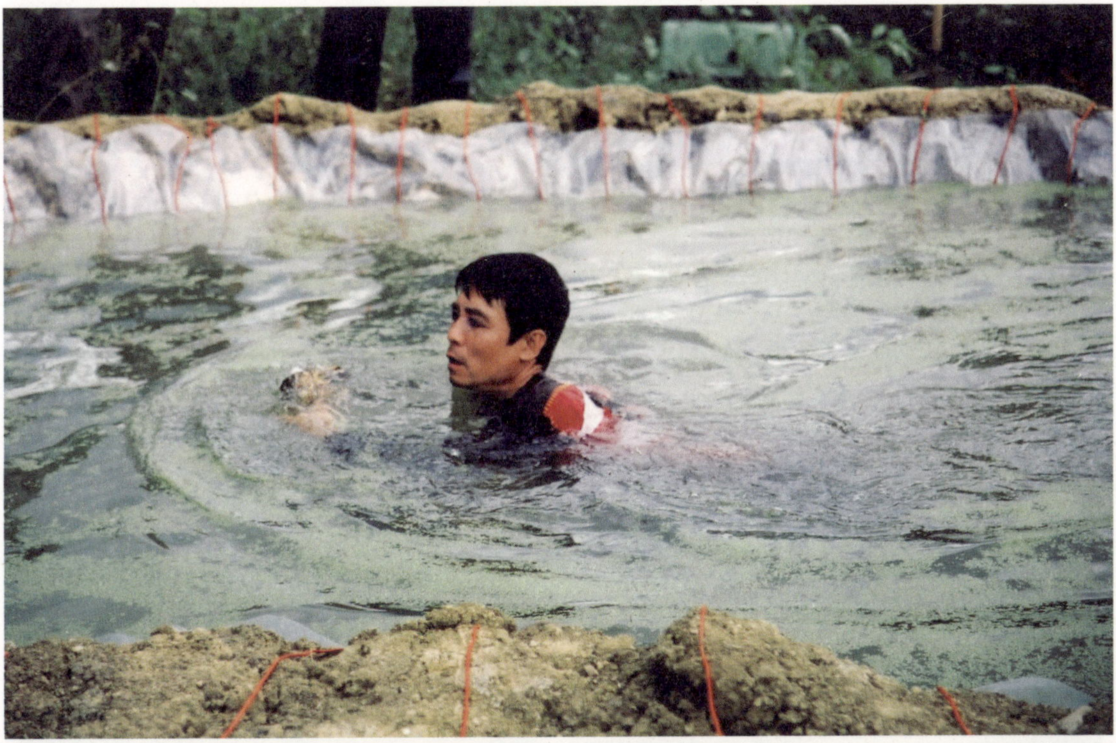

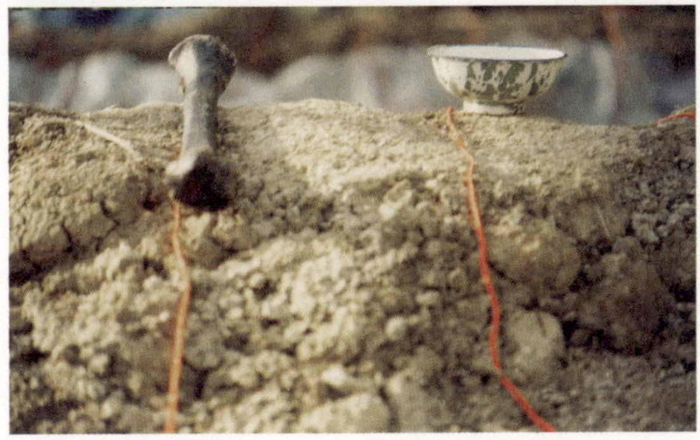

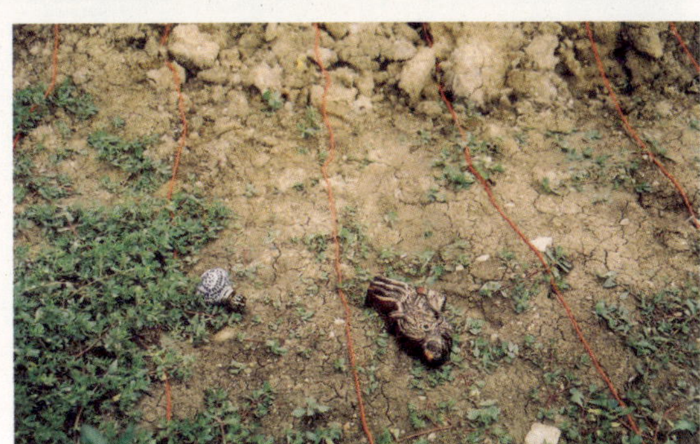

FOODS OF GROUNDS
2003

This installation consists of 39 photographs depicting everyday meals of the Vietnamese working class. Focusing on the core of daily existence, the images capture the relationship between people and food in various settings – whether it's the intimacy of family dining, workplaces, the vibrancy of street food stalls, or traditional local markets. The photographs were installed on the floor and slightly covered with 20kg of paddy rice, along with a text written by the artist on the gallery walls. As the audience enters the space, they are allowed to interact with the artwork, from stepping on the scattered paddy rice, creating the appearance of broken grains, to sweeping aside the rice to reveal the photographs and then carefully covering them again. This staging of the work was intended to alter the viewer's connection with the artwork. Notably, the capacity to cultivate fresh paddy rice became the focal point for many generations of Vietnamese immigrants in America who come from rice-growing regions. Visiting the installation, some of them scrutinise the rice thoroughly, almost as if seeing rice grains for the first time, as recent generations no longer inhabit the rice-cultivating culture.

Foods of Grounds was exhibited at CAVE Gallery in New York in 2003.

Trần Lương, *Foods of Grounds*, 2003, installation, set of 39 photographs and paddy rice grain, 30 x 45 cm (each photograph). Installation view at Cave Gallery.

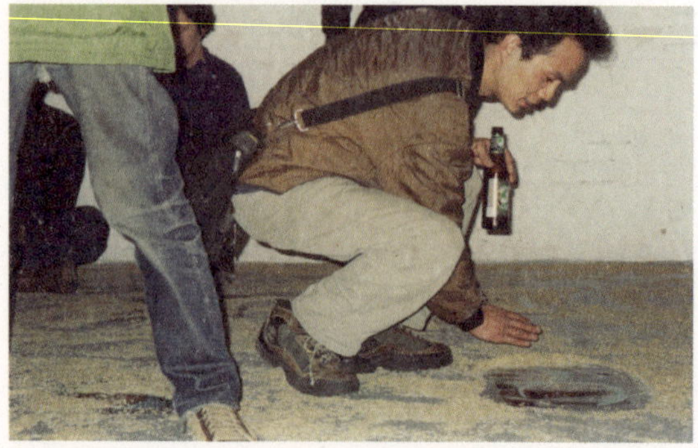

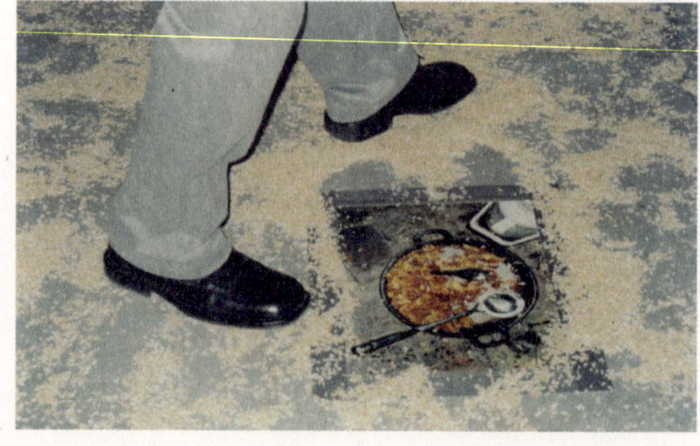

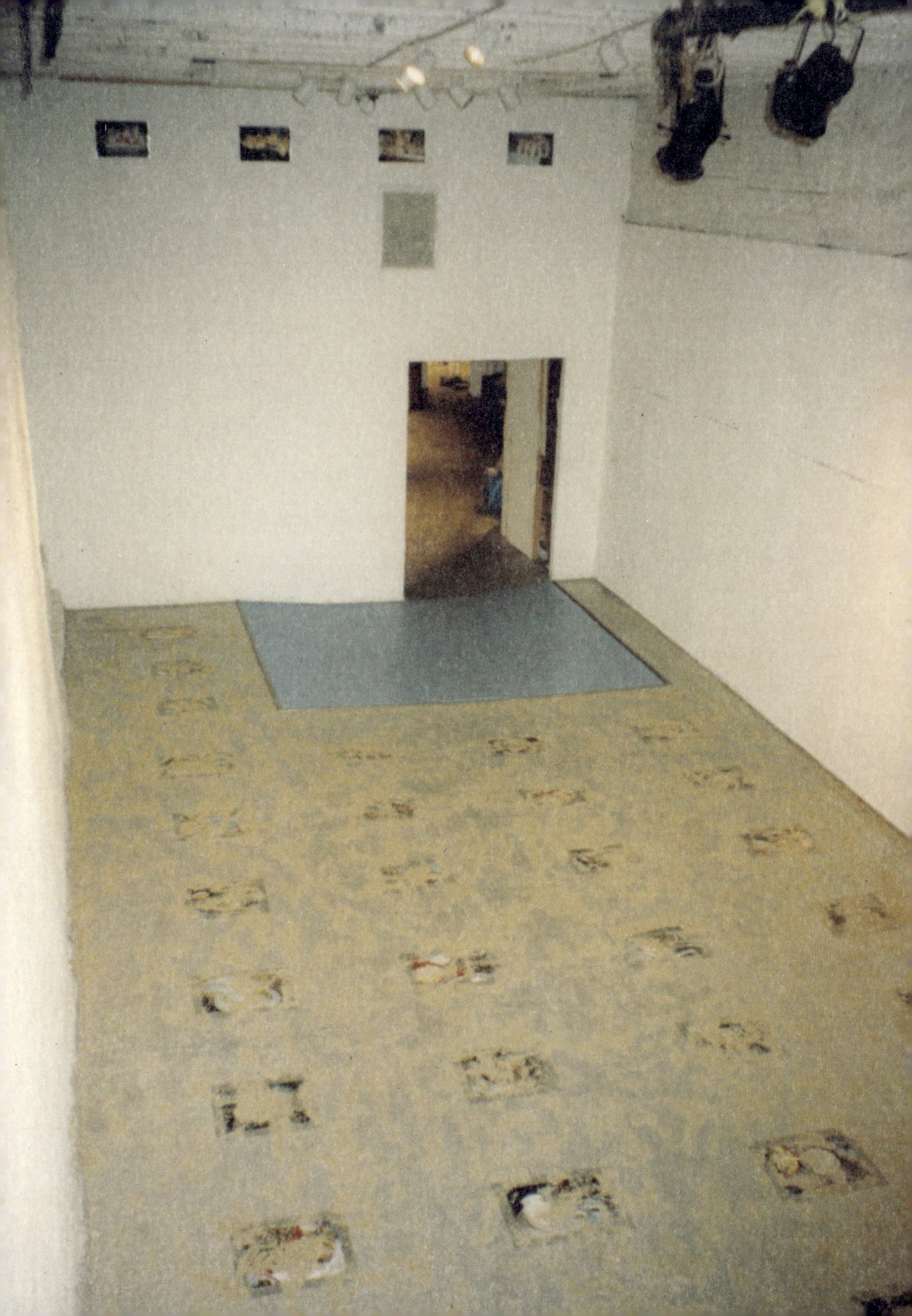

DIRECT AND INDIRECT

2003

8TH NIPAF INTERNATIONAL PERFORMANCE ART FESTIVAL TOKYO, JAPAN

He adopts a crouched position; his head is upside down and he is looking through his own legs. He tries to approach each individual in the audience, shake their hands and interact. Through this action, the artist seeks to create an atmosphere of closer and more direct communication, albeit in a very unusual posture in which the faces and gazes of both characters are reversed. The artist says that putting yourself in a state of seeing things upside down is related to facing biological challenges, as it changes the way the brain and senses process information. It acts as a strategy to provoke criticism, questioning the distance between individuals in the hustle and bustle of urban life.

The performance lasts for 35 minutes and begins with the artist crouching at a distance from the audience. He takes out his camera and takes a photo of the audience from an inverted position. At the beginning of the interaction, viewers are a bit shy, but after a minute of interacting by touching each other's hands and arms, many viewers realise that it is simply a different way of greeting and reading each other; a bit strange, but attractive in its own way. Some people even actively try to get their faces close to the artist's face. When the artist interacts with the last person from the first row of spectators, the performance ends.

The piece was performed live in a gallery in Tokyo as part of the 2003 NIPAF Performance Festival.

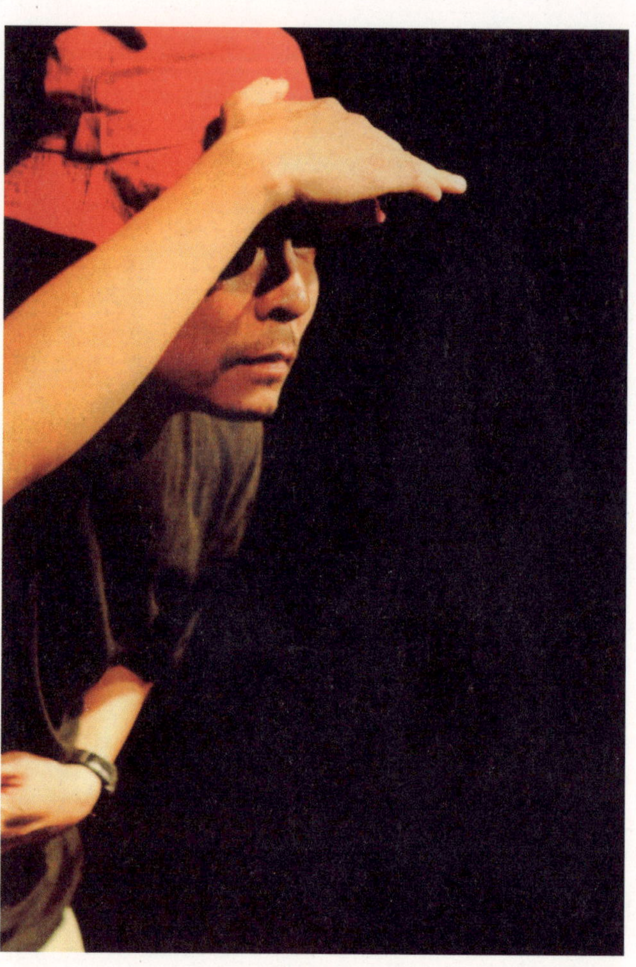

Trần Lương, *Direct and indirect*, 2003, photo documentation of performance, approx 35'. 8th Nipaf International Performance Art Festival, Tokyo, Japan.

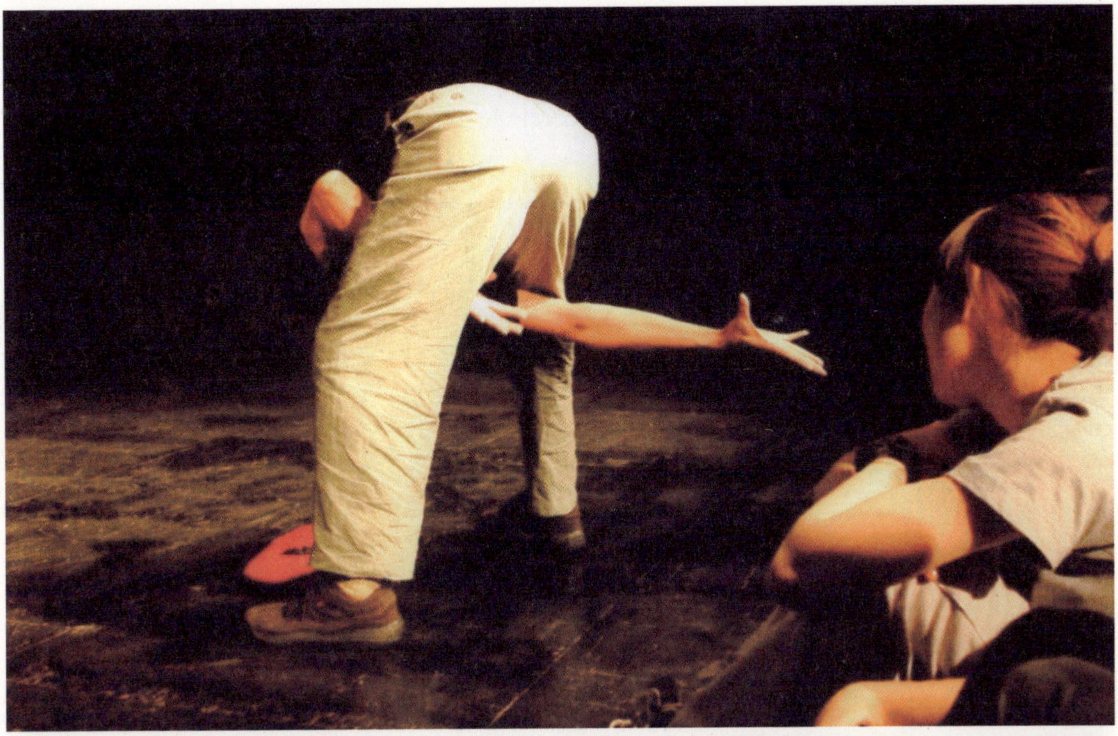

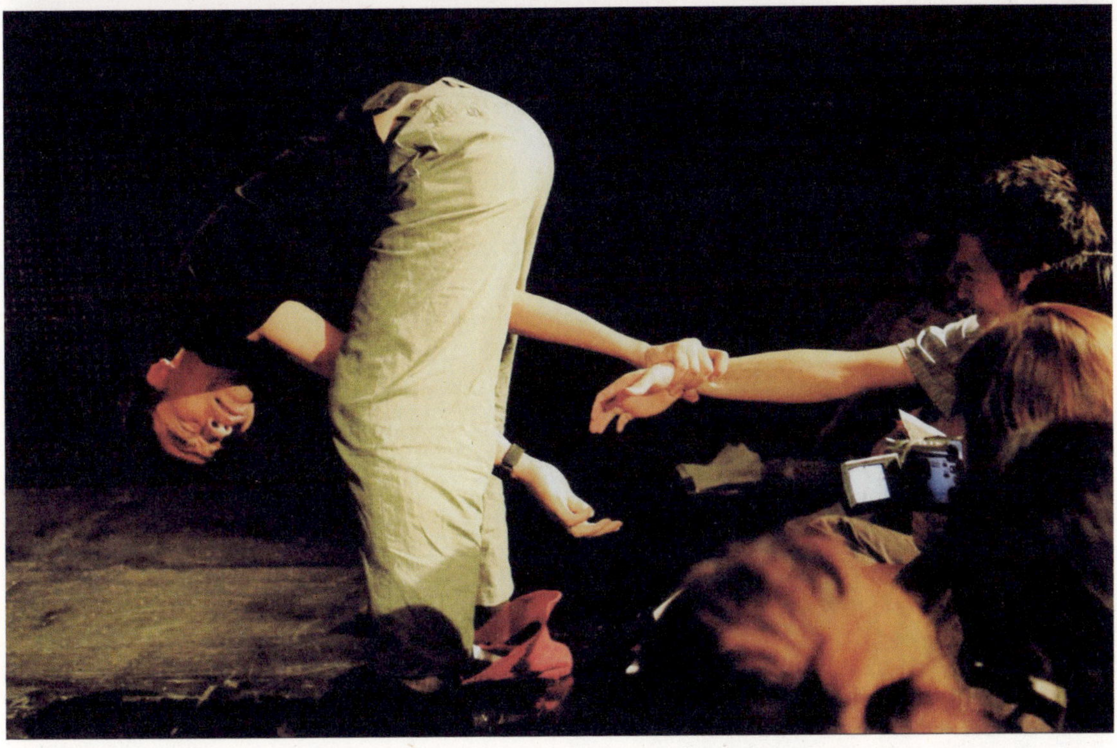

SWEATY
2003

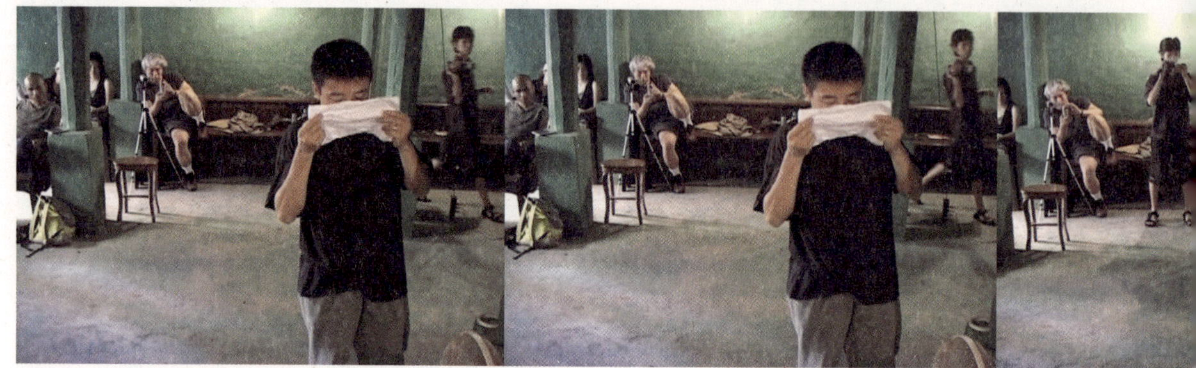

In 2003, Trần Lương organised an art performance event with the group of artists at Nhà Sàn Studio. The scorching summer heat, coupled with the busy preparations for the art event, left him dirty and soaked in sweat. Instantly, he improvised a performance using white sheets of paper, pressing them against his body to absorb the sweat and dust. These sheets were later mounted on the walls and columns in the room, displayed as drawings depicting the body's condition. This act recalls the stone-rubbing (Chinese rubbing) technique, a common exercise used for archiving and studying antiques at Hà Nội University of Fine Arts. In 2003, performance art was still not widely recognised in Vietnam. Both artists and the audience often found performances challenging to understand and approached them with skepticism. The artist's spontaneous performance served as a suggestion for bridging the gap between drawing practices and body-based practices.

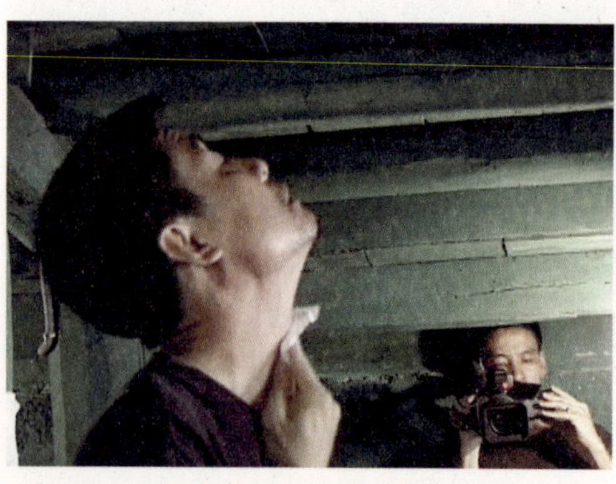

Trần Lương, *Sweaty*, 2003, video documentation of performance, 9'24". Nhà Sàn Studio.

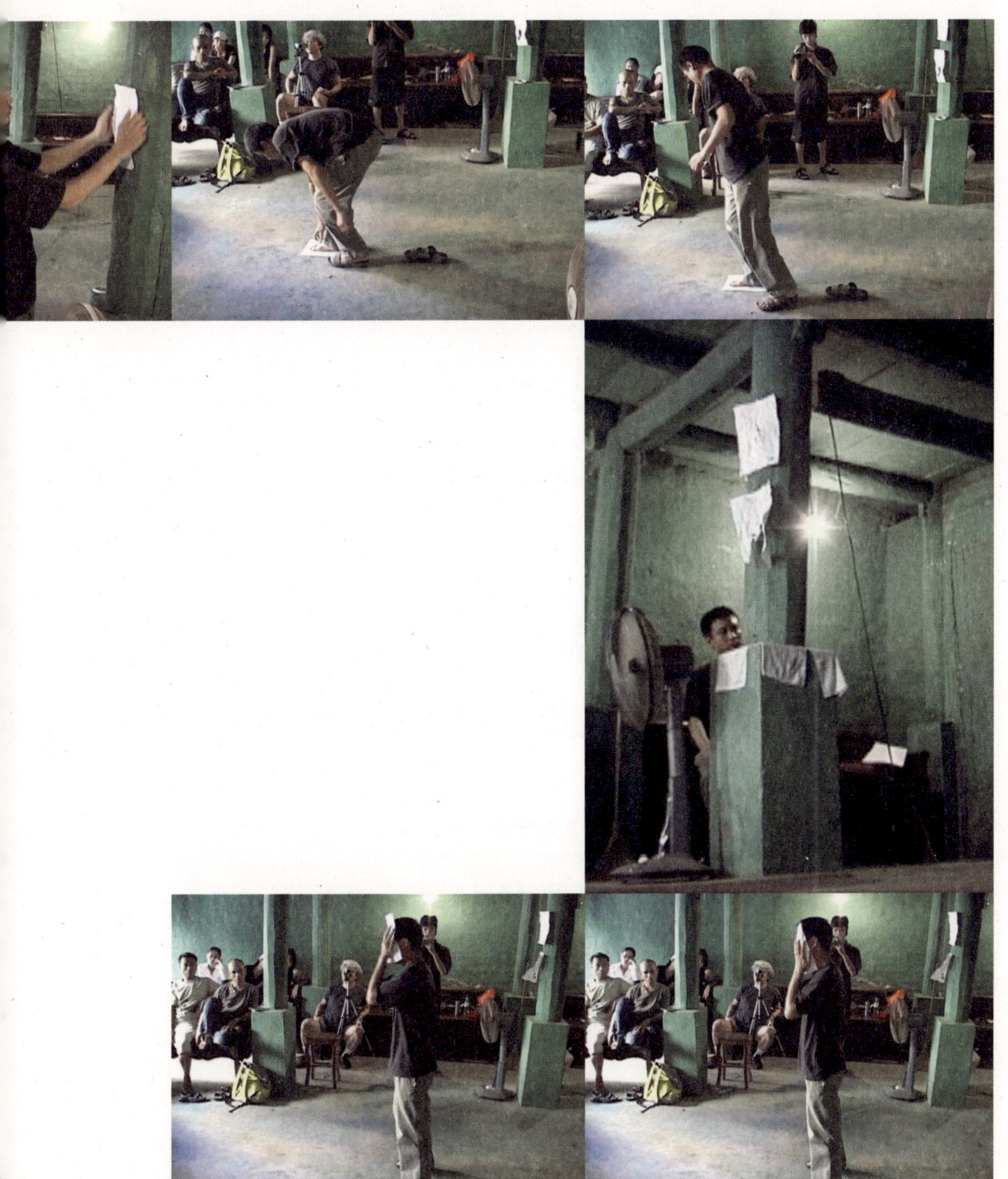

FAIRY TALE SOUP - CHỬ ĐỒNG TỬ AND TIÊN DUNG

2003

Again legends appear!
Legends of street corners
In what space and in what circumstances?
Reverie and romance?
Less pragmatic and more pessimistic?
How much hope and how much desperation?...

- Artist statement, *Fairy Tale Soup* Project

Through a performance for camera, Trần Lương plays the role of a host at a grand, kitschy wedding in the style of the 2000s, where he recounts the love story of a poor fisherman called Chử Đồng Tử and the Princess Tiên Dung. The tale, rewritten in a modern setting and supplemented with sarcastic anecdotes, relates to the lives of the protagonists and their different social classes.

The image of a very poor working class man suddenly and quickly gaining power and wealth is reminiscent of images of communist leaders. It is a satire surrounding the sudden change in class and power, which in fact happened in Vietnam. At the end of the story Lương remained faithful to the content of the ancient story, in which the poor fisherman and the princess leave royal power behind to become hermits. The kitschy, 2000s-style decorative form is typical of what was known as the "subsidy culture" of the Cold War period and the early 2000s. It reflects a popular culture composed of pure façade with no substance. Flashy, confusing and obscure. Weddings in this period were mostly decorated with pieces of painted Styrofoam, along with painted and plastic flowers.

The idea of retelling fairy tales later developed into the exhibition titled *Fairy Tale Soup*, which showcased installation video works of 14 artists in the courtyard of the Hà Nội Opera House.

Trần Lương, *Fairy Tale Soup - Chử Đồng Tử and Tiên Dung*, 2003, video, 14'40".

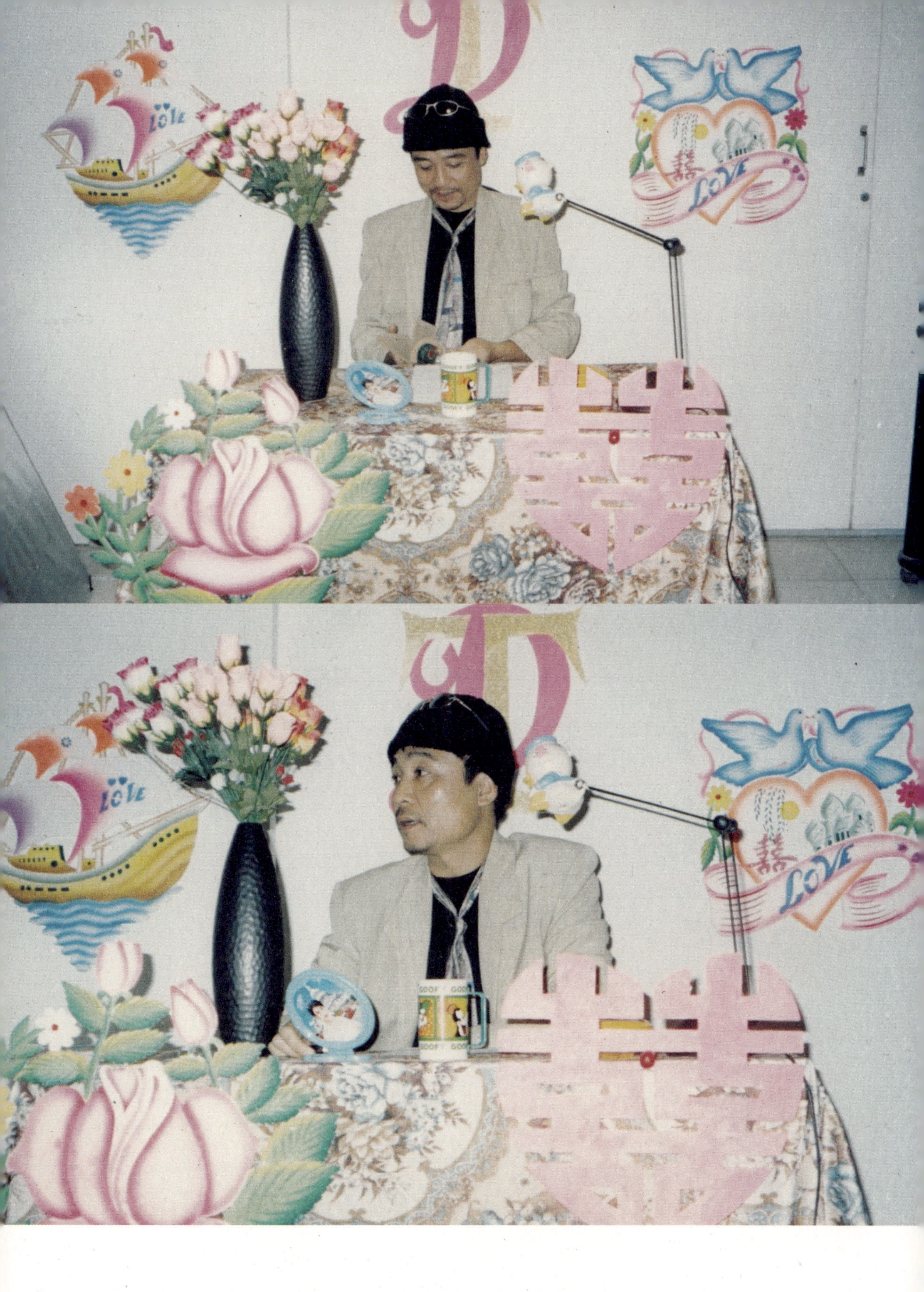
LOVE
LOVE
LOVE
LOVE

WE ARE WHAT WE EAT, WE ARE HOW WE EAT, WE ARE WHERE WE EAT

2003 & 2004

We are what we eat... continues Trần Lương's interest in food and eating behaviours. In this work a video showing people dining in various circumstances and moods is projected onto a wall. On the floor, Lương installed a cruciform-shaped booth and displayed 30 rice bowls, each covering an image underneath. These images, collected from newspapers and the internet, captured life in Vietnam during the Cold War era. The audience is invited to eat steamed rice prepared by the artist, while viewing the images and video. The act of eating serves as a thread connecting memories and opens up a dialogue between the past and present and amongst different communities.

The installation was first exhibited in Williamsburg Art and Historical Center (USA) in 2003. In 2004, as part of the Busan Biennale (South Korea), the video was shown as a looped four-channel work, along with 16 ceramic plates placed on stainless steel shelves. The plates held tangled locks of hair, which blended into the black and white printed images creating a unified whole.

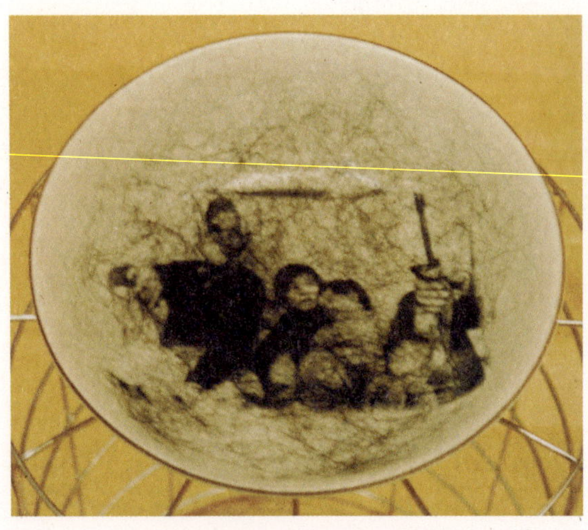

Trần Lương, *We are What we Eat, We are How we Eat, We are Where we Eat*, 2004, 4-channel video installation, 30', photo printing on ceramic plates, round metal cages, 21 x 5.5 cm (each plate). Installation view at Busan Biennale 2004.

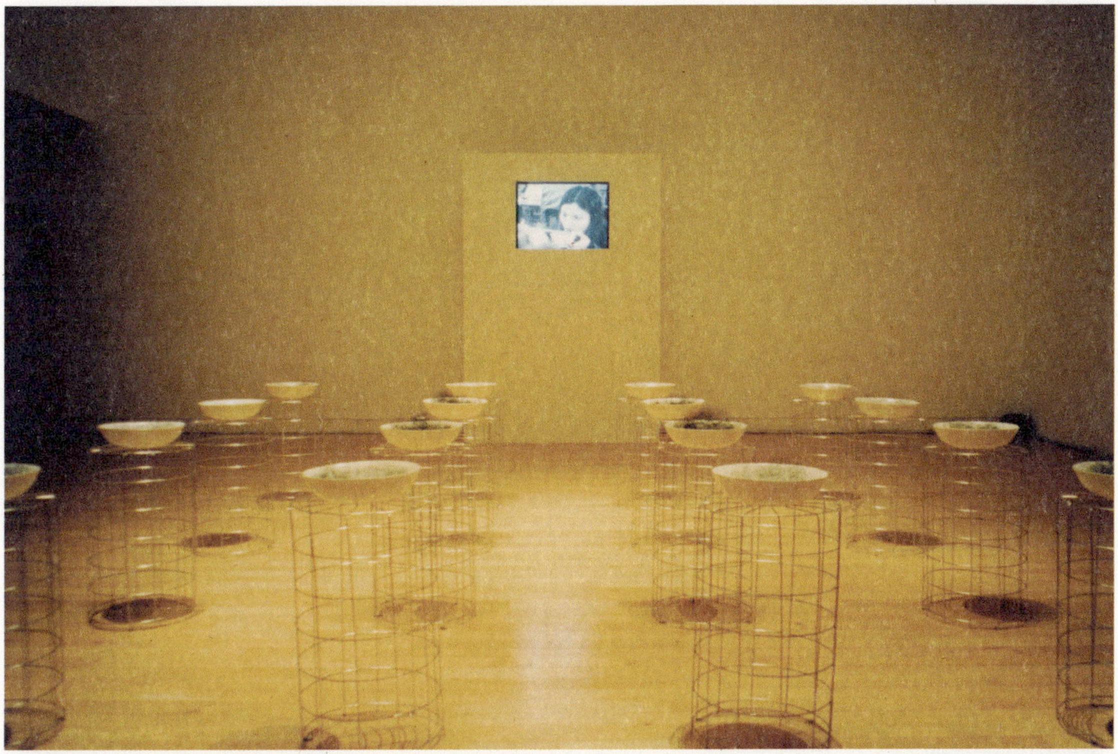

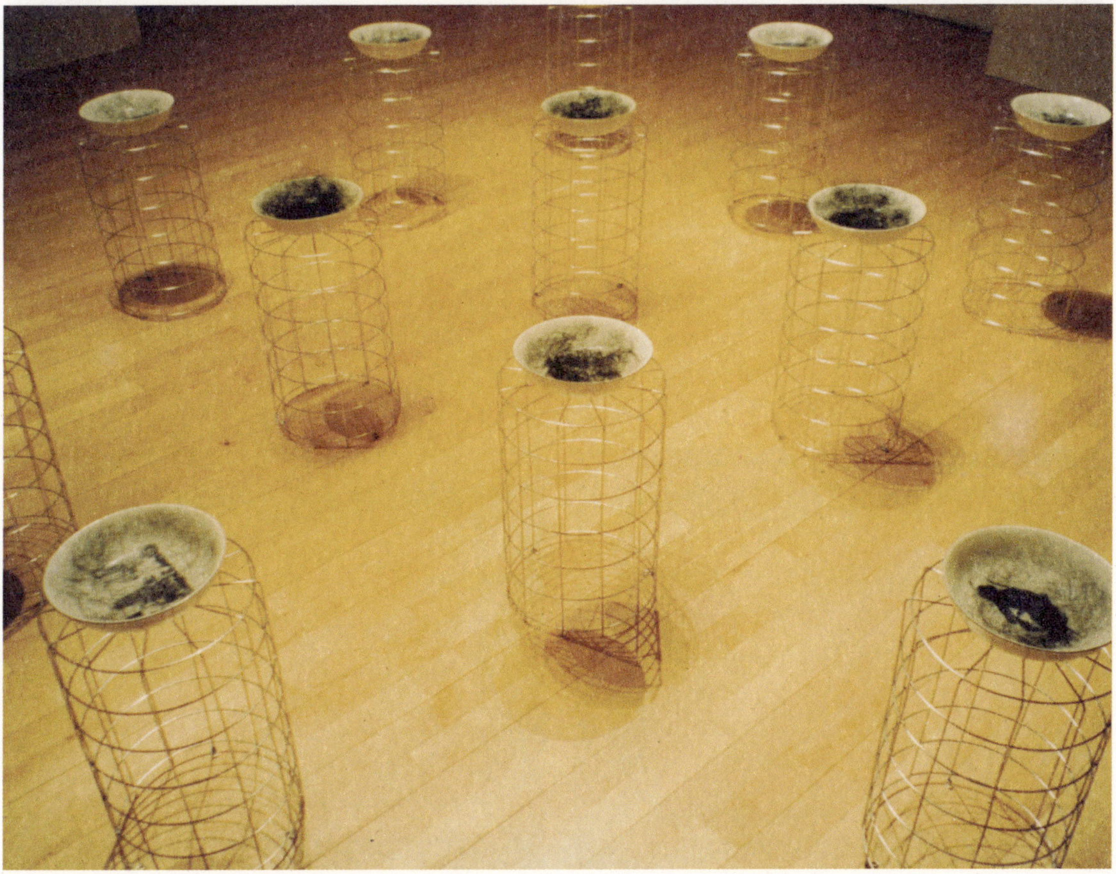

VARIATION FOR DAYS PAST

2004
GOETHE INSTITUT HÀ NỘI

Northern Vietnam's urban areas once boasted a diverse and plentiful bird population. However, since the 1980s, which was marked by population surges and urbanisation, various bird species have gradually lost their habitats and are now facing extinction. *Variation for days past* set up a "stage" within the garden at Goethe Institut Hà Nội. Here, the tranquil scenery surrenders to an invasion of 500 colorful, kitschy plastic birds perched on branches and rooftops. Inside the building, birds perch high around the walls while below them, small frames display lines of dialogue expressing the birds' laments for their impending extinction. These humorous lines evoke a mentally distorted state marked by unease and self-censorship, reminiscent of attitudes that were passed down to the artists generation due to the psychological trauma endured by the previous generation under the cultural censorship of Vietnamese communism.

Trần Lương, *Variation for Days Past*, 2004, site-specific installation, plastic birds, text, recycled film strip frames.

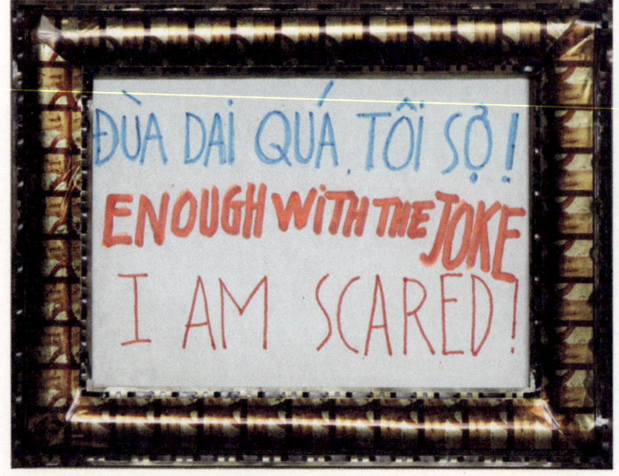

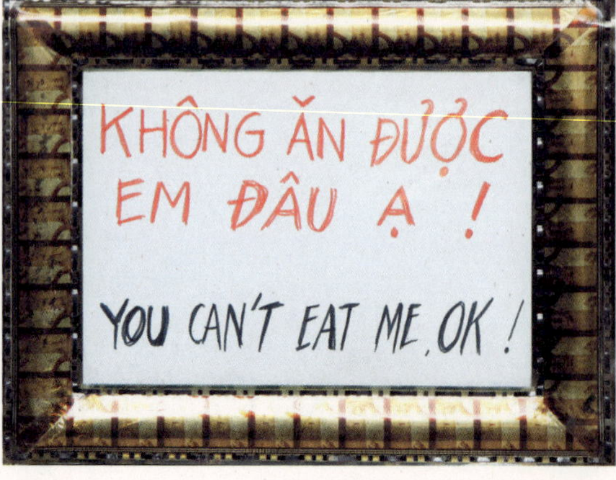

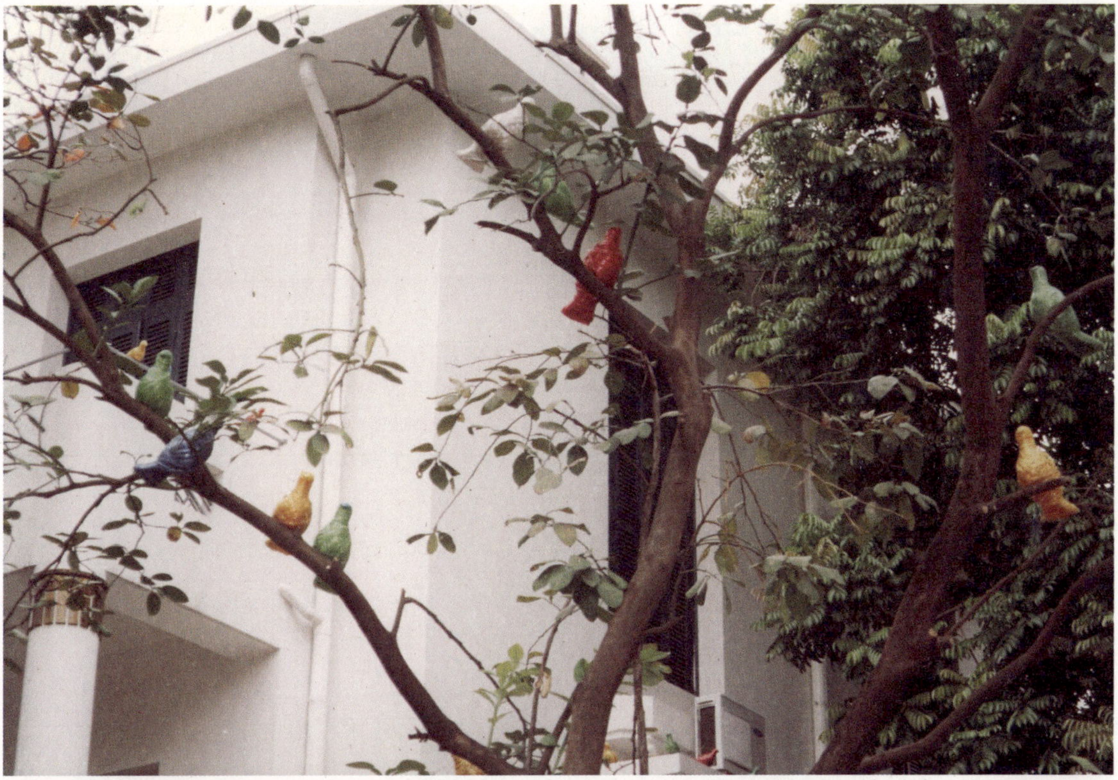

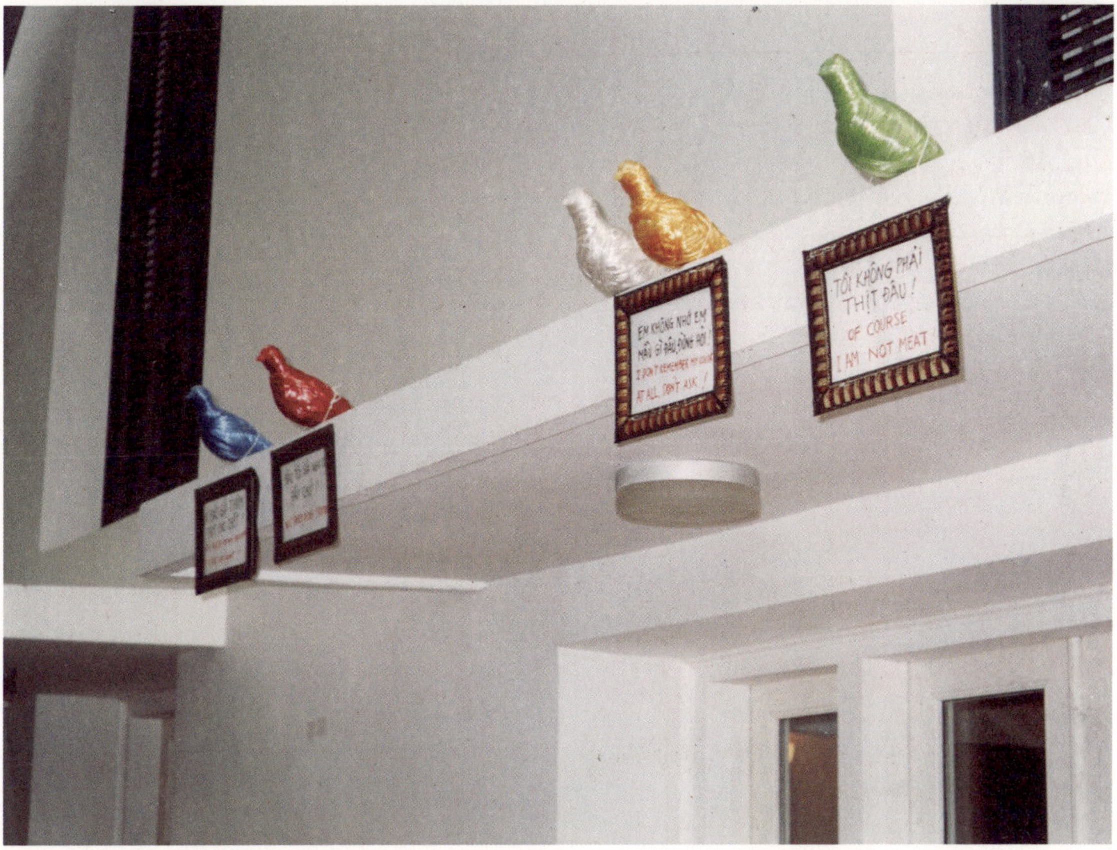
EM KHÔNG NHỚ EM
MẦU GÌ ĐÂU, ĐỪNG HỎI !
I DON'T REMEMBER
AT ALL, DON'T ASK !
TÔI KHÔNG PHẢI
THỊT ĐÂU !
OF COURSE
I AM NOT MEAT

MOVING FORWARDS AND BACKWARDS

2006
CAMBODIA

Moving Forwards and Backwards took place on a pedestrian street along Tonle Sap River in Phnom Penh (Cambodia). Trần Lương, with assistance from a group of Vietnamese and Cambodian artists, invited the pedestrians to brush their teeth using toothbrushes and toothpaste provided by the artist. Gradually, a crowd of people formed on the street, all of them collectively brushing their teeth. Trần Lương moved around talking to people as they brushed their teeth, facilitating conversations about the intertwined history of Vietnam and Cambodia. Despite their mouths frothing with toothpaste, the crowd shared thoughts with each other, fostering a unique connection through this intimate daily ritual. The act of teeth-brushing served as a bridge, allowing people from diverse backgrounds to connect and exchange hidden memories and untold stories. The work also aimed to initiate a dialogue to address the conflict between the two countries, particularly focusing on the period starting from 1978 when the Vietnamese army invaded Cambodia to overthrow the Khmer Rouge regime. The performance, which lasted for more than four hours, was documented and later edited into a video.

Moving Forwards and Backwards was part of the *Hà Nội – Phnom Penh Arts Exchange Program*, 2006.

Trần Lương, *Moving Forwards and Backwards*, 2006, photo documentation of interactive durational performance. Tonle Sap Riverside Path, Phnom Penh, Cambodia.

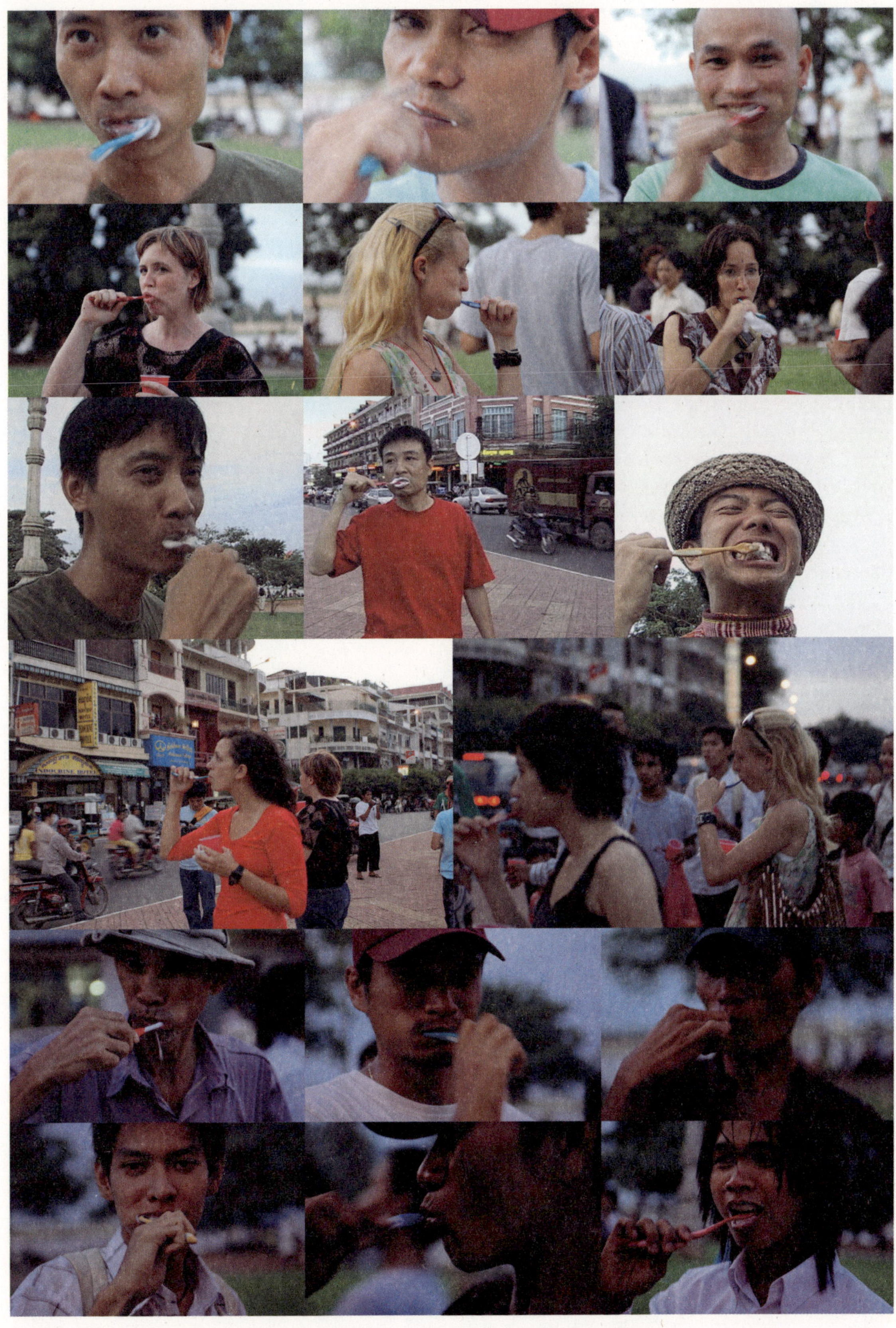

M(A)OUTH - CLEANING
DADAO LIVE ART FESTIVAL 2007

During the Dadao Live Art Festival 2007, Trần Lương undertook a significant action: brushing his teeth in front of the large portrait of Chairman Mao Zedong at the centre of Tiananmen Square. This symbolic act was laden with meaning, representing the erasure of cultural history during China's Cultural Revolution, as well as the artist's personal effort to cleanse himself from the influence of Maoism that he has carried since childhood. The performance ended with the arrival of police and security officers.

While Tiananmen Square was not an official venue of the festival due to strict security protocols, the historical significance of the location moved the artist to spontaneously carry out the action.

Trần Lương, *M(a)outh – Cleaning*, 2007, photo documentation of performance, approx 15'. Tiananmen Square, Beijing, China.

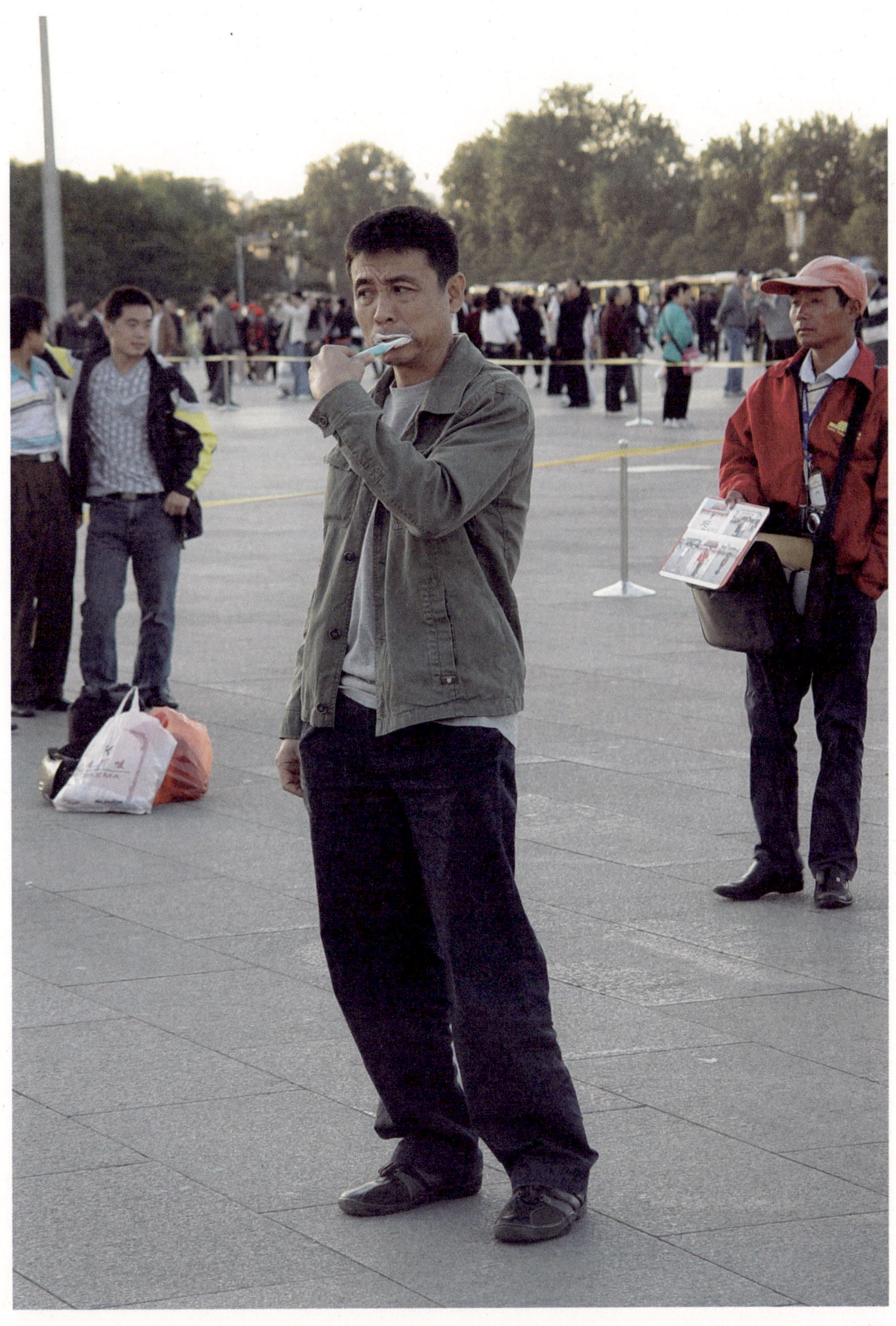

WELTS

2007 – ongoing
Performed on different occasions in Beijing, Yangon, HangZhou, Shanghai, Seoul, Solo-Central Java, Boston, Berlin, Singapore, Amsterdam, Ho Chi Minh City and ChongQing.

The inspiration behind the development of *Welts* stemmed from a moment in 2007 when Lương's son returned from school wearing a red scarf over his shoulders, a symbol of membership to the Ho Chi Minh Young Pioneer Organization. The red scarf had served as one of the few available toys in the artist's youth. Primarily associated with boys, the red scarf was often used in a schoolyard game involving whipping each other. While the game required some skill, it could also turn violent. In *Welts*, the artist connects these elements by permitting the audience to participate and inflict harm on him if they choose to do so. This performance highlights the artist's ongoing fascination with the capacity for violence that people can exhibit when given permission to do so. He states,

> Like seeing myself coming back from hazy memories, I connected thoughts of my son and myself, of past and present, of the scars left on the skin after we played by beating each other with the red scarves, or the scars left in my memories of an interminable miserable time. The many memories and images are still there! But can there be awareness if there is little sensitivity and much callousness? If there is little wildness and much passivity? I suddenly wanted to feel again the startling burning sensation, to re-measure myself and also to receive any possible response from the audience.

Trần Lương, *Welts*, 2007 – ongoing, photo and video documentation of performance in various sites including Beijing, Yangon, HangZhou, Shanghai, Seoul, Solo-Central Java, Boston, Berlin, Singapore, Amsterdam, Ho Chi Minh City and Chongqing.

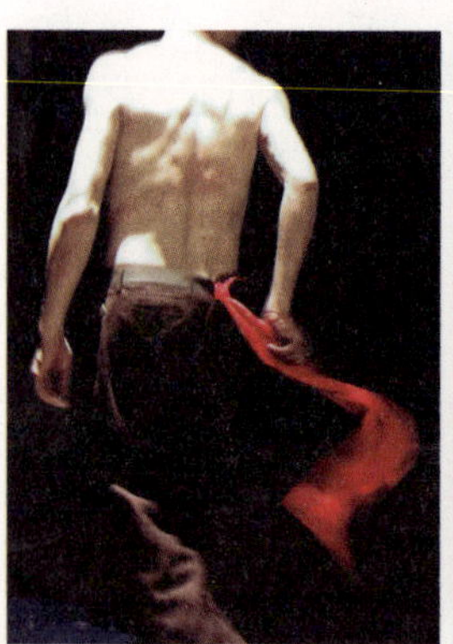
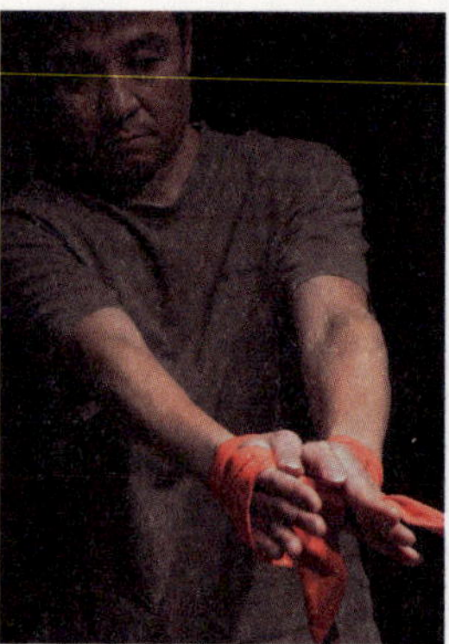
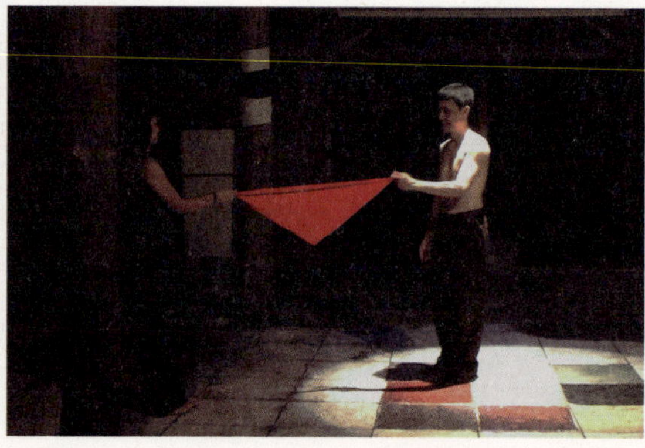

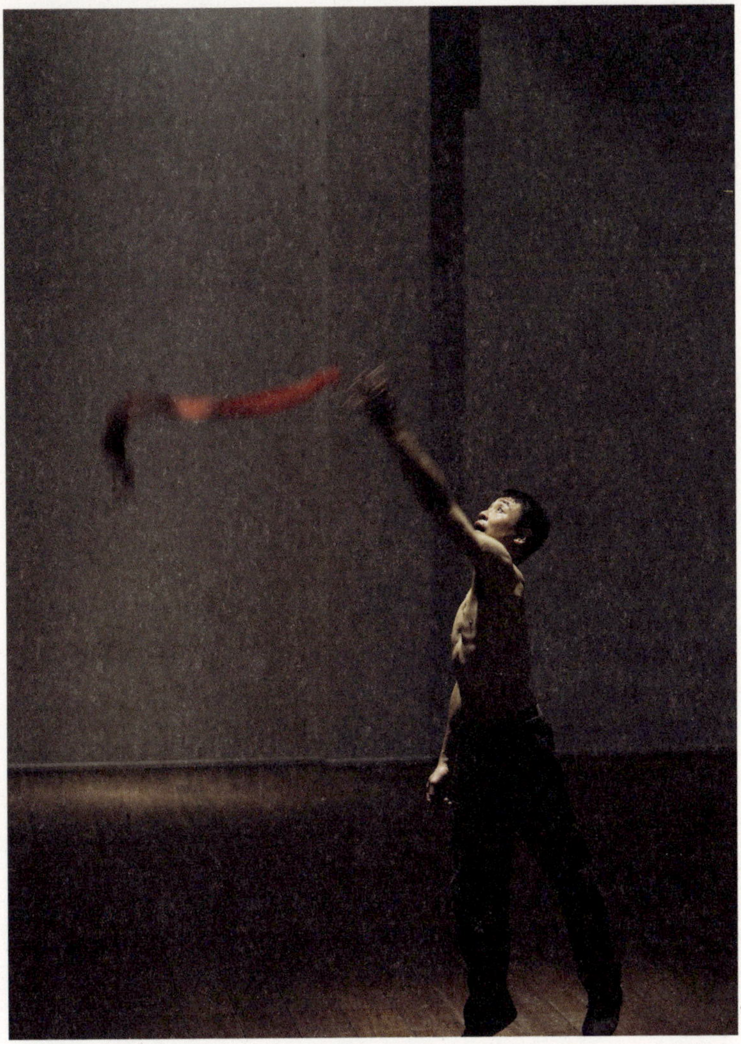

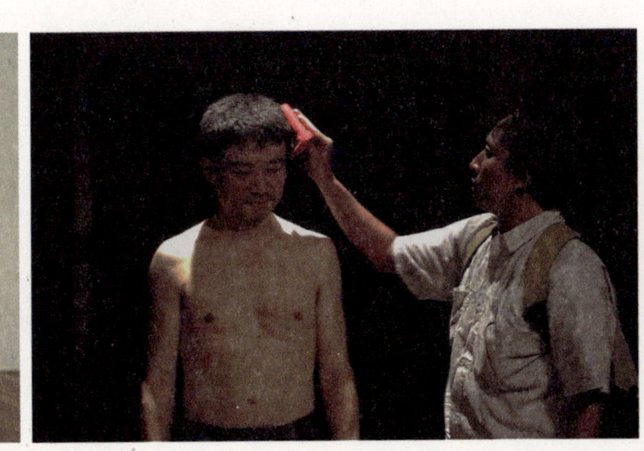

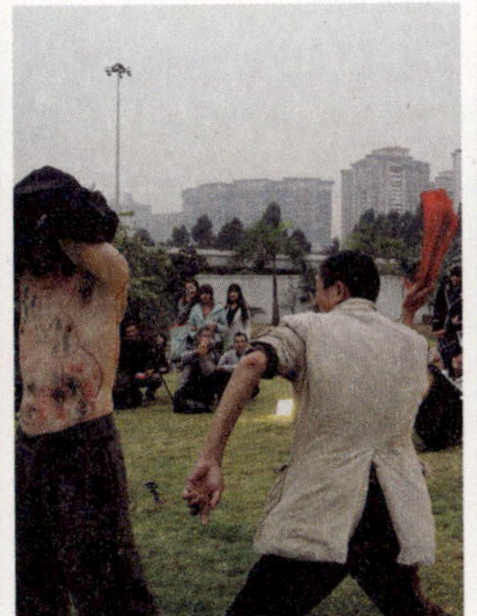

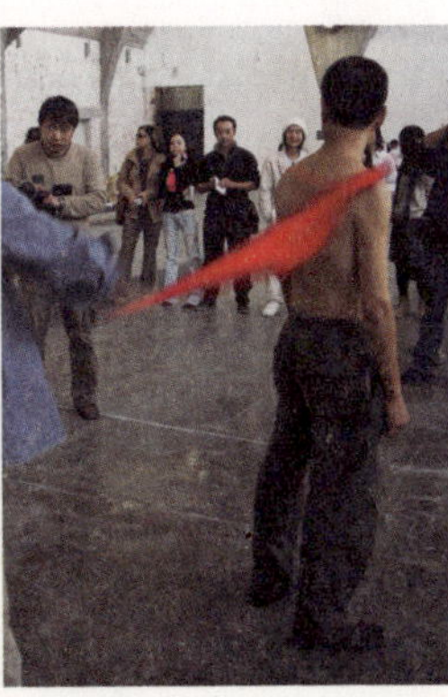

ERUPTION
2008

Eruption was presented as part of a festival with a focus on environmental issues and climate change in Krinjing village at the base of an active volcano called Mount Merapi. The performance began with Lương climbing a tree, engaging in daily rituals like brushing his teeth and washing his clothes. He took off his shirt and washed it with soap, letting the soap suds melt down the tree trunk. Following this, the artist brushed his teeth and ended the performance by shaking a coke bottle until it overflowed. The artist explained that the scents coming from the soap and the coke reference elements of modern life activities. Simultaneously, the image of white foamy soap suds on the tree serves as a metaphor for unusual natural phenomena, such as volcanic ash or a nuclear winter. His aim was to point to the causality between human activity and nature. The artist said that immersing himself in the local life and indigenous culture of the area altered his perspective on the interconnectedness between humanity and nature.

Eruption was performed in the Performance art festival *Perfurbance #4* titled *Global Warming – Global Warning!!* in April 2008. The artwork was performed again in Singapore in June 2008, within the botanical gardens of Singapore Management University (SMU). Interacting with the artificial natural landscape of the urban environment and the strict public regulations of Singapore, the performance had a spirit of human resistance against relentless urbanisation.

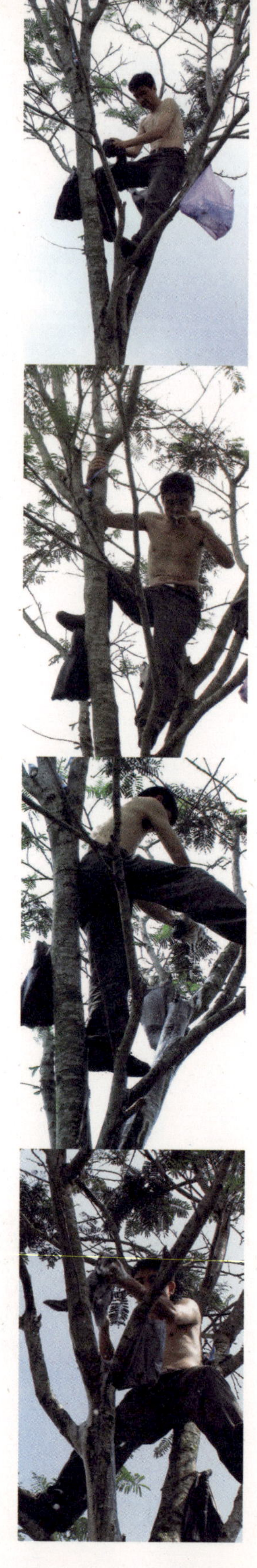

Trần Lương, *Eruption*, 2008, photo documentation of performance. Krinjing Village, Mount Merapi, Java, Indonesia.

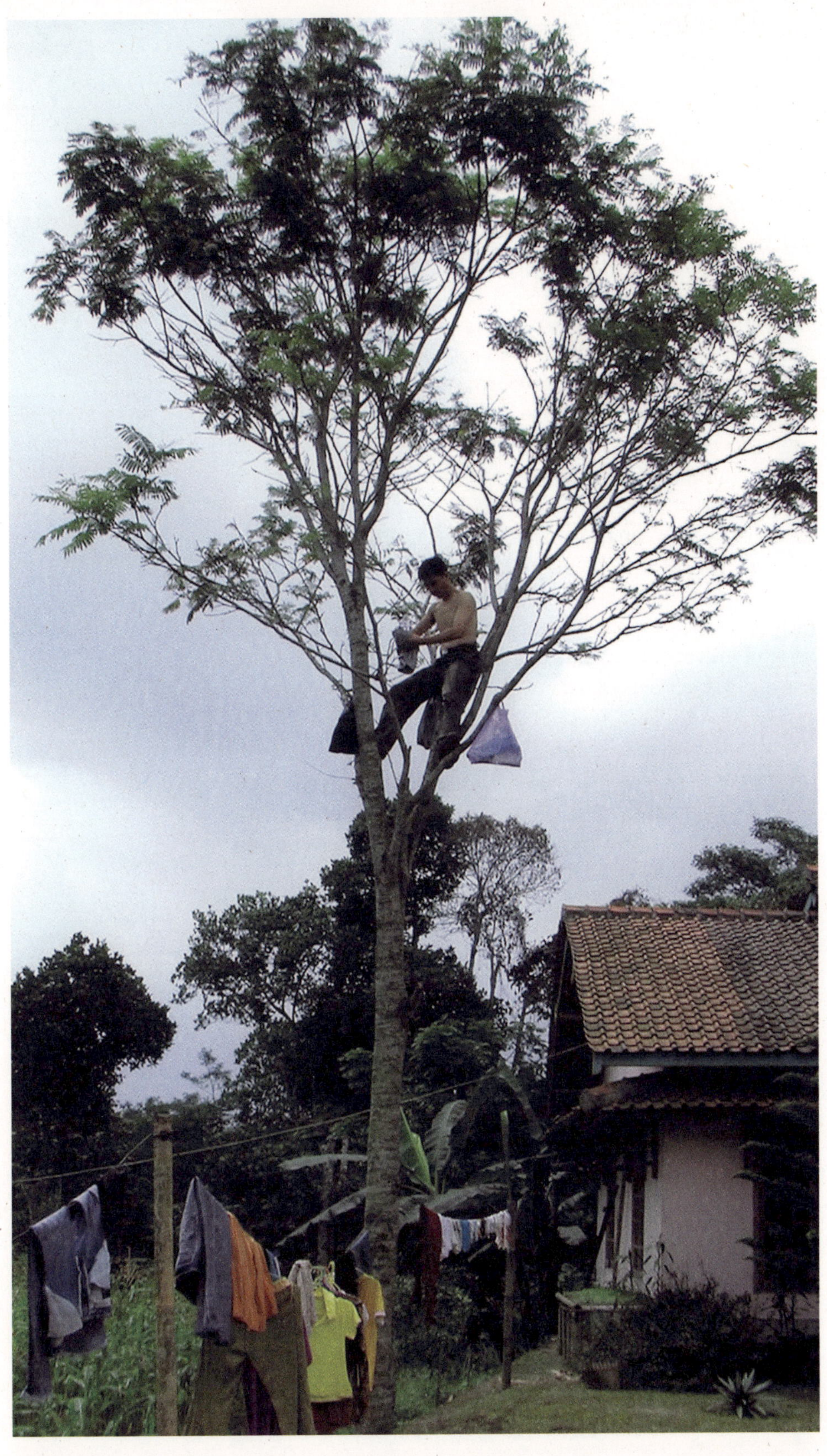

CAMOUFLAGE
2008 & 2009

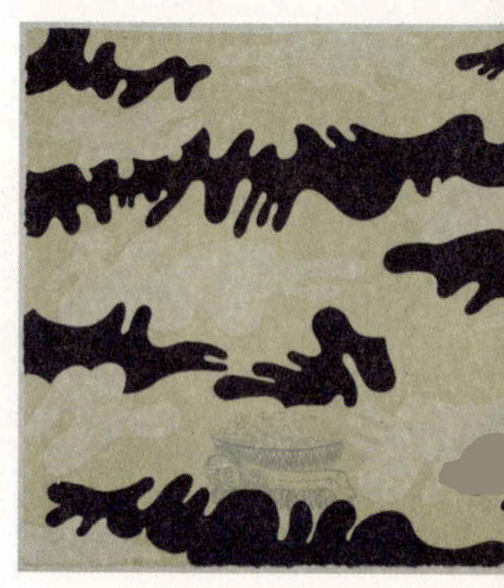

2

Camouflage consists of 70 drawings on Dó paper with black and white camouflage patterns. From these drawings, Trần Lương created a long pathway around the exhibition space, which visitors were invited to walk on. Concealed within the camouflage patterns is a small illustrative drawing, suggesting a clue about an undisclosed event or untold story. For Lương, the pop culture wave in Vietnam intersected with diverse forms of propaganda from the Cold War era, constructing a deceptive camouflage layer that enveloped society. In his statement, he describes this as a pathway of continuous disguise, a chaotic painting that conceals numerous truths awaiting revelation – be they tools, weapons, strategies, or the confusion between consciousness and unconsciousness.

The work was created for the *transPop: Korea Vietnam Remix* exhibition. The project seeks to explore the intersections of contemporary popular culture, including Hallyu (Korean Wave) and V-pop (Vietnamese pop) and the triangulated relationship between Korea, Vietnam and the US, which was forged through the Vietnam War.

1

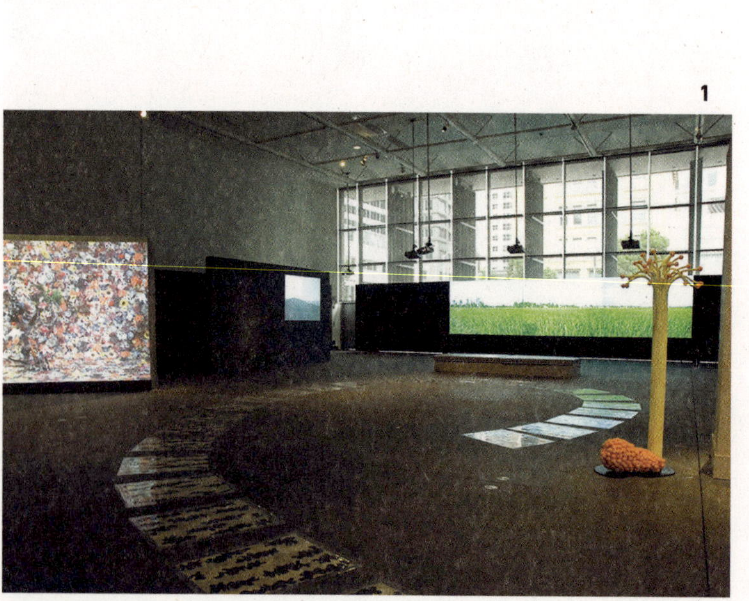

1
Installation View, Yerba Buena Center for the Arts, San Francisco.

2
Trần Lương, *Camouflage*, 2008-2009, Chinese ink, acrylic and gouache on Dó Paper, acrylic board, 60 x 80 cm (each).

3
Installation View, Berlin 2009.

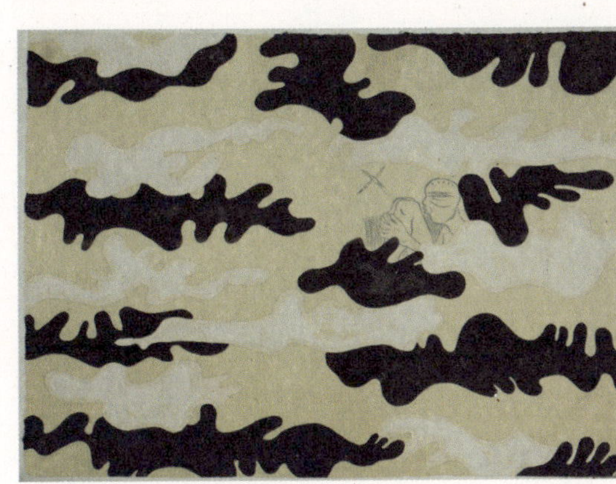

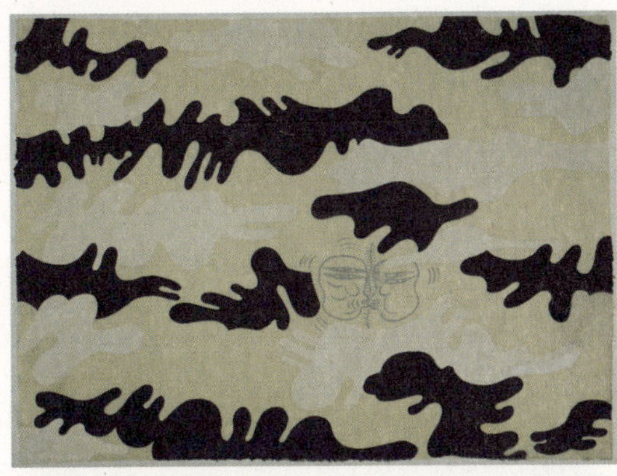

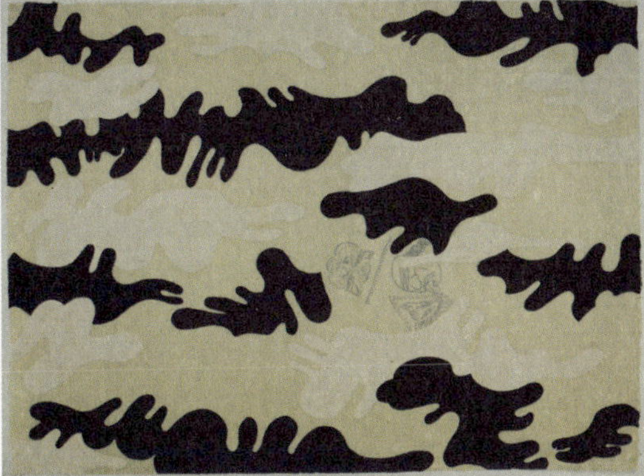

3

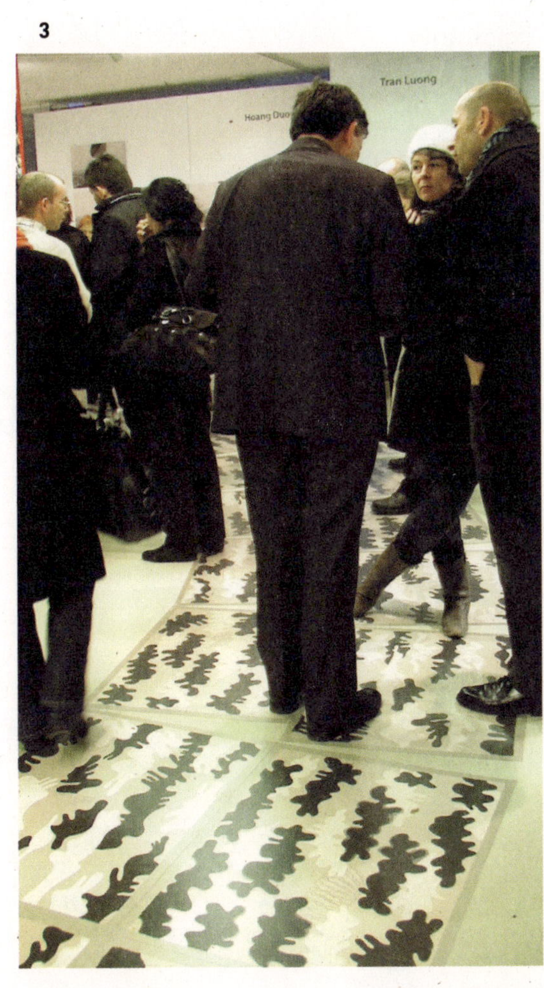

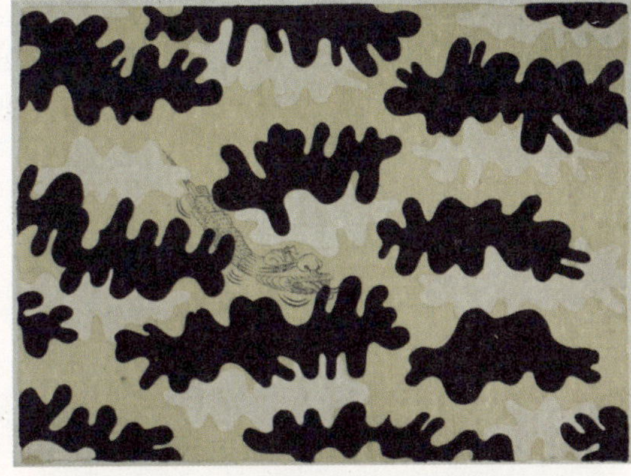

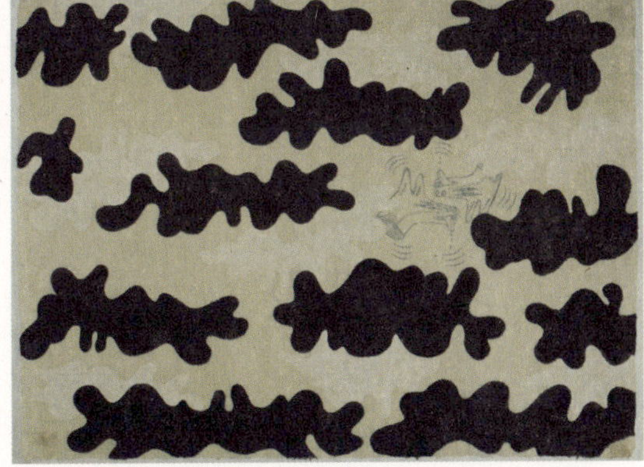

FALL, WINTER, SPRING, SUMMER

2010
Nhà Sàn Studio

Typically, the cycle of four seasons starts with Spring as a symbol of new beginnings and transformation. In *Fall, Winter, Spring, Summer* the artist inverted this cycle to evoke the period when communist forces seized control of the capital, Hà Nội, from the French Government in what is known as the August Revolution. The expression "August's Autumn" is frequently mentioned in songs, poetry and propaganda materials, serving to underscore the contributions of the Communist Party in shaping a new chapter in the nation's history.

The artist began the performance at Nhà Sàn Studio by walking in the dark, prompting the audience with questions about their "personal Spring." As they responded, he wielded a rattan stick, fiercely whipping it through the air. He says "the sound of the rattan stick echoes indelible memories for my generation – the chilling winds of winter, enduring cold and hunger. It recalls childhood beatings and later, the oppression of the regime." In his youth, Lương heard his father and his father's friends talk about censorship and artistic repression through the Nhân Văn Giai Phẩm event. When he became an artist, he also faced censorship, surveillance and threats from the government and the cultural security police. "It's a persistent, still-bleeding wound in our collective consciousness, perpetuating underlying violent tendencies through generations."

Trần Lương, *Fall, winter, spring, summer*, 2010, stills from video documentation of performance at Nhà Sàn Studio.

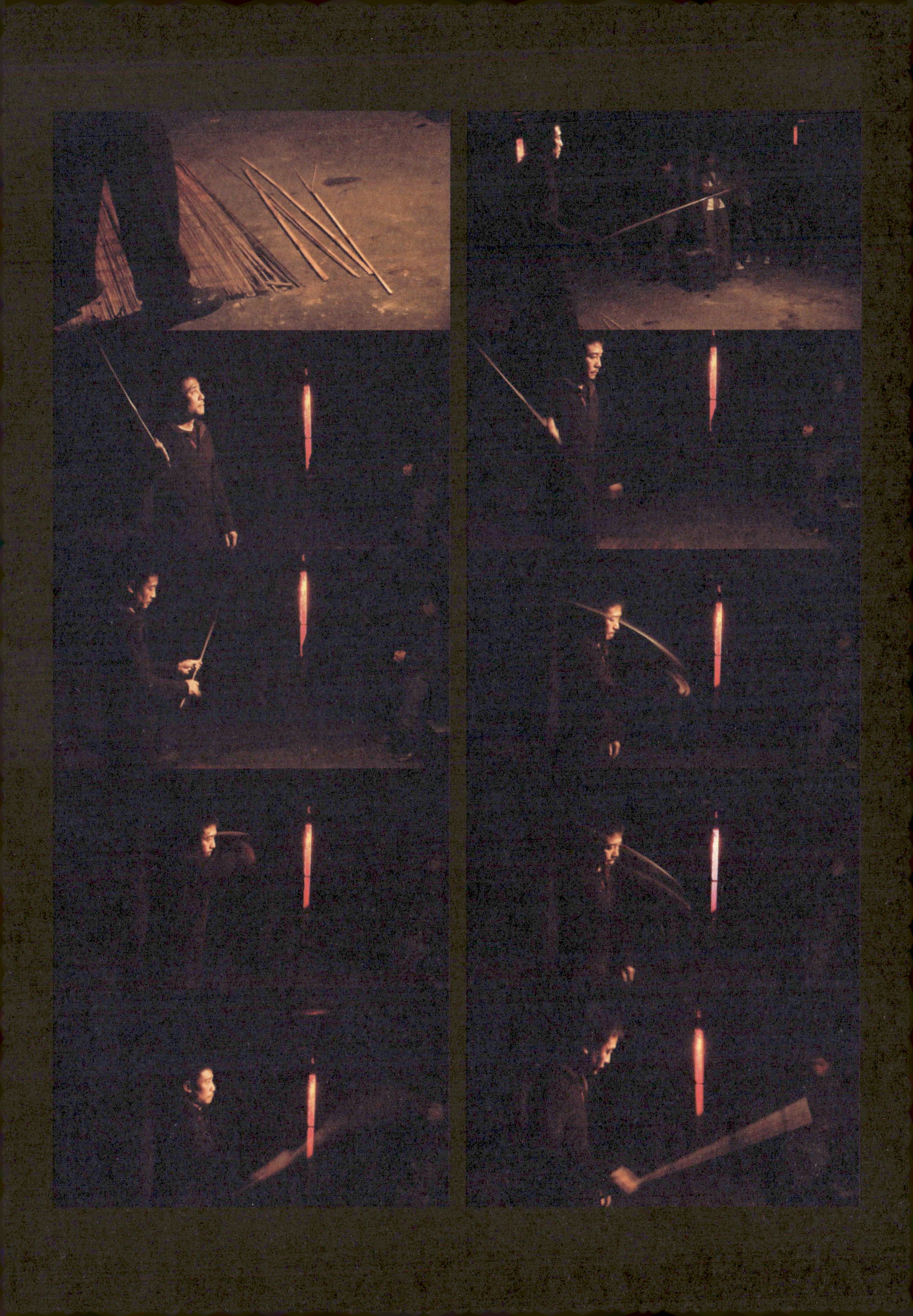

LẬP LÒE
2012

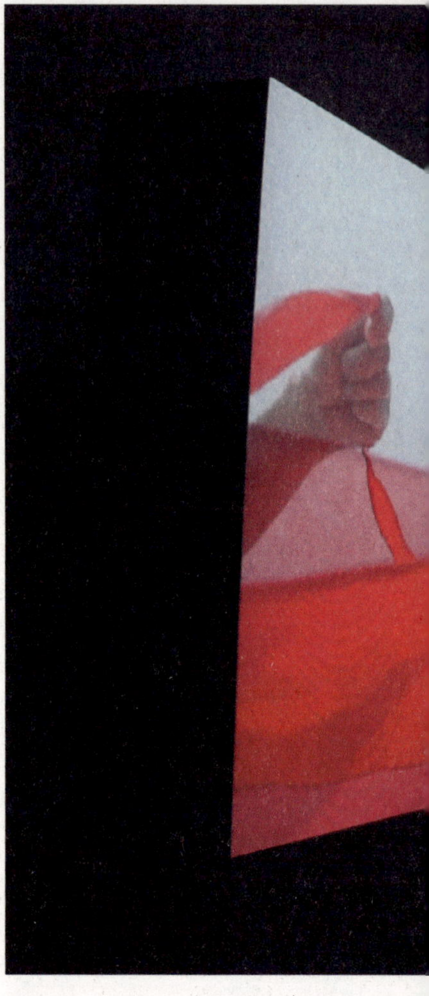

The three-channel video installation Lập Lòe (roughly, "blink" or "flicker") is derived from a performance series *Welts* that began in 2007.

In explanation of the work the artist writes:

> Lập Loè
> The uncertain fates.
> Lightning before the storm.
> The fireflies or battles as seen from afar...
> Efforts of embers, before they are extinguished

Trần Lương, *Lập Lòe*, 2012, 3-channel color video, sound, 5'02" (loop).

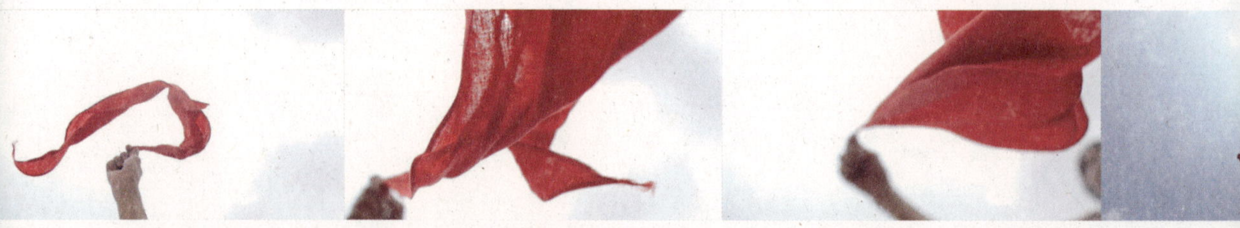

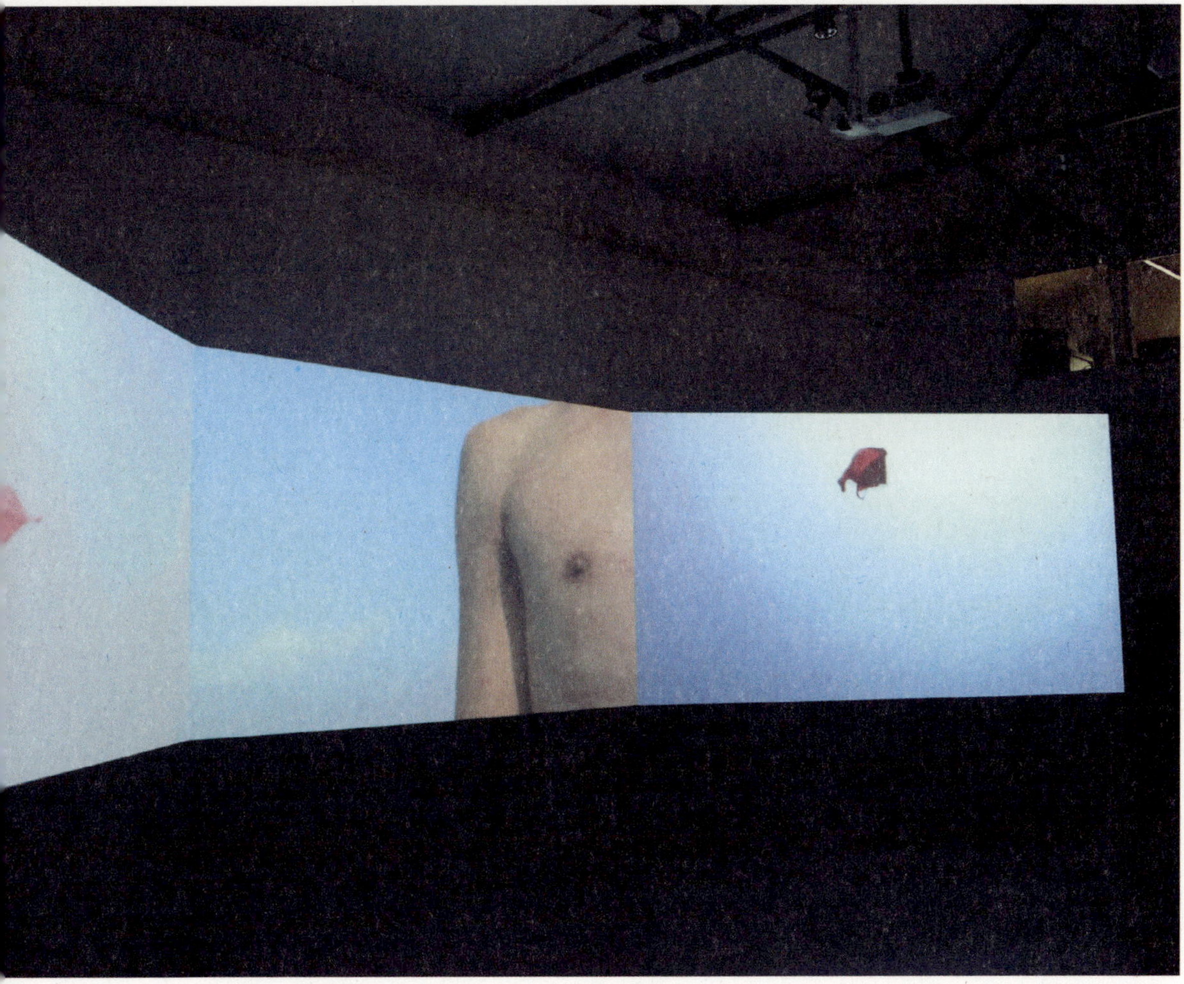

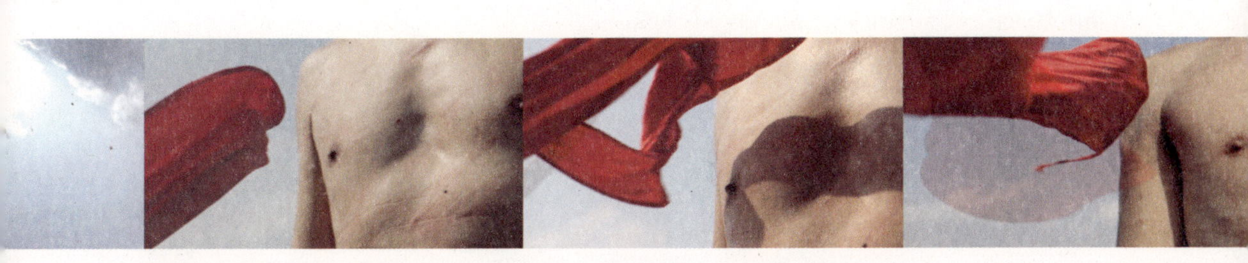

CỌC CẠCH
2013 - ongoing
Performance in various sites

During a visit to a village renowned for its silver and gold leaf craftmanship, Lương was impressed by artisans delicately hammering thin sheets of gold. This sight, coupled with the rhythmic sound, immediately brought to mind the communist propaganda's portrayal of the working class using hammers as a symbol of progress and development. Despite the seemingly peaceful craft, the rhythmic hammering carried underlying tones of violence.

From 2012 to 2014, Lương performed with an anvil and hammer in various locations associated with the working class. These included a mechanical factory, old collective housing, a historic bridge spanning the Red River, and in crowded streets around Hà Nội. Clad in a blue worker's uniform, he sat and continuously hammered a sheet of metal, re-enacting the process of crafting thin golden leaves. The hammering only ceased when his arm muscles grew tired and he could no longer lift the hammer. This action, accompanied by the incessant noise, caused disturbances and piqued public curiosity.

In 2015, he embarked on a 20-day durational performance in Paris, traversing many crowded tourist destinations such as the Eiffel Tower, the Louvre Museum and the interior of the Palais de Tokyo.

> "Cọc Cạch stretches the body's biological tolerance to the limit, challenging muscle function, while testing stamina in response to the pressure from the public. The massive clanging sound of the hammer serves as a warning bell, a premonition of the violence and conflicts still lurking in contemporary society, intensified by the escalating complexities of migration and religious issues."
>
> \- Artist statement, *Cọc Cạch*

Cọc Cạch was later developed into another ongoing project starting in 2015, which includes workshops and artwork involving onomatopoeic text and reading aloud.

1
Trần Lương, *Cọc Cạch* on Sở Mountain, Chương Mỹ, Hà Nội.

2,3,4
Trần Lương, *Cọc Cạch*, 2013 – ongoing, photo and video documentation of durational performance, various sites.

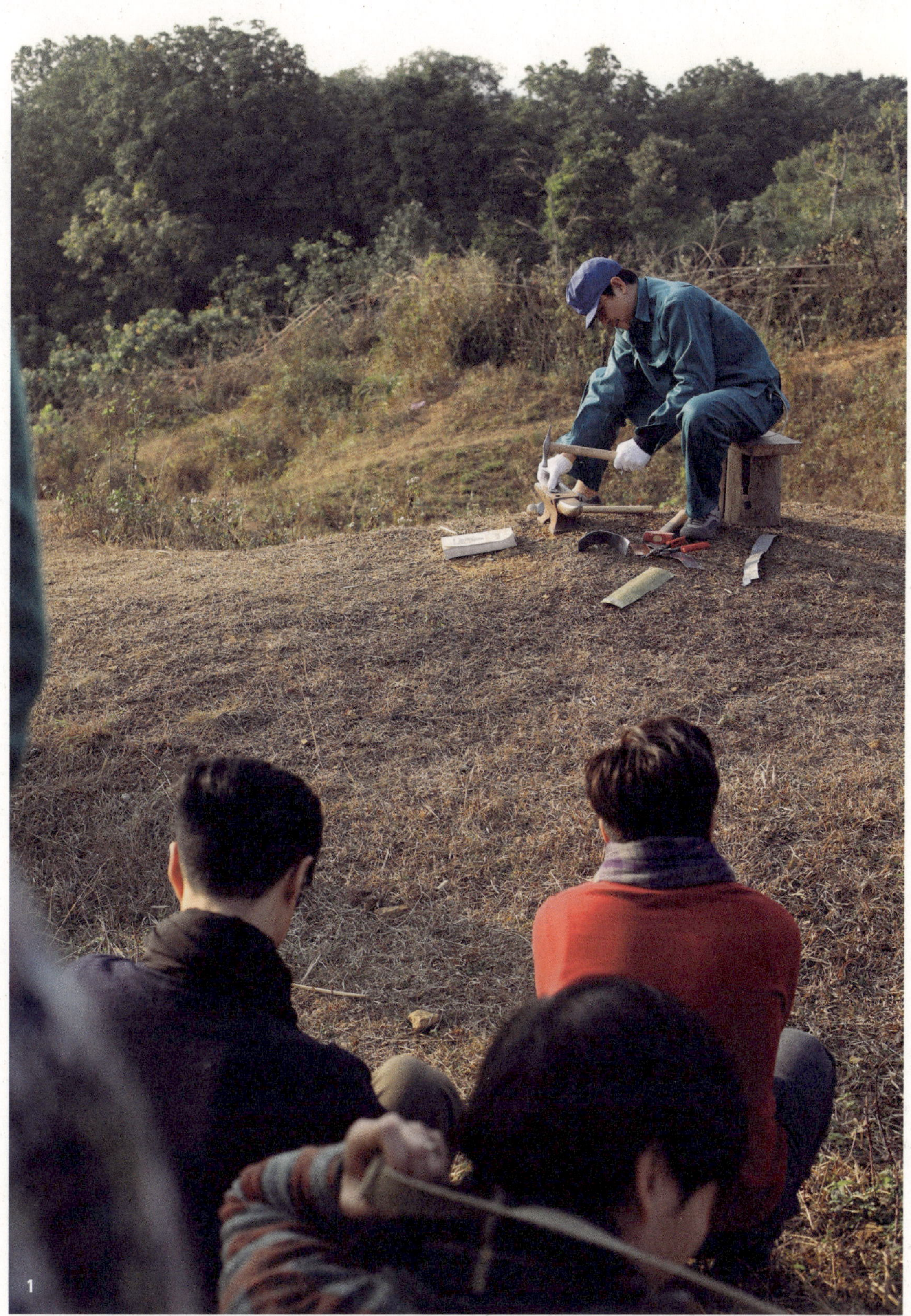

1

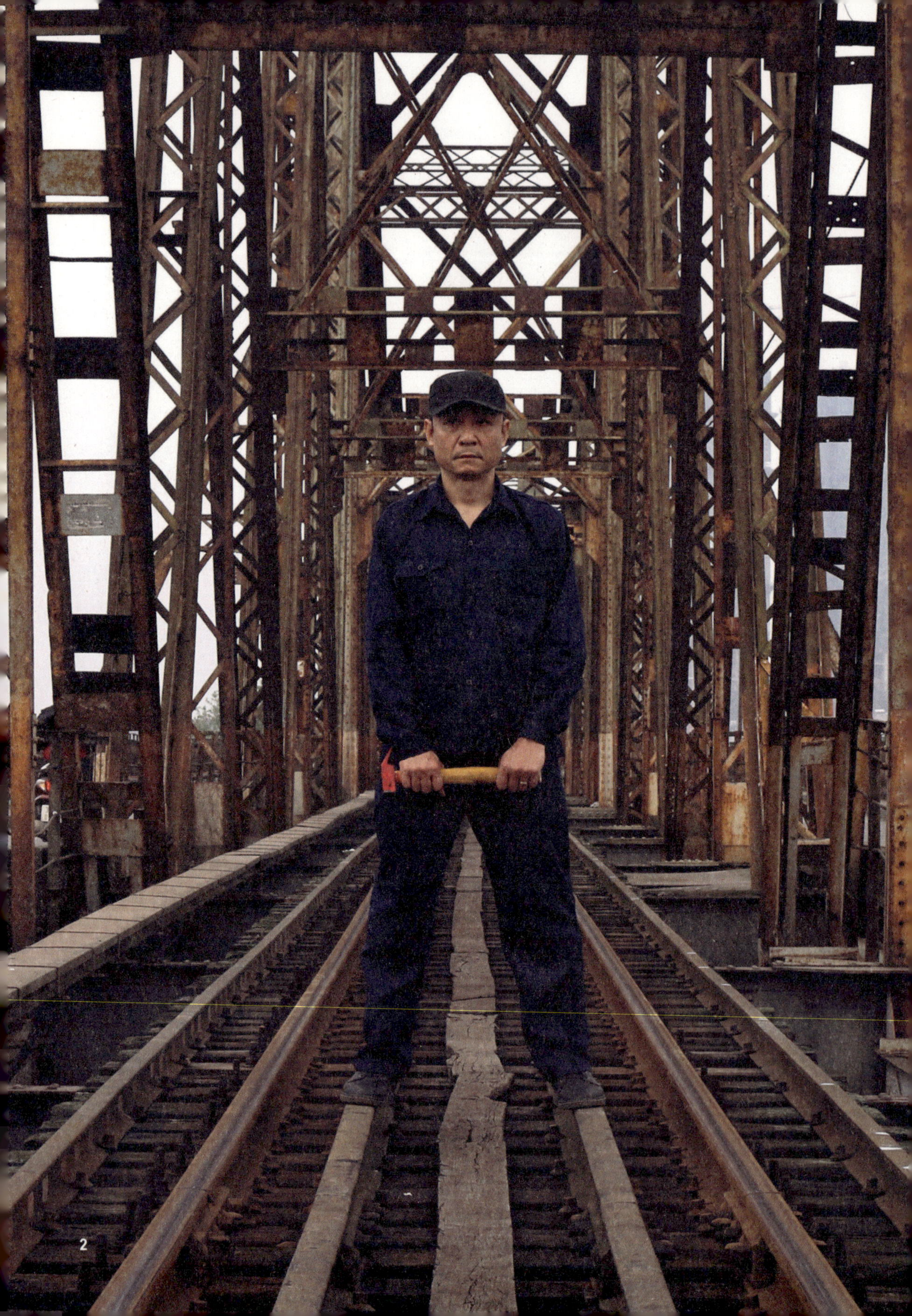

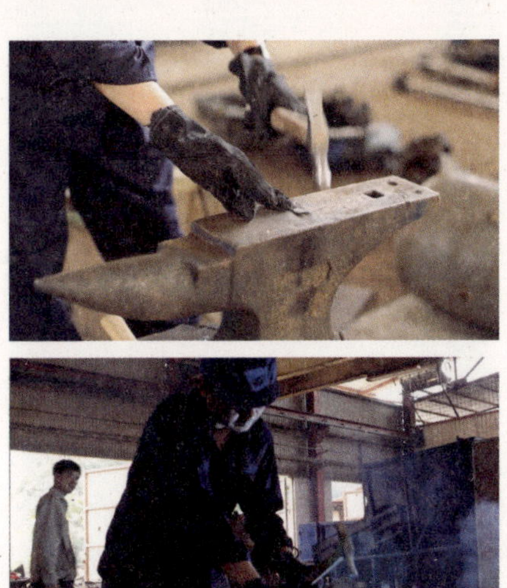

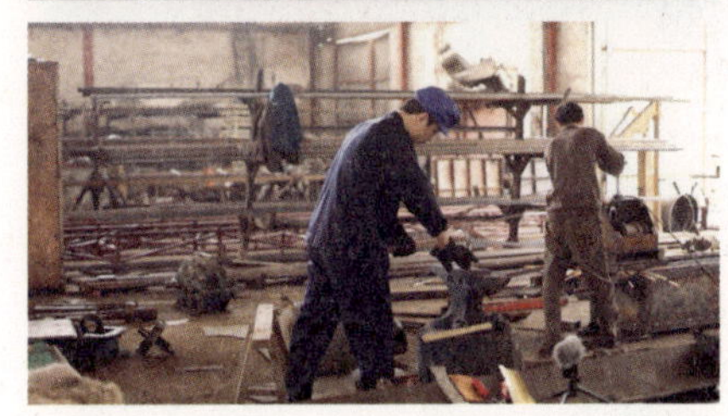

3

4

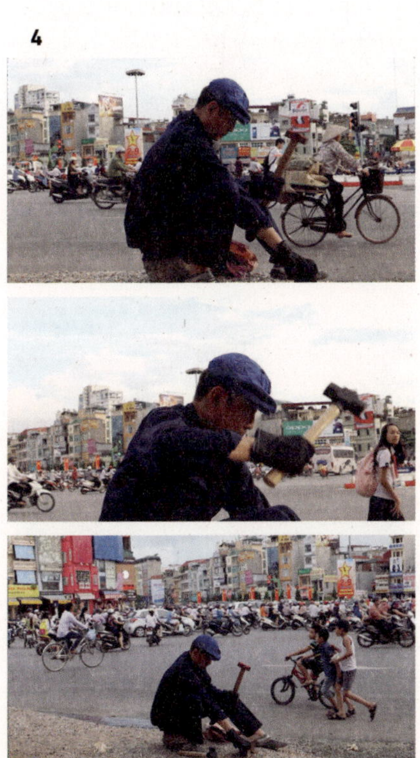

CỌC CẠCH SOUND-BASED PROJECT

2015 – ongoing
Workshop, discussion and sound recording

In Vietnamese "Cọc Cạch" means mismatching pairs of people or things. It also embodies the onomatopoeic sound of two objects clashing, describing something almost broken or not operating smoothly, that creates high intensity noise. For this project the artist selected 21 onomatopoeic words from the Vietnamese language that evoke hitting, smashing, crushing, falling, breaking or exploding. The artist organised a series of workshops for groups of three to six people of different genders and ages. Each participant delved into historical references, studying and practising the origins of these words. They were invited to pronounce the words with the intention of being as close and honest as possible to the sound of its origin, aiming to capture the sound's essence rather than simply reading them.

The artist compiled recordings of the workshop participants' voices, blending them into a choral sound piece. To date, recordings from 80 participants have been collected, with the voice archive continuing to grow.

coong,

cùm,

cộc,

cọc,

cạch,

cốc,

cóc,

cách,

cắc,

keng,

kinh,

kồng,

xoảng,

choang,

chat,

bùm,

bing,

boong,

bịch,

bộp,

bốp.

ABOUT THE HIDING OF THE GIANT JELLYFISH
THAILAND BIENNALE 2018

A site-specific installation along the Ao Nang Beach walkway in Krabi province (Thailand), this work consisted of a soft latex mattress beneath the walkway's pavement, rendering the artwork nearly invisible, seamlessly merging with the coastal landscape. As the visitor steps onto the walkway the ground suddenly sinks, creating a sensation of traversing a soft, animate entity beneath the surface. In places of natural beauty, such as Krabi, tourists typically look outward to enjoy the scenery, offering a brief respite from everyday concerns. The unexpected descent of a footstep disrupts this tranquility. The physical imbalance triggers a sense of awakening, prompting contemplation of personal, social, and biological realities.

The work also contains an interactive soundscape played randomly as visitors walk along the walkway, including the sound of shifting grounds before an earthquake, the laughter of a crowd, the sound of dolphins and seagulls among sea waves, the distorted television soundwave from a political campaign and the sharp sound of a meteorite that bypasses Earth, among other sounds.

This work was commissioned for the Thailand Biennale 2018, *Edge of the Wonderland*, which took place outdoors across several natural sites in Krabi, a well-known tourist destination.

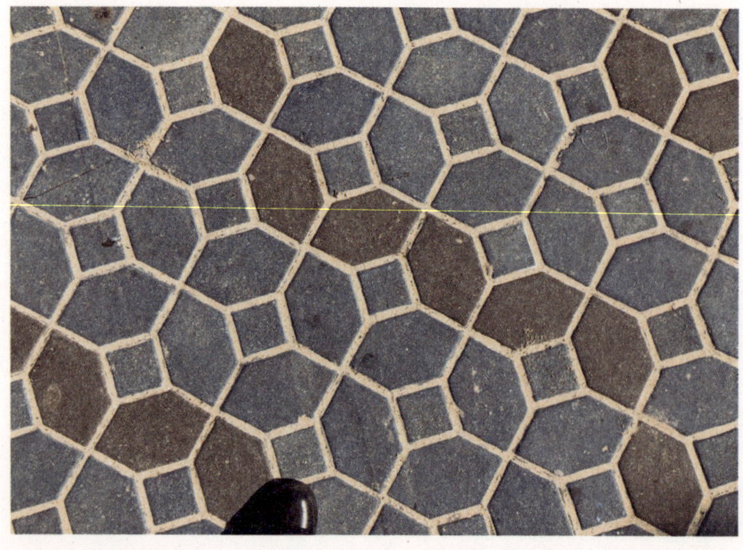

Trần Lương, *About the Hiding of the Giant Jelly Fish*, 2018, site-specific installation, bricks, PU foam, rubber, silicone, interactive sound system. Installation view at Ao Nang beach, Krabi, Thailand. Courtesy of Thailand Biennale, Krabi 2018.

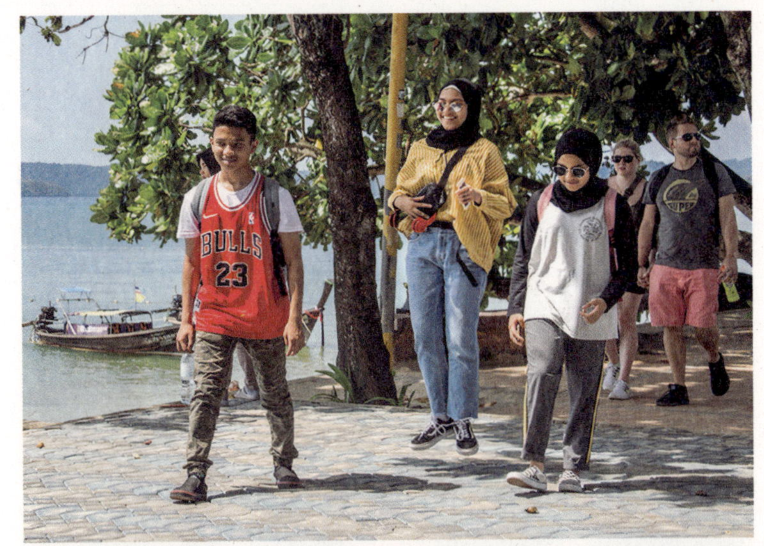
BULLS
23

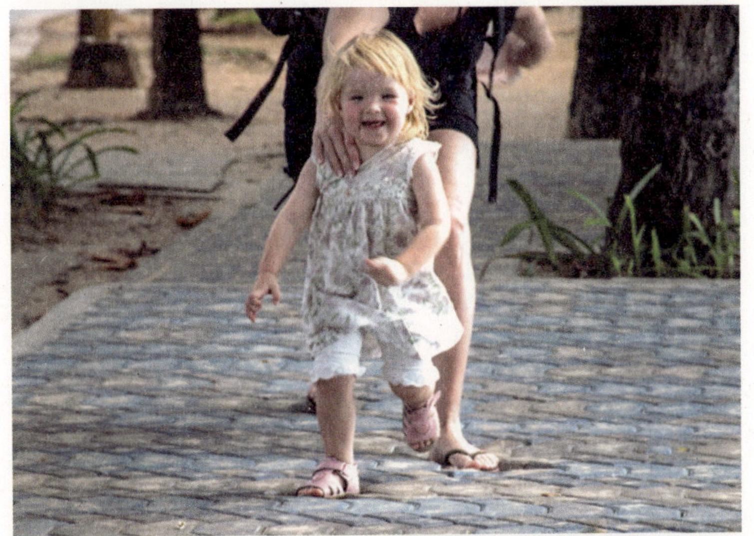

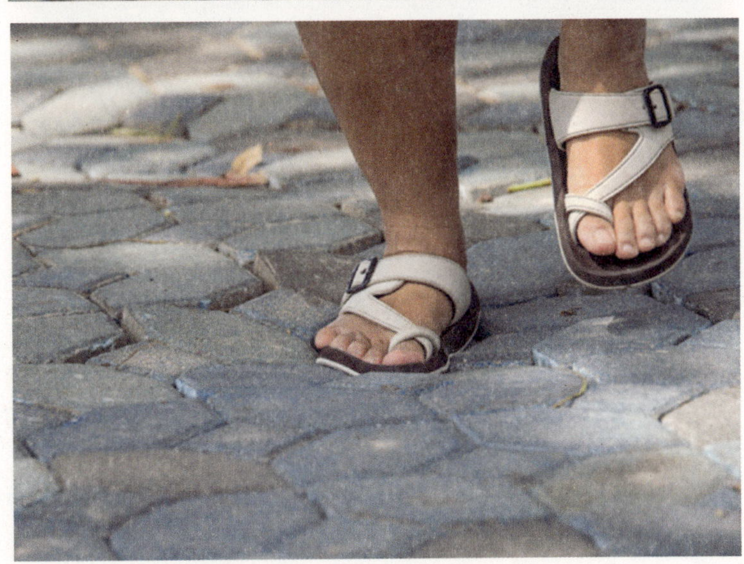

ERUTUF / YROTSIH (History Backward)
2018

Through his engagement with local and indigenous communities, the artist continues to learn about their deep connection to nature and practices of reciprocity grounded in co-existence. Maori people have said that walking backwards into the future underlines First Nation people's relationship to the present, past and future. In this action, the artist covers his head and walks backwards, unable to see, which forces him to slow down and be attentive to senses other than sight. During the performance, the word ERUTUF ('future' spelled backwards) was written on the artist's back and the word YROTSIH ('history' spelled backwards) was written on his chest.

ERUTUF / YROTSIH was performed in Lublin and Bialystok, during *Asia Live! Vietnam Performance 2018* in Poland. It was later performed in Berlin in front of the Volksbuehne Theater.

Trần Lương, *ERUTUF / YROTSIH*, 2018, photo documentation of performance, Lublin & Bialystok (Poland) and Berlin.

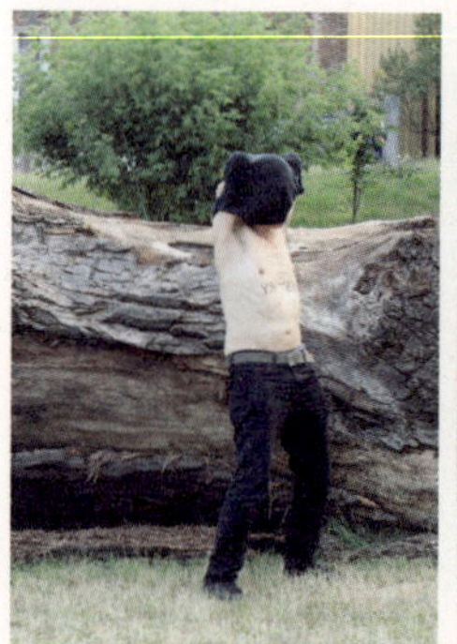
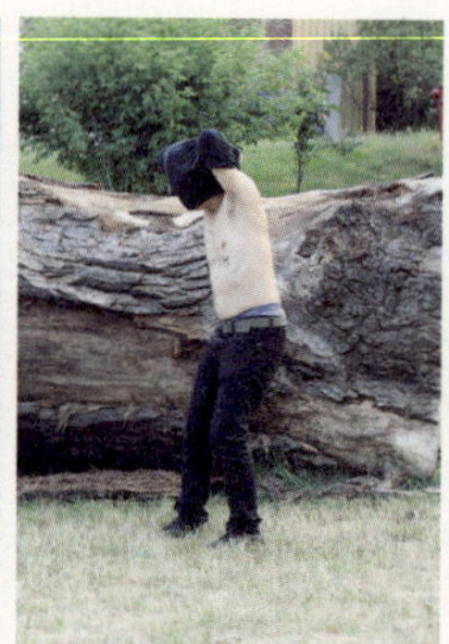
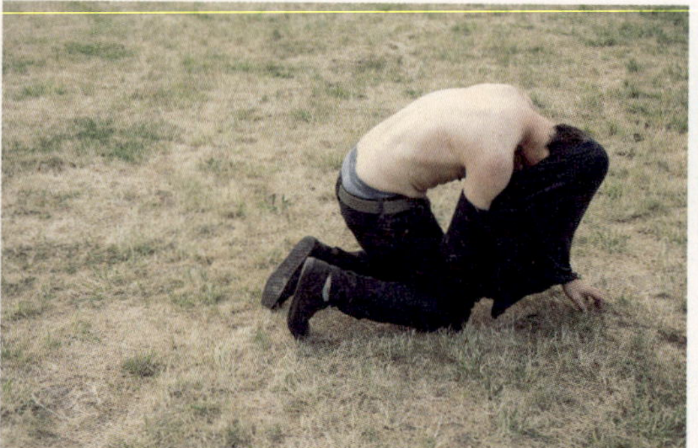
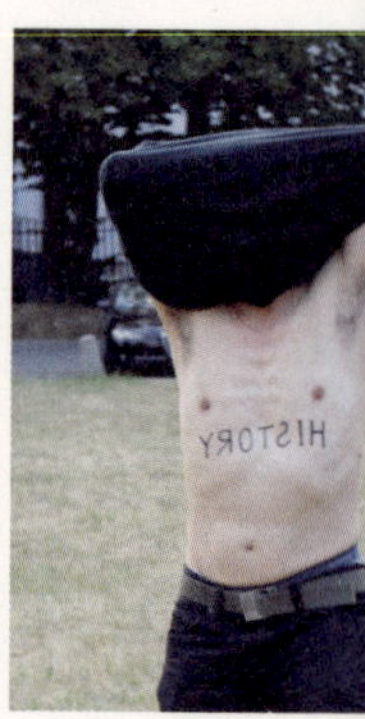

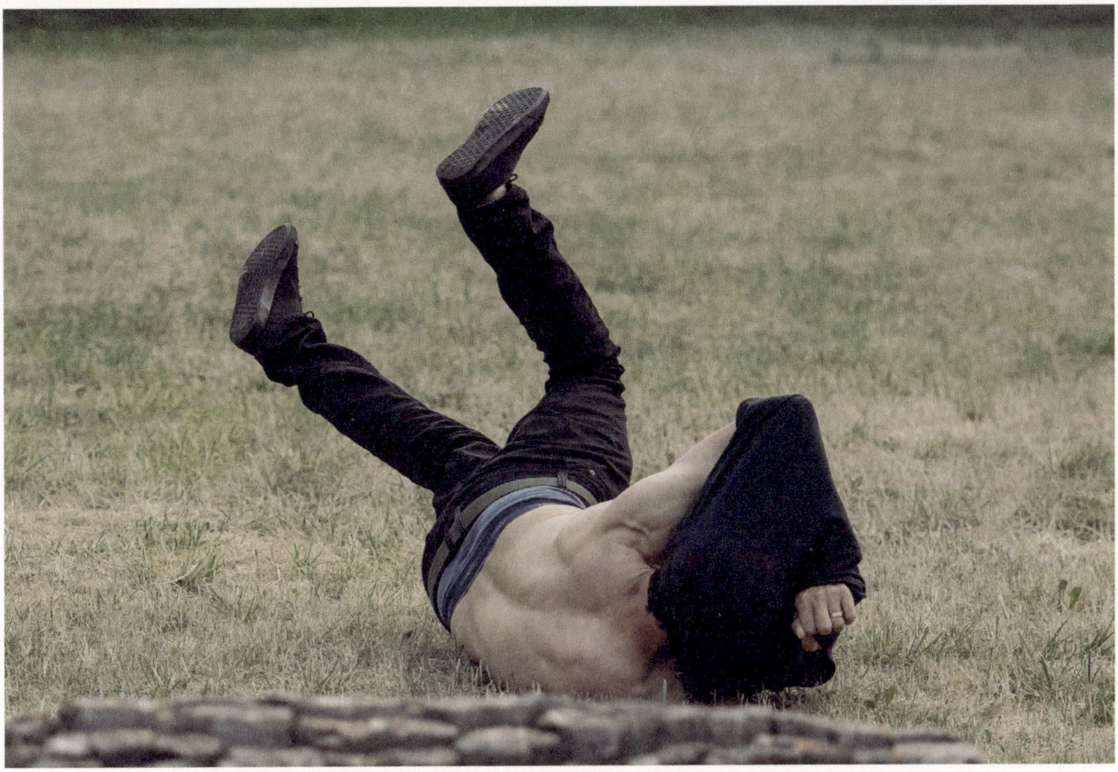

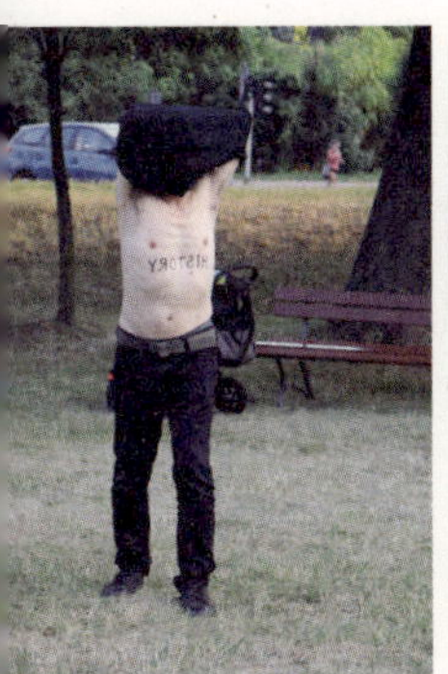
HISTORY

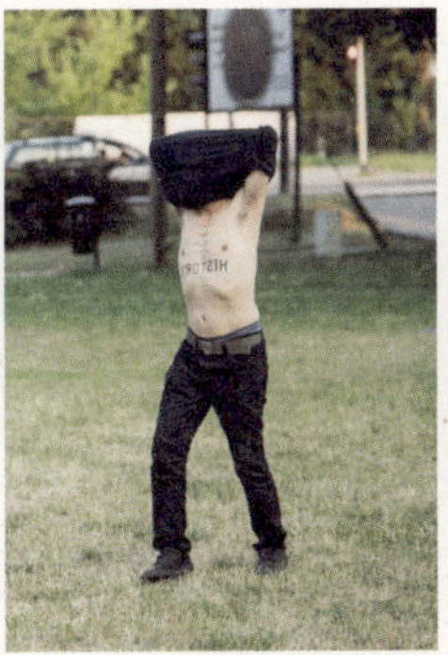

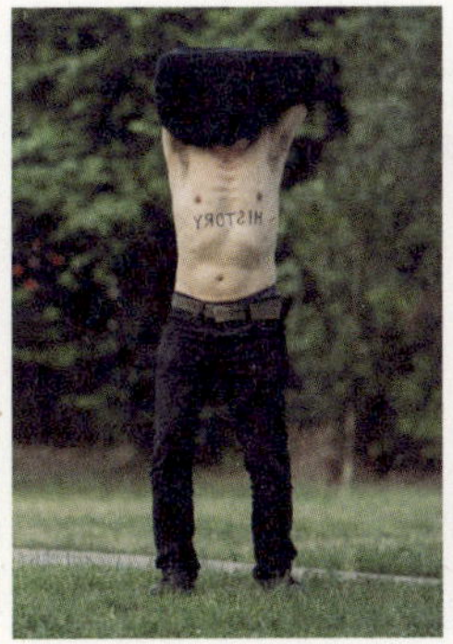

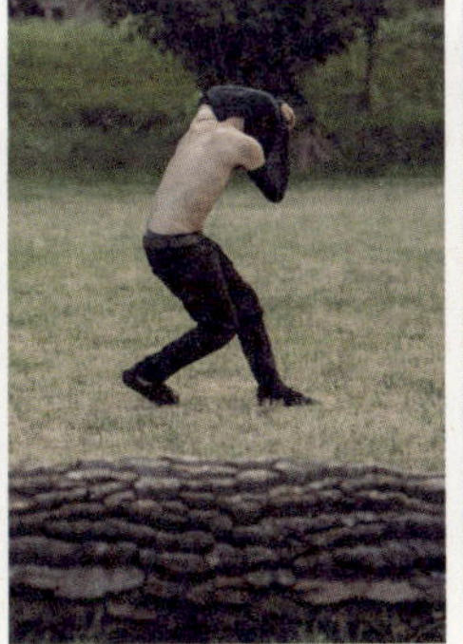

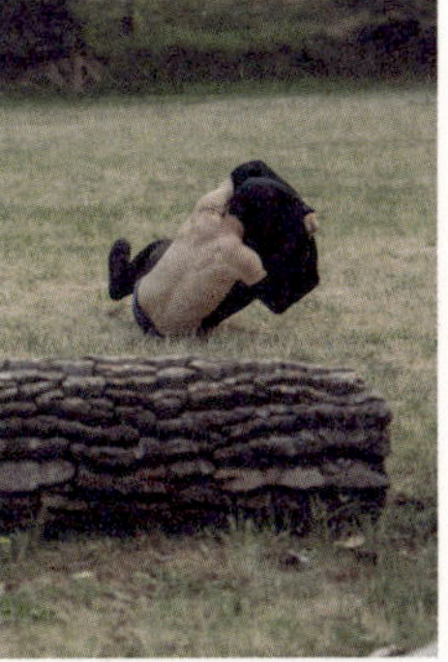

MEKONG STUDY
2019
Nanjing

During the performance, the artist stands upright with his head tilted towards the sky, holding a 1.5-litre water bottle in his mouth. Inside the upside-down bottle, swim a school of live redfish. To prevent choking on the water as it bears down on his throat, and to provide oxygen for the fish swimming in the bottle, the artist continuously blows air upwards. However, the need to maintain this breathing method causes fatigue after about 15 minutes, leading to occasional choking and water spraying from the artist's mouth. The performance lasted for 30 minutes until the artist became too exhausted to continue tilting his head upward.

Mekong Study reflects water management strategies, particularly the construction of numerous hydropower dams upstream of the Mekong River over the past 25 years. These dams have had significant impacts on the downstream region, including Thailand, Laos, Cambodia and Vietnam, triggering an ecological crisis and altering the cultural landscape.

In 2019, the live performance took place at the opening of the exhibition *Polyphony: Southeast Asia* in Nanjing, China.

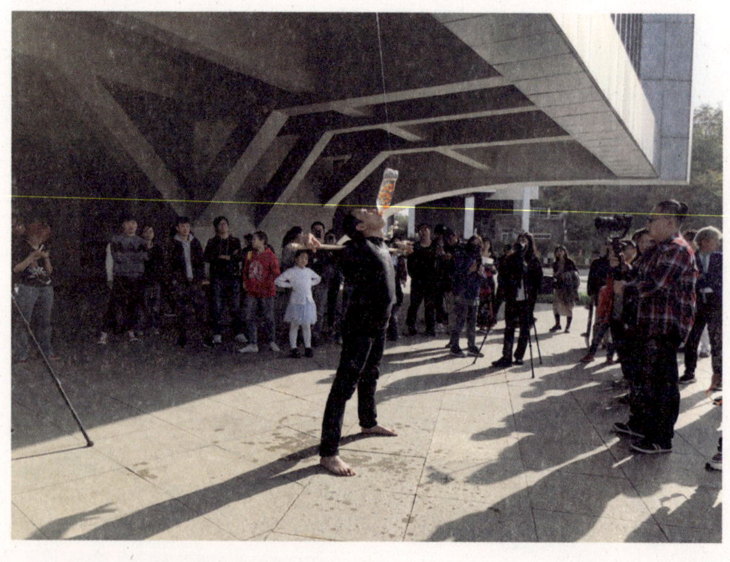

Trần Lương, *Mekong Study*, 2019, photo documentation of performance, approx 20'. Nanjing, China.

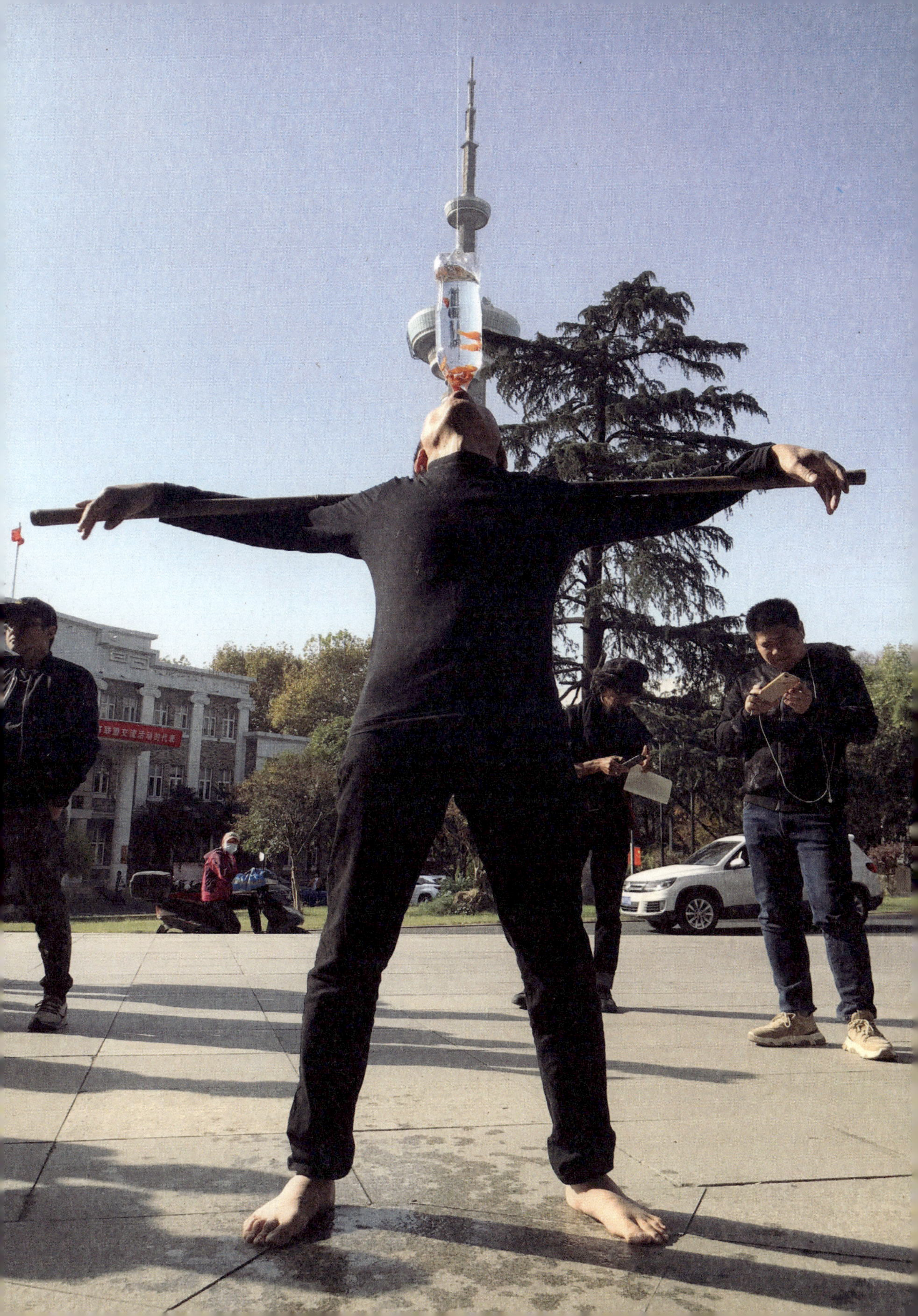

LẾCH-PƠ-CHÙA-PHO-MẦN

November 2023

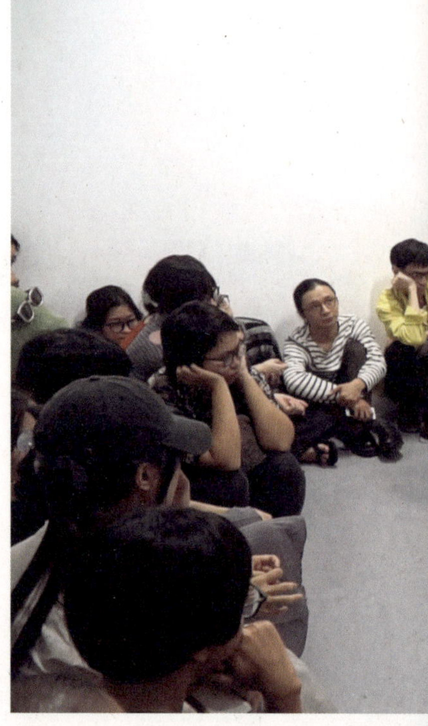

This performance evening was initiated by Hà Nội based artist Vũ Đức Toàn, driven by his concerns about the lecture performance format commonly found in the West but rarely used in the Vietnamese context. The artists were invited to share their concepts of what a lecture performance is. The event, presented by Á Space in Hà Nội, featured many artists, including Trần Lương.

Trần Lương's performance consisted of two parts. The first was the performance of unrelated objects appearing together in a space, with a person – assumed to be the performance artist – standing amidst them. It seemed the artist had disappointed the audience, his purpose seemingly only to support the transformation of the objects. An ice cube melted as a towel gradually absorbed the water. A candle burned out. A massage machine moved aimlessly on the floor. The coffee in a cup gradually ran out. A banana played the role of the sickle before being gnawed on. Even the big toe went numb from the attempt to compose poetry.

While in the first part, the objects were performing while the artist stayed still and speechless, in the second part he talked about the performances of those who never perform; perhaps unaware of performance art's existence. He spoke of something supposedly called "pre-performance phenomena", events in life that inherently contain all the elements of a performance artwork. These "stories" or phenomena in history have become raw materials for later refinement into performance art. Or perhaps Trần Lương's lecture performance was itself an extreme attempt to construct a theory full of illusions.

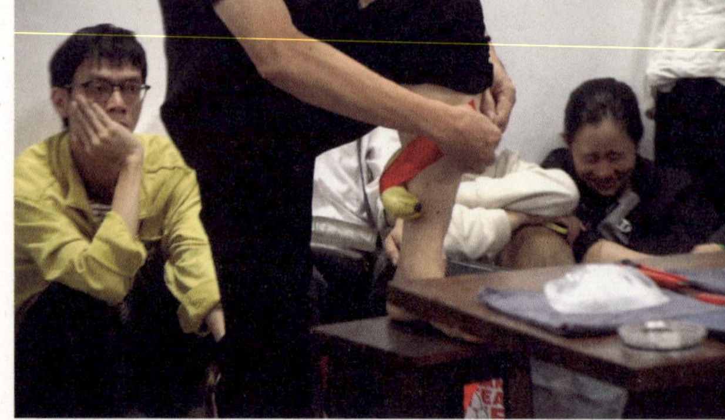

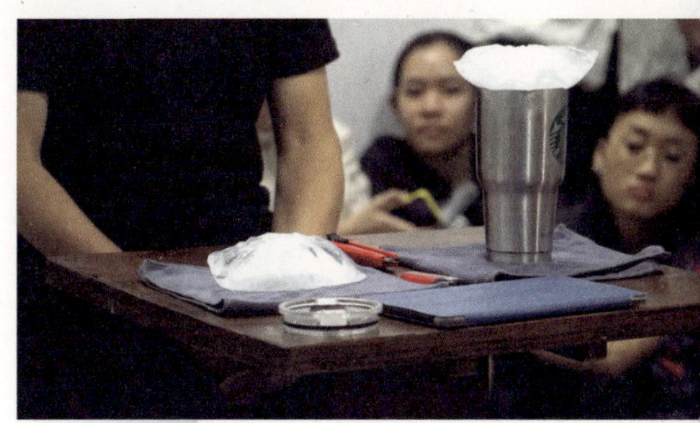

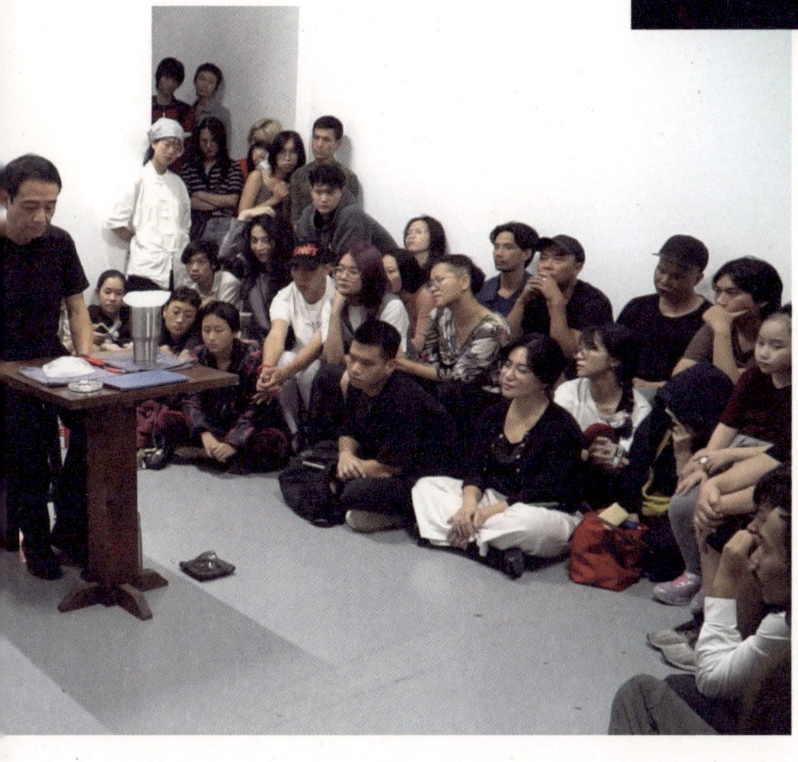

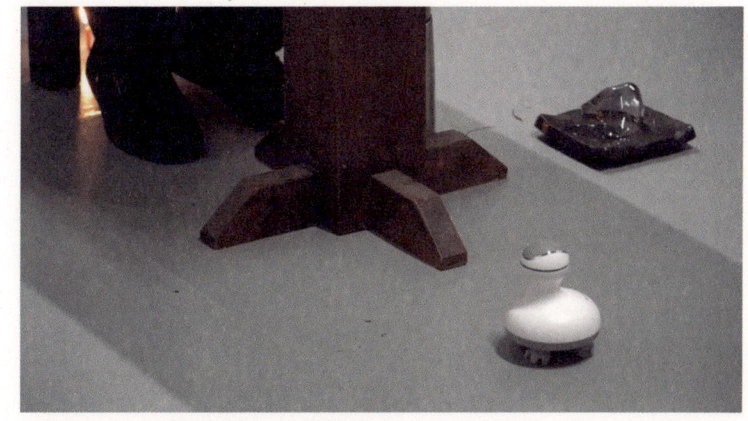

Trần Lương, *Lếch-Pơ-Chùa-Pho-Mần*, November 2023, photo documentation of performance, 35'. *4th Quarter Report*, Á Space, Hà Nội, Vietnam.

SELECTION OF CURATED PROJECTS

2001–2016

This archive presents a selection of exhibitions curated and often fully organised and coordinated by Trần Lương. The selection was made in collaboration with the artist and Trần Lương and APD team member, Flinh, during my stay in Hà Nội in 2023. Flinh has devoted a great amount of time to compiling information and building narratives around many of these projects. Through this selection we have focused on group exhibitions Lương curated, rather than solo exhibitions. The archive presents a selection of exhibitions, projects, festivals and field trips, providing an understanding of his curatorial engagements locally, regionally and internationally when presenting art from Vietnam. Locally presented and curated projects were often self-initiated and self-organised, and so through the creation of this archive, we have tried to understand the conditions of these encounters in terms of economy, resources and affective connections. We chose not to include workshops or exhibition programs that were presented in the art centres that Lương ran, such as Nhà Sàn or Hà Nội Contemporary Art Center, despite these programs being not only conceived, but also coordinated by Trần Lương and his peers – work that he understands as part of the curatorial role of facilitating. The selection of projects is presented chronologically in the book, and we have done our best to obtain proper visual representation of these exhibitions. We hope that this archive serves as a tool for future research on re-writing curatorial histories.

MẠO KHÊ COAL MINE PROJECT 2001

LOCATION: Mạo Khê Coal Mine, Quảng Ninh Province, Vietnam DATE: October 2001 DURATION: 15 days CURATOR: Trần Lương (Director of Hà Nội Contemporary Art Center from 2000-2003) ORGANISED BY: Hà Nội Contemporary Art Center SUPPORTED BY: Vietnam Fine Arts Association & Mạo Khê Coal Mine PARTICIPATING ARTISTS: Nguyễn Bảo Toàn, Hà Trí Hiếu, Lê Quảng Hà, Lê Hồng Thái, Đinh Quân, Đinh Công Đạt, Đào Anh Khánh, Phạm Ngọc Minh, Lê Vũ, Nguyễn Trí Mạnh, Trần Lương.

In 2001, Trần Lương organised a field trip for 11 artists to Mạo Khê Coal Mine in Quảng Ninh province, Vietnam. He invited artists to live with the miners and refrain from creating artworks. The group spent two weeks eating, working and drinking with the workers. In the last few days of their stay, they began creating works including murals on the walls of the mining complex, performances and graffiti-style interventions on the factory walls, among other works. Lương worked with the Fine Arts Association to obtain permission to enter the 25 square kilometre mining complex. Without a support letter from the Association, the visit would have been impossible. The Association also supported transportation, while the coal mine factory provided accommodation. Other costs for the project were shared by the artists.

The presence of cultural workers in mines has a deep and troubled history in Vietnam. Many intellectuals were sent to work in mines as punishment for their work, while students from the Art Academy would have the option to go and sketch in the mining area during their studies.

After the field trip, an exhibition was organised at Hà Nội Contemporary Art Center in February 2002. The exhibition ran for two weeks and included video footage from the field trip alongside photographs of various works including murals, Trần Lương's performance, installation work by Nguyễn Bảo Toàn & Hà Trí Hiếu at the coal mine factory and graffiti work on the facade of the art centre by Đinh Công Đạt. Đào Anh Khánh presented a live performance at the exhibition opening. The coal mine management board and many mine workers attended the opening of the *Mạo Khê Coal Mine Project* exhibition in Hà Nội.

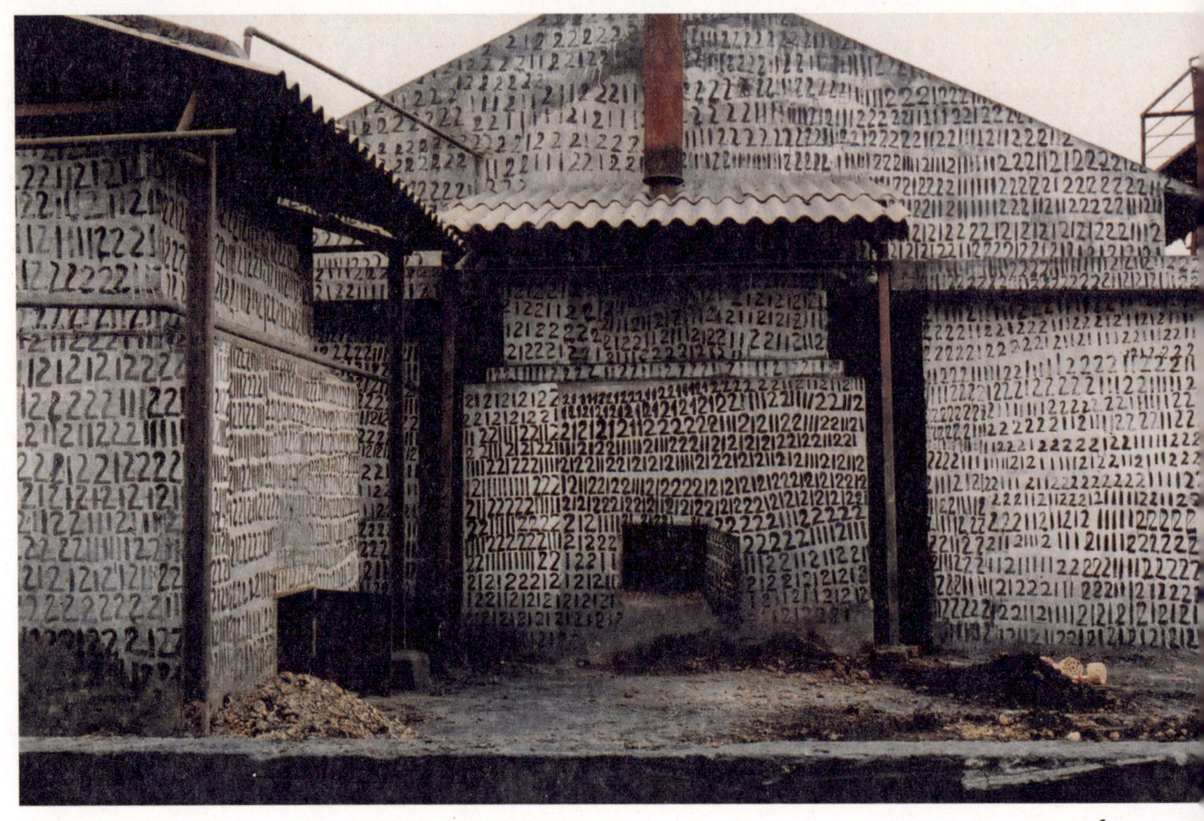

1

1
Đinh Công Đạt, numerical graffiti on Mạo Khê factory buiding. The numbers represent the Vietnamese Traditional Day of Coal Industry on November 12. Courtesy of Trần Lương.

2
Nguyễn Bảo Toàn & Hà Trí Hiếu, *Untitled*, 2001, site-specific installation at Mạo Khê coal mine, utilising miner's boots borrowed from the mine factory storage. Photo: Nguyễn Bảo Toàn. Courtesy of Nguyễn Bảo Toàn and Hà Trí Hiếu.

3
During the field trip, several of the artists painted murals stretching 300 metres along the wall of the coal mine factory. Of the 11 artists from the group, only Đinh Công Đạt did not participate in the mural painting, while artist Đặng Xuân Hoà, who was not part of the group, visited the project and joined in the mural painting. Each artist painted a section approximately 25 metres long. The murals incorporate impressionistic, expressionistic and abstract forms, reflecting the artists' emotional responses to their immersion in the lives of the miners. Additionally, some paintings highlight the social and political issues contributing to the difficult circumstances faced by the workers, such as distorted images of Asian revolutionary leaders. Courtesy of Trần Lương.

2

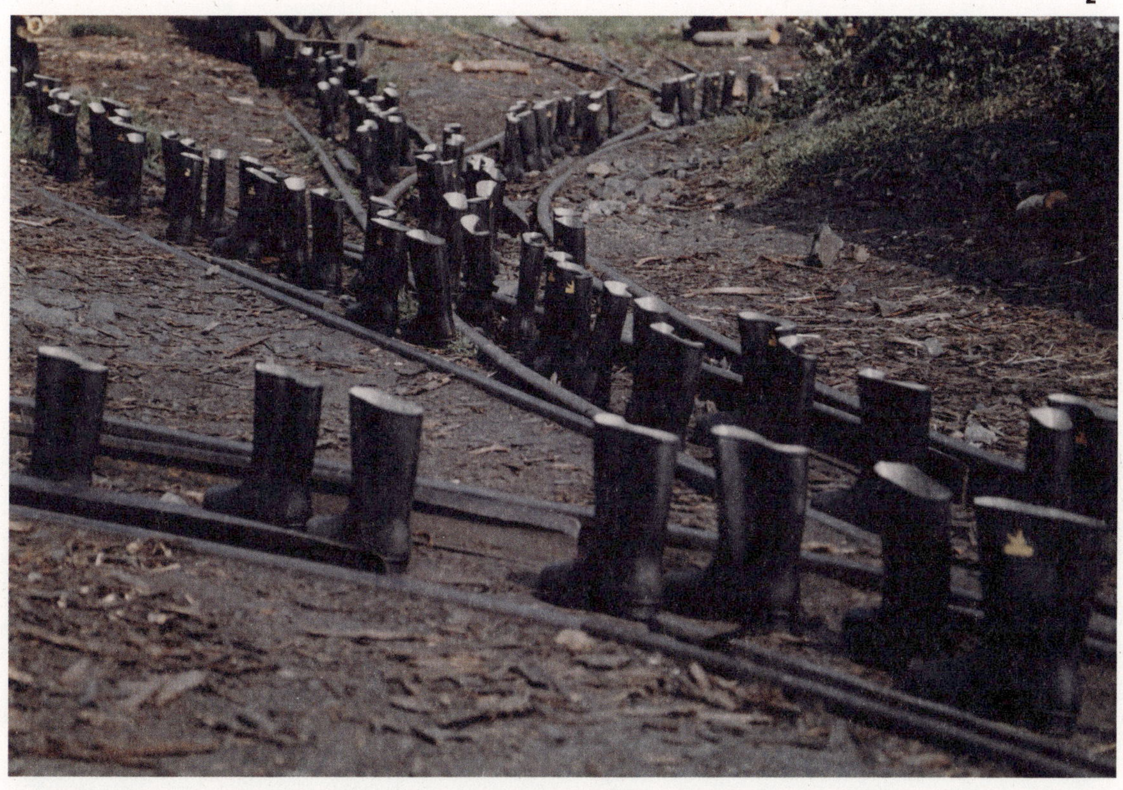

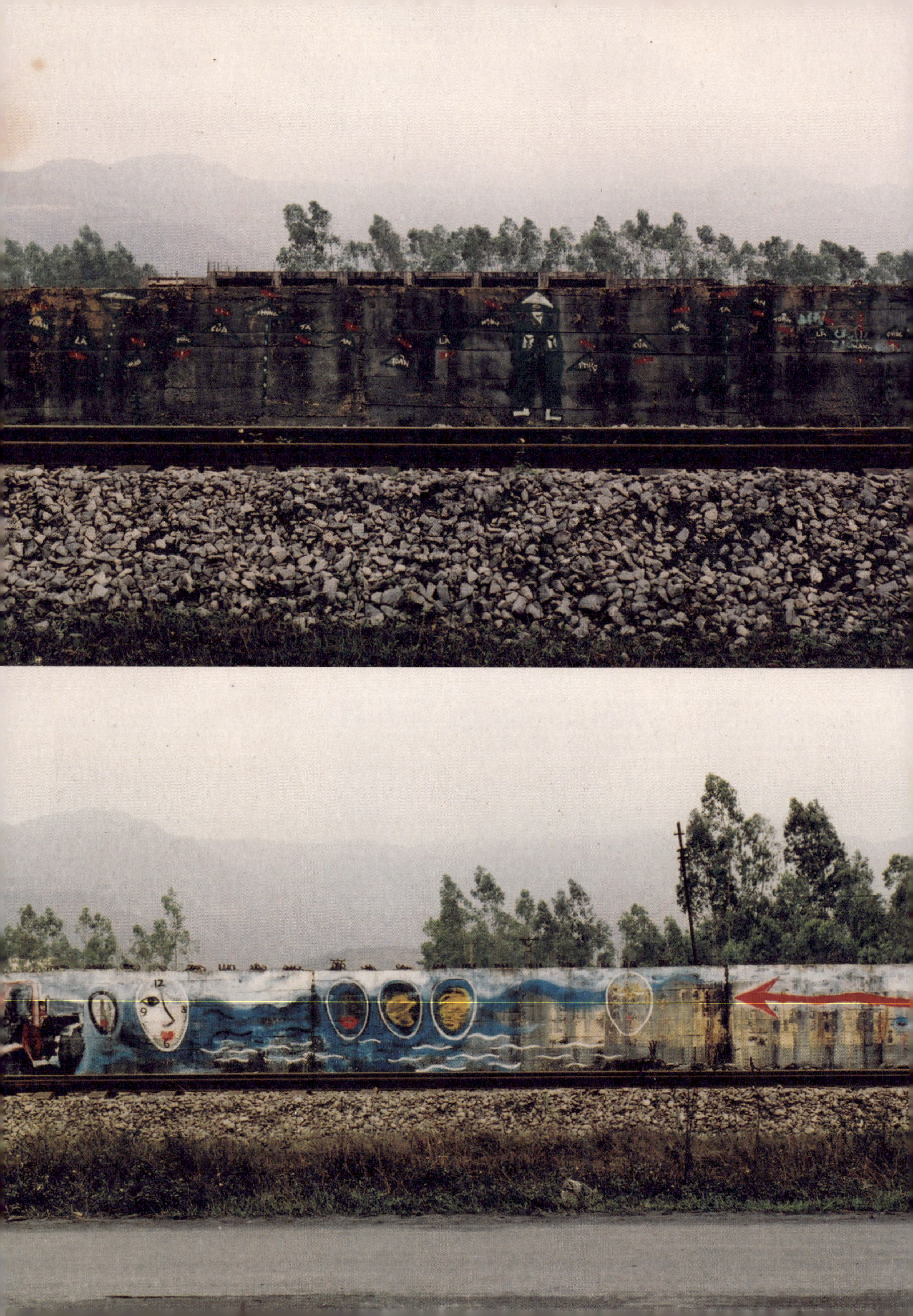
TOÀN
LÀ
CỦA
TA
TOÀN
LÀ

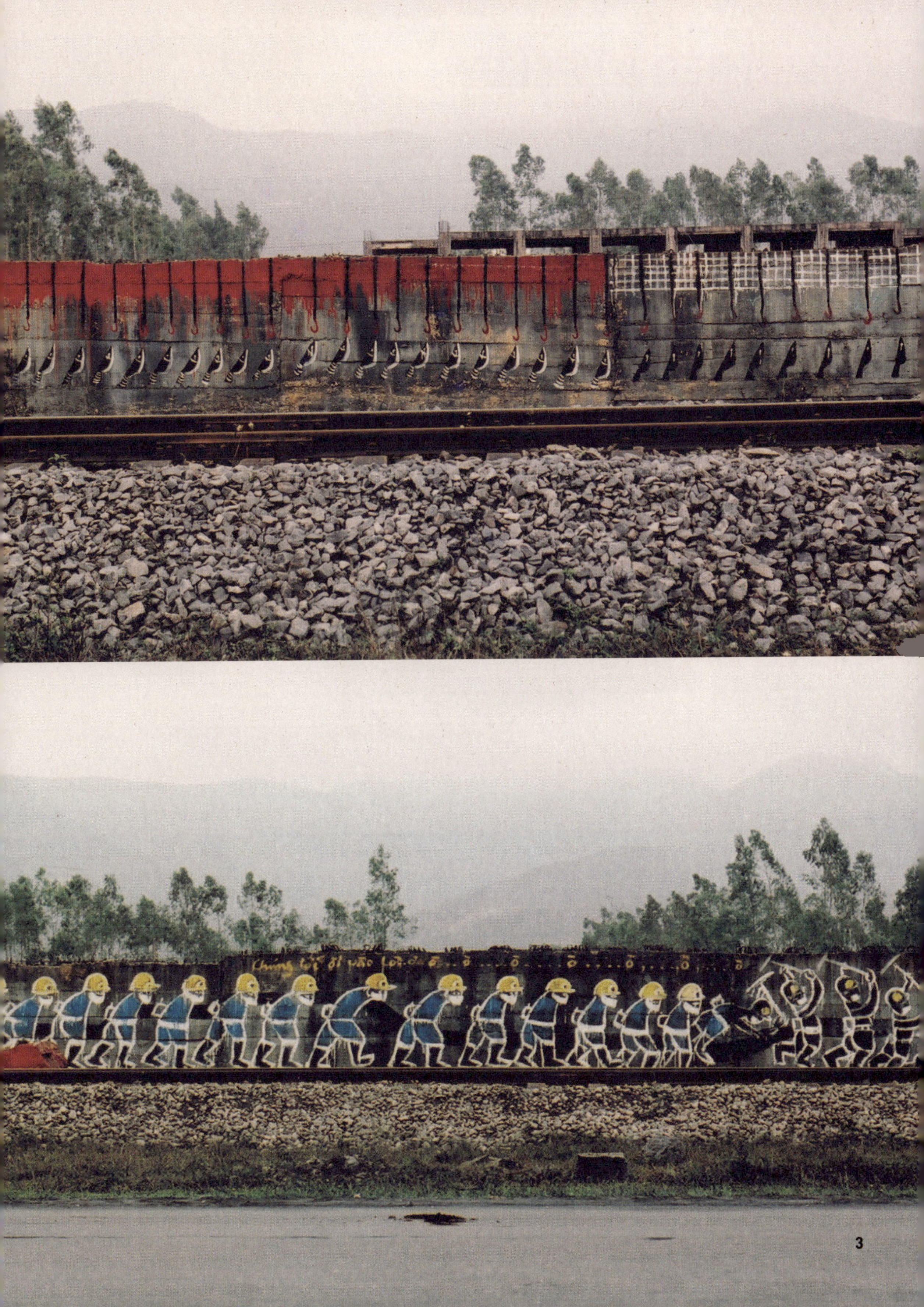

GREEN RED & YELLOW 2003

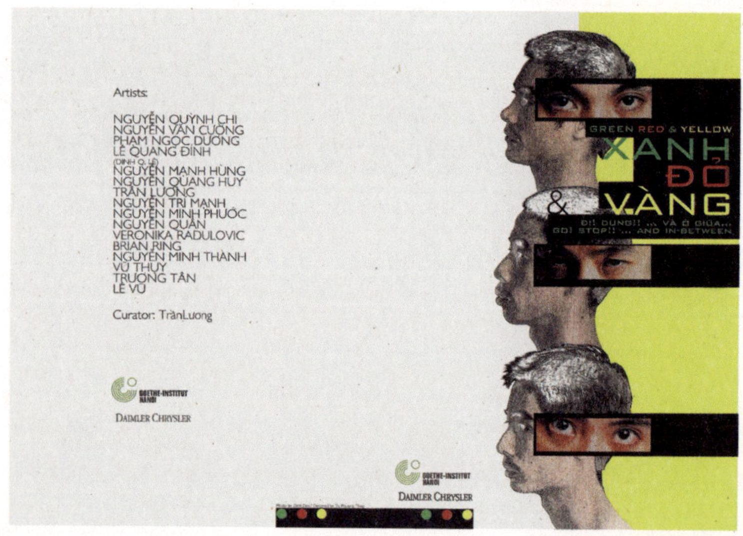

Green Red & Yellow exhibition leaflet, designed by Từ Phương Thảo. Courtesy of Trần Lương.

LOCATION: Construction site of Goethe Institut Hà Nội **DATE:** 3–10 October, 2003 **ORGANISED & CURATED BY:** Trần Lương **SUPPORTED BY:** Goethe Institut Hà Nội (Nguyễn Thái Học Str., Hà Nội) **PARTICIPATING ARTISTS:** Nguyễn Quỳnh Chi, Nguyễn Văn Cường, Phạm Ngọc Dương, Lê Quang Đỉnh, Nguyễn Mạnh Hùng, Nguyễn Quang Huy, Trần Lương, Nguyễn Trí Mạnh, Nguyễn Minh Phước, Nguyễn Quân, Veronika Radulovic, Brian Ring, Nguyễn Minh Thành, Vũ Thụy, Trương Tân, Lê Vũ.

The concept of *Green Red & Yellow* was inspired by a line from a poem written by the poet Lê Đạt: "take the traffic police podium placed in the heart of people,"[1] which refers to the control and censorship of culture and art by the Vietnamese state since 1954. Tran Luong associates the green and red of traffic lights with symbolising binary states of go/stop and right/wrong, while the yellow light represents a "neutral" or "undetermined" state, which he perceives as more humane.

Trần Lương shared this idea and invited 15 artists to create works in response to the theme. The aim of the exhibition was to present a different approach to contemporary art in the context of Vietnam's globalisation with a focus on personal memory, problems related to urbanisation and political issues. The works presented covered various mediums, including painting, installation and video, some of which were interactive and community-engaged (such as the works by Nguyễn Quân, Nguyễn Minh Phước and Vũ Thuỵ), shifting the conventional idea of the artist's role and the form of the artwork. It was the first exhibition in Vietnam where site-specific installations were developed on such a large scale. The exhibition challenged the conservative art circles which suggested that contemporary art should draw on traditional aesthetics and promote Vietnamese identity.

Green Red & Yellow is considered the first large-scale domestic contemporary art exhibition in Vietnam. Given its scale and the constraints of censorship, it couldn't be hosted in either governmental or private venues. Thanks to the dedicated support provided by Mr. Franz Xaver Augustin, Director of the Goethe Institut Hà Nội, the exhibition took place over one week within the premises that were, at the time, undergoing construction for the new institute.

1. Lê Đạt. "Nhân câu chuyện mấy người tự tử". *Nhân Văn (Humanity)* Newspaper, No.1, 20 September 1956, pp. 3. Lê Đạt is a poet, writer and prominent figure within the Nhân Văn Giai Phẩm cultural reform movement, which operated from 1956 to 1958 and was spearheaded by a group of cultural experts including writers, poets, musicians, painters, filmmakers and publishers. Despite the passage of 50 years leading up to the *Green Red & Yellow* exhibition, there had been no noticeable improvement in freedom of expression in Vietnam. This prompted Trần Lương to borrow the concept of traffic light colors in the media to reflect the ongoing censorship and lack of freedom of expression in the country.

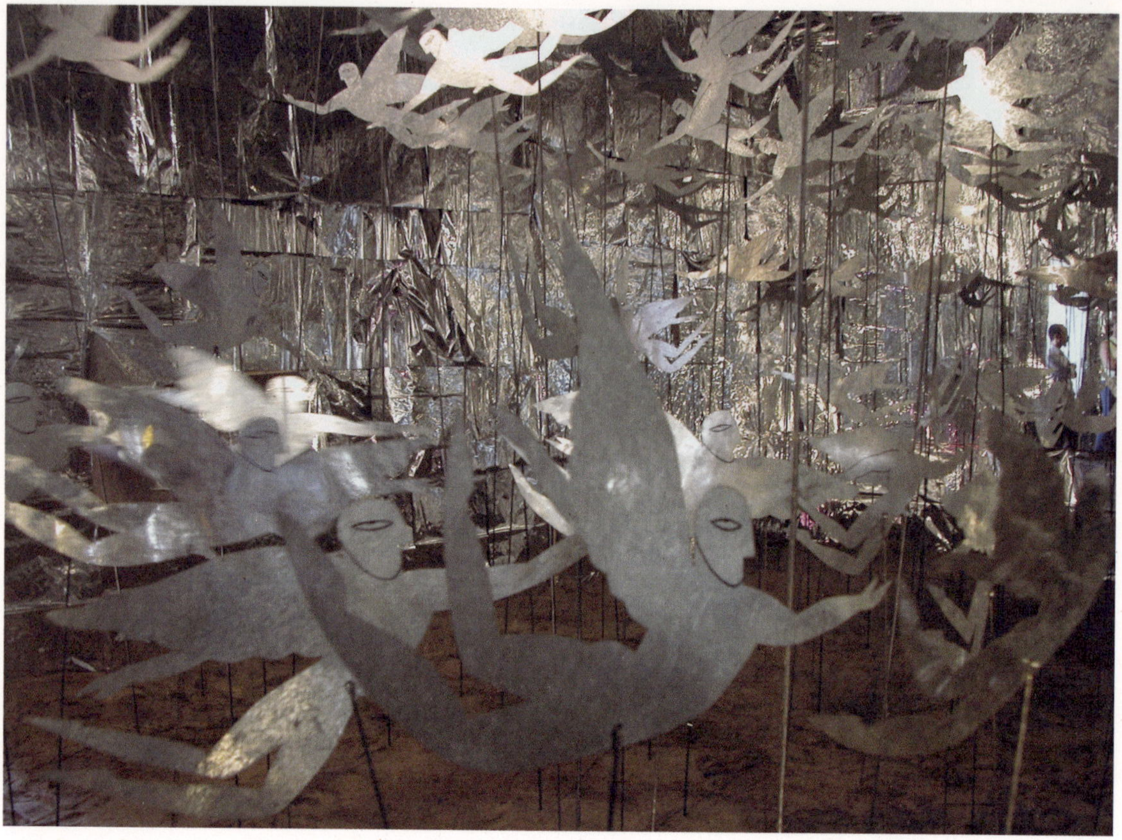

1

2

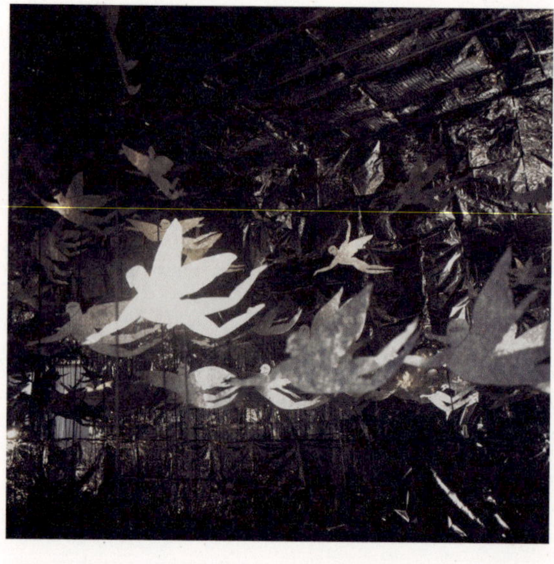

1,2
Trương Tân, *Migratory Birds*, 2003, installation. Courtesy of Trần Lương.

3
Lê Vũ, *The Guise*, 2003, installation with instant noodles. Courtesy of Trần Lương.

4
Veronika Radulovic, *Art is Yellow*, 2003, mixed media, felt pen on plastic tape.

5
Nguyễn Quỳnh Chi, *chairs sold here*, 2003, installation.

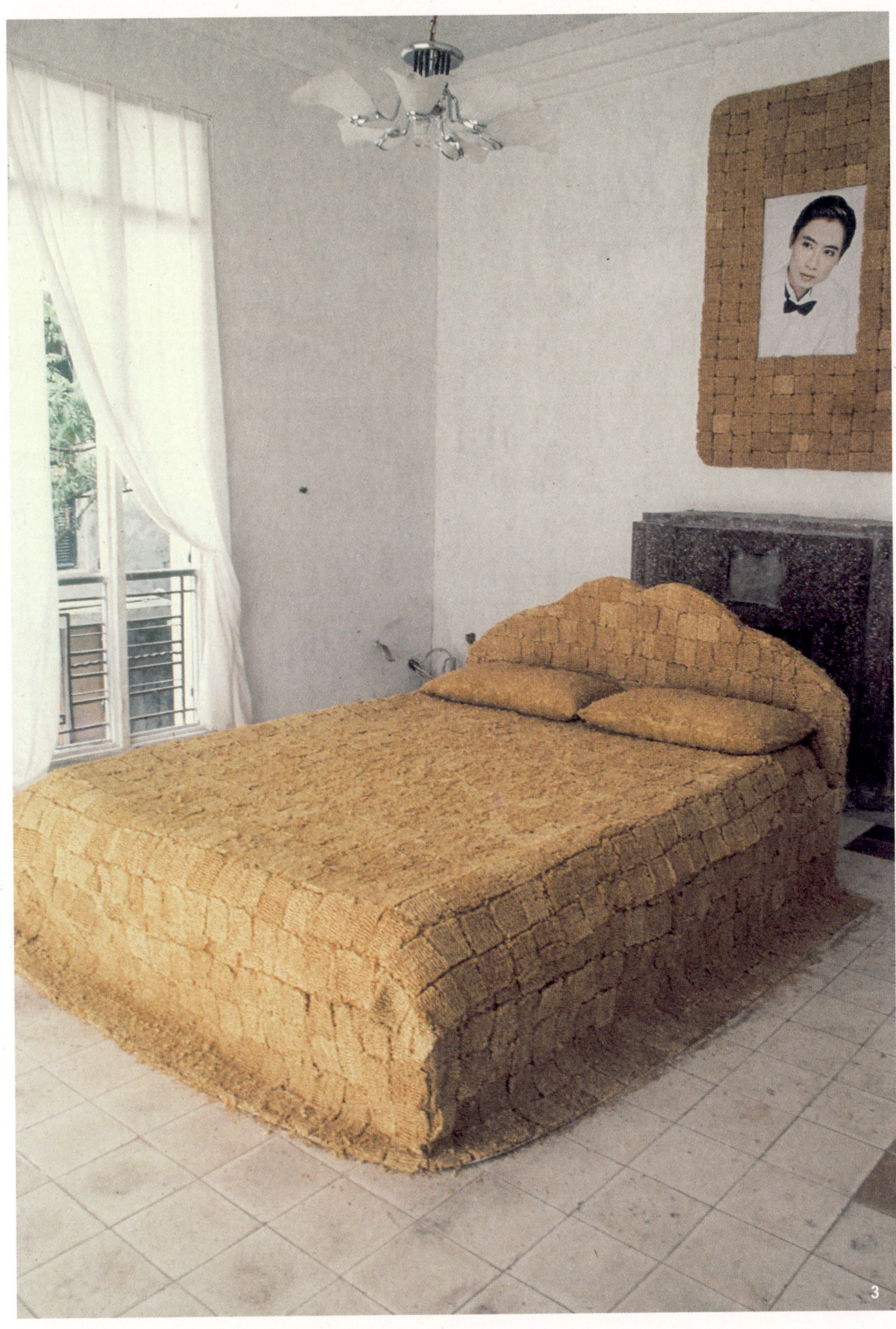

3

4

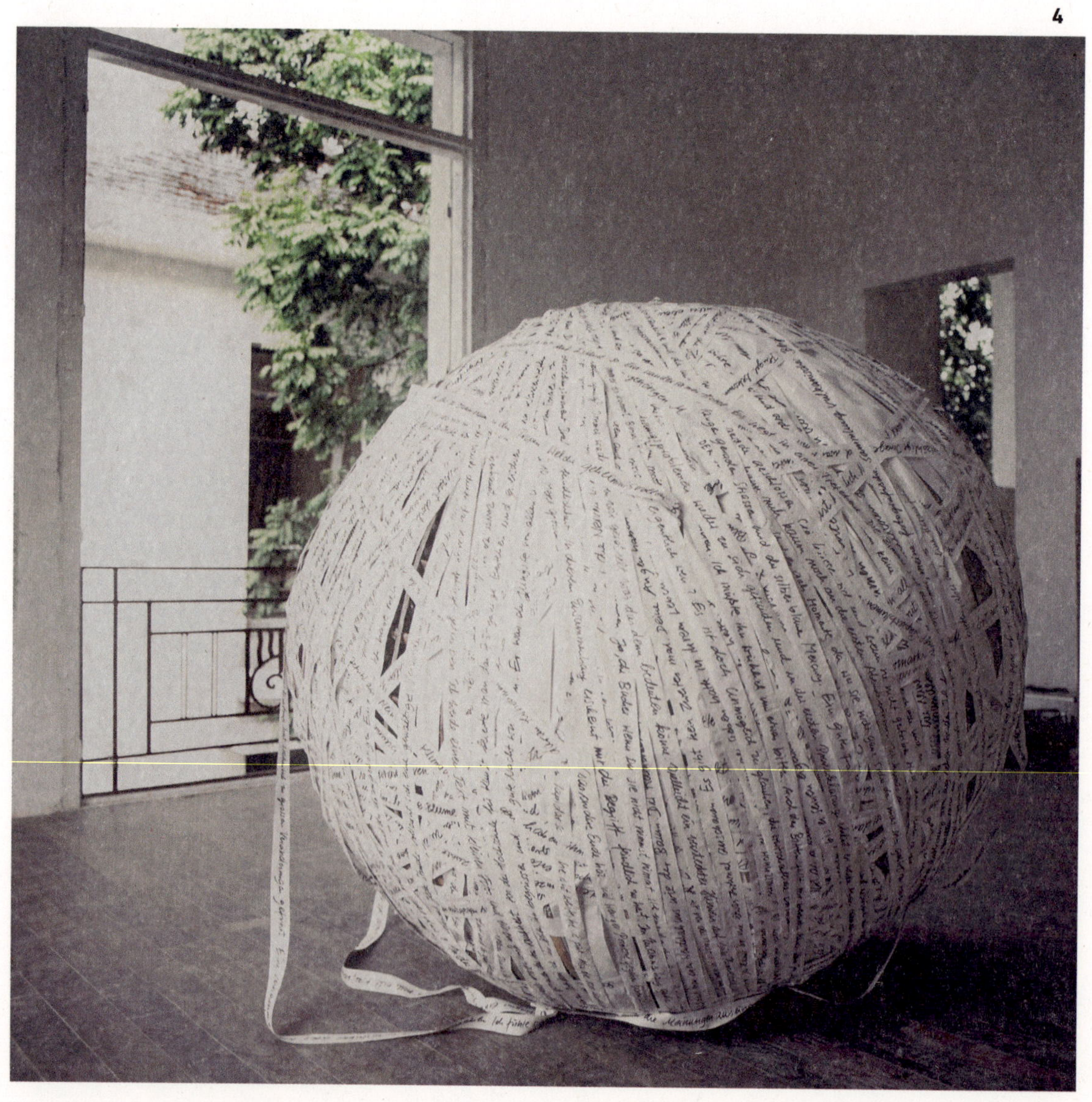

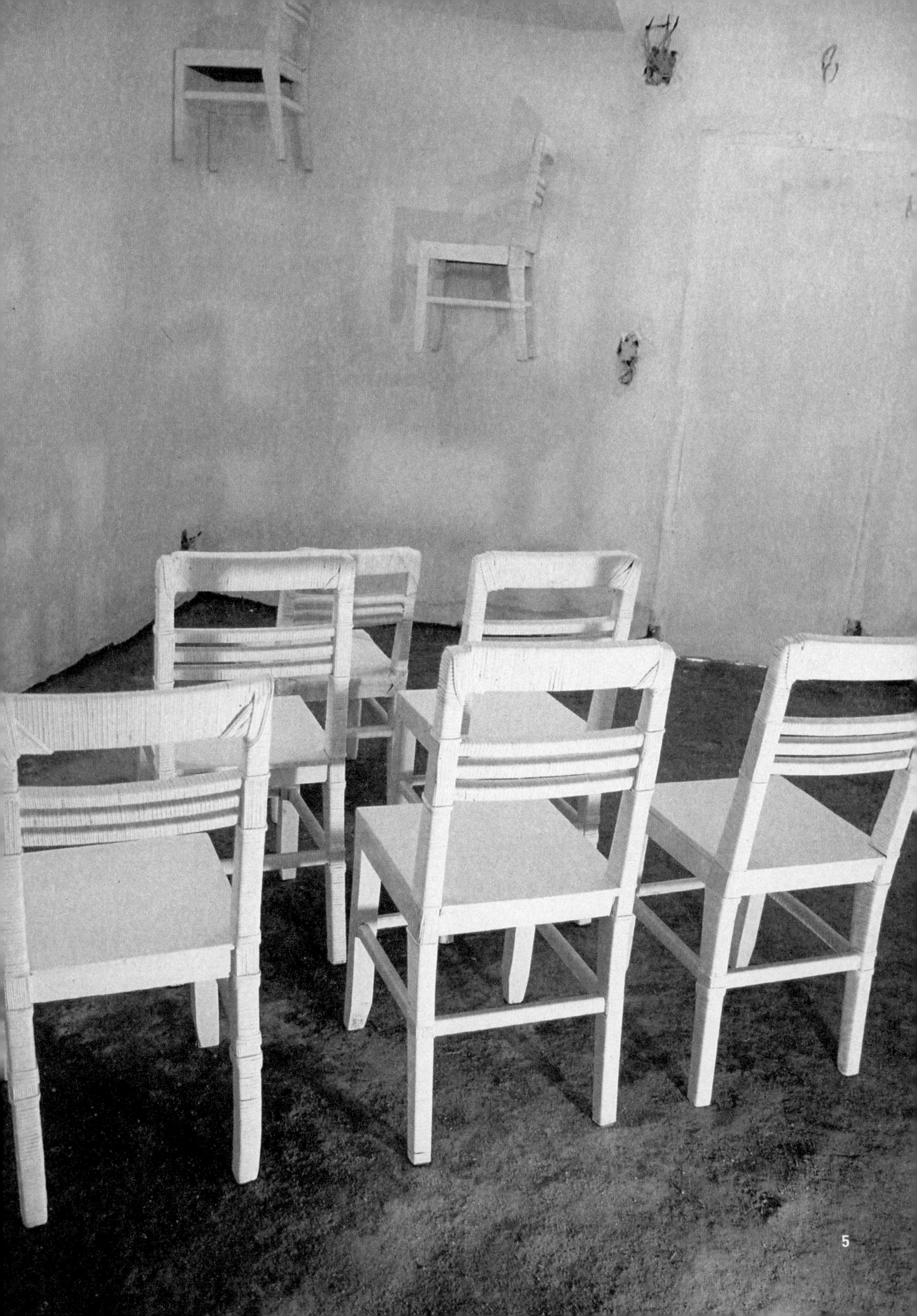

FAIRY TALE SOUP 2003

LOCATION: Hà Nội Opera House Garden DATE: 14 November, 2003 DURATION: half-day CURATOR: Trần Lương SUPPORTED BY: the British Council, SONY Vietnam PARTICIPATING ARTISTS: Trần Lương, Lê Vũ, Phạm Ngọc Dương, Trương Tân, Vũ Thuỵ, Nguyễn Quang Huy, Nguyễn Mạnh Hùng, Nguyễn Minh Phước, Nguyễn Văn Cường, Nguyễn Mạnh Đức, Nguyễn Trí Mạnh, Nguyễn Quỳnh Chi, Nguyễn Xuân Sơn, Vũ Dân Tân, Khuyết Danh.

The idea of this exhibition originated from the video work of the same name by Trần Lương, which includes works such as *Chử Đồng Tử & Tiên Dung* and *Tale of Tò Vò*. In the *Fairy Tale Soup* series Trần Lương performs in front of the camera, reinterpreting folktales within a modern context and infusing them with sarcastic anecdotes. Initially shared with fellow artists at Nhà Sàn Studio, Lương's video work inspired them to create artworks in a similar vein. Shortly thereafter in 2003, he received an invitation to participate in a cultural event from the British Council, celebrating 30 years of UK-Vietnamese diplomatic relations. Given this opportunity, Trần Lương proposed curating the *Fairy Tale Soup* exhibition, which brought together video works from 14 artists.

The exhibition was installed in the garden of the Hà Nội Opera House, featuring a display of 15 TV sets strategically arranged throughout the space to screen video art by 14 artists, each retelling folktales. These works, which were interwoven with allegorical narratives critiquing contemporary society, prompted viewers to consider how culture and information are conveyed and distorted through mass media.

Trần Lương's contribution to the exhibition included the installation of three water tanks positioned along the main pathway of the garden. Filled with bubbling water, smoke and objects resembling giant pots of soup (each with a diameter of 2.5 metres and a height of 80 cm), the tanks served as striking visual focal points. They also acted as the main connecting thread between the various video artworks dispersed within the vast 2000-square-metre space. As part of the interactive experience, audience members were invited to throw their belongings into the tanks, creating a playful and welcoming atmosphere that allowed them to deepen their understanding of the artwork and become active participants in the exhibition. The interactive nature of the installation further enhanced the audience's connection to the concept of *Fairy Tale Soup*.

Situated in a public space in the heart of Hà Nội, the exhibition provided an opportunity for a diverse audience to engage with artwork in a natural setting, free from the confines of traditional gallery or museum spaces.

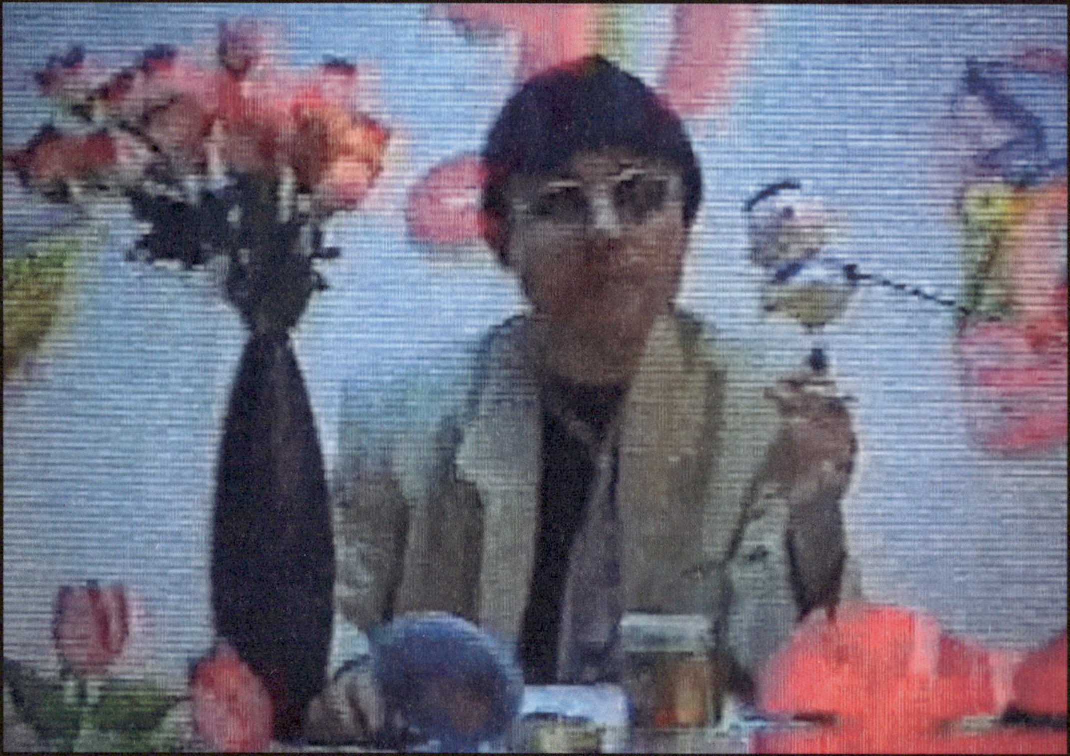

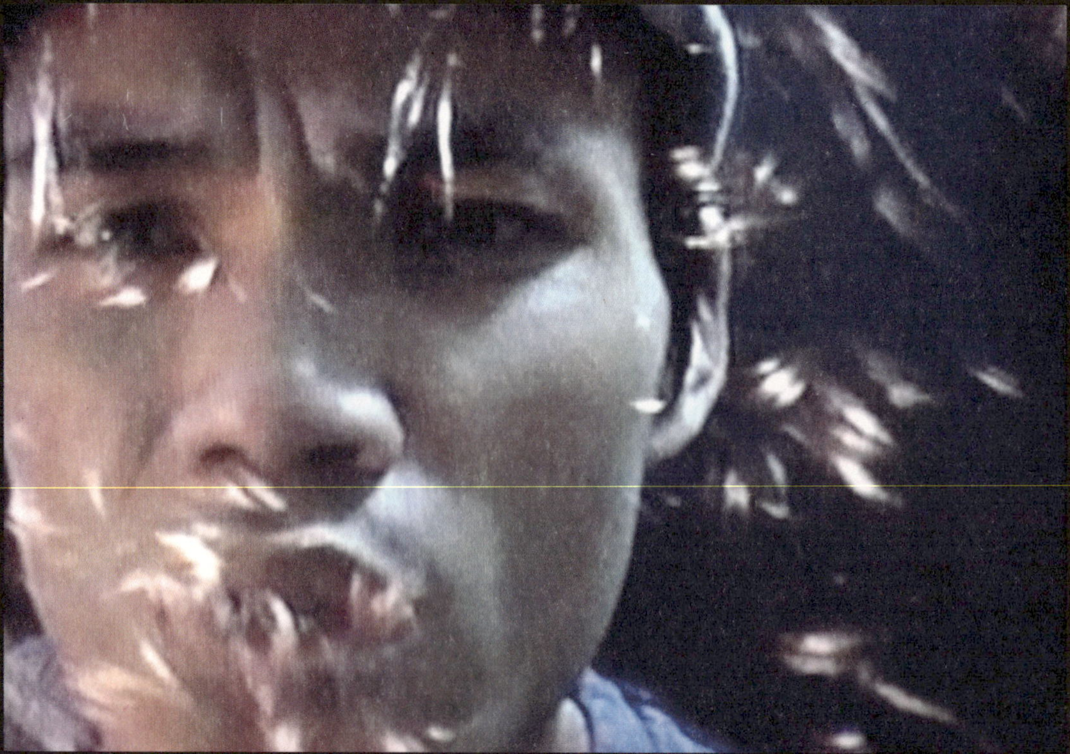

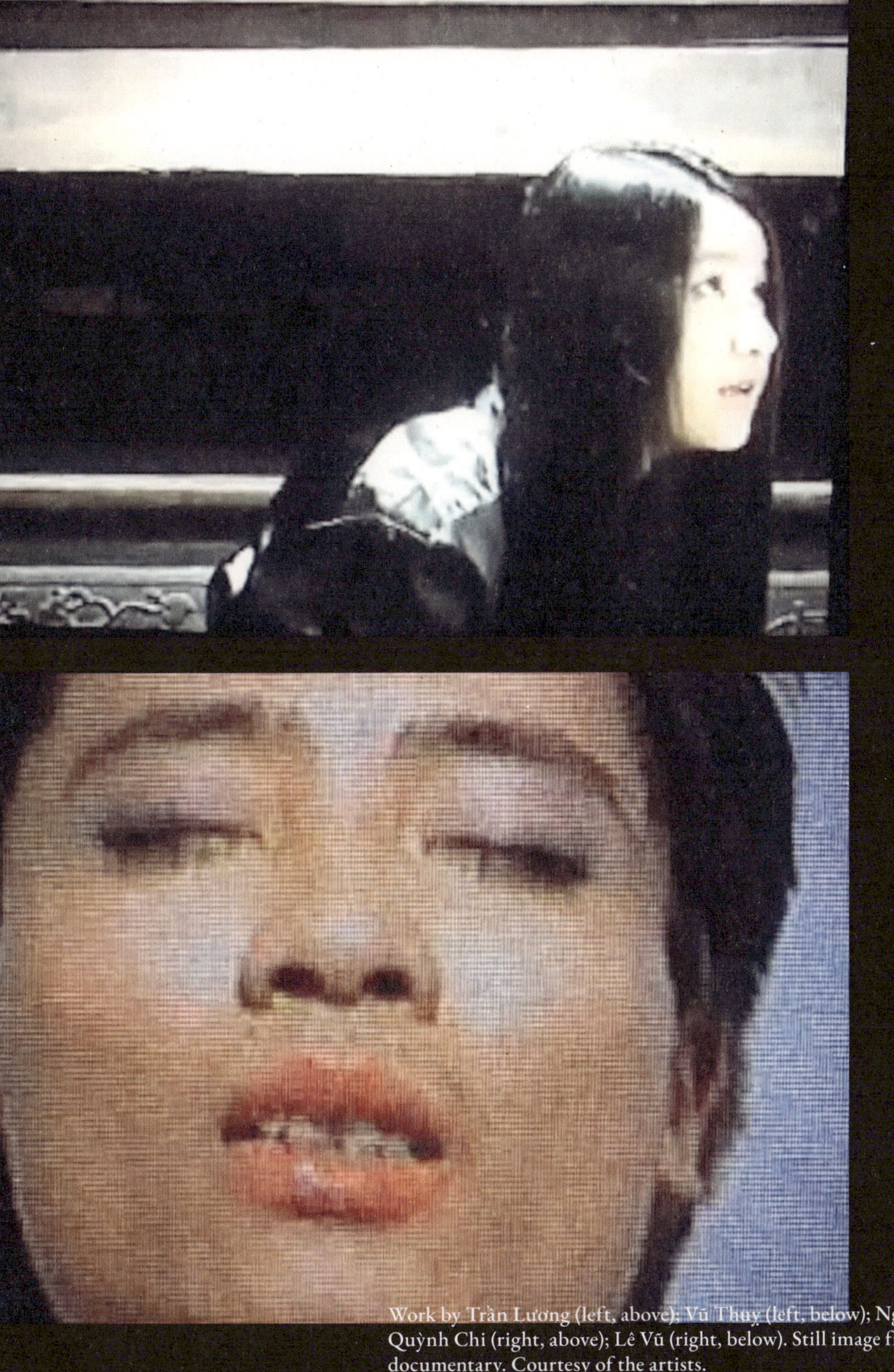

Work by Trần Lương (left, above); Vũ Thụy (left, below); Nguyễn Quỳnh Chi (right, above); Lê Vũ (right, below). Still image from video documentary. Courtesy of the artists.

LIM DIM PERFORMANCE ART FESTIVAL 2004

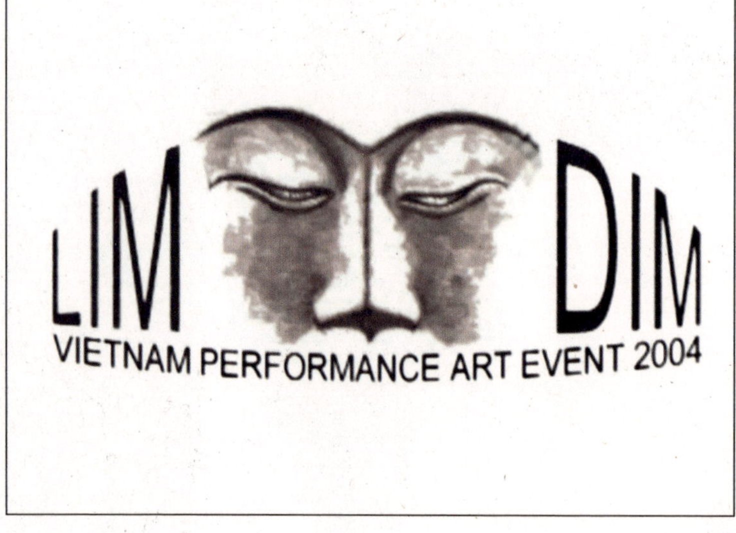

Key visual for *Lim Dim Festival*, designed by artist Nguyễn Minh Thành, featuring a drawing of a Buddha face at its centre. The term "lim dim" in Vietnamese describes half-closed eyes, reflecting a state of meditation and introspection inspired by Buddha's teachings. It also implies a twilight state, a suspicious attitude, or the act of squinting to observe prey.

VENUE: Goethe Institut Hà Nội, British Council, Bến Bạc Restaurant, La Ferme du Colvert Camp, Ryllega Gallery DATE: 9–14 October, 2004 ORGANISED & CURATED BY: Trần Lương SUPPORTED BY: Goethe Institut Hà Nội, British Council, Agency for Cultural Affairs (Government of Japan), Bến Bạc Restaurant, La Ferme du Colvert Camp, Ryllega Gallery. PARTICIPATING ARTISTS: Kirsten Norrie, Jason Lim, Matthias Bolz, Volker Jaeke, Seiji Shimoda, Osamu Kuroda, Yukio Saegusa, Makoto Maruyama, Noriko Ohashi, Rei Shibata, Midori Kadokura, Machi, Mari Tanikawa, Nguyễn Huy An, Phạm Ngọc Dương, Nguyễn Mạnh Hùng, Nguyễn Quang Huy, Nguyễn Hồng Hải, Nguyễn Đức Lợi, Nguyễn Phương Linh, Nguyễn Trí Mạnh, Vũ Hồng Ninh, Nguyễn Minh Phước, Nguyễn Xuân Sơn, Trương Tân, Vũ Nhật Tân, Phạm Đức Tùng, Lê Vũ, Trần Lương.

Lim Dim was an international performance art festival initiated by Trần Lương. The event included live performances, two workshops for students and volunteers and a symposium. Artists from Germany, Singapore, the UK and Japan joined Vietnamese artists, with support from foreign cultural institutions and local private companies.

Performance art has played a crucial role in driving the development of contemporary art in Vietnam since the early 1990s. The dynamic nature of performances has enabled artists to experiment, engage with socio-political issues and adapt to local censorship conditions. The initiation of Lim Dim aimed to continue promoting this art form in the local art scene and establish connections within the Southeast Asian art network, aligning with the rising of performance art festivals in the region during the early 2000s.

Four live performance sessions and two workshops were held at various locations, including the Goethe Institut, the courtyard of the British Council, Ryllega Gallery, two outdoor sites in the mountain area of Hòa Bình and at Bến Bạc Restaurant along the bank of the Red River in Hà Nội. The Lim Dim sites were chosen with the aim of reaching diverse audiences. Previously, interacting with art had been confined to a small group of artists and art lovers in semi-public settings. This opportunity allowed artists to penetrate the locality and receive interactive energy through various landscapes, from urban to natural, while ensuring accessibility to diverse audiences. Different types of sites were chosen from international cultural institutes to semi-public places in the city, alternative art spaces, restaurants and outdoor spaces in the mountains. Trần Lương invited artists to develop new works after visiting each site, and the ideas and arrangements for each session were openly discussed with everyone involved. Live performances took place in semi-public spaces like the Goethe Institut and British Council, as a strategy to avoid intervention from the cultural police, while remaining accessible to the public. However, the third session at the Hòa Bình site, was forced to stop midway through by a group of undercover police. The last session at Bến Bạc Restaurant was shut down before it even began by undercover police officers who threatened the host and artist. After canceling the performance Trần Lương, the artist and restaurant owner invited all the guests to dinner, which evolved into a discussion about censorship and the future of experimental art.

Lim Dim represented a significant milestone, inspiring the art community and nurturing the growth of a new generation of artists who would go on to develop various forms of performance art festivals in the ensuing decades.

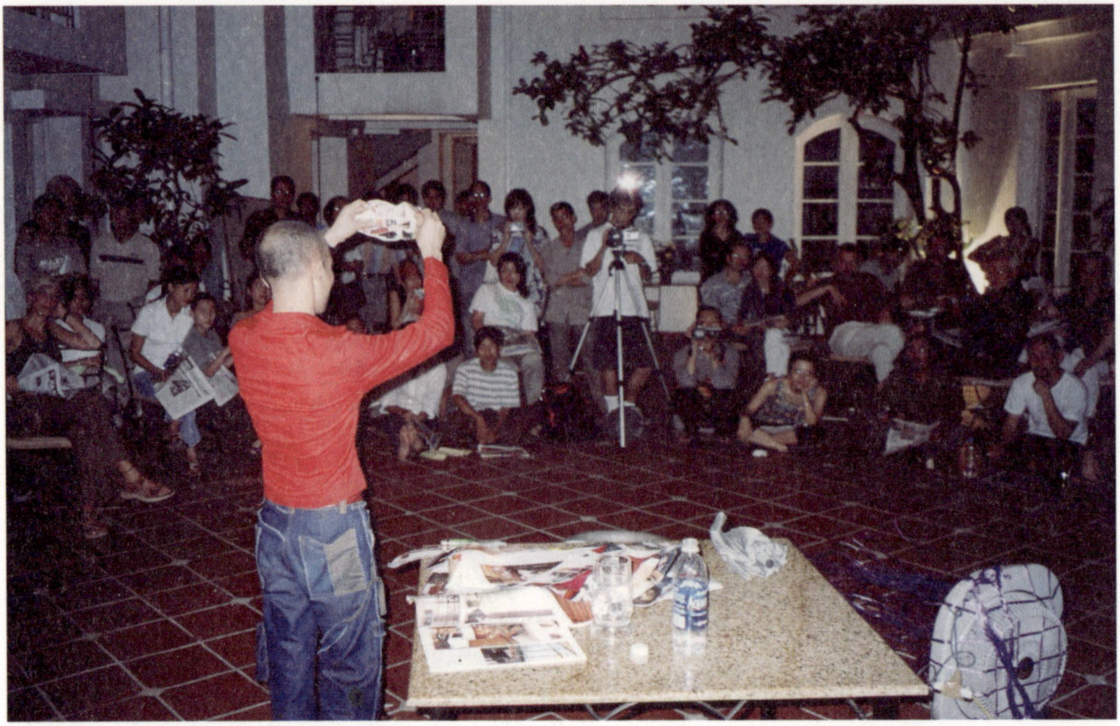

Trương Tân (in a red shirt) during a live performance in the courtyard of the Goethe Institut Hà Nội. Courtesy of Trần Lương.

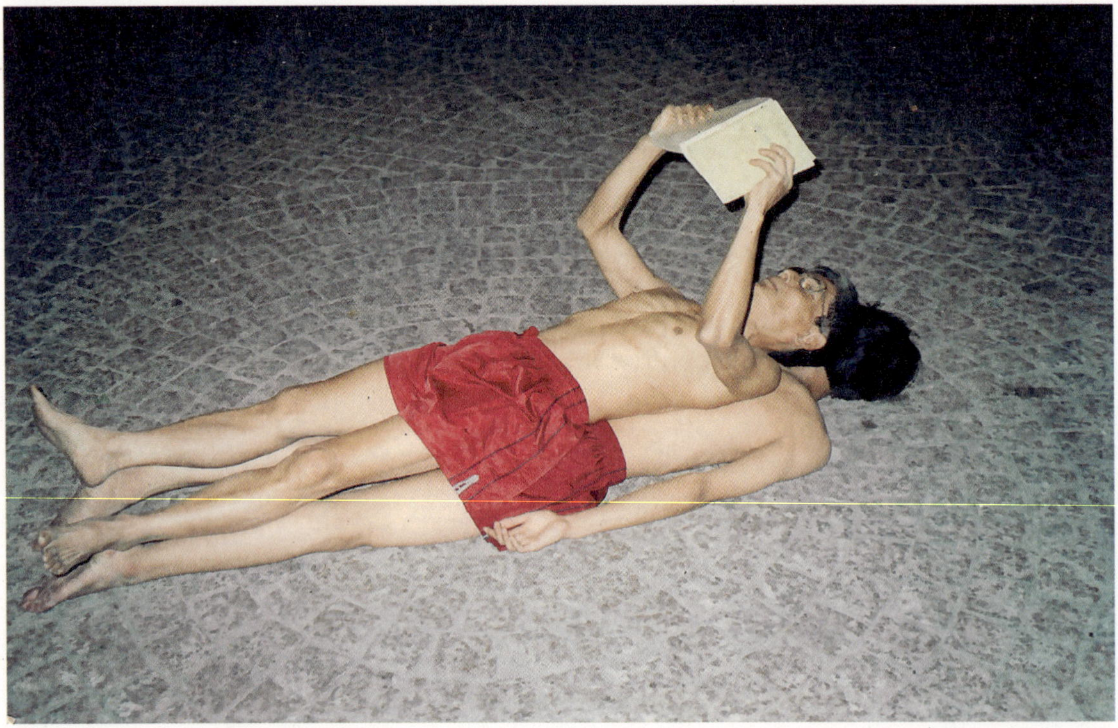

Lê Vũ, *Inheritance*, 2004, durational performance with artist's father, in the courtyard of the British Council. Lê Vũ lies face down on the pavement, while his father lies on him, reading "The Tale of Kieu" (Truyện Kiều), a classic poem that has inspired generations. Courtesy of Trần Lương.

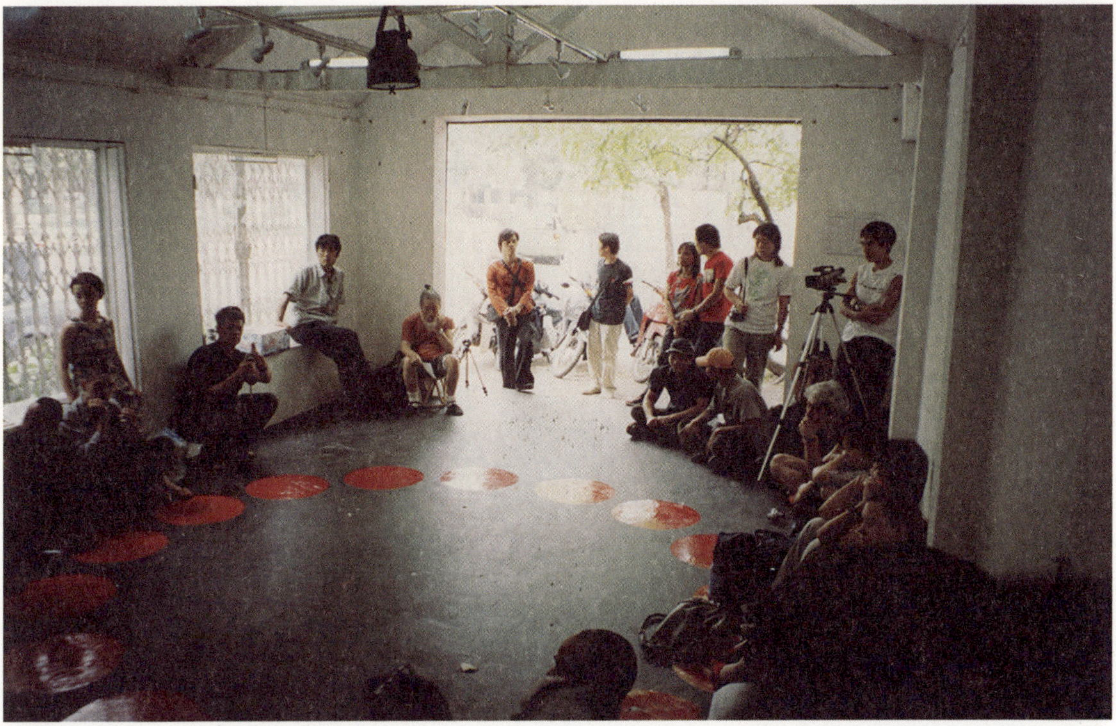

Performance workshop for young artists and students at Ryllega Gallery. Courtesy of Trần Lương.

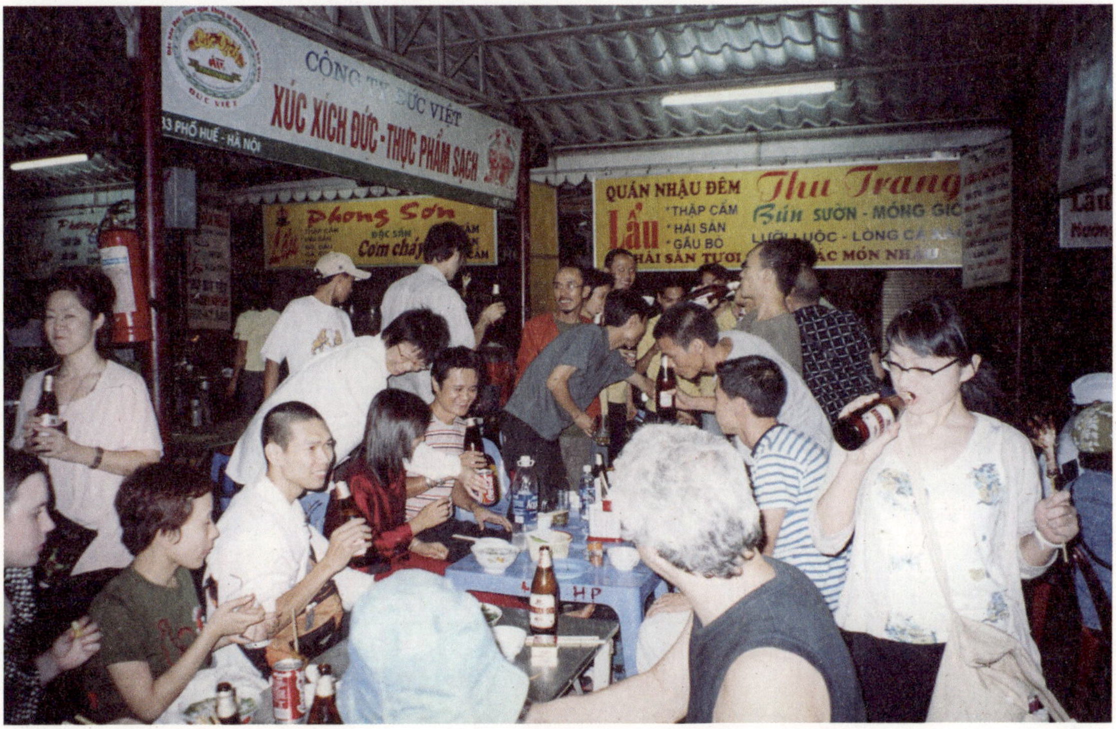

Every performance evening concluded with artists gathering and celebrating at the local night market. Courtesy of Trần Lương.

HÀ NỘI & PHNOM PENH ART EXCHANGE 2006

LOCATION: Reyum Institute of Arts & Culture, Phnom Penh, Cambodia DATE: July, 2006 DURATION: Two weeks ORGANISED BY: Trần Lương, Reyum Institute of Arts & Culture (Ly Daravuth & Ingrid Muan) SUPPORTED BY: Asian Culture Council PARTICIPATING ARTISTS: Trần Lương, Lê Vũ, Nguyễn Minh Phước, Nguyễn Quang Huy, Nguyễn Minh Thành, Trương Tân, Nguyễn Thuý Hằng, Nguyễn Trí Mạnh, Vũ Thuy.

The *Hà Nội & Phnom Penh Art Exchange* program in 2006 was initiated by Trần Lương and sponsored by ACC New York.[1] Nine Vietnamese artists participated in the project, in collaboration with Reyum Institute of Arts and Culture, an NGO dedicated to Cambodian arts and culture, founded by Ingrid Muan and Ly Daravuth. The project formed part of an art exchange series proposed by Trần Lương to ACC, beginning with two cities, Kunming (China)[2] and Phnom Penh (Cambodia). The primary focus was to research the geographical, historical and cultural connections between these countries and Vietnam, as well as to expand and connect the contemporary art network in the region.

The program began with a four-day road trip from Hà Nội to Phnom Penh, first by train from Hà Nội to Ho Chi Minh City, then by bus from Ho Chi Minh City to Phnom Penh. The aim was to allow the artists to experience the transition of the natural environment and culture along the journey. The residency lasted for two weeks. In Phnom Penh, Ly Daravuth, the founder of Reyum, shared presentations on the history and culture of Cambodia, while Trần Lương introduced contemporary Vietnamese art at the Reyum Gallery. These presentations led to discussions and exchanges about shared historical experiences and cultural intersections between the two countries, as well as the approaches to and challenges of developing contemporary art.

In Cambodia in 2006, there was no community of contemporary artists. Only a few Khmer artists from overseas had returned, but they were still very reserved and did not engage in public art activities. Vietnamese artists held a series of workshops with students from the Reyum Art School, which provides free art classes for children from socially marginalised backgrounds who cannot afford to attend regular school. The workshops included practical exercises in Vietnamese lacquer art, performance and installation. During the workshops, each artist collaborated with students to create artworks, either collectively or individually. These works were later exhibited in the Reyum Art School's space, where Trí Mạnh also performed alongside the students at the exhibition opening. Additionally, Trần Lương conducted an interactive performance workshop titled *Moving Forwards and Backwards*.

1. ACC is the Asian Culture Council, an organisation that sponsors Asian artists to attend residencies in New York City.

2. The trip to Kunming took place earlier in 2005. However, the program failed as the artists were prohibited from leaving the country at the Lào Cai border, and all DVD materials and accompanying artworks were confiscated without explanation.

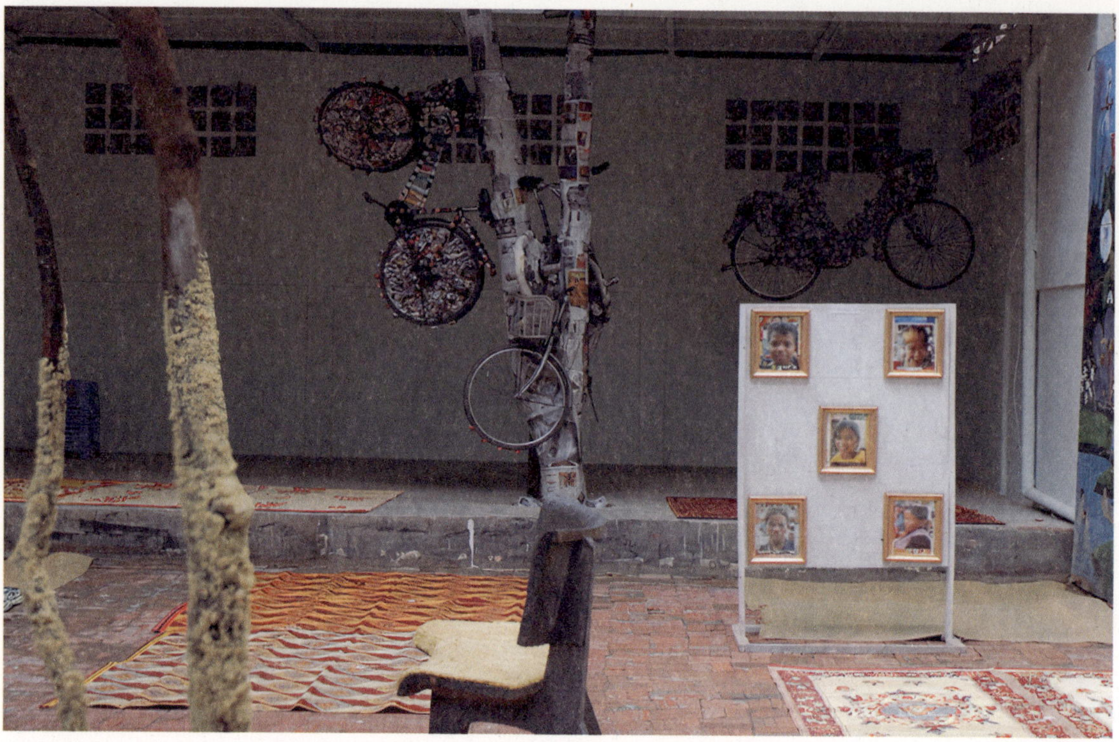

1

2

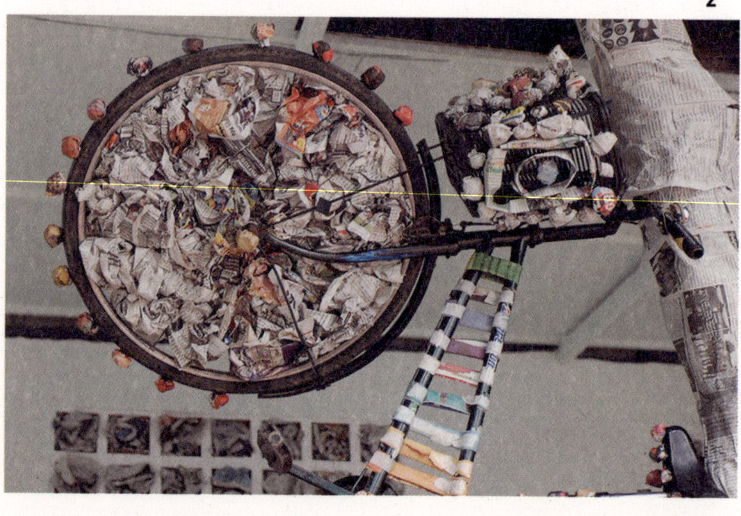

1,2,3
Exhibition in Reyum Art school space featuring trees covered with instant noodles by Lê Vũ and students, alongside a neon light installation in the shape of Buddha by Nguyễn Quang Huy, among other works. Photos: Le Vu. Courtesy of Trần Lương.

3

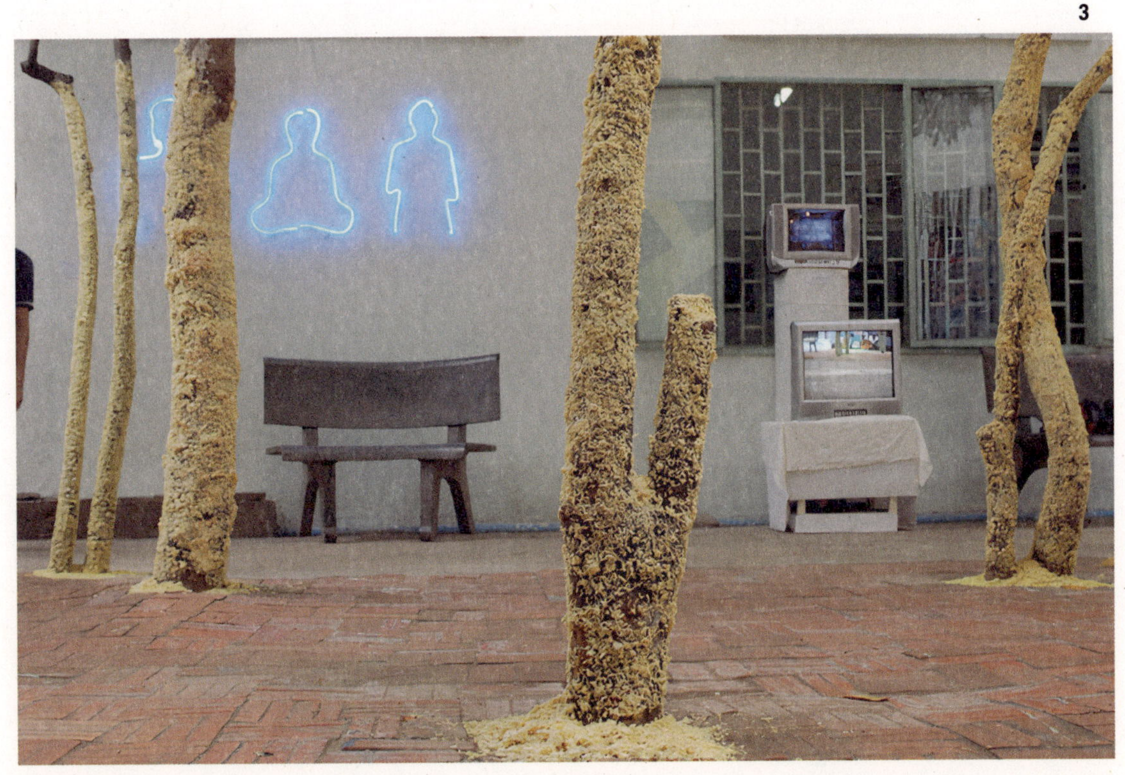

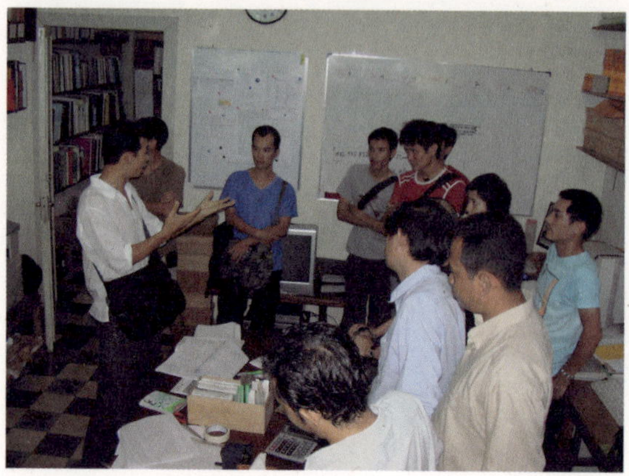

4

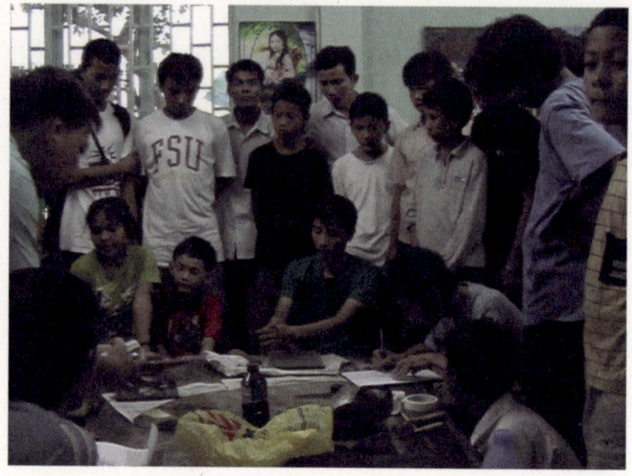

5

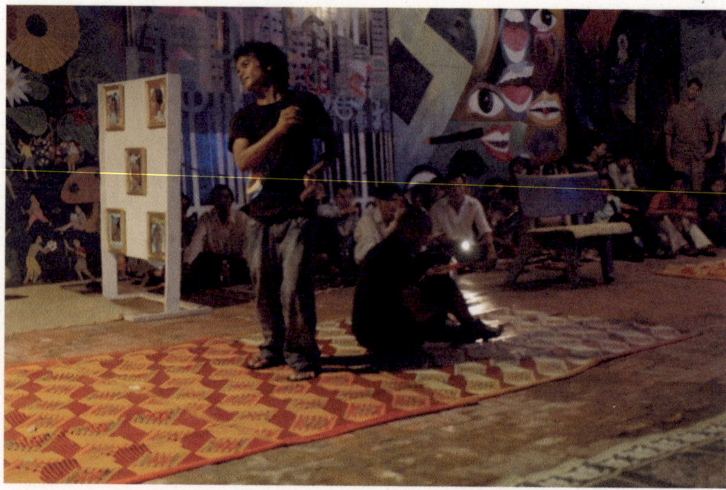

6

4
Ly Daravuth (on the left in the white shirt) introducing Reyum Institute to Vietnamese artists on the first day of the exchange program. Courtesy of Trần Lương.

5
Workshop on Vietnamese traditional lacquer art with students of Reyum Art school, led by Vũ Thuỵ. Courtesy of Trần Lương.

6
Live performance by student Chea Sopheary and Vietnamese artist Trương Tân. Courtesy of Trần Lương.

7
Nguyễn Trí Mạnh performing with students at the exhibition opening, Engaging in a rhythm and clapping game while wearing glasses whose lenses had been obscured with red paint. Courtesy of Trần Lương.

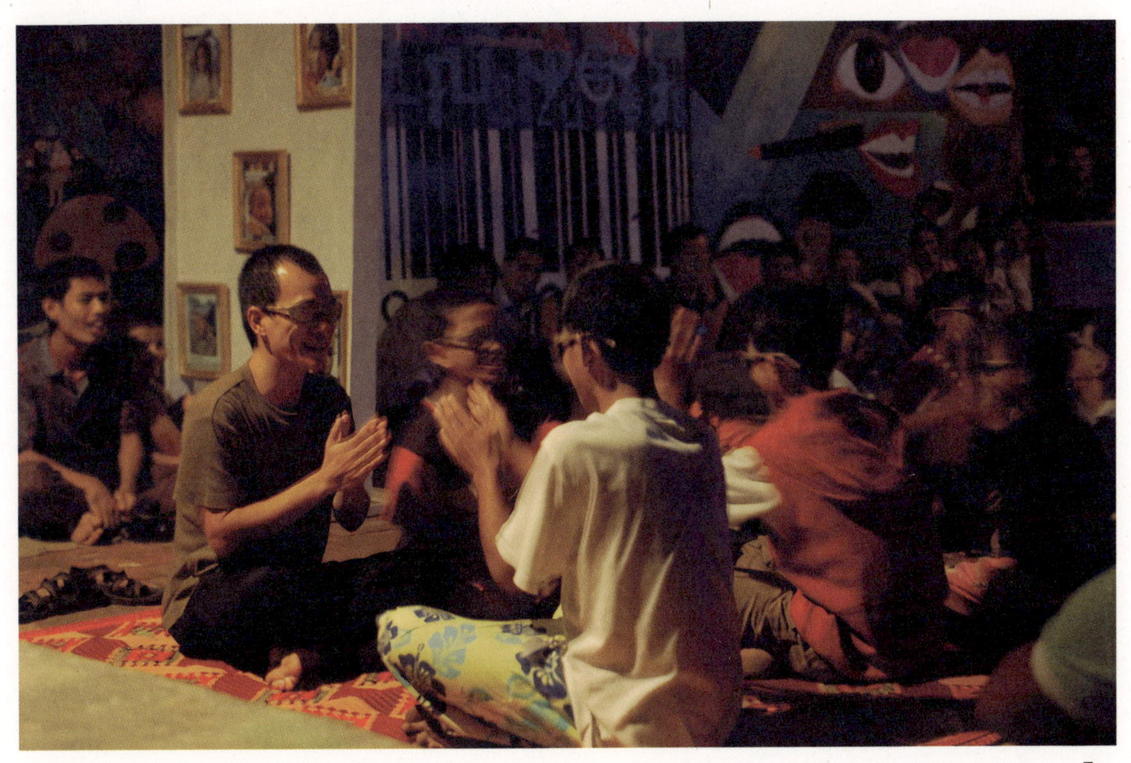

7

NEW FACES - THE FIRST VIETNAMESE YOUNG FINE ARTS FESTIVAL 2007

VENUE: Museum of Hà Nội University of Fine Arts DATE: 15–19 March, 2007 CURATORS: Trần Lương, Đào Minh Tri ORGANISED BY: Ho Chi Minh City Fine Arts Association SUPPORTED BY: Fine Arts Department (Ministry of Culture & Information), The Alliance of Arts and Literature Associations of Vietnam, Swedish International Development Cooperation Agency (Sida), Denmark Cultural Development and Exchange Fund (CDEF) PARTICIPATING ARTISTS: Nguyễn Huy An, Lê Trần Hậu Anh, Mai Anh Dũng, Phạm Ngọc Dương, Lý Trần Quỳnh Giang, Lại thị Diệu Hà, Nguyễn Hồng Hải, Nguyễn Xuân Hoàng, Nguyễn Kim Hoàng, Phạm Gia Hợp, Nguyễn Thế Hùng, Nguyễn Quang Huy, Trần Việt Hưng, Bùi Công Khánh, Nguyễn Ngọc Lâm, Đinh Gia Lê, Nguyễn Phương Linh, Ngô Hồng Lĩnh, Nguyễn Xuân Long, Nguyễn Đức Lợi, Ngô Văn Lực, Ly Hoàng Ly, Nguyễn Thị Thanh Mai, Hoàng Tưởng Minh, Tiến Trọng Nghĩa, Phan Thị Thảo Nguyên, Minh Nguyệt, Vũ Hồng Ninh, Đinh Thị Thắm Poong, Phan Đình Phúc, Nguyễn Văn Phúc, Phan Phương, Trần Kiến Quốc, Siu Quý, Nguyễn Sơn, Lê Kinh Tài , Trần Minh Tâm, Đinh Nhật Tân, Phạm Ngọc Viễn Thành, Trần Hậu Yên Thế, Đinh Khắc Thịnh, Mạc Hoàng Thượng, Trịnh Minh Tiến, Nguyễn Huy Tính, Đỗ Xuân Tịnh, Lê Quý Tông, Nguyễn Thị Thanh Trúc, Lê Việt Trung, Nguyễn Anh Tuấn (Tuấn Mami), Nguyễn Sỹ Tuấn, Khổng Đỗ Tuyền, Đào Long Vân, Lương Văn Việt, Lê Vũ.

New Faces was the inaugural *Young Fine Arts Festival*, a triennial exhibition dedicated specifically to young Vietnamese artists. Initiated by the Fine Arts Association and the Ministry of Culture, the project enlisted Trần Lương as curator, alongside Mr. Đào Minh Tri, President of the Fine Arts Association in Ho Chi Minh City.

The exhibition lasted for five days and was held at the Vietnam University of Fine Arts, utilising both the school museum and the wider campus for displaying and showcasing 54 artworks by artists from across the country. The selection process occurred in two ways. The official method, through the Association, involved an open call where artists submitted proposals with images of their artwork, and the jury selected pieces. Simultaneously, Lương convinced the Association to allow him to work differently; he travelled around, met with artists, encouraged them and commissioned new works. Aware of art censorship, he negotiated with artists to make slight adjustments to their work without altering the main idea, ensuring their pieces could still be selected. The curatorial process not only involved selecting artworks but also persuading and negotiating with artists and the council, sometimes strategising to evade censorship from the Ministry of Culture.

Although there weren't many breakthroughs in artistic ideas, the 2007 festival marked a formal shift transpiring within the traditional bastions of academic art and conservative circles. The event sparked considerable interest among artists, critics and the media. While some lauded the government and the art institution's embrace of contemporary art, others viewed the state's involvement as superficial. The event arose as an inevitable necessity, influenced by the spontaneous development of contemporary art over the previous decade in Vietnam. The second festival was held in 2011 and the project continues to take place every three years.

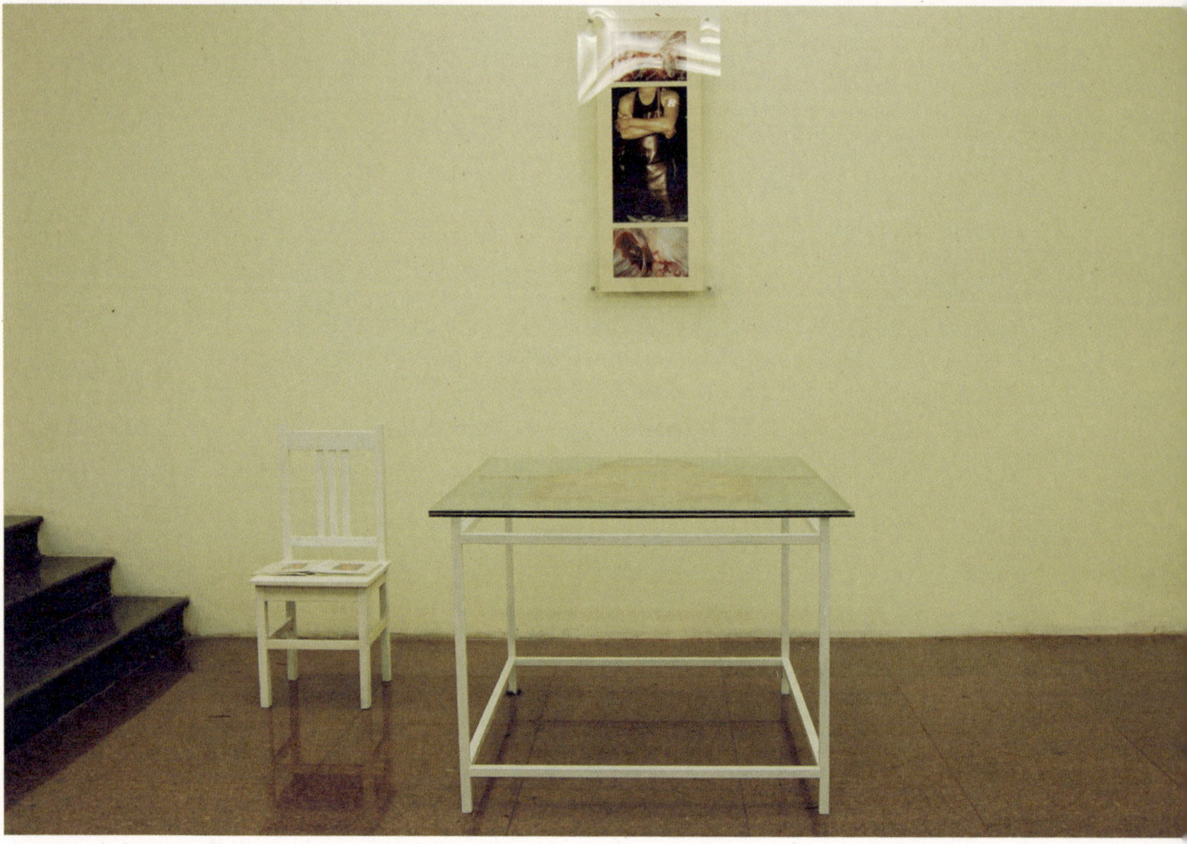

1

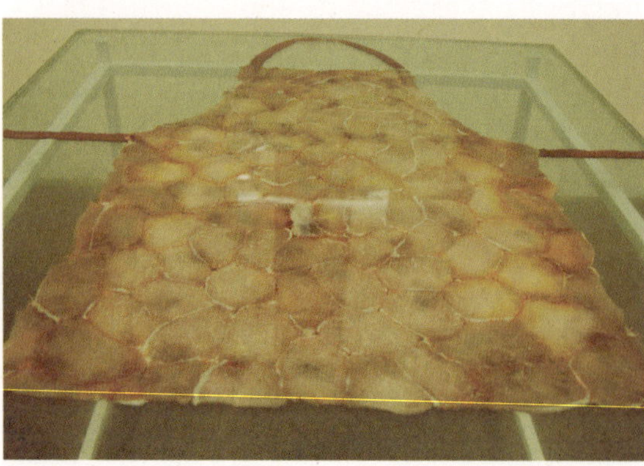

2

1,2

Phan Thảo Nguyên, *Apron*, 2007, installation for pork, glass table, chair and photograph.

3

Nguyễn Huy An (seated on the floor) presents his installation work to the jury board, while Trần Lương explains the work. On the morning of the opening, before the exhibition was open to the public, the jury board, the Fine Arts Association and officials from the Ministry of Culture organised a final walkthrough of the exhibition. During the walkthrough, all the artworks, including performances, were presented and explained thoroughly for final approval. Photo: Nguyễn Thu Hà.

4

Installation view: (foreground) Phạm Ngọc Dương, *Vulture and Turtle*, 2006, silver-gilt wooden sculpture; (background) Lý Trần Quỳnh Giang, *A Gang*, and *Weary Branches*, 2006, wood carving. Photo: Trần Lương.

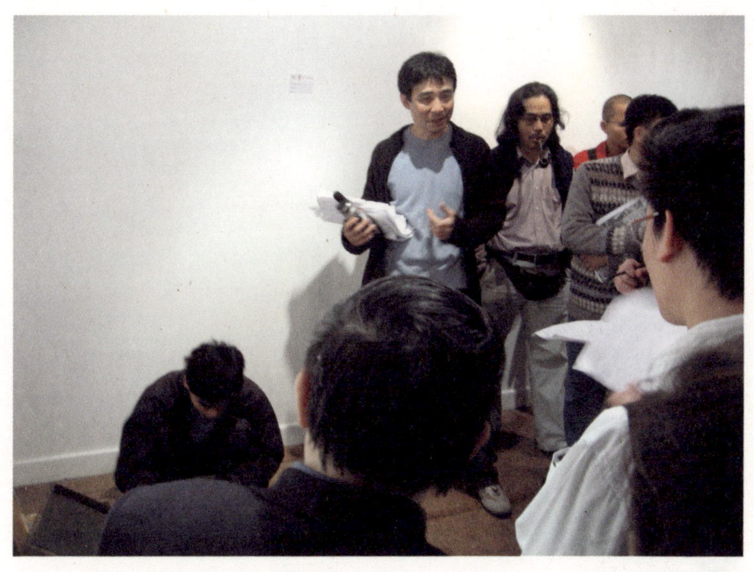

3

4

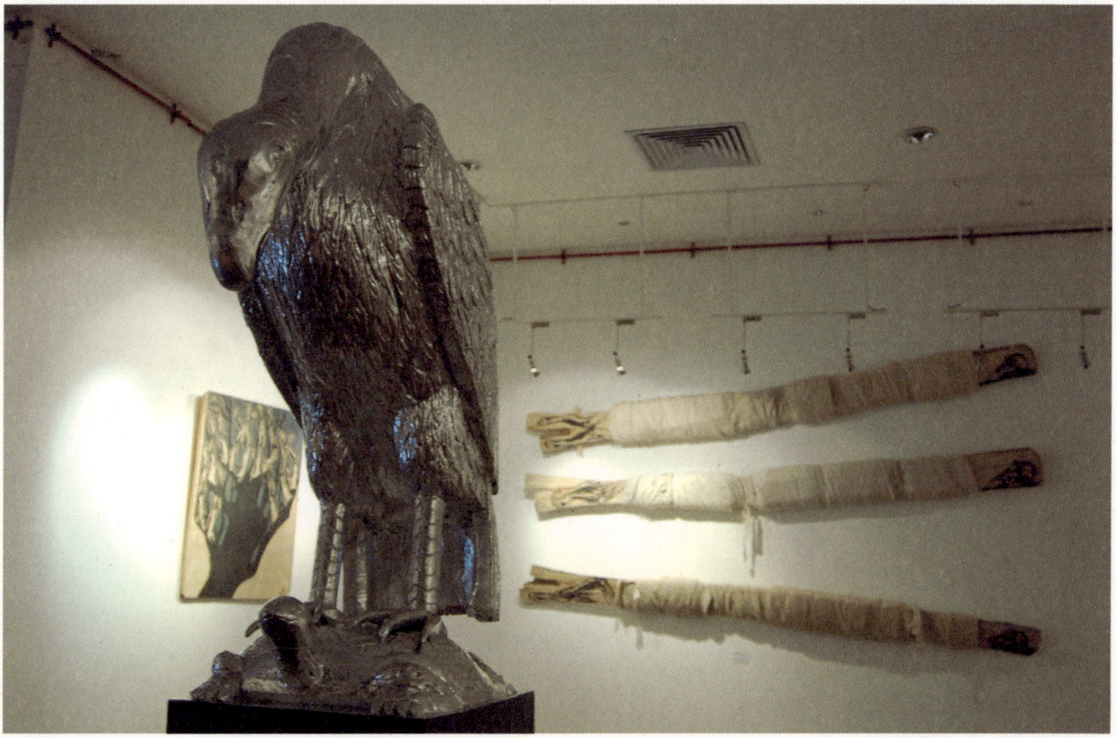

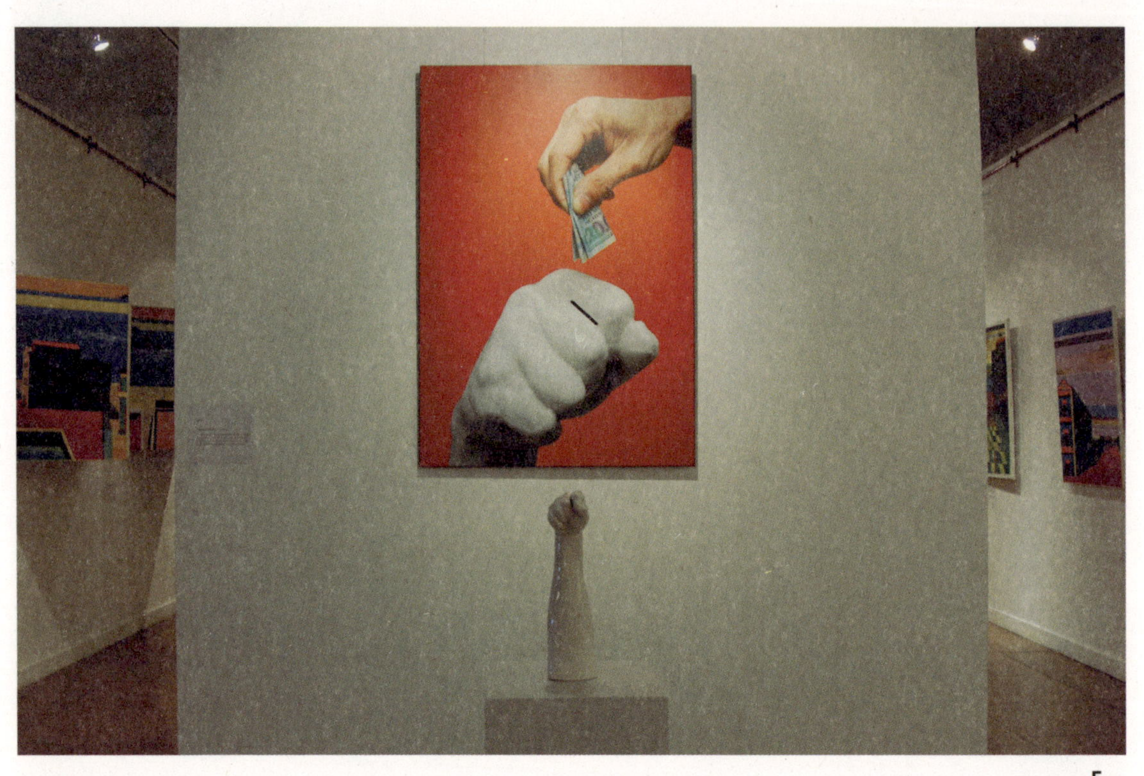

5

5
Lê Vũ, *Saving*, 2007, ceramic and photograph. Photo: Trần Lương.

6
Nguyễn Hồng Hải, *20 and* ..., 2007, installation. Photo: Trần Lương.

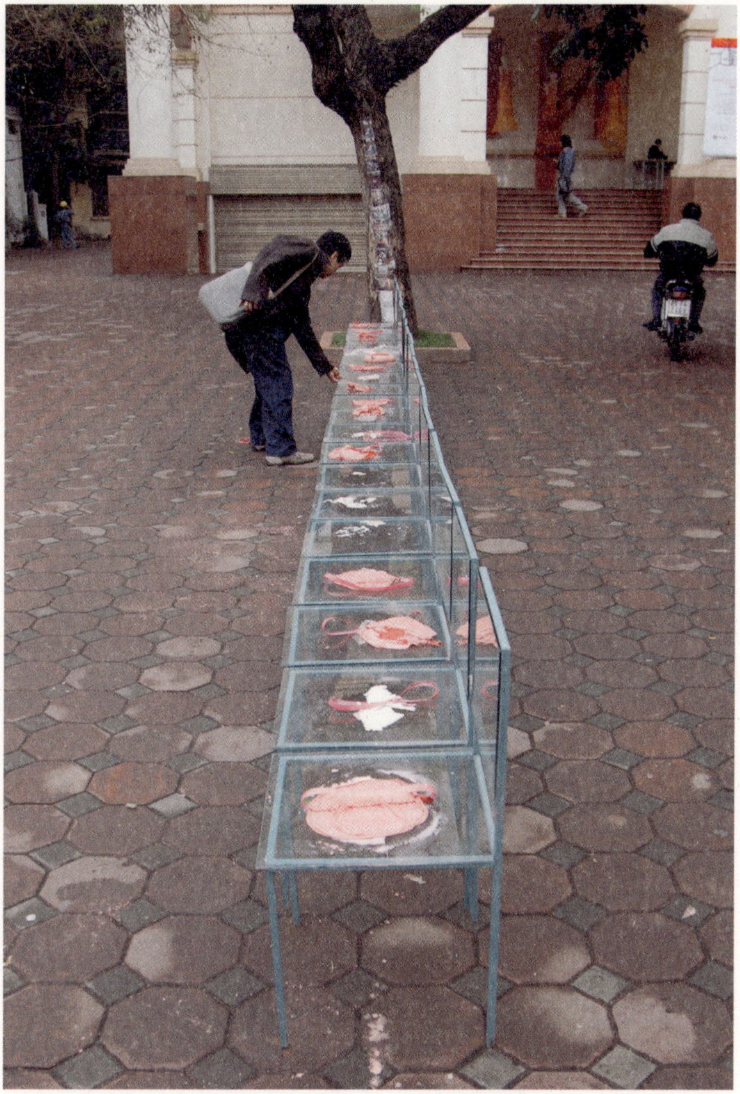

6

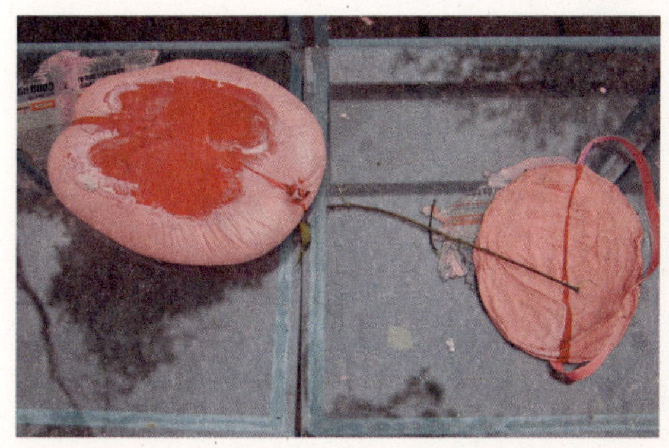

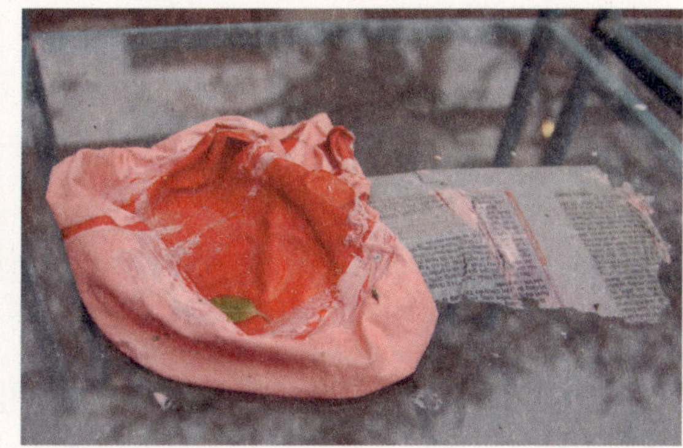

KẾT NỐI: VIETNAM SINGAPORE PERFORMANCE ART EVENT 2008

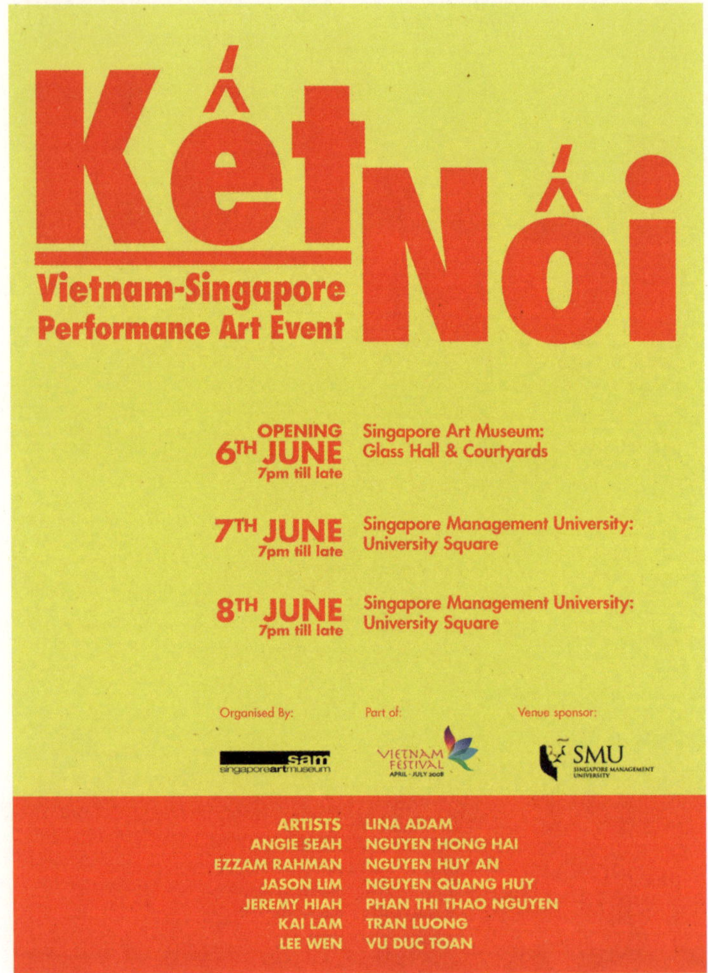

Poster, *Kết Nối: Vietnam-Singapore Performance Art Event*.

LOCATION: Post Museum, Singapore Art Museum, Singapore Management University DATE: 27 May–8 June, 2008 CURATORS: Trần Lương, Lee Wen, Jason Lim COORDINATOR: Tan Siuli ORGANISED BY: Singapore Art Museum ARTISTS: anGie Seah, Kai Lam, Jason Lim, Lee Wen, Jeremy Hiah, Lina Adam, Ezzam Rahman, Nguyễn Huy An, Nguyễn Hồng Hải, Phan Thị Thảo Nguyên, Nguyễn Quang Huy, Trần Lương, Vũ Đức Toàn.

Kết Nối (meaning "to connect" in Vietnamese) was an exchange program between young contemporary artists from Vietnam and Singapore, primarily focused on sharing experiences of practising performance art within their local contexts. Despite their differing economic and social conditions, the two countries share a common history of colonisation and struggles with issues of freedom of expression under current governance (performance art was banned in Singapore until 2004). Additionally, many performance art festivals in Southeast Asia primarily showcase artists' works, with little emphasis on post-performance exchange or discussion.

The program aimed to stimulate dialogue among artists and curators to cultivate a theoretical understanding of performance art within the Southeast Asian context. Spanning ten days at the Singapore Post Museum space, it encompassed dynamic discussions and workshops moderated by Singaporean artists Lee Wen, Jason Lim and Trần Lương. These workshops, led by artists of diverse backgrounds and practices, varied in duration from half-day sessions to intensive nine-day workshops, and covered topics such as experimenting with electronic sound (Kai Lam) and learning traditional techniques for germinating rice seeds (Trần Lương). Additionally, activities such as outdoor barbecues, discussions and group improvisation performances were also included. This multidirectional dialogue fostered an environment where artists could openly share their creative processes, while also gaining insights and inspiration from their peers. For Vietnamese artists, it was an opportunity to develop a theoretical understanding of performance art and learn essential event organisation and management skills, which were lacking in Vietnam's educational landscape. The workshops closed with a series of performances over three nights by participating artists, which took place at the Singapore Art Museum and within the premises of the Singapore Management University.

Kết Nối: Vietnam - Singapore was part of the exhibition *Post-Đổi Mới: Vietnamese Art After 1990*, curated by Joyce Fan. The show was the visual art component of the Vietnam Festival celebrating 35 years of diplomatic ties between Singapore and Vietnam.

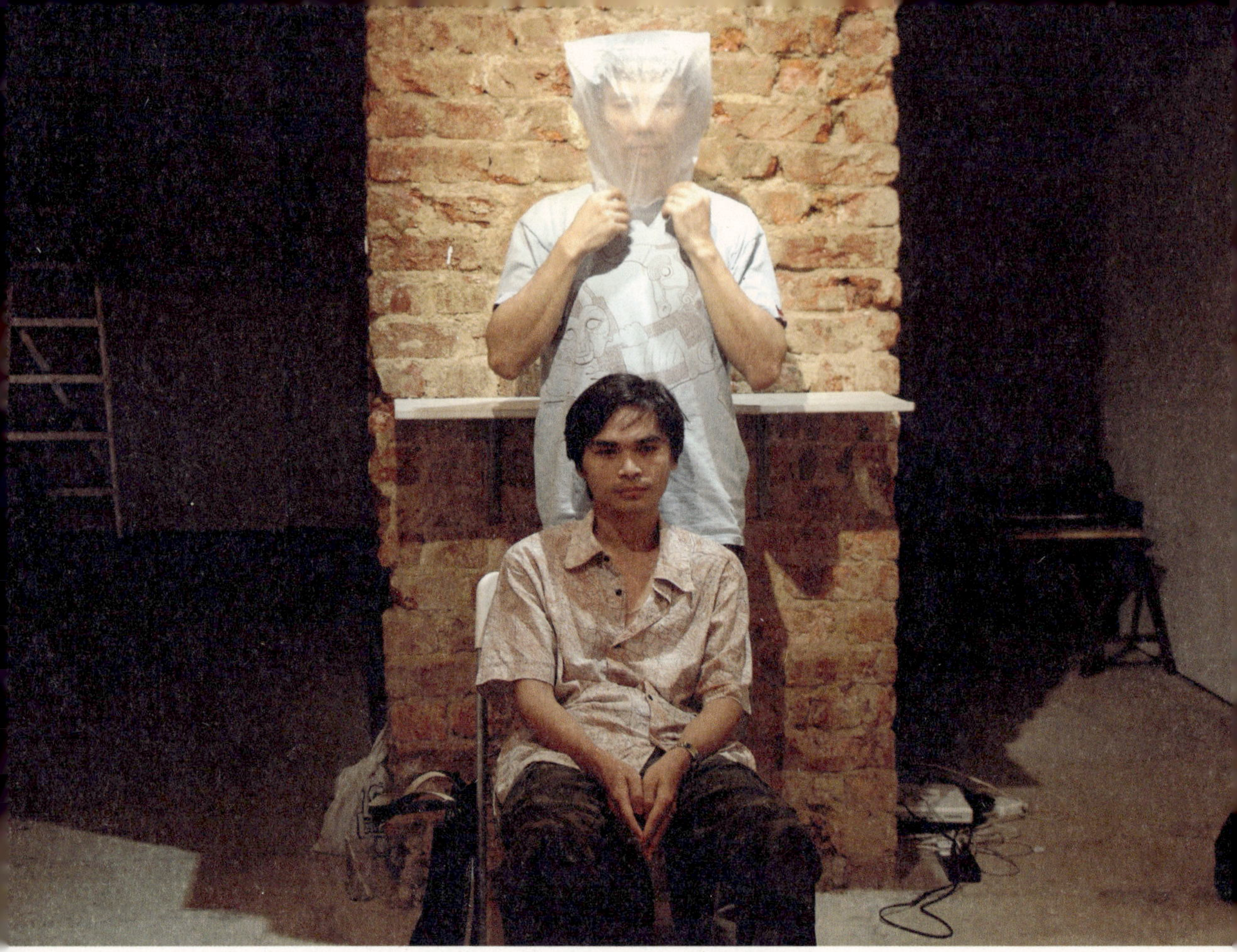

2

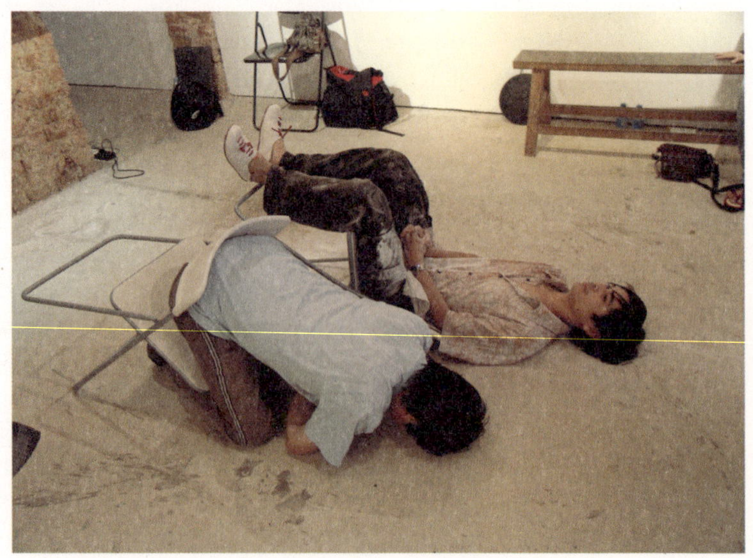

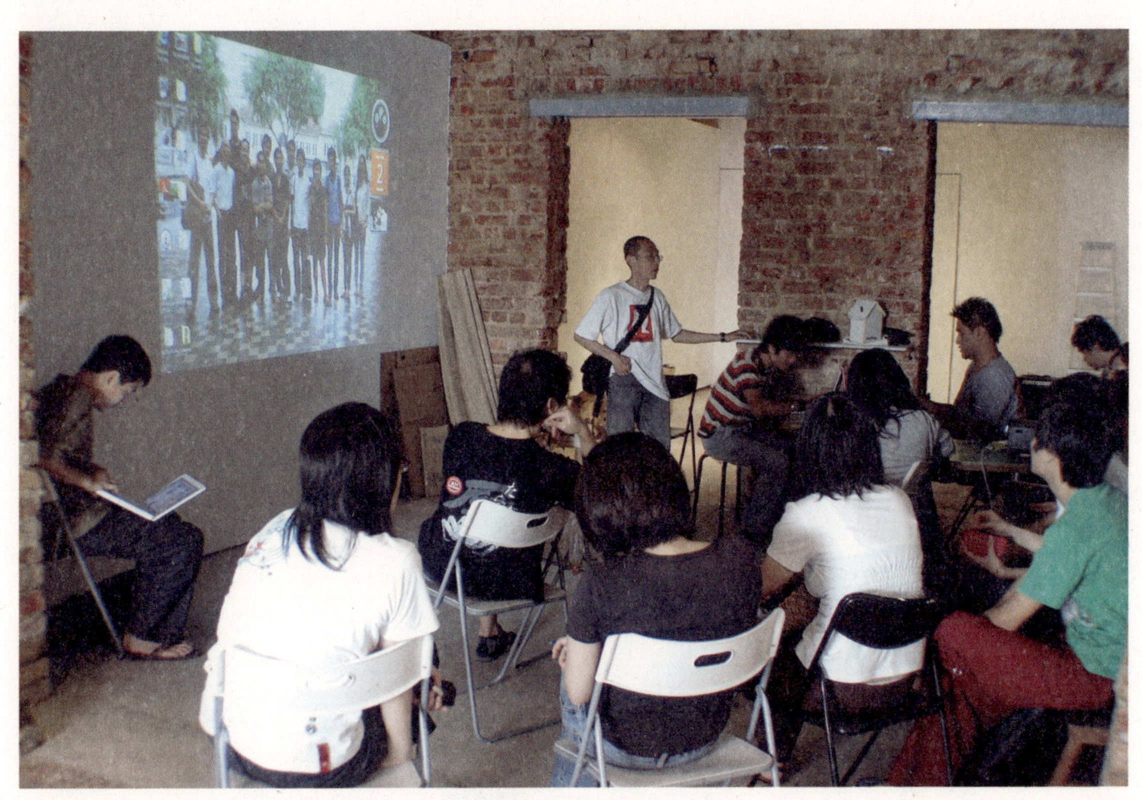

3

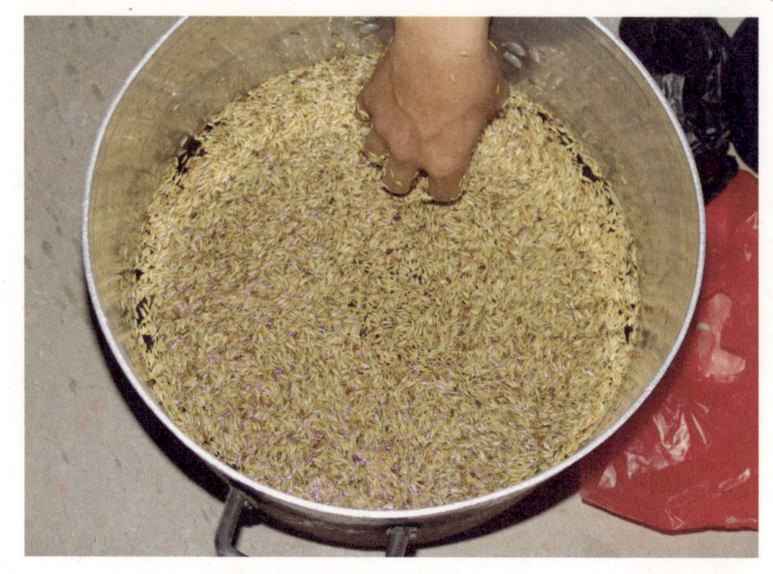

4

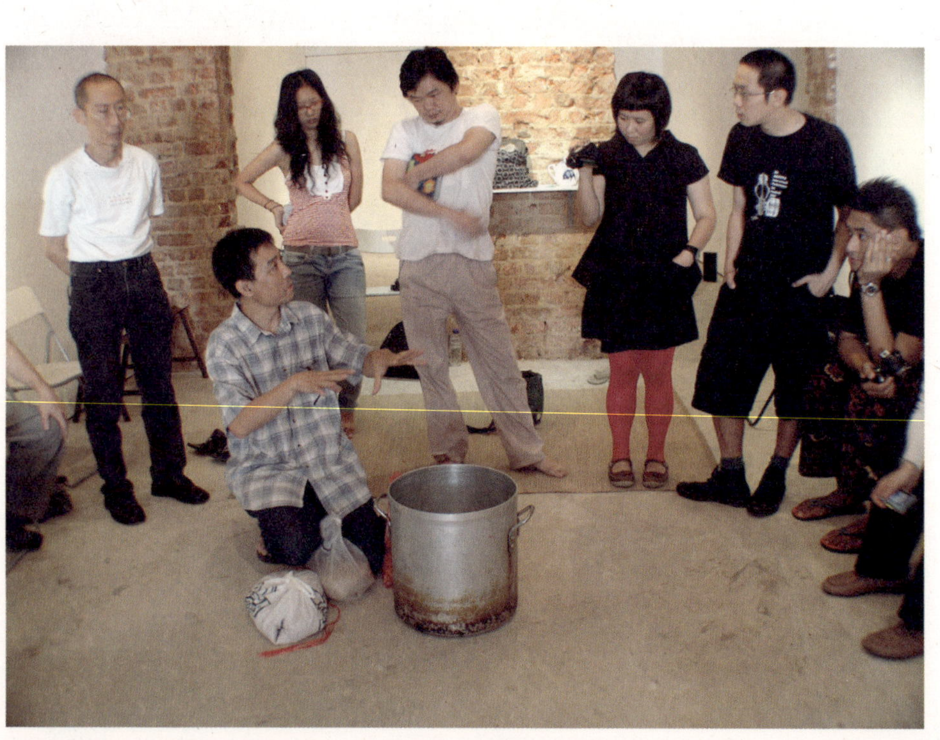

5

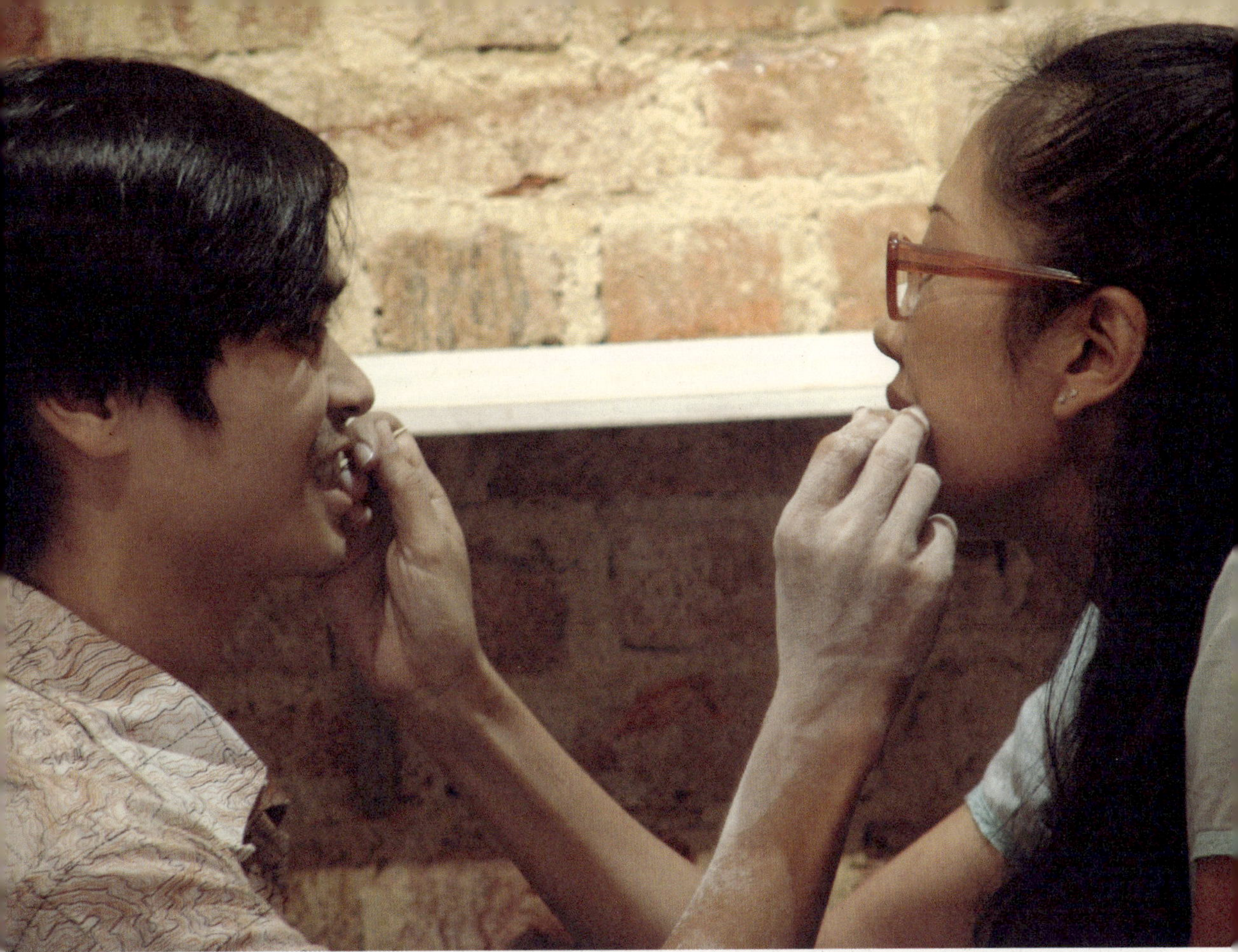

6

1,2

Nguyễn Hồng Hải (pink shirt) and Jason Lim (blue shirt) participate in a group improvisation performance session. Lee Wen Archive. Courtesy of Lee Wen and Asia Art Archive.

3

Trần Lương prepares for the presentation on Vietnamese performance art with participating artists. Courtesy of Trần Lương.

4,5

Trần Lương demonstrates the traditional method for germinating rice seeds to the participating artists. Courtesy of Trần Lương.

6

Tooth-picking performance by Nguyễn Hồng Hải (left). Lee Wen Archive. Courtesy of Lee Wen and Asia Art Archive.

LIM DIM 2009

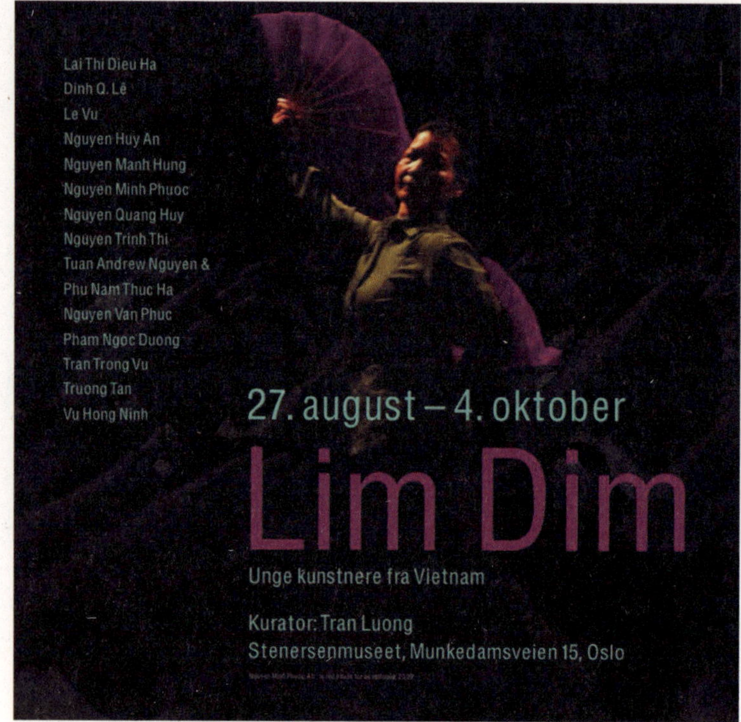

Lim Dim exhibition leaflet.

VENUE: The Stenersen Museum, Oslo, Norway DATE: 27 August–4 October, 2009 CURATOR: Trần Lương ORGANISED BY: The Stenersen Museum, The Du store verden! Network SUPPORTED BY: Art Council Norway, Fritt Ord, Norwegian Embassy of Hà Nội, Municipality of Oslo ARTISTS: Lại Thị Diệu Hà, Đinh Q.Lê, Lê Vũ, Nguyễn Huy An, Nguyễn Mạnh Hùng, Nguyễn Minh Phước, Nguyễn Quang Huy, Nguyễn Trinh Thi, Tuấn Andrew Nguyễn & Phù Nam Thúc Hà, Nguyễn Văn Phúc, Phạm Ngọc Dương, Trần Trọng Vũ, Trương Tân, Vũ Hồng Ninh.

Lim Dim was an exhibition that showcased contemporary Vietnamese art, providing insights into the practices and evolution of contemporary art in Vietnam since 2000 through a collective of socially interconnected artists. Born in different historical periods of Vietnam, the participating artists have diverse upbringings, perspectives on life, beliefs and artistic concerns, which sometimes clashed. Despite the generational gaps, they shared camaraderie, often bonding over meals and drinks and a shared experience of the outsider status of official non-recognition. The exhibition featured both old and newly commissioned works, presenting a medley of perspectives, including reflections on Vietnam's tumultuous history (by artists Đinh Q.Lê and Nguyễn Văn Phúc), skeptical views on identity and religion within the contemporary context (by Phạm Ngọc Dương, Vũ Hồng Ninh and Nguyễn Quang Huy) and challenges to societal prejudices against artists themselves (as seen in works by Lại Diệu Hà and Trương Tân).

Lim Dim marked the first medium-sized exhibition of Vietnamese contemporary art presented in a Western country, offering a very rare opportunity for Vietnamese domestic contemporary art to appear independently. This also marked the first time an exhibition addressed post-war issues, contributing to the historical recognition and evaluation of the generation of artists who grew up during the "open door" period. Previously, individual Vietnamese artists or groups living outside of Vietnam made only sporadic appearances in exhibitions related to the Cold War, in which artist lists often mixed foreign artists with Vietnamese artists living overseas.

The term "lim dim" in Vietnamese refers to partially closed eyes. It implies a sense of twilight and a cautious and suspicious attitude. The artworks included in the exhibition were linked to the central issues of social transformation in the early 2000s, capturing significant events spanning from ideological shifts to economic realities, evoking a sense of doubt and introspection. They reflected the collective mood of the Vietnamese people, many of whom, if not disillusioned, exhibit indifference towards the state apparatus, religion and societal ethics.

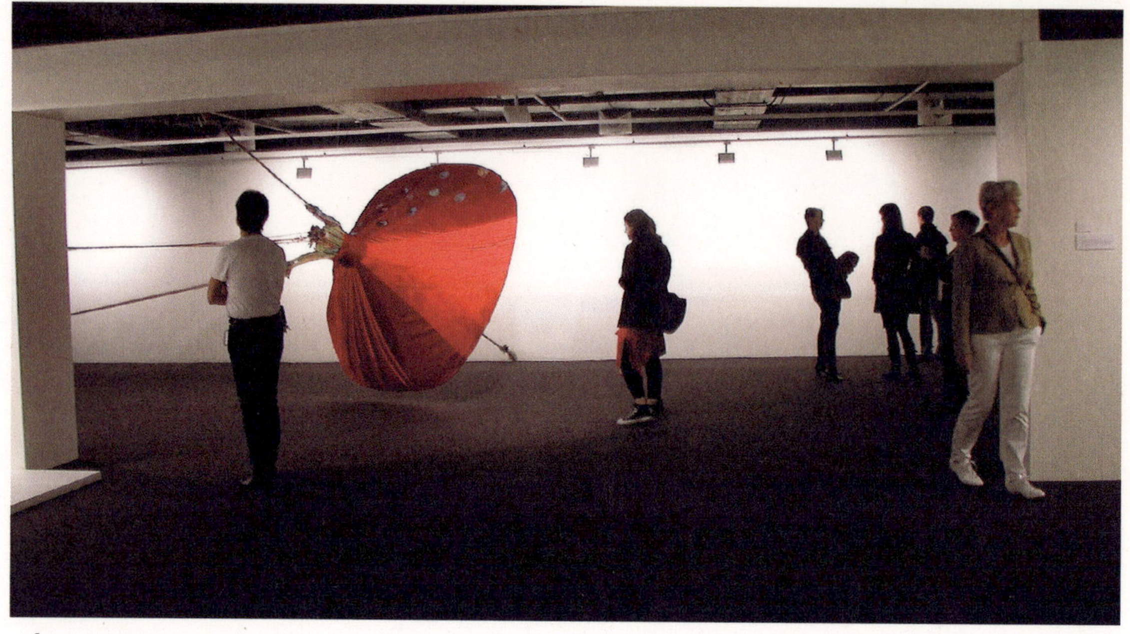

1

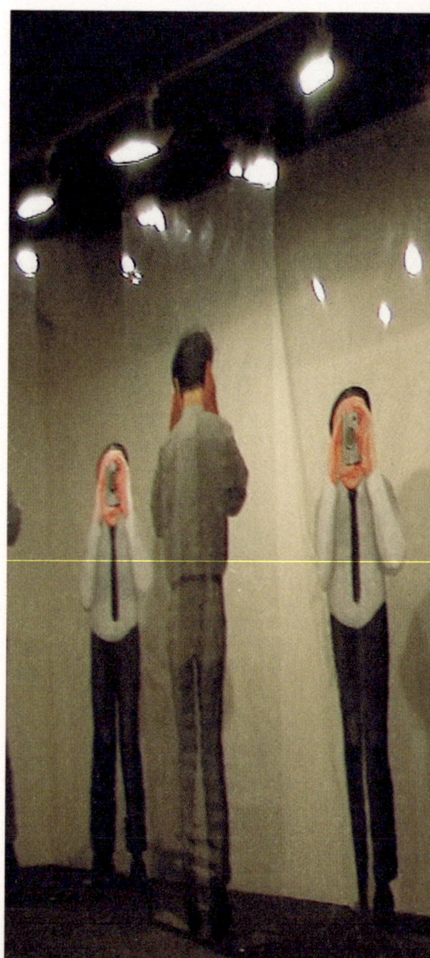

3

1
Trương Tân, *Dancer*, 2006, installation with metal, fabric, elastic rope, 300 x 400 x 800 cm. Installation view. Courtesy of Trần Lương.

2
Nguyễn Quang Huy, *Unknown Women*, 2005, mixed media installation. Installation view. Photo: Sidsel de Jong.

3
Trần Trọng Vũ, *Subject or Object*, 2009, installation with painting on transparent nylon sheets, set of 8 pairs, 100 x 270 cm (each). Installation view. Courtesy of Trần Lương.

4
Nguyễn Mạnh Hùng, *Apartment Block*, 2009, installation detail.

5
Nguyễn Mạnh Hùng, *Apartment Block*, 2009, wood, metal, plastic, paper and electric system, 70 x 70 x 300 cm. Installation view. Photo: Sidsel de Jong.

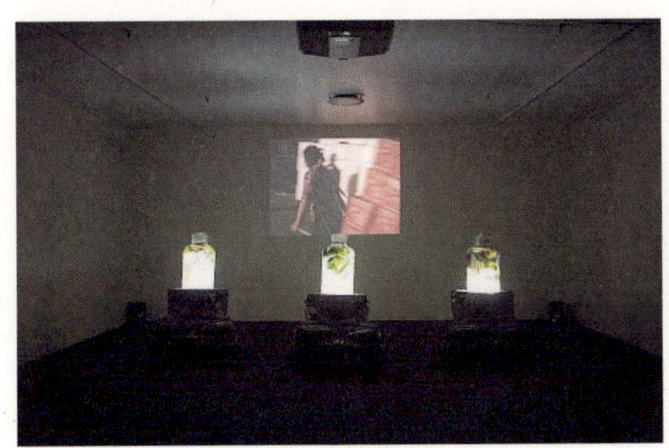

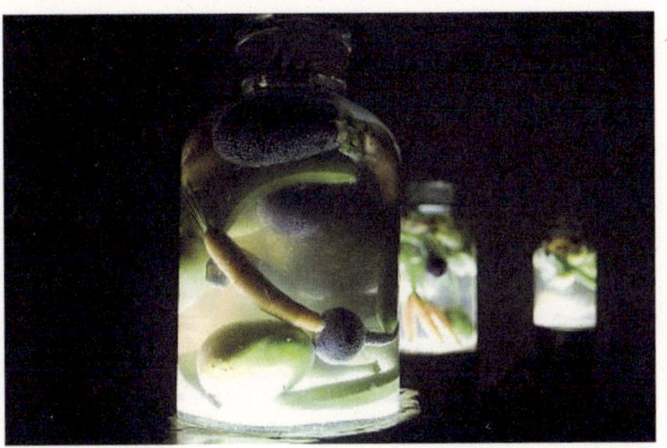

2

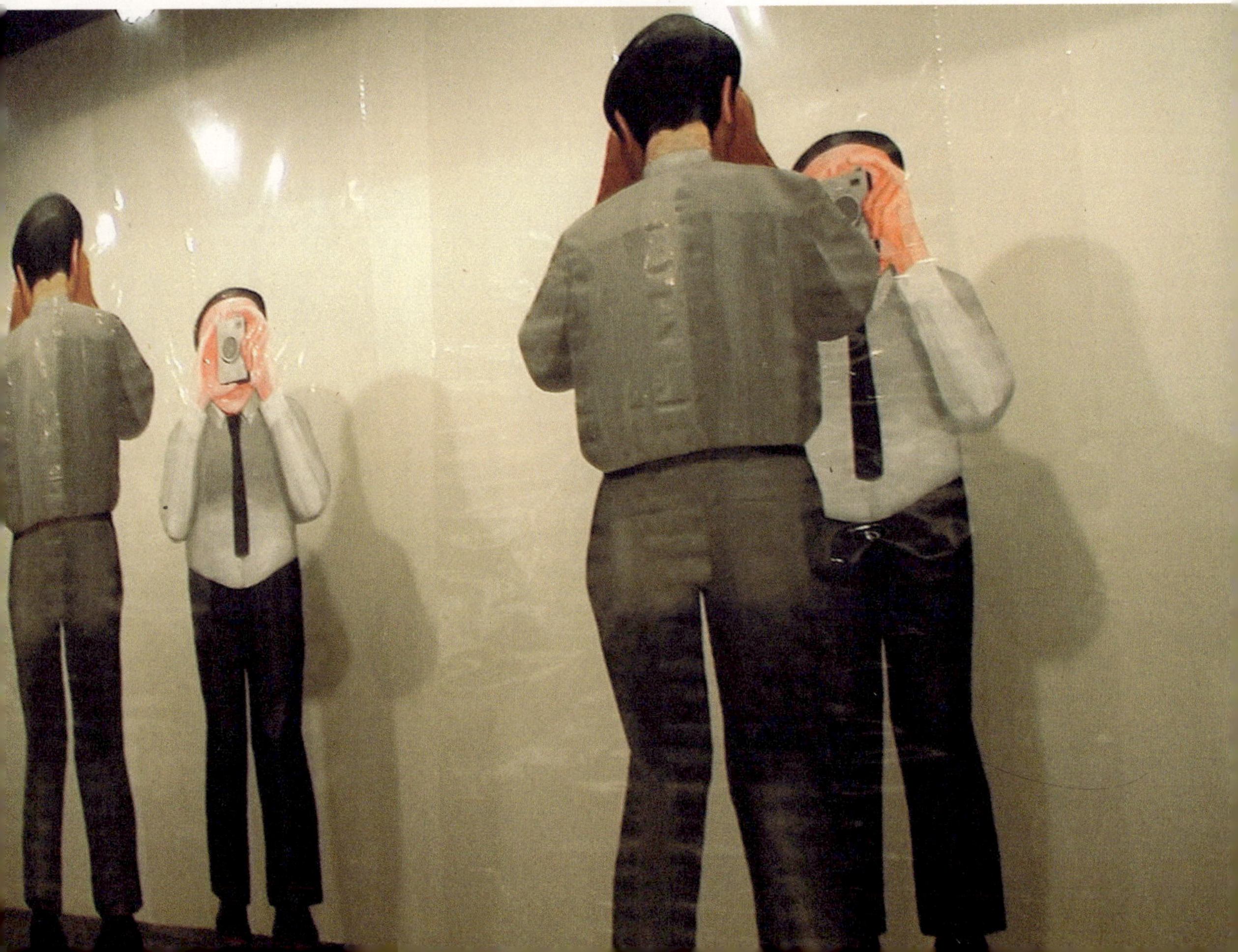

4

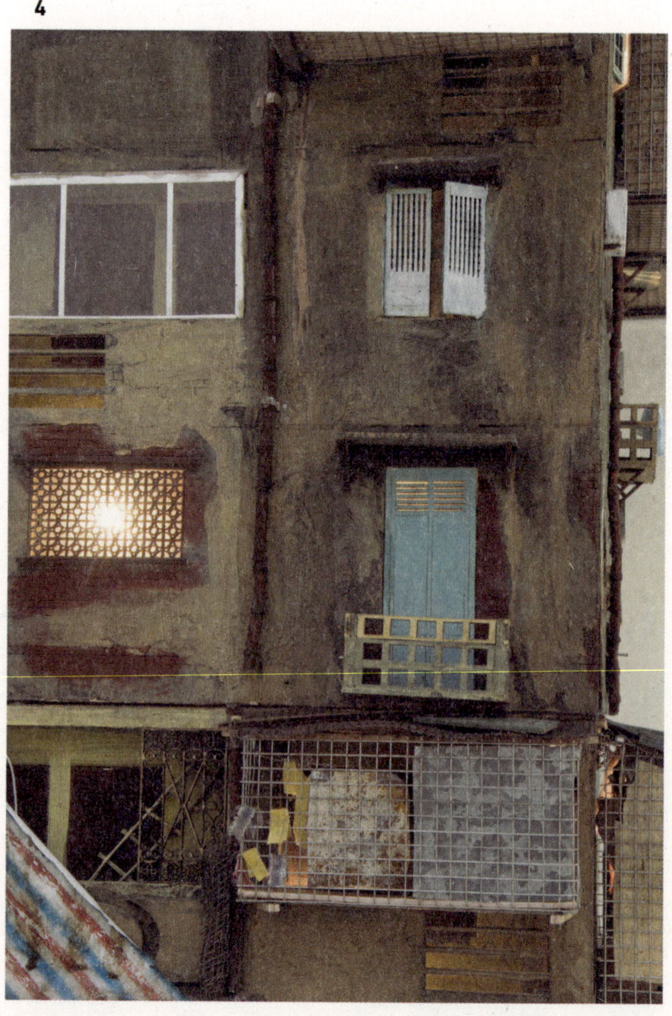

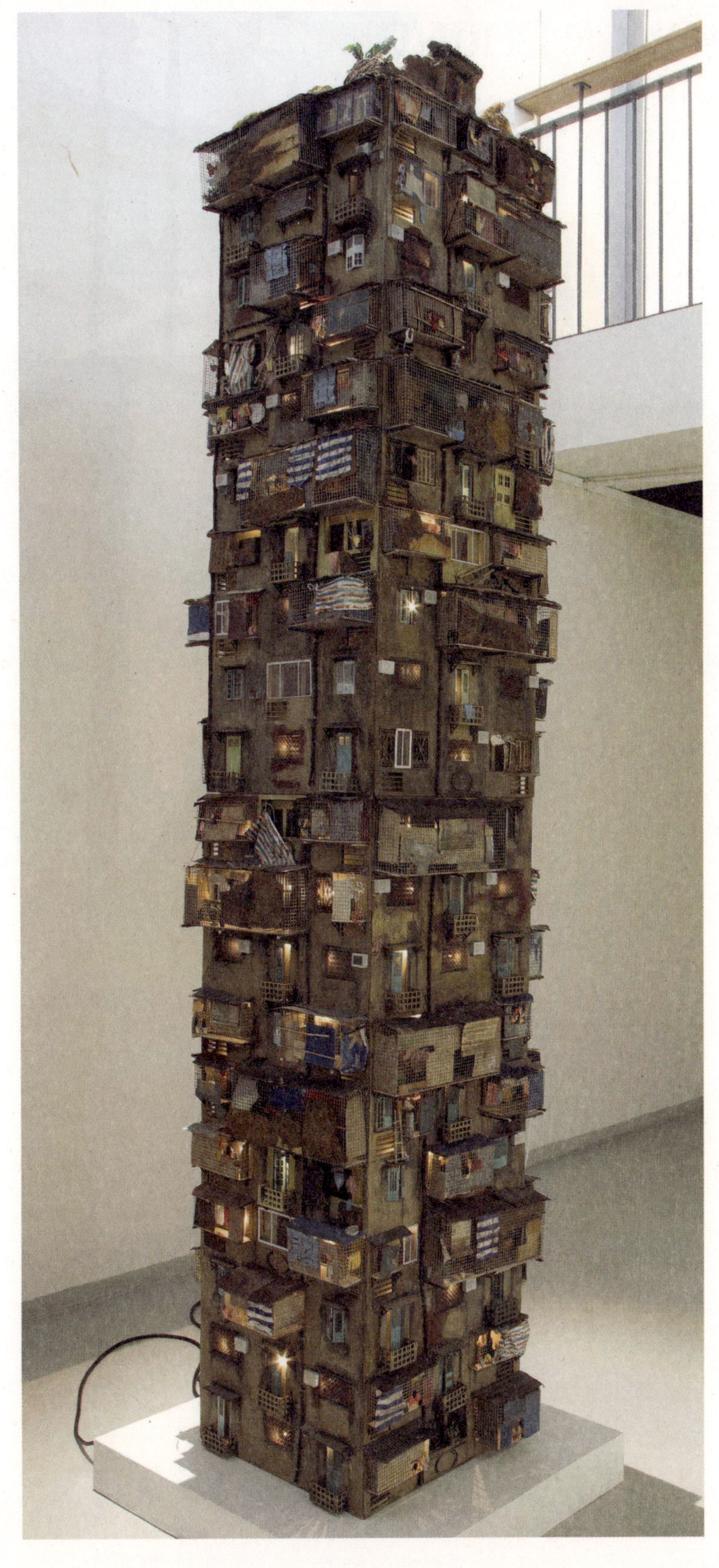

5

PHẬP PHỒNG 2011

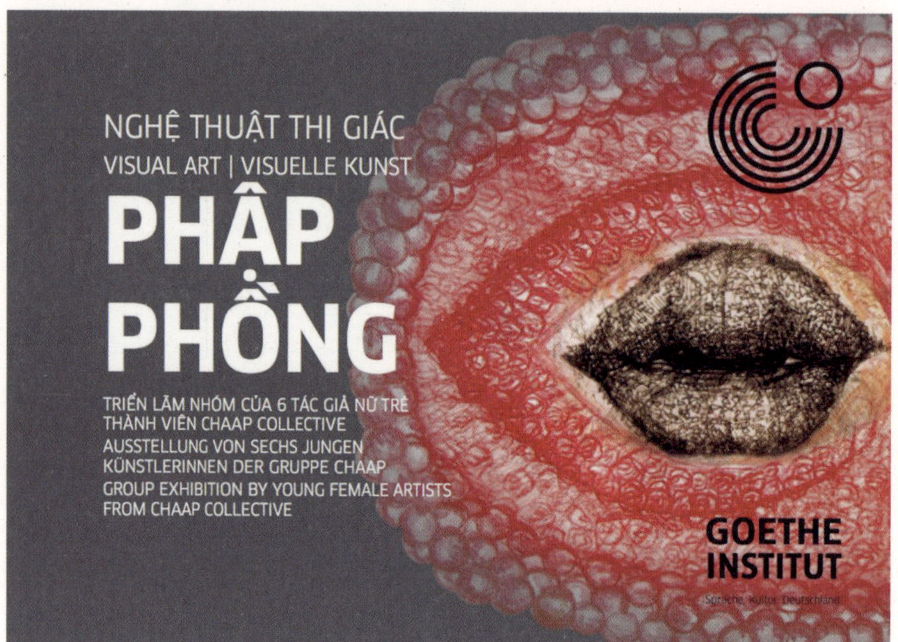

Phập Phồng exhibition poster.

VENUE: Goethe Institut Hà Nội DATE: 1–13 December, 2011 CURATOR: Trần Lương SUPPORTED BY: Goethe Institut Hà Nội ARTISTS: Nguyễn Thị Hoài Thơ, Phạm Thu Thuỷ, Hường By Nguyễn, Phạm Hồng, Võ Ngọc Huế, Hà Thị Hồng Ngân.

Phập Phồng was an exhibition introducing the works of six young female artists from Chập Collective, featuring installations, performances and videos. Chập Collective, also known as Chập Art, started out as a group of young men and women. However, after about a year, only eight members of the group remained, all of whom were female students who had come from remote provinces. Having grown up amidst limited access to information and educational opportunities, they converged in Hà Nội in 2009, aiming to create a platform for practice and discourse on contemporary art for students. This initiative emerged in a climate marked by a growing demand for education on contemporary art, particularly following the momentum of the Young Fine Arts Festival in 2007.

A figurative term, "phập phồng" describes the rising and falling of an object with a thin, sensuous and dynamic surface. The exhibited pieces delved into personal narratives and the lived experiences of the artists, laying bare the wounds and frustrations of being a woman in Vietnamese society, where patriarchal ideologies continue to exert significant influence in most regions. Different states of "phập phồng" are hinted at through the arrangement of artworks. Installations resembling the shape of vulva and breasts, crafted from soft, colorful and organic materials, were strategically positioned outdoors at the exhibition entrance and within the courtyard, serving as a playful and provocative exploration of femininity. Conversely, artworks within the exhibition space explored societal norms and prejudices regarding appearance, employing materials such as steel, spikes and razor blades to symbolize internalised and repressed emotions.

The title, *Phập Phồng*, was proposed by the curator following discussions with the artists and an exploration of their personal backgrounds. Common themes identified and agreed upon within the group included issues of poverty, lack of education and the absence of a sexual revolution. All works within the exhibition were commissioned by the curator with funds from Goethe Institut and the entire process of development, from conceptualisation to production, was mentored by Trần Lương. The works reflected the ongoing struggle for self-awareness and self-assessment of women's roles within familial relationships, communist society and the remnants of Confucianism.

In terms of materials and methods, the works challenged traditional stereotypes of femininity, featuring motifs such as lips, traditional áo dài garments, uterine entrances and brides in wedding dresses portrayed as alluring, colourful "traps". The works drew audiences in with these traditional cultural images and appealing materials such as crimson-lit entrances and wedding flower arrangements, before confronting them with elements crafted from materials such as razor blades, sharp steel spikes and a headband made of solid ice.

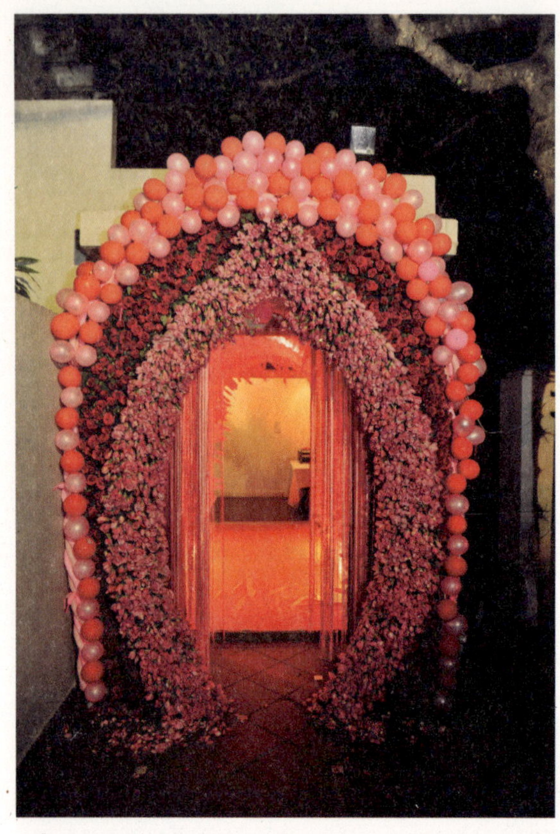

1

1
Hường By Nguyễn, *Gate of Immortality*, 2011, installation at exhibition entrance with flowers and balloons. Courtesy of Trần Lương.

2
Nguyễn Thị Hoài Thơ, *Loofah Trellis*, 2011, mixed-media installation. Courtesy of Trần Lương.

3
Võ Ngọc Huế, *Mother's Story*, 2011, live performance. Courtesy of Trần Lương.

2

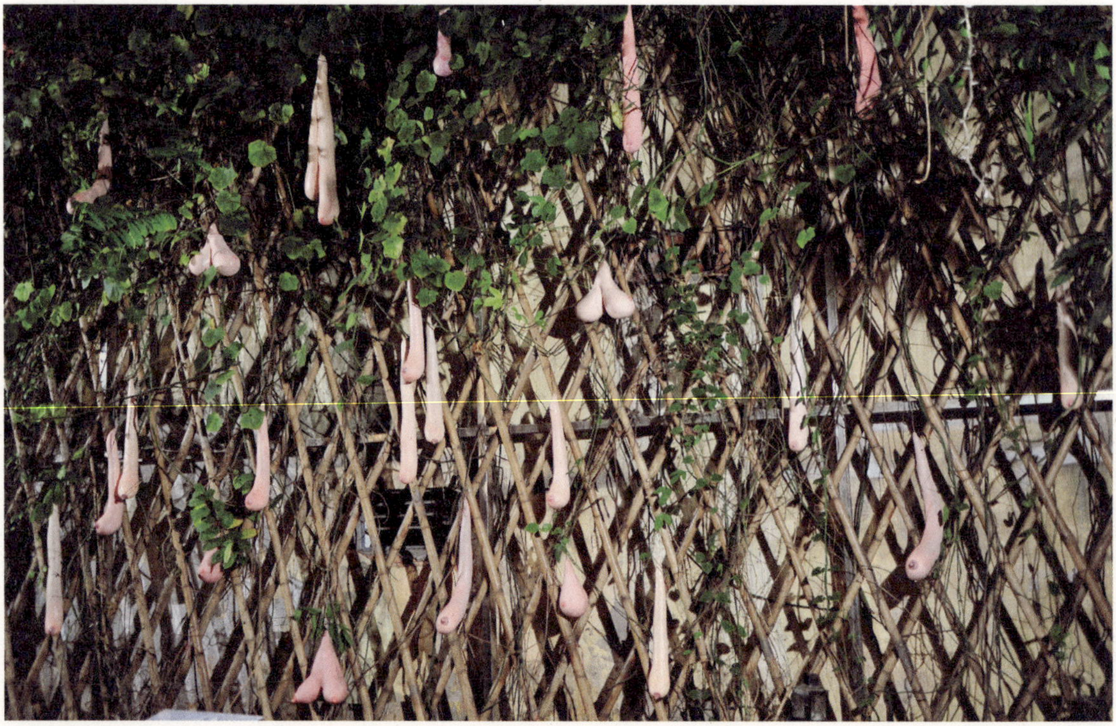

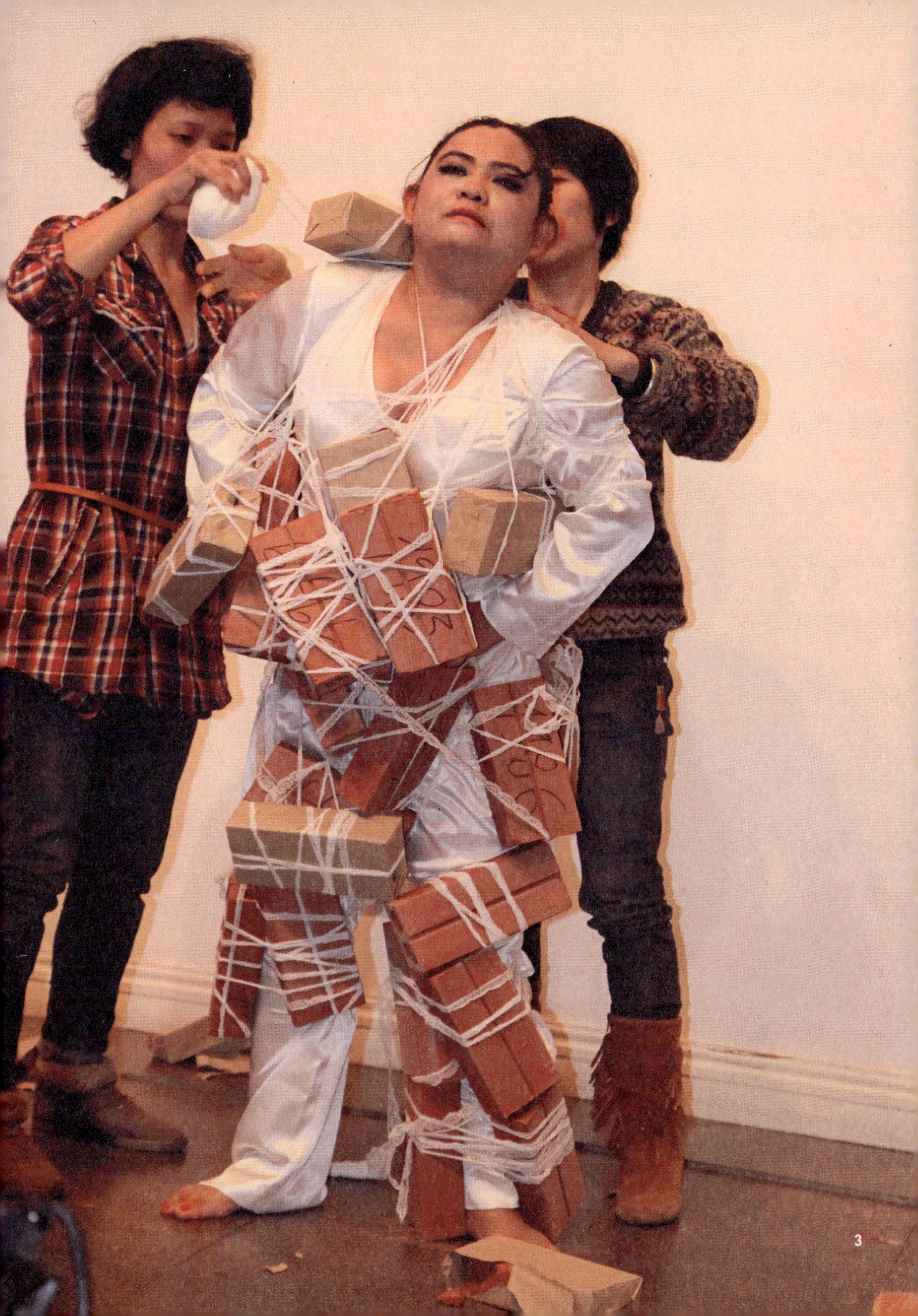

3

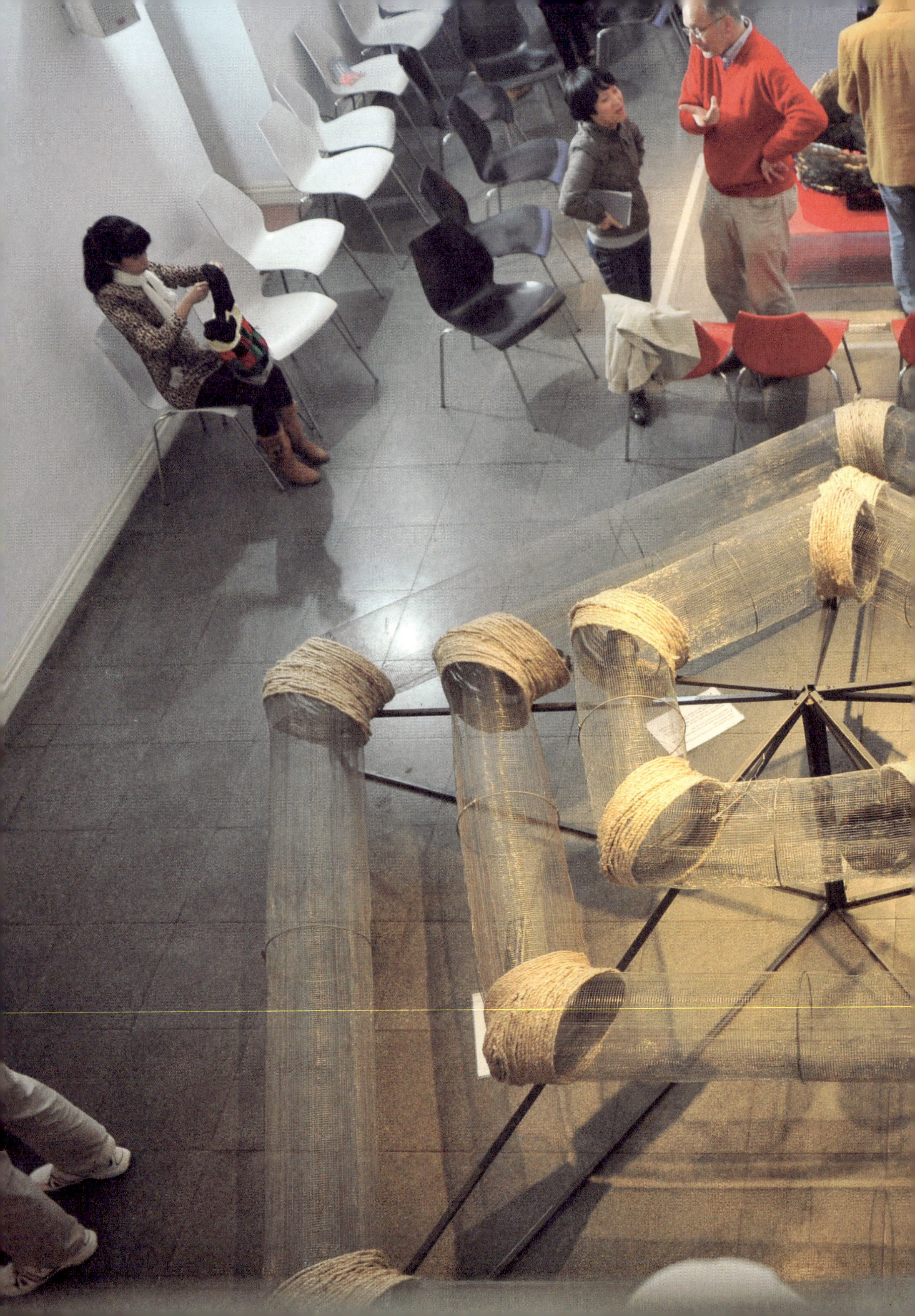

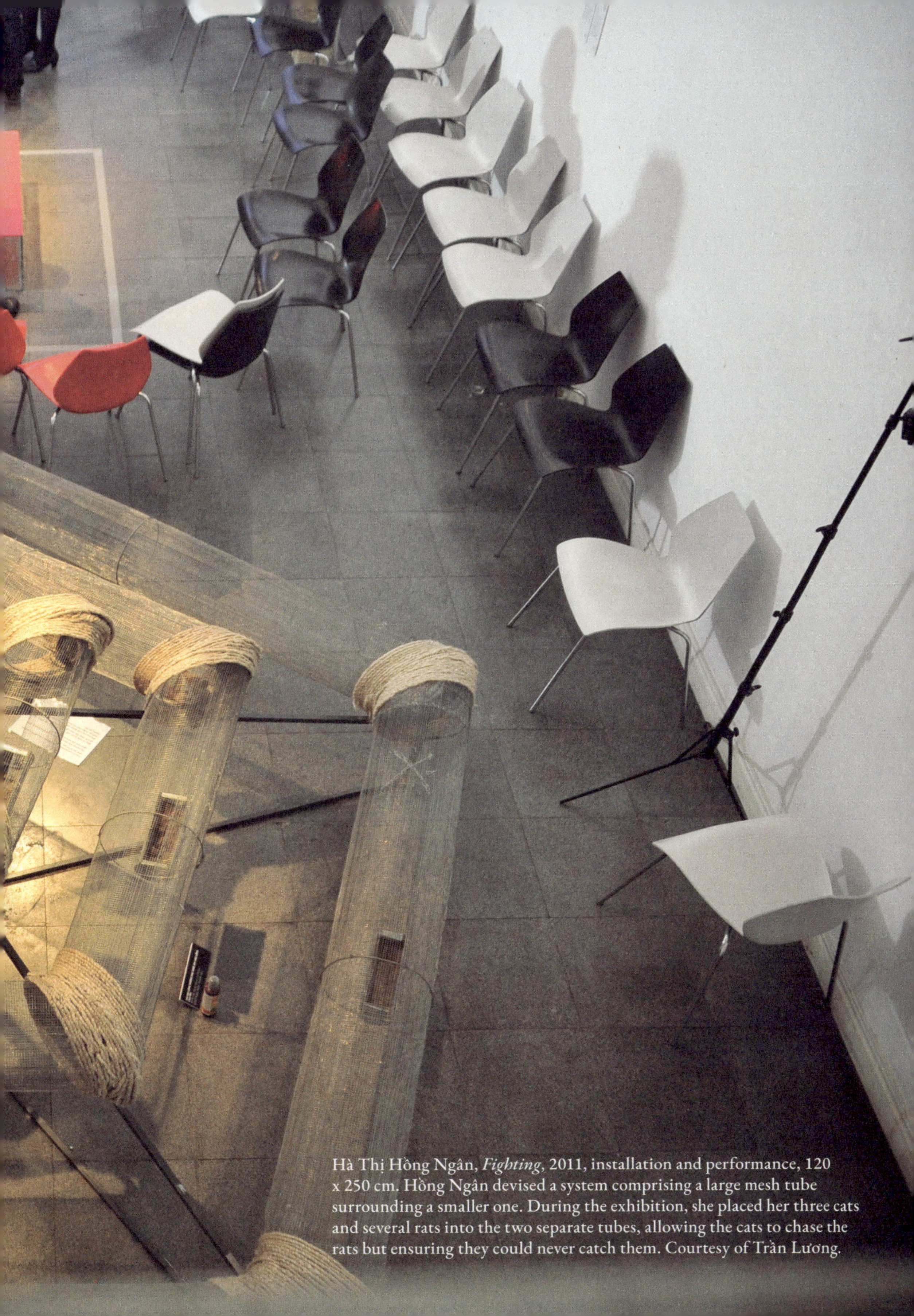

Hà Thị Hồng Ngân, *Fighting*, 2011, installation and performance, 120 x 250 cm. Hồng Ngân devised a system comprising a large mesh tube surrounding a smaller one. During the exhibition, she placed her three cats and several rats into the two separate tubes, allowing the cats to chase the rats but ensuring they could never catch them. Courtesy of Trần Lương.

RIVERSCAPES IN FLUX 2011–2013

VENUE: Vietnam National Fine Arts Museum, Goethe Institut Hà Nội DATE: 12–29 April, 2012 TOURING VENUES: Cactus Art Gallery, Ho Chi Minh City, Vietnam 12 May–26 May, 2012; | g23 Art Gallery, Bangkok, Thailand 22 June–22 July, 2012; Sa Sa Bassac, Phnom Penh, Cambodia 18 October–11 November, 2012; Metropolitan Museum of Manila, Philippines 15 March–13 April, 2013; LANGGENG Art Foundation, Yogyakarta, Indonesia 6–19 June, 2013 CURATORS: Trần Lương, Apisak Sonjod, Erin Gleeson, Ade Darmawan, Iola Lenzi & Claro Jr. Ramirez ORGANISED BY: Goethe Institut Vietnam SUPPORTED BY: DB Schenker, GIZ ARTISTS: Nguyễn Thị Thanh Mai, Phan Thảo Nguyên, Lương Huệ Trinh, Nguyễn Thế Sơn, Anothai Nitibhon & Jean David Ciallouet, Jedsada Tangtrakulwong, Sutthirat Supaparinya, Lim Sokchanlina, Than Sok, Vuth Lyno, Achmad Krisgatha, Budi Dharmawan, Mahardika Yudha, Wok the Rock, Aung Ko, Goldie Poblador, Jon Romero.

Rivers are considered one of the most important natural elements shaping the social, cultural and religious life in most Southeast Asian countries. They serve as connectors not only for cultural exchange but also for river and maritime trade routes. In the context of the 21st century, economic development, industrialisation and hydropower exploitation are causing damage and degradation to the ecological environment. This has led to conflicts between governments and local individuals and communities, as well as between nations sharing common watercourses.

Initiated by the Goethe Institut in Vietnam, *Riverscapes IN FLUX*, aimed to investigate the cultural landscapes of rivers and raise public awareness of the ecological and socio-economic challenges that the riverscapes in these countries are currently facing. The project collaborated with Goethe Institutes in Thailand, Myanmar, the Philippines, Cambodia and Indonesia.

With the participation of six invited curators and 17 regional artists selected through an open call, the project's curators worked with the artists during field research, artwork development and exhibition production. The process included four months of fieldwork in river areas such as the Red River and Cửu Long River (Vietnam), Tonle Sap (Cambodia), Chi River and Ping river (Thailand) and Angke River (Indonesia), with a focus on engaging with local communities. Additionally, workshops and lectures were held in Goethe Institut Hà Nội and Cần Thơ University to discuss climate change issues in the Mekong Delta region. This made Riverscapes IN FLUX a complex art project, as it combined elements of a social development project with an interdisciplinary approach.

The *Riverscapes IN FLUX* exhibition presented 17 artworks comprising multimedia installations, photo series, videos and object installations. The exhibition celebrated its opening in Hà Nội and was subsequently shown in Ho Chi Minh City, Bangkok, Phnom Penh, Manila and Yogyakarta, accompanied by film screenings and various educational and cultural activities.

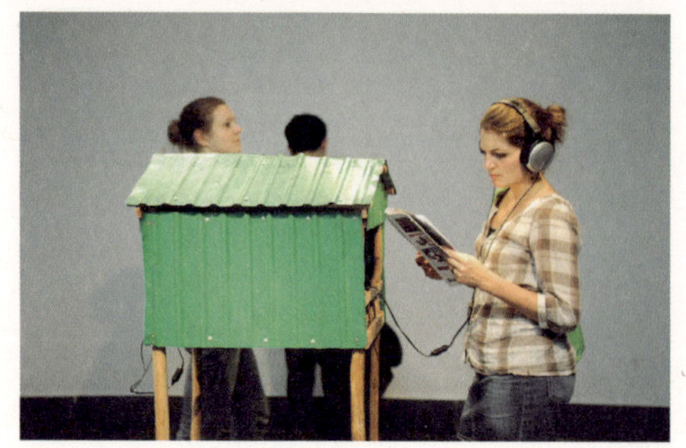

1

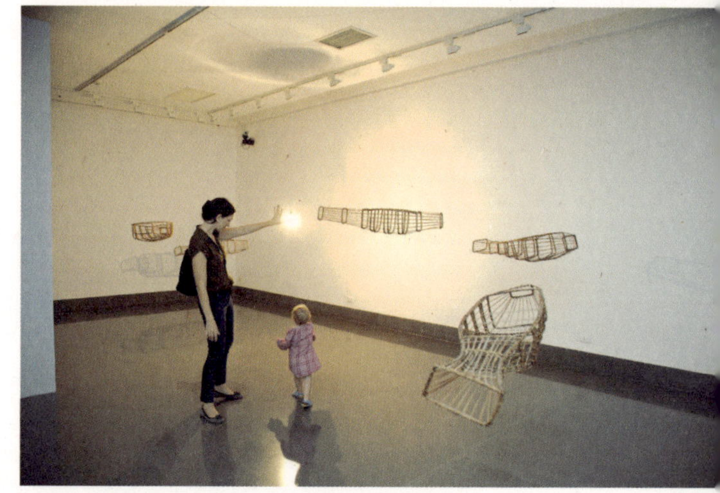

2

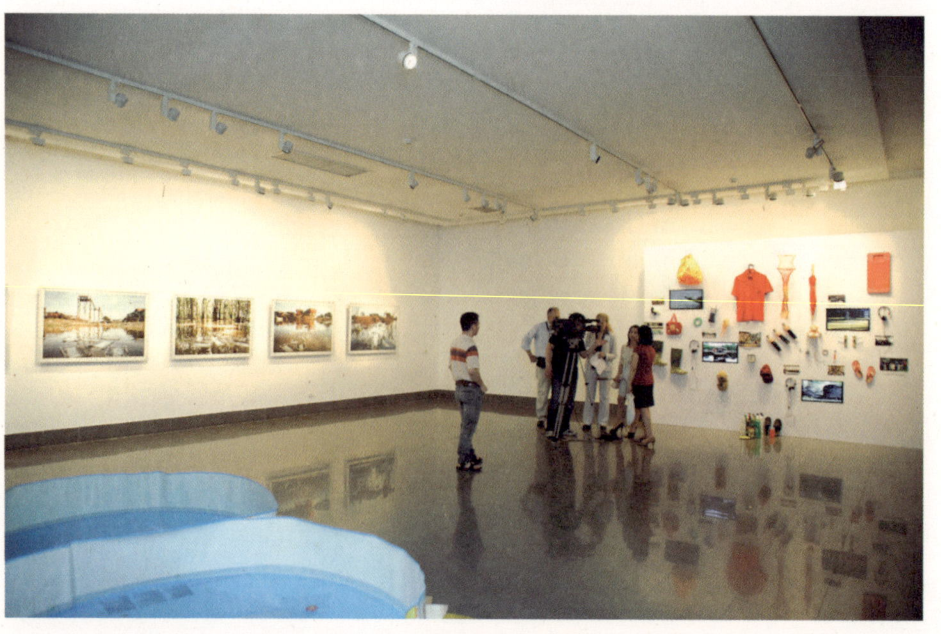

3

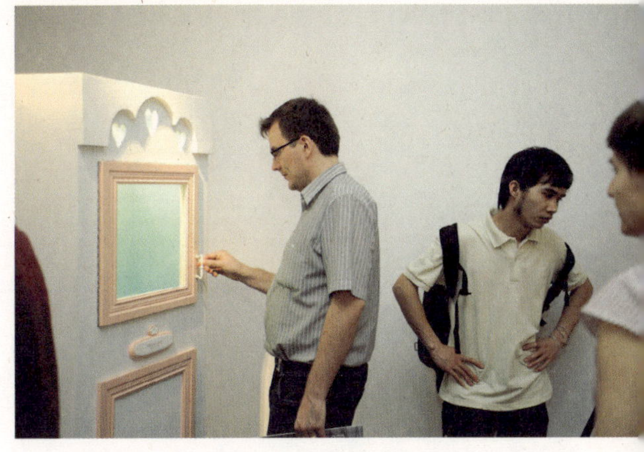

4

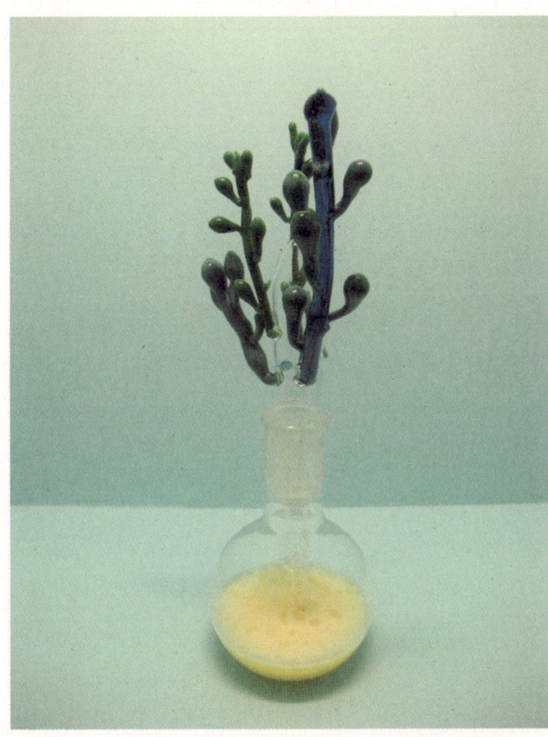

5

1
Vuth Lyno, *Rise and Fall*, 2012, sound installation.

2
Jedsada Tangtrakulwong, *Chi River*, 2012, installation with sound.

3
Installation view at Vietnam National Fine Arts Museum. Foreground: Anothai Nitibhon & Jean David Cuallouet, *Loi Krathong*, 2012, multimedia two-channel video installation; Left (on wall): Lim Sokchanlina, *Rising Tonle Sap*, 2012, digital photography; Right (on wall): Mahardika Yudha, *Shifting Live Objects Into Inanimate*, 2012, four-channel video with found-object installation.

4,5
Goldie Poblador, *The Fragrance of The Marikina River*, 2012, interactive mixed-media installation with hand-blown glass bottles, light-cabinets and scent.

6
Aung Ko, *The Sights Viewed from Boats*, 2012, mixed media installation with found objects.

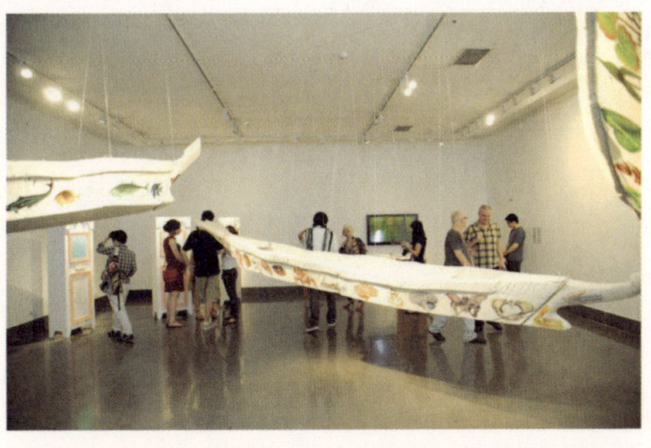

6

Photo 1,2,3,4,6: Hoàng Đức Thịnh
Photo 5: Natalia Kraevskaia

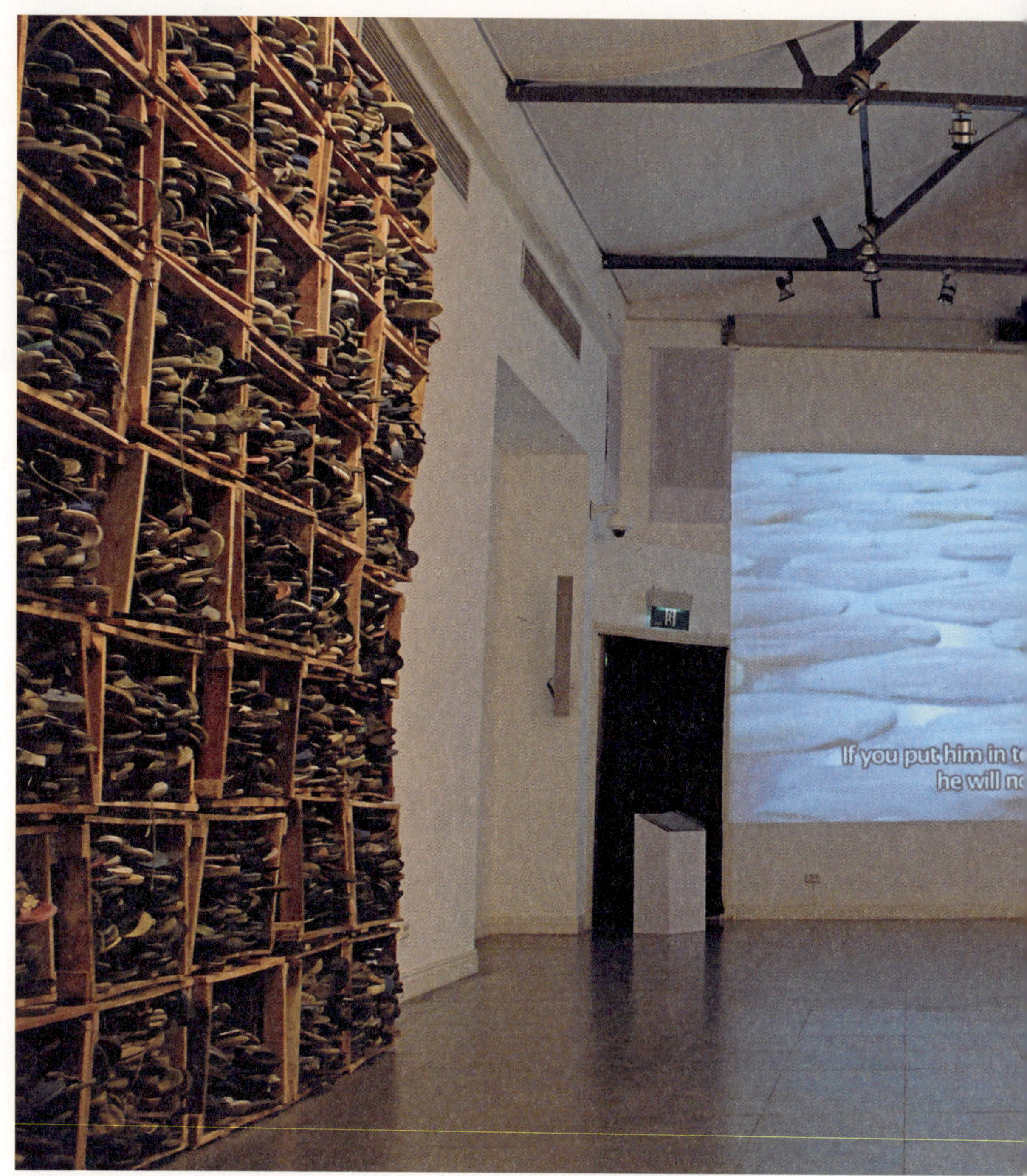
If you put him in
he will

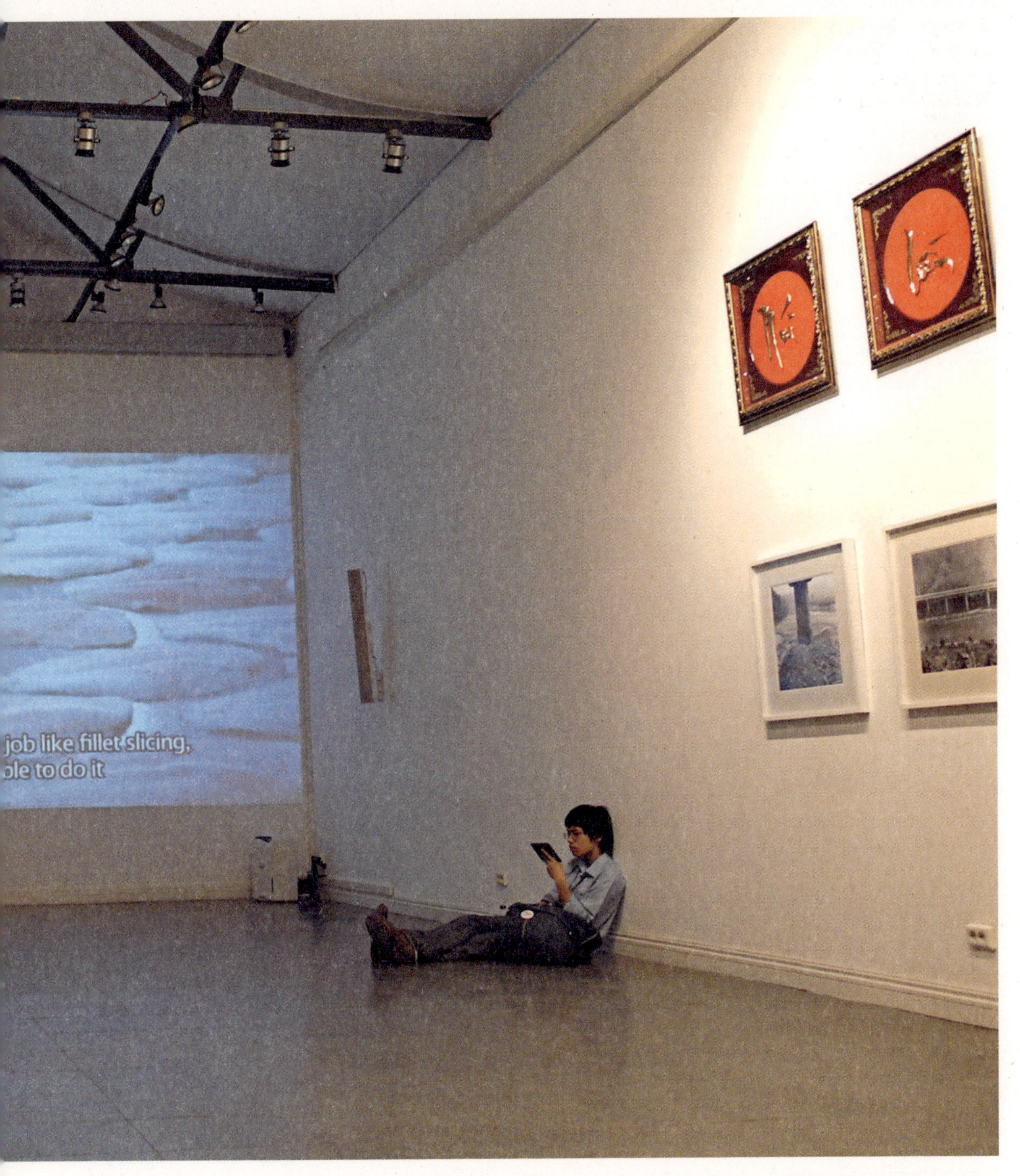

Installation view at Goethe Institut Hà Nội.
(Left wall) Nguyễn Thị Thanh Mai, *The Vestiges*, 2012, installation, with 60 wooden crates and slippers; (centre) Phan Thao Nguyen, *Mekông Mechanical*, 2012, video installation with documentary album; (right wall) Nguyễn Thế Sơn, *Mountains Links with Mountains, River Links with Rivers*, 2012, mixed-media installation, photography Ultra Printing and Relievo. Photo: Trần Lương.

4TH SINGAPORE BIENNALE IF THE WORLD CHANGED 2013

LOCATION: Singapore Art Museum, National Museum of Singapore, Peranakan Museum, Singapore Management University, Waterloo Centre, National Library, Fort Canning Park, Our Museum @ Taman Jurong. DATE: Oct 26, 2013–Feb 16, 2014 CURATORS: 27 curators based in Southeast Asia SINGAPORE Tan Boon Hui, Khairuddin Hori, Joyce Toh, Tan Siu Li, Michelle Ho, David Chew, Naomi Wang, Fairuz Iman Ismail, Tay Swee Lin, Seng Yu Jin, Tamares Goh, Charmaine Toh MALAYSIA Faizal Sidik, Yee I-Lann INDONESIA Aminudin TH Siregar "Ucok", Mia Maria PHILIPPINES Claro Ramirez, Kawayan de Guia, Charlie Co, Abraham Garcia Jr THAILAND Ark Fongsmut, Angkrit Ajchariyasophon VIETNAM Trần Lương, Nguyễn Như Huy CAMBODIA Erin Gleeson LAOS Misouda Heuangsoukkhoun MYANMAR Aye Ko ORGANISED BY: Singapore Art Museum SUPPORTED BY: Ministry of Culture, Community and Youth, National Arts Council and National Heritage Board in Singapore PARTICIPATING ARTISTS: (82 artists) Ahmad Abu Bakar, Irwan Ahmett & Tita Salina, Jainal Amambing, Ang Sookoon, AX(iS) Art Project, Zcongklod Bangyikhan, Boo Junfeng, Sharon Chin, Chris Chong Chan Fui, Kiri Dalena, Marisa Darasavath, Leslie de Chavez, Guo Yixiu, Iswanto Hartono & Raqs Media Collective, Adrian Ho, Dusadee Huntrakul, Joo Choon Lin, Toni Kanwa, Khvay Samnang, KOMVNI, Lai Chee Kien, Erica Lai, Lâm Hiếu Thuận, Urich Lau, Lê Brothers, Sean Lee, Lee Wen, Kamin Lertchaiprasert, Liao Jiekai, Hazel Lim, Lim Shing Ee & Kazunori Takeishi, Nikki Luna, Manny Montelibano, Moon Kyungwon & Jeon Joonho, Kumari Nahappan, Nasirun, Ng Joon Kiat, Krit Ngamsom, Nge Lay, Nguyễn Thị Hoài Thơ, Nguyễn Huy An, Nguyễn Trinh Thi, Ưu Đàm Trần Nguyễn, Oanh Phi Phi, Nipan Oranniwesna, Anon Pairot, Bounpaul Phothyzan, Po Po Poodien, Eko Prawoto, Anggun Priambodo, François Roche, Rosid, Sai Hua Kuan, Albert Samreth, Tisna Sanjaya, Svay Sareth, Angie Seah, Jeremy Sharma, Shieko Reto, Patama Roonrakwit, Siete Pesos, Leroy Sofyan, Shirley Soh, Speak Cryptic, Prateep Suthathongthai, Samart Suwannarat, Talaandig Artists, Grace Tan, Royston Tan, Tan Wei Kheng, Boonsri Tangtrongsin, Tay Bee Aye, teamLab, Chi Too, Nguyễn Trần Nam, Trần Tuấn, Nopchai Ungkavatanapong, Suzann Victor, Oscar Villamiel, Vũ Hồng Ninh, Ken + Julia Yonetani, Mahardika Yudha, Zulkifli Yusoff, Robert Zhao Renhui, ZNC.

The 4th Singapore Biennale was held in 2013 under the title *If the World Changed*, showcasing the works of 82 artists and art collectives. The main focus of SB 2013 was to present contemporary art in the Southeast Asia region, often characterised by its social engagement and exploration of issues such as environmental degradation, loss of physical heritage and censorship in art.

The biennale adopted a bold new collaborative curatorial structure, involving a team of 27 curators from Southeast Asia. This platform enabled curators in the region to share knowledge and experiences, some of whom had expertise in theoretical work and institutional settings, while others were self-taught and more experienced in activism in non-urban areas. Workshops and roundtable discussions took place concurrently with the artwork selection and commissioning process. Without separate country pavilions, the curators focused on creating combinations and harmonies among individual works, drawing out diverse nuances from different countries.

Trần Lương, one of the invited curators of the exhibition, presented seven works by artists Nguyễn Thị Hoài Thơ, Nguyễn Huy An, Nguyễn Trinh Thi, Ưu Đàm Trần Nguyễn, Nguyễn Trần Nam, Trần Tuấn and Vũ Hồng Ninh. The selected works, some of which were newly commissioned, largely reflected contemporary social issues in Vietnamese society, including art censorship, feminism, urbanisation and the commercialisation of Buddhism. In addition to the content, Trần Lương also emphasised the material elements of the works and their interactivity with the audience in public spaces, situating them within the context of Singapore, which is known for its orderliness and strict requirements regarding public behaviour. To achieve this, he successfully persuaded and negotiated conditions with the curators and organising committee, adapting the artworks to better fit and engage with their surroundings.

Due to the collaborative nature of SB 2013 involving 27 curators from countries in the region, coordination of the curation process was very complicated. The artworks were not separated by country, but were blended together based on the suitability of each work to the site, considering the context of the content, visual relationships between adjacent works and the cohesion and relations within clusters of works. The Biennale was presented in five different buildings and spaces, all of which were historical buildings or functioned as libraries, making more than half of the works site-specific, commissioned works. Through research and negotiation with the organisers, Trần Lương successfully chose suitable locations for each artwork, positioning them in prominent areas with high interaction with the audience, such as the main front yard, the lobby and SAM's central courtyard.

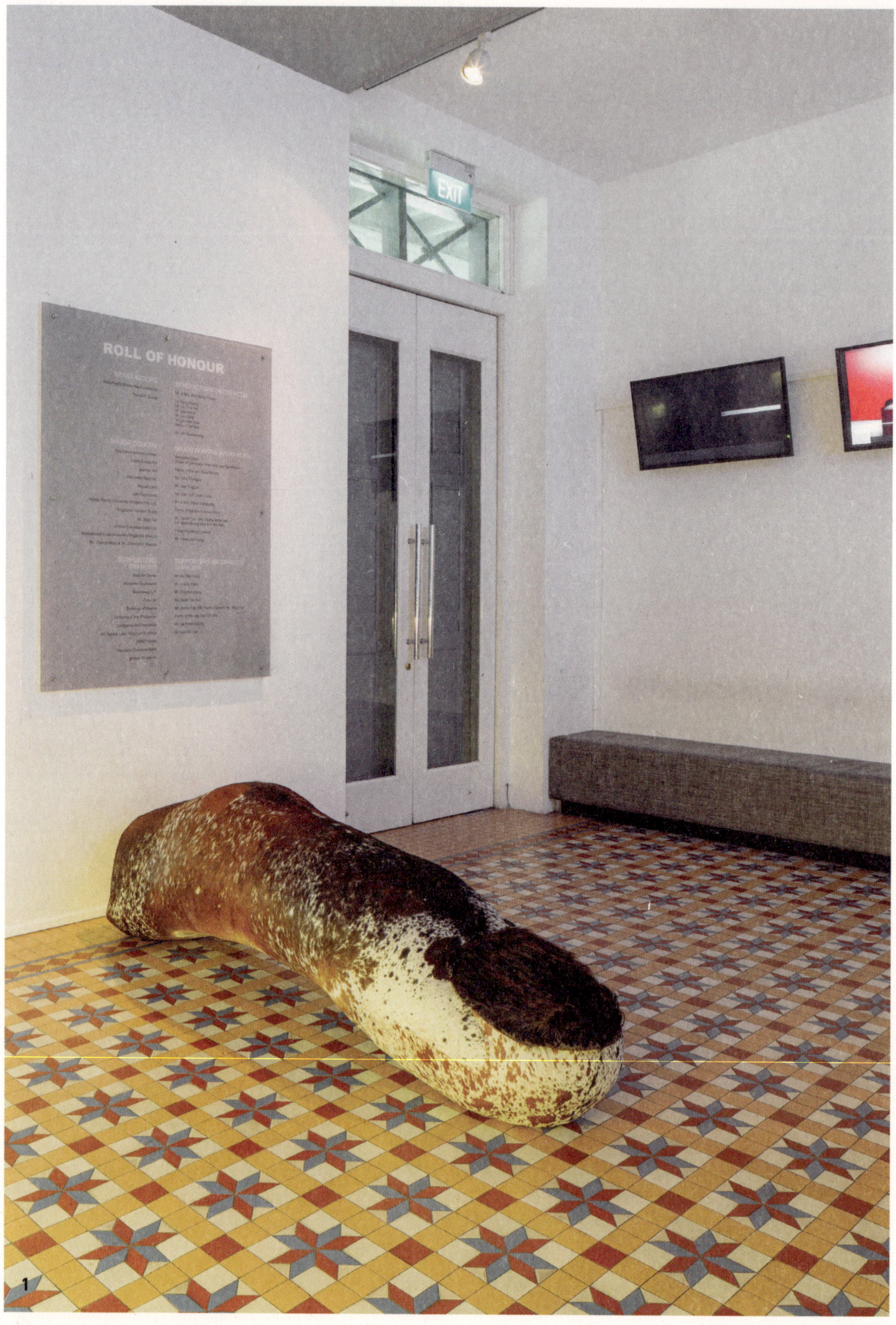

1

1
Trần Tuấn, *Forefinger*, 2013, mixed media, set of 4, dimensions variable. Singapore Biennale 2013 Commision. Courtesy of the Singpore Art Museum.

2
Nguyễn Trinh Thi, *Unsubtitled*, 2010, video projection on wooden cut-outs, dimensions variable. Singapore Biennale 2013 Commision. Courtesy of Singapore Art Museum.

3
Ưu Đàm Trần Nguyễn, *Waltz of The Machine Equestrians*, 2012, single channel video, 5'. Courtesy of artist.

4
Nguyễn Huy An, *The Great Puddle*, 2009, installation with Chinese ink and plywood, 800 x 500 cm. Courtesy of Singapore Art Museum.

2

3

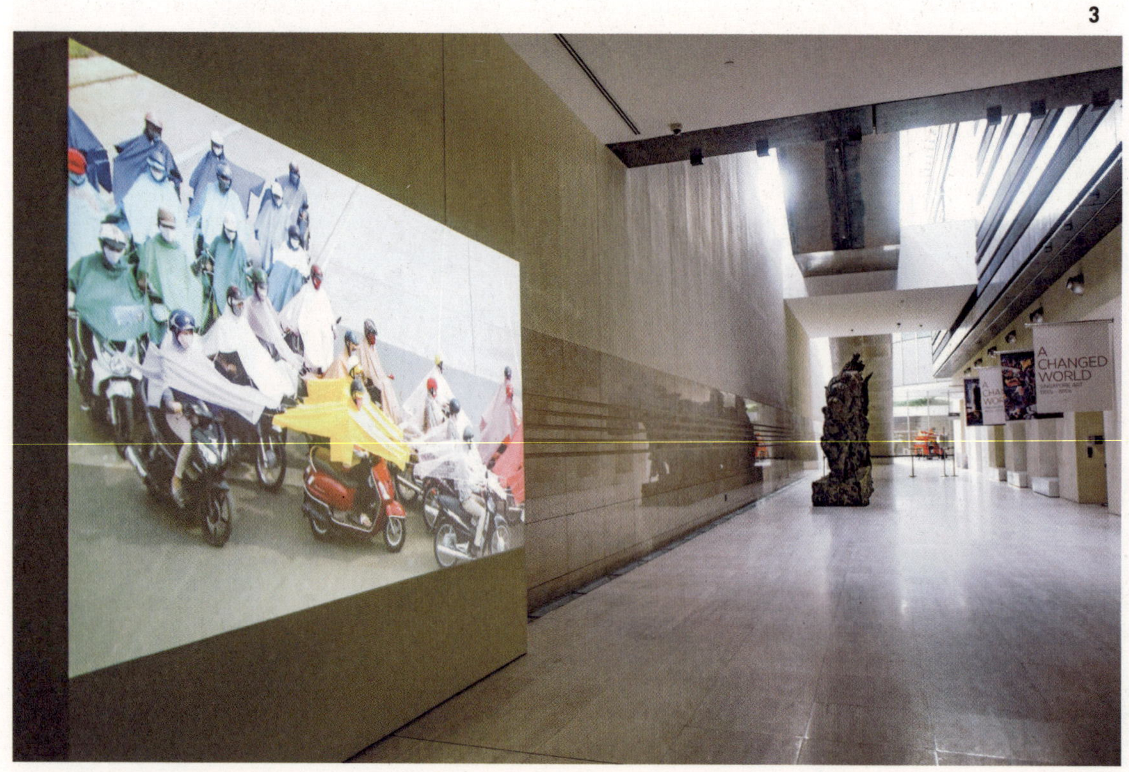

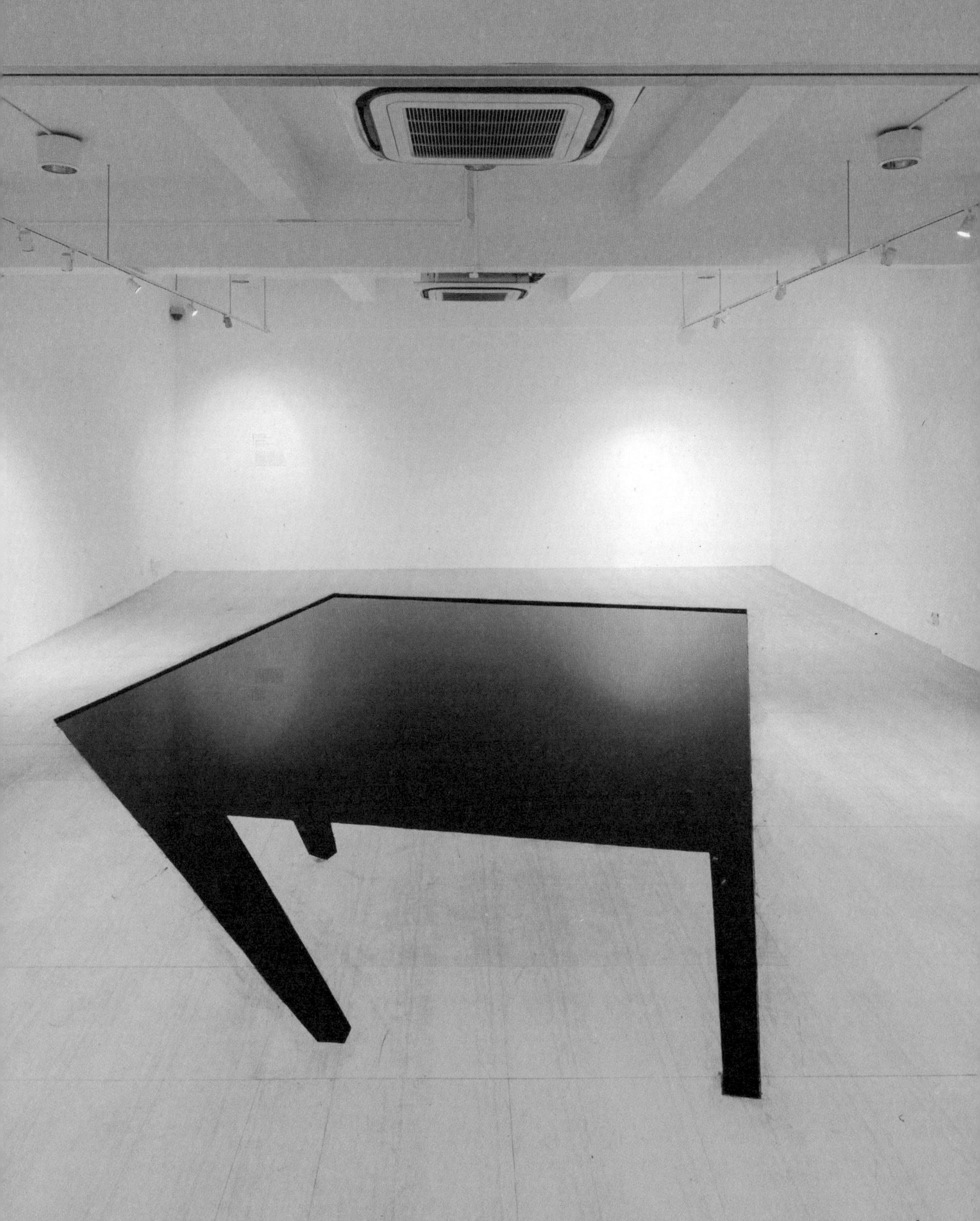

JOURNEY OF GREEN VIETNAM 2010–2014

LOCATION OF FINAL EXHIBITION: Museum of Vietnam University of Fine Arts DATE: 10–16 November, 2014 CURATOR: Trần Lương ORGANISED BY: Film No.1 Joint Stock Company, Talis Media SUPPORTED BY: The Ministry of Culture, Sports & Tourism, Ministry of Natural Resources and Environment, Vietnam PARTICIPATING ARTISTS: Trần Tuấn, Nguyễn Thế Sơn, Lương Huệ Trinh, Trương Công Tùng, Phan Thảo Nguyên, Nguyễn Na Sơn, Đỗ Doãn Hoàng, Đặng Đức Tuệ, Trần Lương.

Journey of Green Vietnam was a social development project focused on the regions facing environmental issues in Vietnam, with the goal of providing documentary information to raise community awareness and influence policymaking. Initiated by Nguyễn Mỹ Linh, founder of Talis Media), the project enlisted the participation of numerous journalists, reporters, photographers, singers and artists. As project advisor, Trần Lương incorporated artistic elements to develop the project across various dimensions; expanding approaches to information dissemination, community engagement through artistic activities and promotion of the project through popular singers and MCs.

In addition to advising, Trần Lương involved artists in field trips as he had done previously. Over four years, ten field trips were conducted, spanning mountainous areas (Tây Nguyên, Mường Nhé), coastal regions (Cà Mau and the Mekong Delta) and industrial zones (Bình Dương and the outskirts of Ho Chi Minh City). These trips aimed to investigate issues related to deforestation, illegal mineral exploitation, freshwater crises due to hydropower, rising sea levels and industrial pollution. Depending on the region, Trần Lương invited one or two local artists to join the field trips and the documentary process. Artists directly engaged in environmental documentary work, a task that often demands a wide range of skills and entails numerous challenges and risks. The costs associated with field trips, as well as artwork and exhibition production were fully covered by the Ministry of Natural Resources and Environment, under the auspices of a project of the Ministry of Culture. This was a rare occurrence, given the Ministry's reputation for stringent censorship of contemporary art addressing social issues. By combining project resources, Trần Lương succeeded in building an art project in a flexible manner, facilitating access to information for artists and diversifying working methods.

The *Journey of Green Vietnam* exhibition showcased the outcomes of the artists' participation in these field trips. Held at the Vietnam University of Fine Arts Museum, the exhibition featured works by six artists, including photography, installations, videos and sound installations, alongside several documentary photo series by journalists Na Sơn, Đặng Đức Tuệ and Đỗ Doãn Hoàng. The project served as a source of motivation for young artist communities to engage with environmental issues and promote awareness of art's role in community development. Some artists have continued to develop works based on materials gathered during the project's field trips.

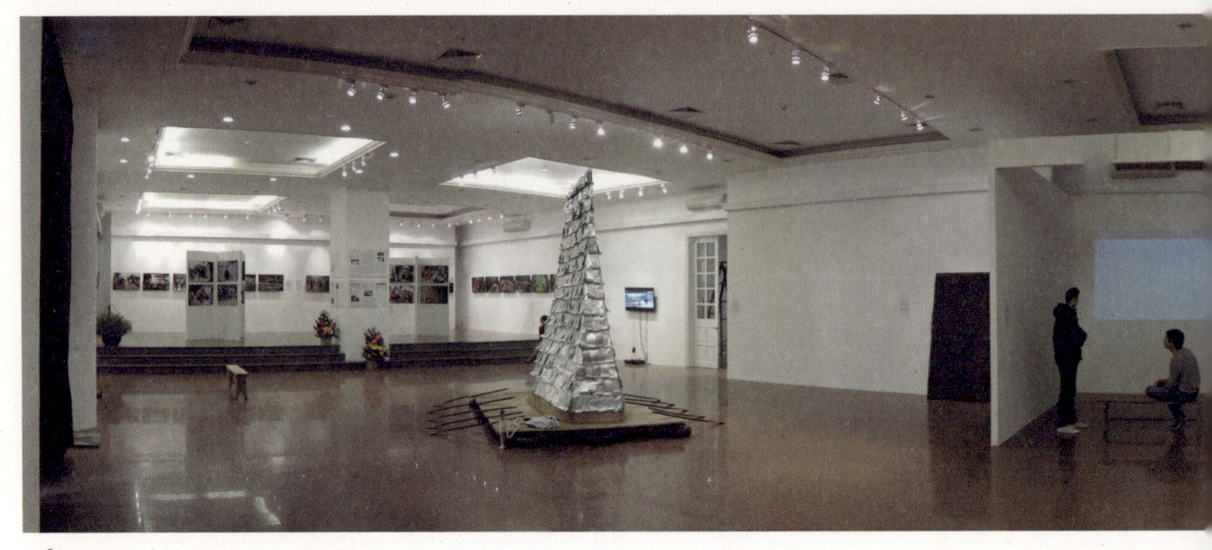
1

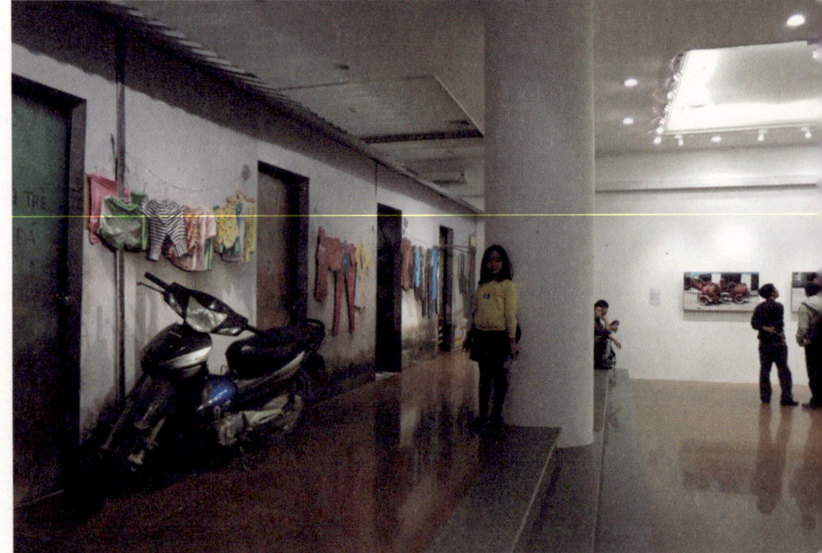
2

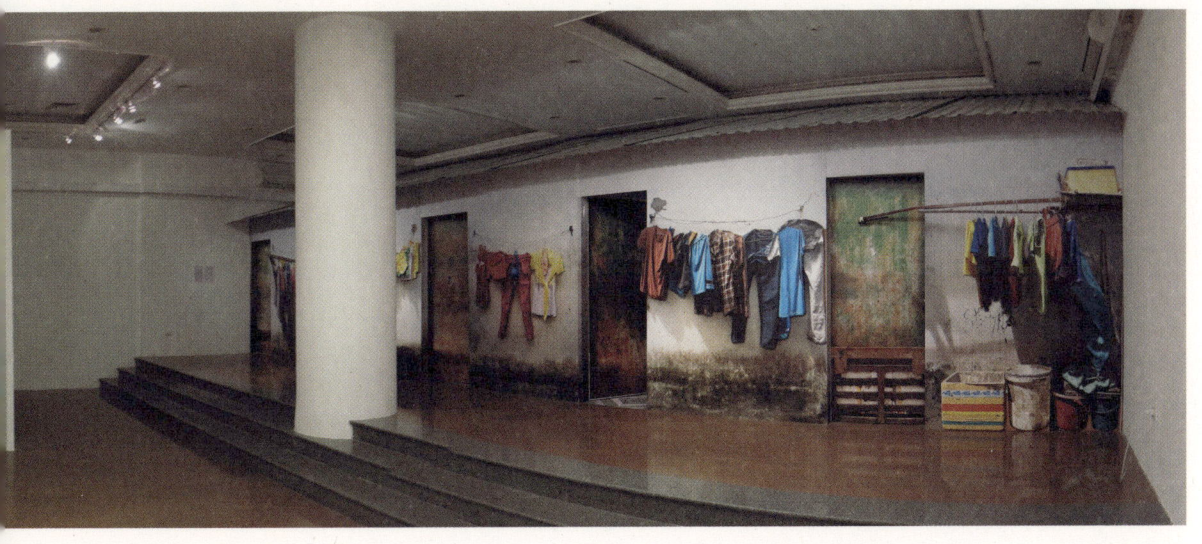

3

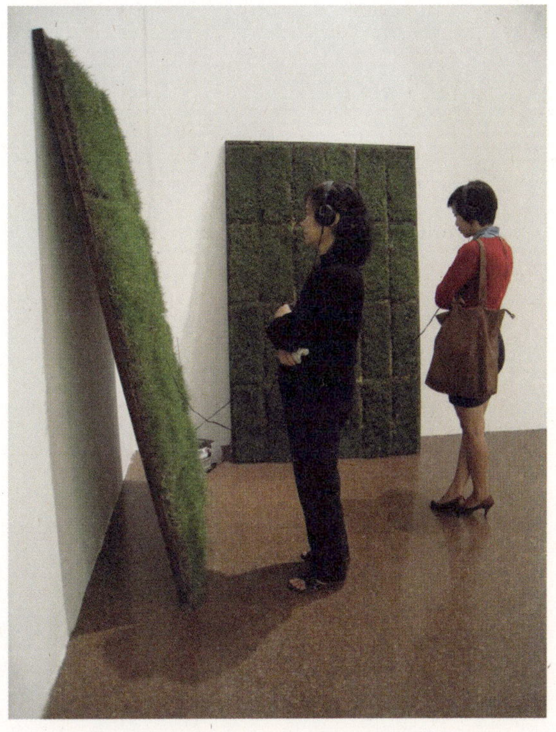

1
Installation view at Museum of Vietnam University of Fine Arts. Photo: Nguyễn Thế Sơn.
Left (on wall): Photography series by journalists Nguyễn Na Sơn, Đỗ Doãn Hoàng and Đặng Đức Tuệ; Left (on ground): Trần Tuấn, *Bè Rông*, 2014, installation with recycled metal cans, 400 x 600 x 400 cm; Middle left: Lương Huệ Trinh, *Illusions*, 2014, sound installation, 13'; Middle right: Trương Công Tùng, *Another place across the river*, single channel video, 8'28, 2014; Right: Nguyễn Thế Sơn, *8m2*, 2014, photography and sound installation, 350 x 1300 cm.

2
Nguyễn Thế Sơn, *8m2*, 2014, photography and sound installation, 350 x 1300 cm. This synthetic artwork simulates the 8m2 living space of a worker, sometimes for a family of four, in Southern industrial zones. The work resulted from the artist's field trip. Photo: Nguyễn Thế Sơn.

3
Lương Huệ Trinh, *Illusions*, 2014, sound installation, 13'. Photo: Trần Lương.

MIỀN MÉO MIÊNG / CONTEMPORÅRY ART FROM VIETNAM 2015

VENUE: Bildmuseet, Umeå, Sweden DATE: 14 June–01 November, 2015 CURATOR: Trần Lương CURATORIAL ASSISTANT: Lê Thuận Uyên ORGANISED BY: Bildmuseet, Umeå University ARTISTS: Nguyễn Huy An, Triệu Minh Hải, Nguyễn Mạnh Hùng, Trần Thị Kim Ngọc, Bàng Nhất Linh, Nguyễn Phương Linh, Nguyễn Trần Nam, Vũ Hồng Ninh, Nguyễn Thế Sơn, Nguyễn Trinh Thi, Trần Tuấn, Trương Công Tùng, Ưu Đàm Trần Nguyễn, Phạm Trần Việt Nam.

Miền Méo Miệng / Contemporary Art from Vietnam is one of the most comprehensive presentations of Vietnamese art that has ever been presented in Sweden. The theme of the show, *Miền Méo Miệng* (translated as "the land of distortion"), was inspired by the Vietnamese saying "roll your tongue seven times before speaking." Caution, consideration and contortion have been required to express one's opinion in Vietnamese society since feudal times. The exhibition also addressed issues related to freedom of expression, self-censorship as a consequence of the aftermath of war and government oppression in the country.

Most of the artworks were created within two years of the exhibition and some were made specifically for the show. The artworks in Miền Méo Miệng were divided into two groups based on different approaches to history. The first group approached history through personal materials, as well as local, historical and social events. These works gave the audience insight into the socio-political setting in the local context of Vietnam, countering the biased image about the country defined by the Vietnam War as portrayed in Hollywood movies or in Communist propaganda. The second group took a rather more indirect approach, examining the past and present from a perspective distant in both space and time. Their method involved re-examining history from a more global perspective, potentially avoiding censorship and making the works more accessible to an international audience.

The significance of the second group of works lies in the fact that they were created by Vietnamese artists living outside of Vietnam. As global citizens, these artists view Vietnam and its history from the perspective of a democratic society. On the other hand, these artists had all returned to live in Vietnam part-time, and had adopted a vague and metaphorical language in their works, avoiding clear expressions and attitudes due to fear of discrimination and causing difficulties with the communist government, which may increase their risk of deportation.

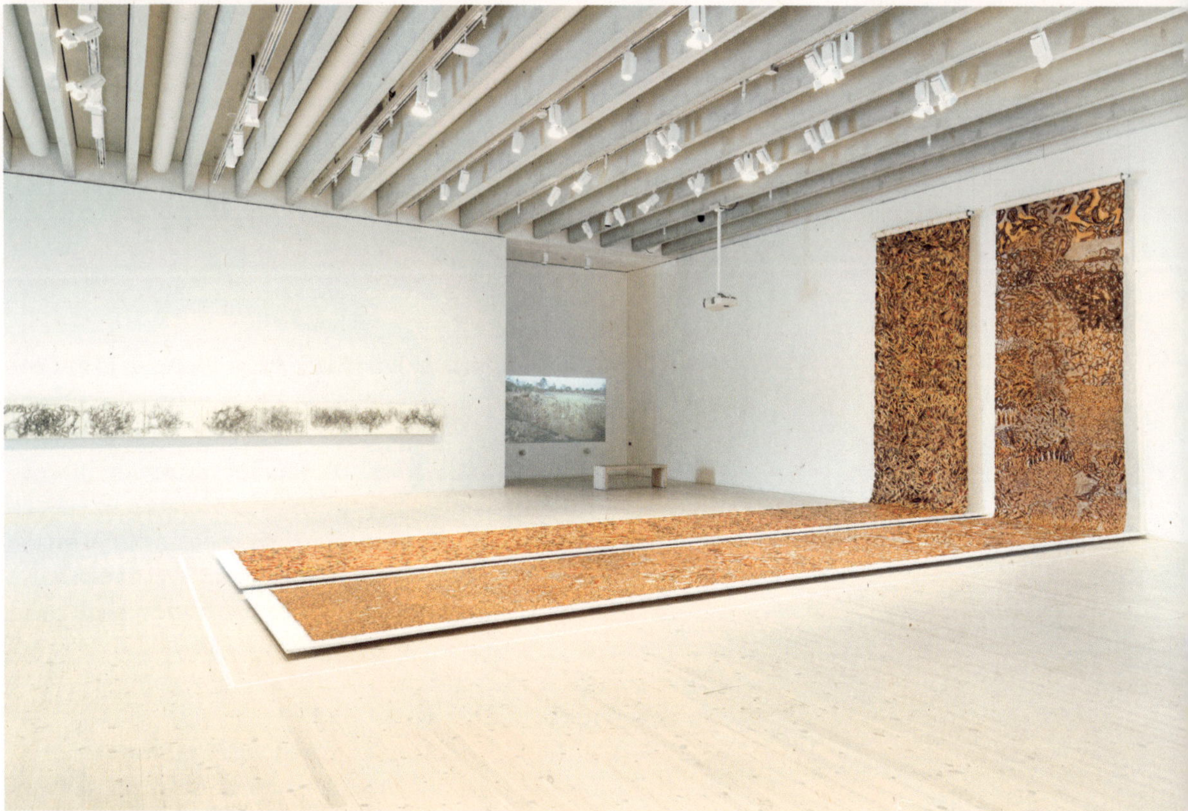

1

2

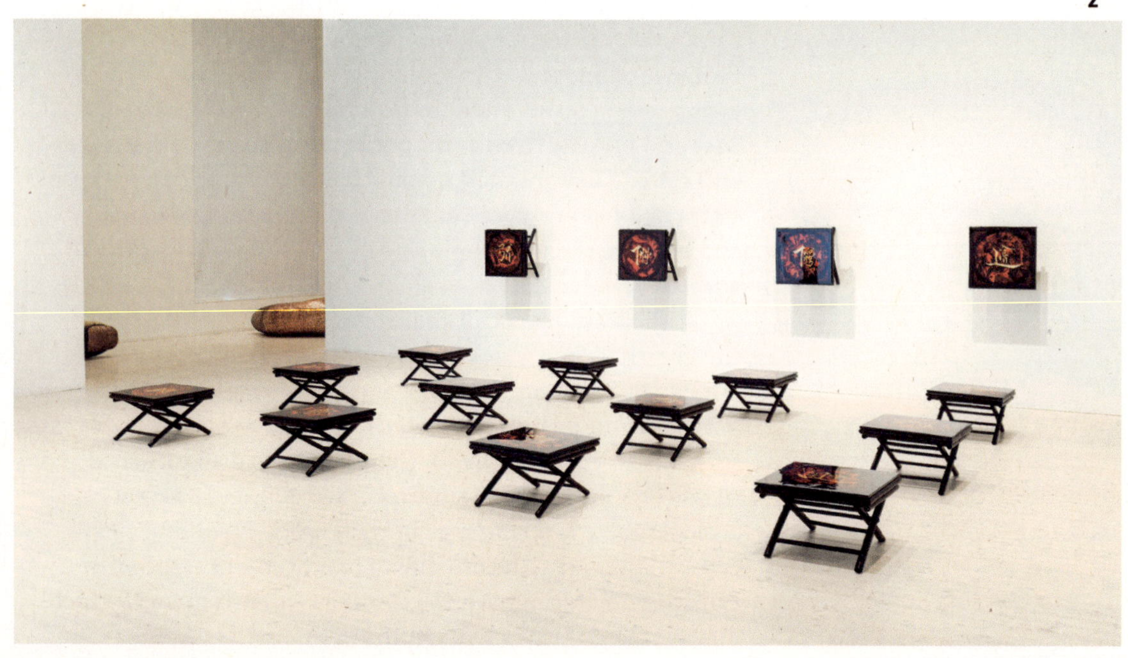

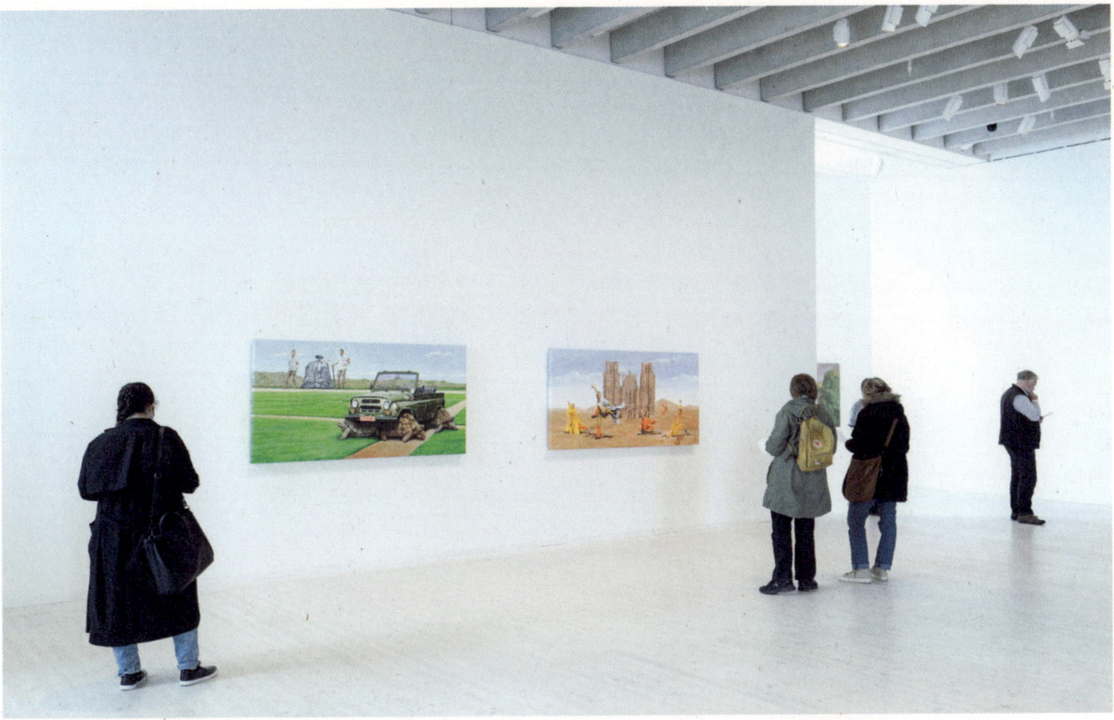

3

1
Phạm Trần Việt Nam, *Oration for ten types of human beings*, 2014-2015, oil on canvas with embroidered details, 168 x 2000 cm. Installation view. Photo: Mikael Lundgren.

2
Nguyễn Thế Sơn, *The Stories of 16 Coffee Tables*, 16 coffee tables with lacquer tabletop, 60 x 60 x 50 cm (each). Installation view. Photo: Mikael Lundgren.

3
Nguyễn Mạnh Hùng, *Patrol, Treasure, Occupy Landscape*, 2014-2015, acrylic on canvas, 200 x 100 cm. Installation view. Photo: Polly Yassin.

4
Trần Tuấn, *Forefinger*, 2013/2015, set of 4, dimensions variable. Installation view. Photo: Polly Yassin.

4

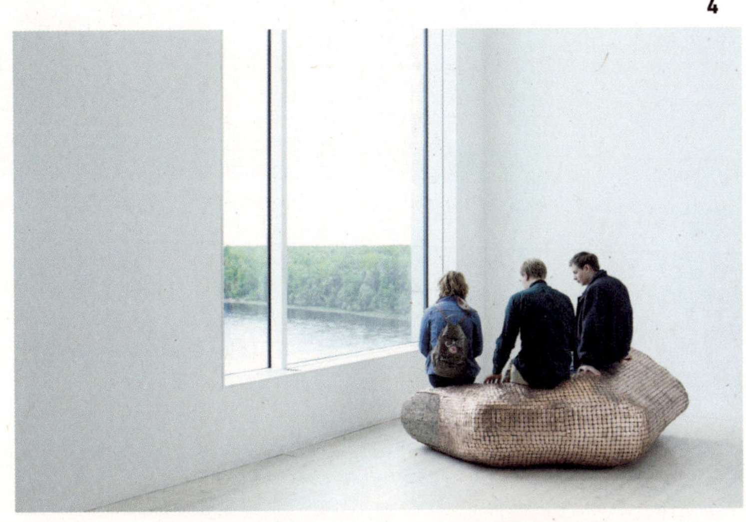

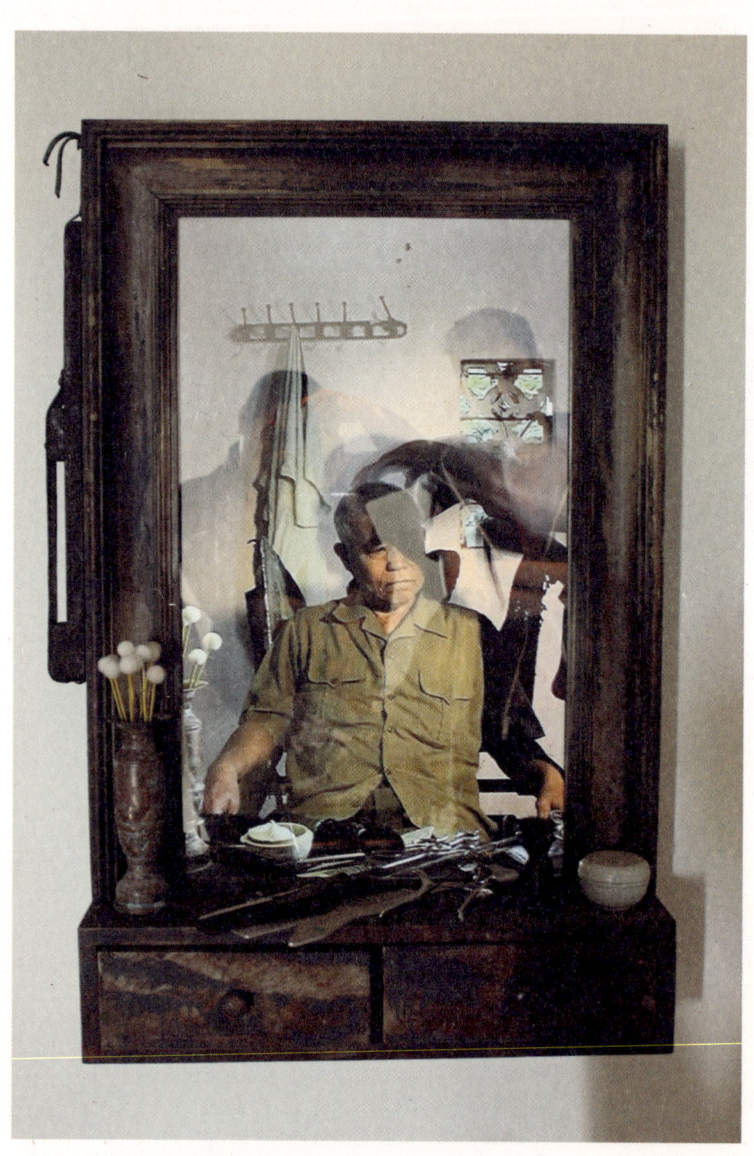

Bàng Nhất Linh, *The Vacant Chair*, 2015, installation with chair made of an aircraft fighter pilot's seat, video loop. Installation view. Photo: Trần Lương.

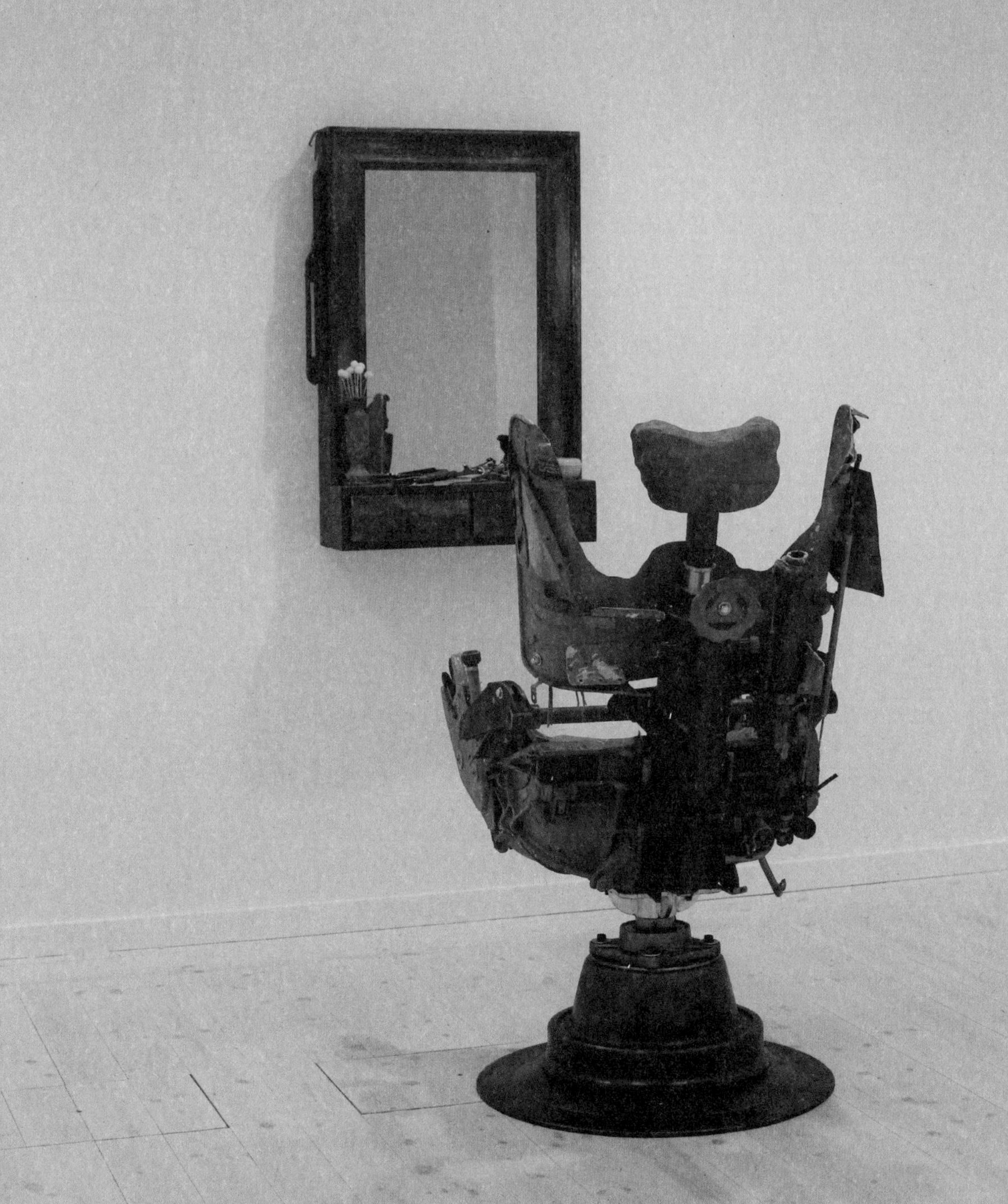

NHÂN VĂN - GIAI PHẨM PERIODICALS[1] / TAIPEI BIENNALE 2016: GESTURES AND ARCHIVES OF THE PRESENT, GENEALOGIES OF THE FUTURE 2016

LOCATION: Taipei Fine Arts Museum DATE: 10 September, 2016–5 February, 2017 CURATOR: Trần Lương ASSISTANTS: Triệu Minh Hải, Lê Thuận Uyên, Lê Hương Quỳnh

The archival project *Nhân Văn – Giai Phẩm* is Trần Lương's ongoing research project, which was shown for the first time at the 2016 Taipei Biennale.

Nhân Văn – Giai Phẩm Periodicals is a series of journals and newspapers that were published in Vietnam over a ten-month period, from February to December 1956. Nhân Văn Giai Phẩm (NVGP) aimed to foster a cultural and art reform movement in Vietnam following the country's independence in 1954, but it was quickly suppressed by the new government. All related documents and works were confiscated and banned from public access, dissemination or publishing until the present time. The archive, displayed at the *Taipei Biennale 2016*, includes a comprehensive collection of books, posthumous manuscripts and sketches by artists, along with two documentary videos about the poets of the NVGP group.

Trần Lương first conceived the idea of the NVGP archive when his father, Mr. Trần Công, a prominent figure within the group, fell ill in 2014. NVGP had a profound impact on Trần Lương, shaping both his life and his artistic direction. Growing up with his father's artist friends, he was immersed in an artistic milieu, yet witnessed the hardships and injustices of societal rejection towards them. These experiences deeply motivated him to start collecting materials, conduct research and establish an archive. For him, this project involved exploring his family's history and presenting NVGP's works to the public with fresh perspectives, reshaping the group's cultural significance for lessons relevant to today. The archive received enthusiastic and reliable support from the artists' families and Mr. Thái Kế Toại, a former police lieutenant colonel. Mr. Toại reviewed the entire NVGP case file and provided significant support to the artists during the hardships of the 1970s-1980s.

Curated by Corinne Diserens, the Taipei Biennial 2016 at Taipei Fine Arts Museum explored the politics of historiography with around 80 participating artists. Themed *Gestures and Archives of the Present, Genealogies of the Future*, it delved into artists' role in challenging power dynamics in public archives.

1. "Nhân Văn – Giai Phẩm (Humanities - Masterwork/ Work of Beauty) was an ideological movement that originated within the Communist Party of Vietnam during the struggle against France led by Ho Chi Minh (1948-1954). It manifested as a literary revolution and a demand for democratisation in North Vietnam between 1954 and 1960 across various domains such as philosophy, ideology, law, education, art, literature, and journalism through various publications. The movement was initiated by artists and intellectuals, most of whom had participated in the army during the anti-French Resistance War. The organisation was later suppressed, its members publicly tried for attempting to overthrow the people's authority, and hundreds of professors, teachers, students, writers, filmmakers, musicians, artists, architects, reporters, publishers and civil servants in several public institutions were subjected to punishment.[...]"

   - Thái Kế Toại, "NHÂN VĂN – GIAI PHẨM: a democratic movement, a failed literary revolution," in *2016 Taipei Biennial Catalogue: Gestures and Archives of the Present, Genealogies of the future*, ed. Corinne Diserens (Taipei: Taipei Fine Arts Museum, 2017), 367.

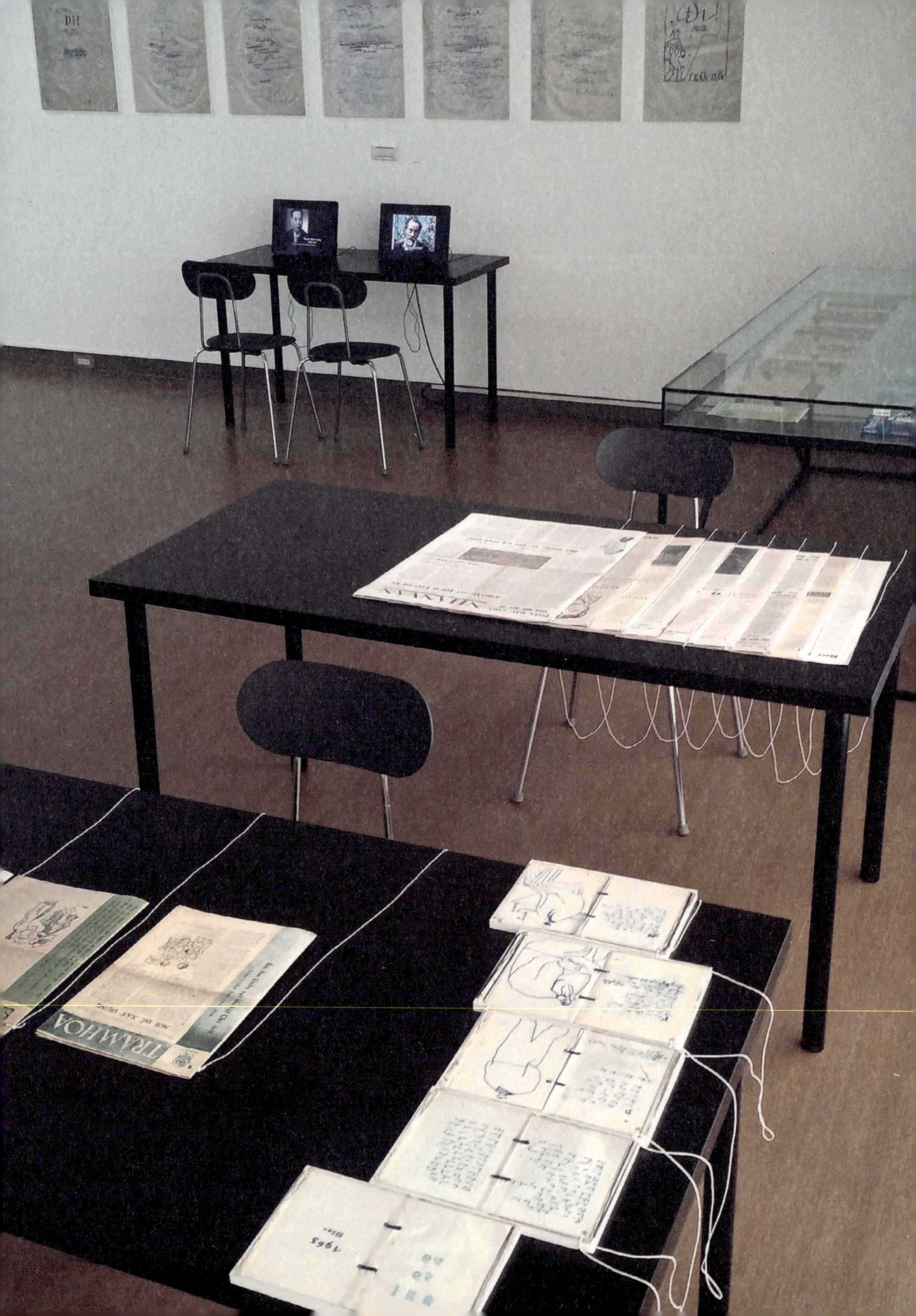

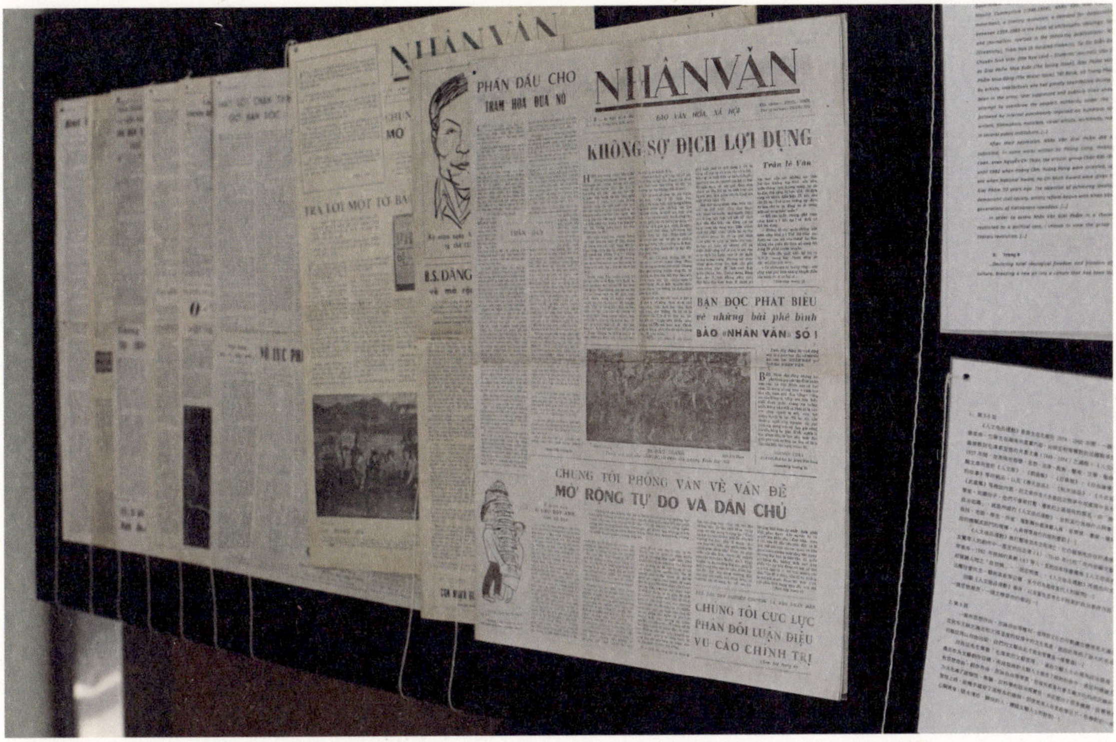

1

1 Replicas of Nhân Văn (Humanities) Newspapers. Photo: Triệu Minh Hải

2 Display of replicas of Giai Phẩm Periodicals, along with other publications of Nhân Văn – Giai Phẩm poets.

2

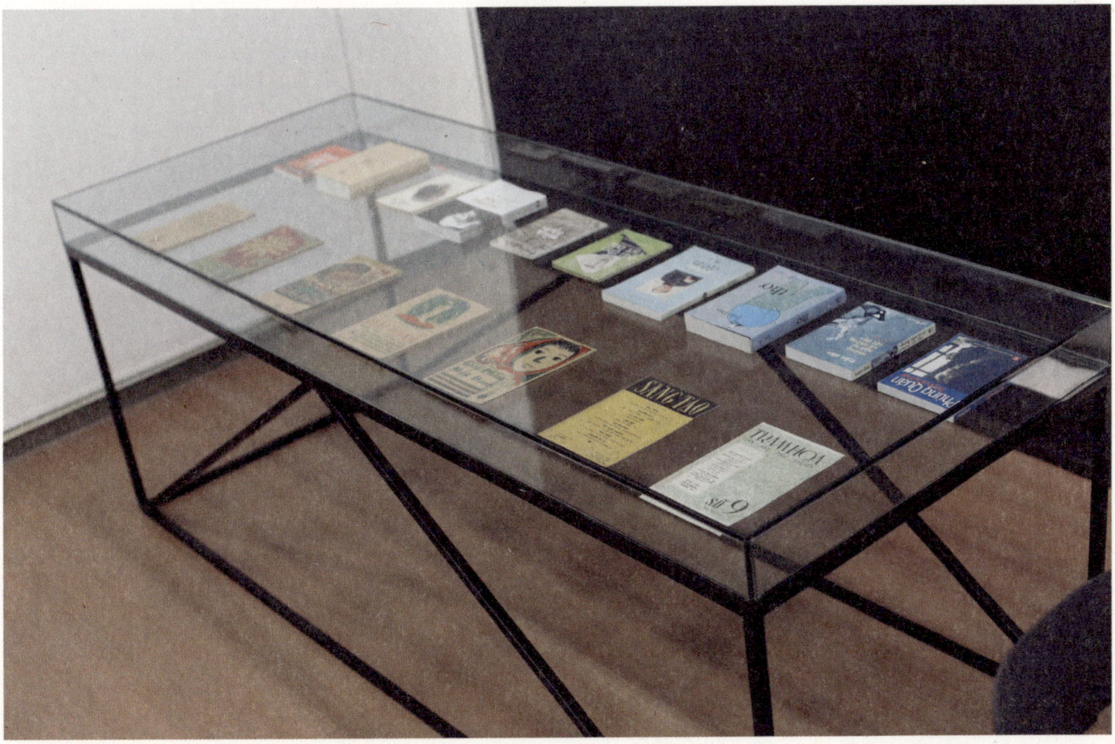

NAVIGATING 'ĐỔI MỚI' - CURATING AS A COMPASS POINT

by **Lê Thuận Uyên**

To date, Trần Lương still uses the English word "curator" to refer to his and his colleagues' practices, despite the widespread circulation of the translated term "giám tuyển" within the artistic community and mainstream media.[1] Lương thinks that the Vietnamese version does not quite encapsulate the complexity and nuances of curatorial work in a context-specific art landscape.[2] Borrowing the word from English, he maintains a degree of distance between the user and the word itself, suggesting a more fluid interpretation of the role, unrestricted by predefined understandings.

The notion of fine art as an independent discipline was officially introduced to Vietnam in 1925 with the establishment of the École Supérieure des Beaux-Arts de l'Indochine (the Indochina Advanced School of Fine art).[3] Despite efforts to research and incorporate local materials such as silk and lacquer into the school's curriculum, it largely remained an extension of French modernist thought. As Vietnam underwent major socio-political upheavals, the school and in general the art structure, had to adapt to changing circumstances amidst periods of war, constant displacement, the influences of Soviet ideology and aesthetics (from both the Eastern bloc and from China during isolation), the Đổi Mới era of free-market reforms and finally a globalised yet fragmented world. These perpetual changes within less than a century have hindered the establishment of a sustainable model for the development of art and culture, let alone its implementation. Post-Đổi Mới Vietnam inherited such a unique context that it would be impossible to simply apply a Western curatorial framework.

In a society without adequate cultural infrastructure for art and culture such as Vietnam (and indeed many other Southeast Asian countries), the role of curator was adopted as an improvised response to the need for space for artistic experimentation, the facilitation of contemporary art development and the provision of counter narratives to existing outsider representations of Vietnamese art on the international stage. There was (and to some extent still is) no

1. In Vietnamese, *giám tuyển* is a Sino-Vietnamese word, with giám meaning 'look closely at, to take care of something' and *tuyển* meaning 'to select, to nominate.' The term refers to the act of creating space for and giving attention and care to something. It is close to the original meaning of the English word.

2. From here on, I refer to Trần Lương as Lương, not as Trần. Using the first name is the way Vietnamese people address one another.

3. Pre-French occupation, art – referring to painting, music, poetry – was part of the holistic knowledge of scholars (mandarins). Other art forms existed in communal and religious architecture and were created collectively.

distinction between museum curators, commercial curators and independent curators, given that a structured system for art creation and circulation was absent.

As curatorial work did not emerge in the Vietnamese art scene until the late 1990s, Trần Lương's reference points were limited. Nevertheless, Lương was not one to blindly adhere to an existing system. He was aware of the trap of a one-size-fits-all model. Over time, through his hands-on approach to a multitude of projects as well as through active participation in the global art system as an artist/representative from Vietnam, Lương has formulated his own curatorial method. While the system's deficiencies can pose challenges, they also afford Lương an opportunity to envision modes of curating that cater to local voices and their needs – those not only of his own generation but also younger practitioners who inherited analogous social conditions.

//

I was first introduced to Lương in 2014 by Đỗ Tường Linh[4] I had just returned to Vietnam from the UK and joined an artist-run space called Nhà Sàn Collective as their manager. I felt compelled to meet as many people as I could so as to learn about the scene. At the time, I was already aware of Trần Lương's position as an important senior figure and his reputation as an uncompromising, blunt and politically vocal artist/curator. We sat down at a casual restaurant inside the publicly owned Trúc Bạch guest house, seated at a plastic table and stools, drinking beer over lunch. The setting was an interesting overlay of time and aesthetics.

Still green experience-wise, I did not arrive prepared. Fortunately, Trần Lương came with questions and initiated the conversation. At the end of lunch, he told me that the best way to learn about Vietnamese contemporary art was to jump straight into it. He mentioned that occasionally he would enlist an assistant to help him with ongoing curatorial projects, suggesting I consider such a role if I ever wanted to become a curator. I was puzzled. For someone with no artistic background of any sort, the role of a curatorial assistant had never occurred to me. I was quite content with focusing on more managerial and administrative tasks. Six months later, I called him and said I had quit my day job as a reporter and was ready to learn more. Lương paused for a while and presented me with a long list of the downsides of working as a curator – financial precarity, the lack of a legal system of support and the disproportionate relation between immense

4. A curator/ researcher now based between the US and Vietnam. She is known for her intergenerational knowledge of the contemporary art scene and is the connector of many artistic collaborations.

work effort and recognition. He questioned whether it was the spotlight and dazzle that I was seeking, cautioning that, if so, this career path might not be suitable. I responded with an affirmation of my intention, to which he said, "You know, you cannot make haste when it comes to art."

For nearly four years, from mid 2014 to late 2018, I worked part time as Lương's assistant, although our collaborations extended beyond that timeframe. There was no defined scope of work. Lương allowed me to choose the projects I wanted to work on – often involving exhibitions, personal archive organisation, artistic research and community-based initiatives – and determine my own level of commitment. While I learned a lot from him and earned his respect as a colleague, our mentor-mentee relationship was not without its trials and tribulations. For the most part, it boiled down to our levels of proximity to the art scene and our disparate historical backgrounds and experiences. Lương who was born during the Vietnam War,[5] was raised in an isolated, ideologically homogenous, culturally suffocating and economically deprived country, and so harboured a much more critical stance towards the authoritarian regime than someone like me. I belonged to the post-Đổi Mới generation and had enjoyed greater access to mobility and freedom, and thus I was more tolerant of the strictly state-controlled governance model. These divergent perspectives sometimes led to conflicting views on the role of art as a significant agent of change in society. Additionally, as an outsider to the art landscape,[6] I was at a distance from the art historical movements, events and communities that Lương had been involved in or had witnessed first-hand. Consequently, I lacked both the understanding of how the scene functioned, and the flexible approach to working with more senior artists,[7] a language that Lương was much more fluent in. Nevertheless, this initial obstacle eventually became a thread of my practice as I learned to value intergenerational knowledge through my years working with Trần Lương.

Now that I have gained more experience and have gradually honed my own voice as a curator, I am able to identify the trajectories of Lương's practice and pinpoint how his approach to curating has informed mine. From time to time, I imagine a conversation with my younger self. In her green days, if I had been there with her, what wisdom would I have shared? The following is an imagined conversation between myself today and that younger self.

5. In Vietnam, the Vietnam War is called the "Resistance War Against America."

6. I did not study art and did not know anyone in the art scene until my return to Vietnam in 2014.

7. Both in age and in their practical experience.

//

It's been a few months since I became Trần Lương's curatorial assistant and I understand now that curating is not exactly a walk in the park. It must have been even more challenging in the 1990s-2000s in Vietnam. Perhaps the work is even more demanding because, in each project, Lương always chooses to invite artists to make new work. Assuming the roles of curator, organiser, fundraiser and translator, he talks about having to 'hand-hold' artists. However, I think he genuinely enjoys working in close collaboration with them. Onlookers have critiqued him for being too deeply involved in the final outcome of the work or for 'grooming' the artists beyond their pace. There are times when I can feel the tension between him and the artists. Lương is an artist himself, which means he can make artworks on his own terms and timing. So why does he bother working with artists in such a vigilant manner knowing it may earn him notoriety? As his assistant and trainee, should I (and could I) follow in his footsteps when I am not fluent in the artists' languages of art making?

One thing that I've observed about Lương is that he does not distinguish between his various forms of practice. To him, art and life are inseparable and thus the curatorial process should be in synergy with how one lives their life. His conception of the relationship between curator and artist is not merely professional and transactional; instead, it is personal. I use the adjective personal loosely here as it does not nesscessarily mean he only works with those he has an existing friendship with. What I want to emphasize is his care for the artists, treating them as friends, or even as brothers and sisters.[8] Consequently, he pays close attention to their thought processes, considering how their personal memories and everyday living conditions impact and inform the way they make their works. Observers may raise their eyebrows at such an approach and how the politics of intimacy might manifest in the final outcome of a curatorial project. Then again, critics must acknowledge that the filter through which they view Lương is one that is perhaps not entirely applicable to Vietnam. Gestures are context specific. Symbols are context specific. Aesthetic expressions also correlate with context. Thus, in order to thoroughly comprehend artistic articulations, and eventually interpret them into public presentations, Lương's choice of

8. In Vietnam, the words brother and sister do not denote blood relation. Rather, they refer to a relationship with care, love and compassion that is comparable to kinship.

maintaining close proximity to the artists (in all permitable aspects) is a choice. It is his curatorial framework.

In addition to his framework, let's zoom out and unpack Trần Lương's intuitive vision. In order to do that, I must take you back to the heyday of contemporary art in Vietnam and reiterate that Trần Lương, like many of his counterparts in the region, became a curator as an improvised response to the lack of organised facilitation of experimental art activities. In a way, he understood that sporadic, spontaneous appearances could not gather a collective force strong enough to lead to long-lasting impact. Moreover, he was incredibly attuned to the political climate of post-Đổi Mới society and seized the opportunity to negotiate for a larger, freer space for artistic expression. There was an unspoken need to represent those with shared aspirations.

Another note for you to consider is the social context into which Lương was born, one in which bombs were still raging overhead. His childhood years were spent in various places, allowing him to see both the harsh reality and the beauty of life beyond the city of Hà Nội. Growing up during wartime meant that uniformity was a camouflage and collective solidarity was crucial for maintaining social order and consolidating the war effort. Individuality was not a virtue at the time, as strict application of the nationalist-communist ideology permeated all aspects of society. At the dawn of change, in the 1990s, as the state apparatus began to slightly relax its grip on cultural matters in an attempt to accommodate new economic rhythms, the sanctioning of distinctive personal identity was set in motion, welcoming a new chapter.[9] Simultaneously, as the country opened its doors to the world and curious eyes turned to Vietnam to search for unheard stories, free-thinking artists had an alternative platform through which they could exhibit their independent, critical voices.

For Lương, perhaps having a distinct and critical approach to his practice (regardless of the forms through which it manifested) was a bold and much needed response to the prolonged stalemate of the local art system. One example of this would be his involvement in the establishment and curatorship of Nhà Sàn Studio in 1998.[10] Sceptical about the possibility of integrating experimental forms such as installation, performance and video art into the official art system at the time, Lương found an alternative way to mobilise resources and support for the artists who ventured beyond conventional practices. There was a strongly felt desire on his part to forge a new aesthetic – a bold, evocative

9. Despite this fact, there were still numerous restrictions due to the obscure terms of cultural policy and the lack of adequate independent support systems.

10. A space that Trần Lương co-founded with artist Nguyễn Mạnh Đức, dedicated to the experimentation of new artistic articulations. Located inside Đức's home – a Mường ethnic wooden house on stilts – the exhibition space hosted many bold, critical works as well as other artistic events that facilitated conversation around experimental, contemporary art.

language that could present more truthful accounts of what was going on.

Trần Lương taught himself many skills, from Western art history to English, budgeting, and many other tasks that neither the educational institutions nor the domestic workplace at the time equipped their associates with. Moreover, he was always aware of his slightly more privileged position,[11] which enabled him to be more perceptive about the surrounding social unfolding. For his generation, remnants of Confucian teachings still resonated, leading to the belief that it was morally righteous to uphold the quality of a *junzi* – a distinguished, moral person who acts more and speaks less, who is loyal to his cause, possesses knowledge, practises self-discipline and who places humanism at his core. Thus, the courteous thing to do was to pass on his experience, to inform and guide his younger colleagues. And one effective way to do that was through his curatorial projects. *Green, Red & Yellow* (2003) was an exhibition that manifested a clear, consolidated approach to exhibition making or curating. After developing his curatorial concept (or a prompt), Lương reached out to invite artists and worked intently with them to develop their ideas into fully formed sketches and production plans. Lương was also in conversation with artists on the spatial arrangement of each artwork. He acted as the negotiator between the artists and the venue, and as a moderator between the artists and their audiences.

11. Both in terms of financial and social capital as he comes from a household of generational intellect.

//

It is true that he takes pride in supporting others. We often talk about Eastern martial arts fiction and recount tales of heroic acts. I think that is why he is quite keen on building infrastructures for the arts in different forms and scales. I now recall that Trần Lương was also involved in the establishment of another space called Hà Nội Contemporary Art Center (Trung tâm Mỹ thuật đương đại). Right now, he is not associated with any space. What about in the future? I know he often tells me that space is not the most important factor in building a healthy art ecosystem, but I think he's very conscious of space-making and the experiential aspect of physical exhibitions.

Quite rightly so. I don't know where to begin because you are bringing up a very broad topic. I can tell you straight away that he has been the director of a space called APD since

2020.[12] Prior to that he was not associated with any space in particular, however he is always active.

One thing to take away from your comment is his awareness of the physical experience of artworks. This spatial sensibility is cultivated through his performance art practice as well as through his participation in the making of art spaces (Nhà Sàn Studio, Hà Nội Contemporary Art Center, APD) and the programming for various organisations over the years, including the Goethe Institut, L'espace, British Council and the Factory Contemporary Art Center, among others.

Lương impresses organisers and audiences alike with many of his performances, for instance, *Groping for the past / Lần mò quá khứ* (2002, Civitella Ranieri Center, Italy),[13] *Welts* (2007 - ongoing),[14] *M(A)outh-cleaning* (2007, Dadao Live Art Festival, Beijing),[15] and many other works that directly respond to his immediate context. His performative gestures suggest to the audience not only the region that he comes from, but also his attitudes towards the site he is working in and his expression of complex emotions or psychological states of mind that are challenging to articulate verbally. You are probably wondering why I mention his performances? I notice that this performativity bleeds into his curation, for Lương is very mindful of the viewers' behaviour, gestures and reactions upon encountering an artwork. The visual dimension is key to the placement of his artworks, but the sensorial aspect of a display is of no less importance. Manifested in the exhibition format, which is of a much more measured and balanced manner, this trait may have stemmed partly from his bodily experience of making performances in different venues and contexts.

With regards to exhibition making, Lương makes it a serious business to learn about the site in order to interpret his idea in the designated space.[16] Research is therefore key to his exhibition layout process. That being said, Lương is never a curator who works on paper. He understands that the ability of artistic interventions to move, disturb and engage the audience comes from a thorough comprehension of the site. This means that if a project engages with a specific site or community, he always builds field trips into his timeline and encourages artists to stay and engage with the locals. If the project is an exhibition in a foreign country, it's important for Lương as a curator to spend time locally, on-site. This allows him to find ways to facilitate dialogues among the works, aiming for a universally shared understanding that is more accessible to the public. He believes that the works on display should attempt to communicate with the existing

12. The abbreviation for Centre for Art Patronage and Development, an art organisation established in October 2020 with the goal of supporting art creation and promoting socio-cultural development. https://apd.org.vn/en/about-us/

13. Where he dug out soil to create a pond and threw in duckweed along with objects he had collected previously from Vietnam. During his performance, Lương taped a piece of paper with a drawing of open eyes over his eyes and jumped into the pond to fish out the objects.

14. One of Lương's performances that has taken place on various occasions, where the audience members are invited to hit him with a red scarf. The performamce was inspired by him witnessing his son come home from school adorned with a red scarf, proof of his new membership in the Communist Children's Association.

15. Trần Lương brushed his teeth on Tiananmen Square in Beijing, during a visit with other artists and organisers of the Dadao Live Art Festival.

16. Here, exhibition making is not confined to the presentation of artworks in a space that is purposely built for art. It could mean an organised display of artworks in a public or private space, a performance art festival, or a project where art is only a part of the overall programme.

interconnected layers of architectural structure, ambient sound, temperature, light, social history and whatever else is present in the context.

//

I am currently assisting him with the Miền Méo Miệng exhibition. Translating his curatorial text into English causes me a lot of headaches. This is because his analogies are often either visual or tactile, and his references are contextually specific. He is meticulous with his English translation too, as he understands the connotations that the 'wrong' choice of words could have. I notice that Trần Lương seems to have a distinctive approach to naming his projects. Such as, Green, Red and Yellow (2003), Something Fell, Falling and Will fall (2008), LIM DIM (2004 & 2009), Phập Phồng (2011) and Miền Méo Miệng (2015), to name a few. Their commonality lies in their idiomatic sound, embodying an expressive yet playful state of mind. I wonder if this reflects his dark humour or a deliberate strategy to make a statement.

Let's revisit some of the examples you mentioned and unpack them a bit:

LIM DIM is a duplicated word specifically describing the state of one's eyes being partially open while drifting in and out of sleep.[17] The name was used for an international performance art festival in Hà Nội that Trần Lương curated and organised with support from Ryllega Gallery, Goethe Institut Hà Nội, British Council, Bến Bạc Restaurant and La Ferme du Colvert Camp. In 2009, he curated a group exhibition in Oslo showcasing the artworks of Vietnamese artists under the same title.

Something Fell, Falling and Will fall (2008) was a group exhibition for which the curator's statement was written in poetic verse, aimed at evoking an obscure state of mind rather than offering a contextual description of the exhibition.[18]

Phập Phồng (2011) showcased works by six female artists of the Chaap Collective at the Goethe Institut in Hà Nội.[19] The curator's statement served as a prompt for the exhibition, highlighting contrasting attitudes, bodily gestures, states of mind and more.

Miền Méo Miệng (2015) translates literally as "The

17. "...[It] is first and foremost an exhibition of Vietnamese art, but more importantly it is an exhibition that presents a new generation whose work has rarely been shown in Europe. More specifically, the exhibition presents a group of artists who are socially interconnected, who meet regularly for dinner and drinks, exhibit in outsider venues such as the cutting-edge Nhà Sàn Duc Studio, share the outsider status of official non-recognition, and closely observe and consistently challenge everyday order while they are constantly subject to quiet scrutiny. Hence the highly metaphorical title of the exhibition." – From the exhibition catalogue.

18. An exhibition that took place at L'espace in Hà Nội, presenting the works of Nguyễn Huy An, Nguyễn Trần Nam and Nguyễn Hồng Hải. The statement can be accessed here: https://apd.org.vn/en/uncategorized-en/2008-something-fell-falling-and-will-fall/

19. Information on the project can be found here: https://apd.org.vn/en/library/online/2010-2020-en/2011-phap-phong-2/

land of the Distorted." An excerpt from the preface of the exhibition catalogue explains, "consideration and contortion are required in order to express one's opinion in Vietnamese society, a reality with origins in the country's history. A serious and critical message is often hidden behind a seemingly innocent and sometimes humorous statement."[20]

20. Information on the project can be found here: https://apd.org.vn/en/library/online/2010-2020-en/elementor-13835/

Trần Lương is actually a very playful person, finding enjoyment in teasing and witty satire. His sense of humour echoes through his texts, whether it's his artist statement or his curatorial elaborations. Being the son of a filmmaker associated with the Nhân Văn Giai Phẩm movement,[21] Lương grew up surrounded by avant-garde writers and artists of 1950s Hà Nội. Perhaps this environment ignited a literary interest in Lương? Regardless of the influence, Lương started contemplating the auditory and sensory triggers of the Vietnamese language at a young age.

21. The *Nhân Văn-Giai Phẩm* affair was a cultural-political movement in North Vietnam in the second half of the 1950s. Two periodical journals were started during that time, *Nhân Văn* and *Giai Phẩm*; which published critical reviews of repetitive, cliche and hollow works and advocated for freedom of artistic expressions.

From very early on, Lương developed a clear approach to writing his texts: words that embody both sound and visual imagination, titles that intrigue exhibition viewers, statements that enable open and fluid interpretation of the works and writings that project originality as well as personal characteristics. His technique of writing (or rather composing), places emphasis on the indicative power of the text. Using Vietnamese is a deliberate strategy that Lương employs due to its ability to capture and reiterate the nuances of the local sensibility. It suggests a form of cultural memory grounded in climate cycles, habitual routines, folkloric practices and spiritual beliefs. Such textual articulations are proposals for an adhesive agent that can bridge the past and the present, connecting what is happening currently with what is to come.

But such a method does not only target the local audience. The appearance of foreign-sounding words in a Western art space can create a very strong and loud message, especially in the 2000s (and even early 2010s). It was a reclamation of agency, a renegotiation of what the 'Vietnamese narrative' is. What could be more pronounced and resounding than a Vietnamese man representing his and his people's own stories on the international stage? It is important to note that prior to this moment, exhibitions on Vietnamese art were predominantly curated by foreign curators who may not have been fully attuned to the deeply rooted micro-historical narratives and cultural nuances. Language served as a visible marker that could signal insiders' stories. However, Trần

Lương was not oblivious to the potential exoticisation of the language itself. Understanding that meaning can easily be lost in translation, if Lương were to incorporate Vietnamese words, he would not opt for the somewhat standardised method of writing a curatorial text. Hence, he adopted a more prose-like, idiomatic approach that laid out possible connotations and implications of what the terms could mean.

//

Trần Lương takes pride in his engagement with development projects beyond the art landscape and views contemporary art practice as a socially conscious endeavour. He believes that artists should not retreat to their ivory tower, but actively engage with the social issues rooted in their everyday life. He is a keen advocate for artistic conversations (and displays) to take place in unconventional spaces so that artworks have a more direct interaction with the public. Lương is also a fervent critic of what he deems bureaucratic, repetitive and superficial programmes. Essentially, Lương believes that contemporary art should be at the forefront of a wider social movement to remain relevant and meaningful. I don't disagree with his view as I do think that art can open up new questions and inspire people to think in new ways. Then again, don't you think it is a bit coercive and rigid to assume that all artworks must carry such social weight? Can't a project just be deeply personal?

I consider Lương part of what I call 'the sandwiched generation' – those who have experienced both ends of the war and peace spectrum, along with its embedded perplexing moments and complications. This means that he constantly had to navigate through the relays of personal, familial and global histories. He is a hopeless romantic who believes in change. Similar to his revolutionary predecessors, Lương devotes himself to a cause and stays on course until the end. And because of that, being socially relevant is very important to him.

Additionally, as I said at the beginning of our conversation, demonstrating one's critical and creative self unapologetically is a profoundly personal endeavour. Trần Lương is very critical of the repetitive, outdated function of the public cultural institutions and their programming. He often expresses his frustration with the public system's lack of accountability and transparency. For Lương, ownership of one's actions is crucial in building a healthy art landscape. In 2001, he organised the *Mạo Khê Coal Mine* project in an effort to reform the dated and ineffective painting field trips of the Vietnam Fine Art Association.[22] Instead of staying in a public guest house or a hotel, the 11 invited artists lived with the workers in their lodging and followed them to work so as to grasp the precarity of life as a coal miner. The idea was to create direct exposure in order to facilitate possible open conversation that could lead to mutual understanding, shared values and the clashing realities of life in a "modernised and globalised Vietnamese society."[23] Artists should respond to life, instead of merely documenting it through a romanticised or ideologically distorted lens. This project also reflects Lương's view on the artist's positionality in the contemporary context.

The *Mạo Khê* (2001) project inaugurated a series of what would become known as the Outdoor Projects.[24] These include *Fairy Tale Soup* (2003), where video and mixed media installations were presented outdoors in the courtyard of the Vietnam Opera House; *Riverscapes IN FLUX* (2012-2013), which examines the human impact on changing river courses and subsequent environmental degradation; and *Journey of Green Vietnam* (2014), resulting from a long-term field research project under the same name. This project was carried out by the Ministry of Culture, Sports and Tourism, in collaboration with Film No.1 Joint Stock Company and Tali's Company. It aimed to raise community awareness about environmental protection through art and cultural activities. Trần Lương is a keen advocate for contemporary art to be included in the social development conversation, believing that materialistic possession is only one part of the equation, and that art and culture have the power to hold a space for understanding and re-evaluating value systems. Having said that, the common thread among all these projects is Lương's uncompromising artistic demands when it comes to displaying the artworks created from these projects. He relentlessly pushes artists to be responsive to their immediate locality without instrumentalising their artistic language as a tool to tell the stories of others. Lương is first and foremost an artist, which means that even in his very public-oriented undertakings, he reserves an intimate space for the individualistic journey of artmaking.

//

22. A detailed explanation of this project is included in another article in this publication written by Phoebe Scott (p.55-63).

23. A phrase that was often used in mainstream media to talk about the success of Vietnam in the Đổi Mới era.

24. A term coined by Trần Lương himself. Please refer to his Mạo Khê project statement here: https://apd.org.vn/en/library/online/2000-2010-en/2001-mao-khe-coal-mine-project/statement-of-mao-khe-coal-mine-project-steam-rice-man/

Lương has always had an interesting vision of himself in the future. When I was new to this role, he told me countless times that there would come a day when he would sit in a wheelchair and I would be busy juggling multiple projects like he was doing at that time. I would tell him how outdated he was, and he would be proud knowing that I had made it on my own.

...

As I moved cities and took on different job opportunities to explore my own path to curating, my trajectory shifted as a consequence. Trần Lương's imagined future is nowhere in sight as he is still incredibly active, and I am still struggling to formulate my own curatorial methodology. Nevertheless, I can see that he and I have grown to execute our shared vision for the local art scene through different pathways. I adopt a much more laissez-faire curatorial approach, working with artists who may not fit the categories of socially conscious artists, but who are wrestling with the anxiety of a post-human world. My work aims to broaden contemporary art audiences through exhibitions and public programmes geared towards the very general public. Additionally, I focus on capacity building for a network of private donors who have the potential to support art practitioners.

As I continue my journey, I am beginning to map out the threads of my practice more vividly and trace the thoughts that informed such threads. I notice that my idea of time – time for pacing, time spent with the artists, time making dues – is very much influenced by Lương. I am now one of the few curators in Vietnam who often works with artists from across generations, understanding the significant impact of thinking about legacy in an increasingly fragmented world. I've learned to agree to disagree with Lương, realising that influence manifests itself in both harmony and negation. And I carry in my work the infrastructure he has built so that I can tackle different artistic pursuits.

Lê Thuận Uyên
Hà Nội, March 2024

ONGOING WORK WITH COMMUNITIES

For two decades Trần Lương has actively participated in various projects working with communities on the margins across Vietnam. One of his earliest involvements was in 2005 with *Water Droplets*, where he spent months working with both children and adults on Điệp Sơn and Ninh Tân islands. Some of these endeavours have leaked into contemporary art language, as seen in *On the Banks of the Red River* [see pages 134-135] or in exhibition presentations such as the *Journey of Green Vietnam project* [see pages 242-245]. However, the majority of these initiatives remain unarticulated and unrecognised in the broader understanding of the role of art and culture in times of climate disasters, resource scarcity and the widening gaps between different communities – issues that we are all facing today.

Complex and multi-layered, the community initiatives that Trần Lương's has been involved with engage local governments, indigenous elders, local communities with specific needs and young cultural workers. They require complex coordination to execute, involving architects, researchers, geologists, botanists, local farmers and many others with knowledge of the land and its relation with water, climate-adaptive building practices and rituals fostering community resilience, among other issues. The projects are challenging, demanding not only the creation of physical infrastructure but, more importantly, soft infrastructures and relationships essential for integration into the community. Many of these initiatives challenge the knowledge structures, language and vocabulary that Trần Lương himself is accustomed to as an artist.

Reflecting on this part of Lương's work, I cannot help but think that his understanding of the limitations of installation as a form and his gesture of moving away from it, is framed by the specific climate conditions of the tropics and the attendant impossibility of maintaining objects in a museological state of permanence due to humidity, as well as the social urgencies within Vietnamese society. These urgencies are addressed through community initiatives led by Lương at the Sống Foundation, where teams collaborate with various communities in different areas of Vietnam to work on tangible measures aimed at addressing survival on the planet. I would like to propose viewing these socially engaged practices as social installations – gestures and structures that serve a purpose in communities, rather than the creation of museological objects.

This section of the book, featuring conversations between myself and Trần Lương and a text by Linh Lê, offers insight into the ongoing work that Trần Lương has been undertaking in collaboration with the Sống Foundation.

Biljana Ciric

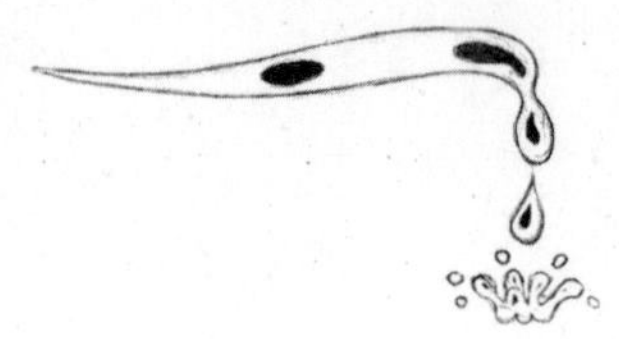

BC: When did your collaboration with the Sống Foundation begin?

TL: It's been ten years already. It started at the beginning of 2013. During those first four years, I was the chair of the Sống Foundation's advisory board, though unofficially. During those initial four years we only worked in areas prone to flooding. I was mainly doing fundraising. I activated the artistic community to donate paintings, which we then auctioned in Hà Nội and Sài Gòn to raise funds.[1] We held these auctions twice a year, and this funding was a major resource that helped the Sống Foundation to survive.

From early 2016 to early 2017, the Sống Foundation started to gain a better reputation in society, allowing us to get more support. We also started to explore crowdfunding and applying for funding from corporations. My job required less fundraising, and from late 2016, we began charting a new direction for Sống. This involved addressing wider problems, such as planting mangrove forests in the Mekong Delta, specifically in Sóc Trăng province. We also planted dry forests in central Vietnam, in Ninh Thuận province, which is the province with the lowest rainfall in the country. We also implemented two Happy Village projects in Quảng Nam province (central Vietnam); one in Bắc Trà My district and another in Nam Trà My district. The reforestation and Happy Village projects continue to this day.

Since then, my involvement has deepened, and I am now in the position of Vice President. These days it is me and the President who are guiding the foundation. I also spent a lot of time travelling around the country, making agreements with local governments and overseeing things on site. Of course, we have local partners and people whom we employ, but it's important for us to also be present on site.

After COVID, we reorganised the Sống Foundation because we still had a lot of people donating money. We're now building something more in-depth and structured. I

1. Vietnamese people usually call Ho Chi Minh City "Sài Gòn" or "Saigon", the city's name before 1975.

am in charge of the *River Ơi* project. "Ơi" means "Hey." River Ơi aims to incorporate additional cultural elements into our projects.

So, last year, as part of the River Ơi project, we organised a group of visual artists to visit Lâng Loan village. Our objective was to discuss and advise people on drawing patterns on the pillars of the Quật house, a structure that has disappeared in the transition from wartime to peacetime. People no longer build these kinds of houses, which in the past served as a community house with a tall roof. Each ethnic group developed a distinctive style for their Quật house, according to the local geography. The common feature among these Rong houses (known as *Quật houses* or "house for worship" by the Xơ Đăng people) is their very special column and roof structure designed to withstand the winds of the high mountains. This structure is very different from the column and roof structures found in houses on the plains.

We researched the patterns and decorative motifs of different community houses. From this research we selected specific decorative motifs used on the columns of the houses of the Xơ Đăng people, where we built the Quật house.

We engaged many experts to contribute documents and opinions, including the former director of the Hà Nội Museum of Ethnology and an old photographer who has made many research trips to the region. In the Central Highlands, we also engaged an ethnographic researcher specializing in the Central Highland region. We have gathered some important monographs, including photos from Catholic monks and colonial documents from France. These documents were brought to Lâng Loan to discuss with local community elders about which samples should be used. The elders discussed the materials for a long time before deciding.

After that, we also discussed the location of the patterns on parts of the Quật house, which was challenging because some details had been completely forgotten after so many decades. The whole process was carried out using the co-design method. Of course, we cannot do things exactly like they used to because materials and climate conditions have changed. We don't have so much wood anymore!

For example, today it is impossible to do traditional thatched roofing. The leaves are still growing there, but the price to collect them is way too expensive compared to using other materials. Simply because the main human resources in the community are young people who have gone to work in industrial zones near big cities. If the old and weak villagers go to collect grass and leaves to roof their houses, the cost will be very high. We had to find another solution to adapt to the situation, while still using materials indigenous to the region. These were some of the discussions we had.

BC: How did you choose Quảng Nam province in central Vietnam? Is it because it is particularly affected by landslides or poverty? What was your decision based on?

TL: We made the decision ourselves by going out into the field, meeting people, seeing the situation and encountering the issues directly. It is very important to have the space to make these connections, otherwise the community will just ignore us, feeling that they don't need us or our project.

BC: Is your work with the Sống Foundation voluntary, or do you receive a salary for it?

TL: Me? For ten years, zero dollars. Sometimes I even contribute my own money. But, you know, in another sense I do it that way to survive. If I were to get paid, the official system would kill me. They hate people like me who constantly raise awareness among poor people. That's why I don't take any money, so they cannot accuse me of not paying taxes.

BC: Can you tell me about the River Ơi project?

TL: River Ơi is a project that focuses on raising awareness about climate change and environmental issues among local people. It addresses problems stemming from broken indigenous community and family structures. We focus on preserving and adapting beliefs, religions, customs and culture in the new status quo. We practise through building site-specific field projects and learn from these experiences. We also try to influence policy, open new directions and replicate successful projects. We are trying to wake up traditional knowledges like sewing and traditional weaving. Ethnic minorities often grow hemp mainly for the fibre to weave thick and durable fabrics. We also try to experiment alongside them, with new materials, trying to understand why certain materials are used. For example, certain natural materials are used to build houses because they contain oils with a strong smell, which means insects will not eat them. Then, we think about how to make new materials as the old ones are disappearing.

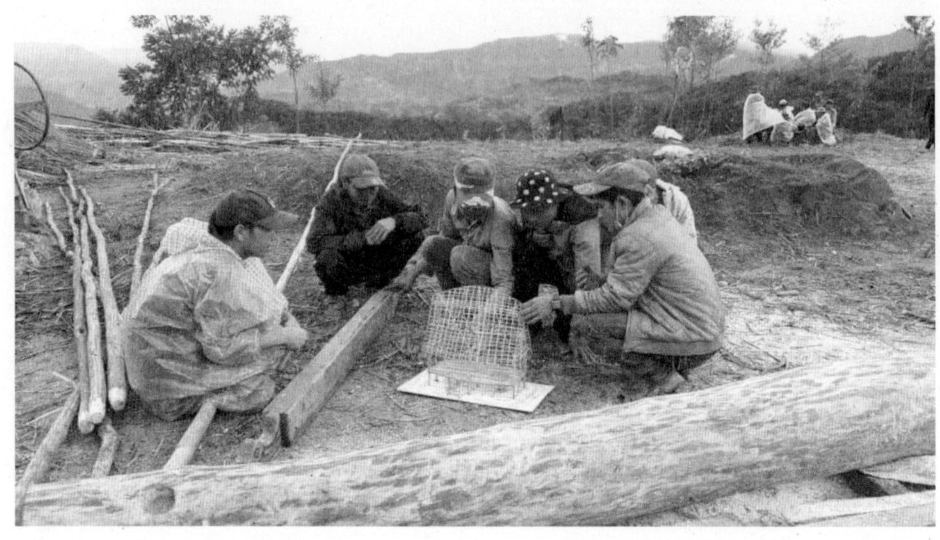
1

2

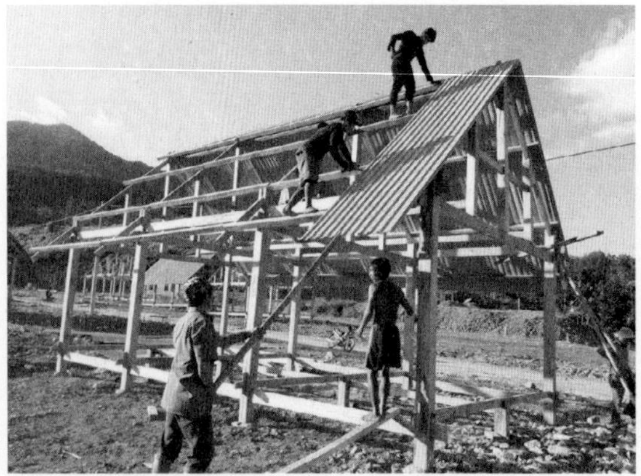
3

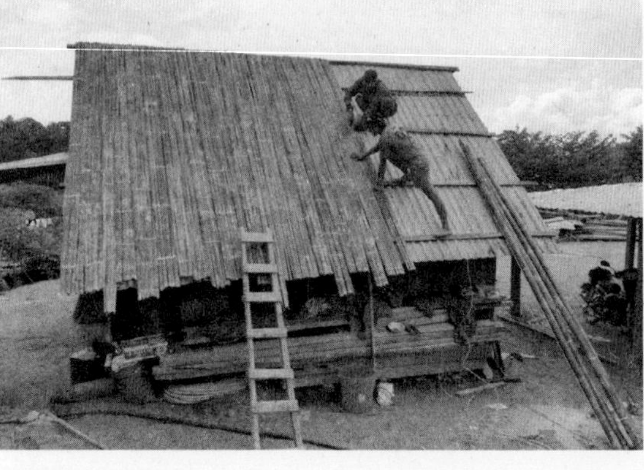

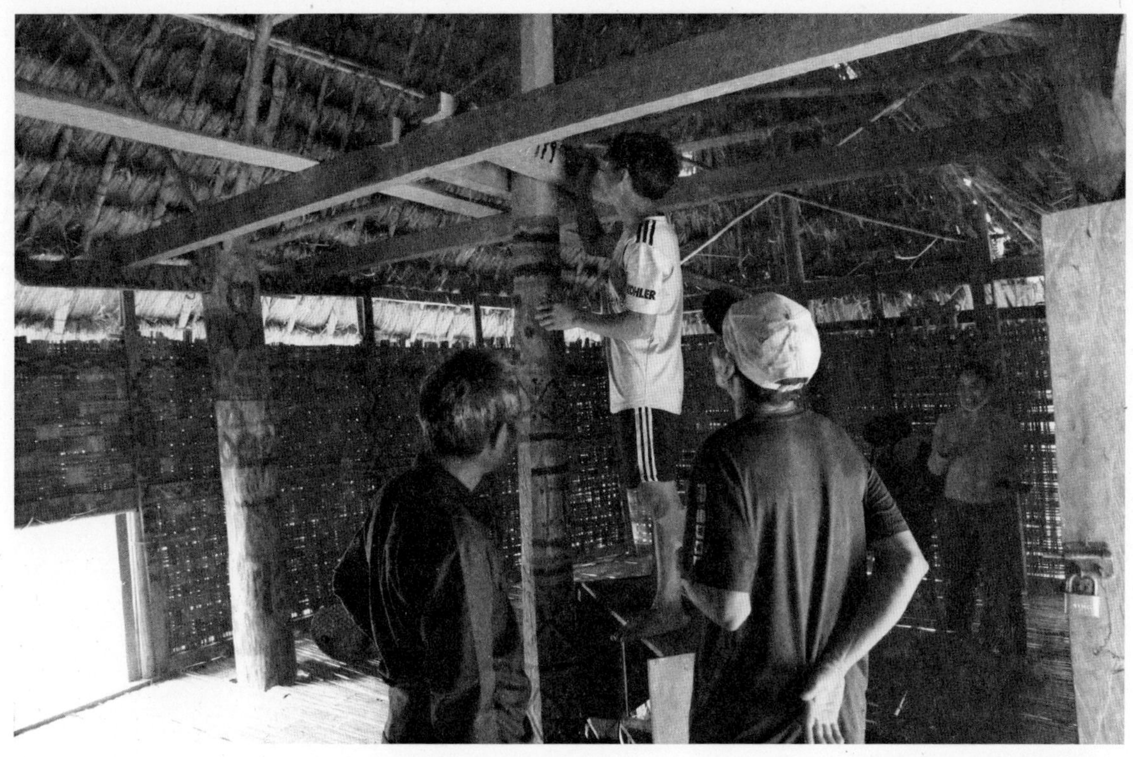

4

1
Mr. Hồ Văn Hai (wearing a grey shirt in the middle), a skilled carpenter from the village, gathered with village elders and young men around the Quật house model. He explained the structure of the Quật house and how to connect the beams, which have bird motifs carved at both ends and are pierced through by two main pillars. After his explanation, tasks were assigned based on each villager's abilities. The construction of the Quật house started in late August 2020. Photo by architect Đinh Bá Vinh.

2
The process of building a resettlement village for seven different Ca Dong villages in Hamlet 3, Bắc Trà My district. When the Sống Foundation took over this project in May 2020, the location had already been chosen by the district authorities, situated near a lowland area. The new resettlement houses were pre-designed in the style of plains houses. During construction, the locals adapted these designs based on their traditional building habits, resulting in unstable structures. Additionally, the new houses were unsuitable for the local weather conditions and traditional living habits. From this project, the Sống Foundation learned many lessons and gained much experience for developing the *Happy Village* project in Lâng Loan village, Nam Trà My (Quảng Nam province).

3
The process of building houses for the Xơ Đăng people in Lâng Loan village in July 2020, Nam Trà My district, involved reconstructing the houses using old house frames transported from the previous village. Architect Đinh Bá Vinh then provided advice and solutions on house modifications and reinforcement. After the houses were completed, the Sống team encouraged the villagers to cover the metal roofs with local bamboo (lồ ô) to reduce heat, minimise rain noise, and maintain traditional aesthetics. The photo shows the kitchen of village chief Hồ Văn Cư, which also serves as the office for the Happy Village project.

4
After the Quật house construction was completed, Trần Lương, along with artists Trịnh Ngân Hạnh and Flinh, sought to rediscover the decorative motifs of the Quật house of the Xơ Đăng people. In June 2023, they visited Lâng Loan village to discuss the decoration of the Quật house with the village elders. Once the ideas were agreed upon, the artists and villagers enthusiastically participated in redecorating the Quật house. Photo by Flinh.

A FIELD NOTE ON FIELD TRIPS

by **Linh Lê**

SEEING WITH YOUR OWN EYES

At 5 am we boarded a bus that took us from Vĩnh Châu, a town in Sóc Trăng province, bound for Lạc Hoà village, where the Sống Foundation[1] has been implementing its forest-regrowth project, Green Happiness,[2] since 2020. After about 20 minutes, the bus dropped us off at an intersection where a smaller, patchy tarmac road led to the field. As we walked, the sleepy town gradually emerged before us, bathed in the warm morning sun, which cast its glistening light on the signature pointy roofs of a Khmer Buddhist temple. Its majesty was juxtaposed against a nearby gigantic windmill and a row of quaint one-story concrete houses. Who would have thought that this landscape, with its inevitable blend of lush nature, rich culture and advanced technology in a small village in the depths of the Mekong Delta, could one day disappear into the water?[3]

A group of local Khmer men, dressed in navy long-sleeved t-shirts (the uniform of the Green Happiness team) arrived with saplings, bundles of bamboo stakes, and rectangular foam boards. Their voices, switching constantly between Vietnamese and Khmer, carried a certain sense of urgency, disrupting the quiet, serene atmosphere. They started lining up all the foam boards in a ditch and loaded saplings, bamboo stakes and other equipment onto them.

At 6:15 am, water began to flow into the ditch. We all started walking alongside the ditch on a slippery dirt path. As we walked, the water level in the ditch started rising and its flow became increasingly fiercer. I was told that people in the Mekong Delta live and work in close relation with "con nước" or tidal schedule, which varies daily. There are days when these men must reach the ditch at 2 am to catch the rising tide because without it, they would have to use mules to transport heavy loads along 15 kilometres of slippery dirt roads and boggy swamps. This human-environmental interdependence, which seems both astonishing and paradoxical to me as someone accustomed to a fixed schedule, is a way of life that

1. Sống Foundation is a Vietnam-based non-profit social fund that was founded by Ms Phạm Thị Hương Giang (Jang Kều) in 2013. With a focus on sustainable community development, its first programme, *Resilient Houses*, has been providing housing solutions and aid to areas that are affected by natural disasters in Vietnam since 2013.

2. Launched in 2020, *Green Happiness* is a programme initiated by the Sống Foundation, which focuses on ecological restoration through afforestation in Ninh Thuận and Sóc Trăng, Vietnam. By planting native species in each area with careful scientific monitoring, the project hopes to restore the green lungs for these areas, while preserving depleting groundwater (Ninh Thuận), and preventing landslides (Sóc Trăng).

3. A 2021 study suggested that the delta will be underwater by the year 2100.
Thu Hang, Ngoc Tai, Hoang Nam, "Vietnam's Mekong Delta, world's youngest river basin, might be first one gone," VNExpress International, September 2, 2023, https://fishbio.com/news/vietnams-mekong-delta-worlds-youngest-river-basin-might-be-first-one-gone/

has been passed down through many generations in the delta. Perched on the foam board, we floated out into a vast body of water that, only two hours later, would reveal its true self as a swamp.

Upon our arrival in the field at around 8am, the men quickly got to work forming into different groups: one using a strong water hose to create a hole in the mud, another quickly planting the saplings, and the last securing the young saplings using three bamboo stakes and a plastic band. The entire operation was carried out with ease, accompanied (surprisingly) by joy, as the workers engaged in constant banter. Some even sang in their native tongues. Three hours later, what had initially appeared to be an endless marsh had transformed into an incubation ground for a future forest of white mangroves, crucial for helping prevent saltwater intrusion and coastal encroachment in Sóc Trăng. Little did I know it had taken the team at the Sống Foundation many years of research, lobbying and costly experimentation to arrive at such a process. Previously, they had been allocated a different area by the local authority. It is a place that Trần Lương, who has served as Sống's Chairman of the Advisory Board since 2013, described to me as "dogs eat rock, chickens eat stone" – a Vietnamese idiom for uninhabitable, barren soil. The first batch of white mangroves died soon after they were planted. After another prolonged period of scientific persuasion and lobbying, which included relationship-building with local authorities, they were allocated the area in Lạc Hoà village, a small town inhabited mostly by Khmer and Teochew people, located at the edge of the Mekong Delta. Yet again, they faced failure as the white mangroves died a few months later due to strong waves and winds from the adjacent sea. The solution to this challenge was the construction of a long bamboo fence along the shoreline where the sea meets the swamp, along with a support system for each newly planted sapling involving three bamboo stakes. Once again, what seemed like a simple solution required tremendous effort in mobilising funds and human resources.

At noon, we all started walking back to the village and, thanks to the high tide, we trudged back with difficulty, unlike the smooth sailing earlier in the day. With each step we took, we sank deeper and deeper. At that moment, I truly grasped the meanings, both literal and metaphorical, of "quagmire", a term inspired by the characteristics of the Mekong Delta, which the American journalist David Halberstam used to describe the US's awkward and confusing position in Vietnam.[4] Even today, when that war has become

4. David Halberstam, *The Making of a Quagmire*, (New York: Random House, 1964).

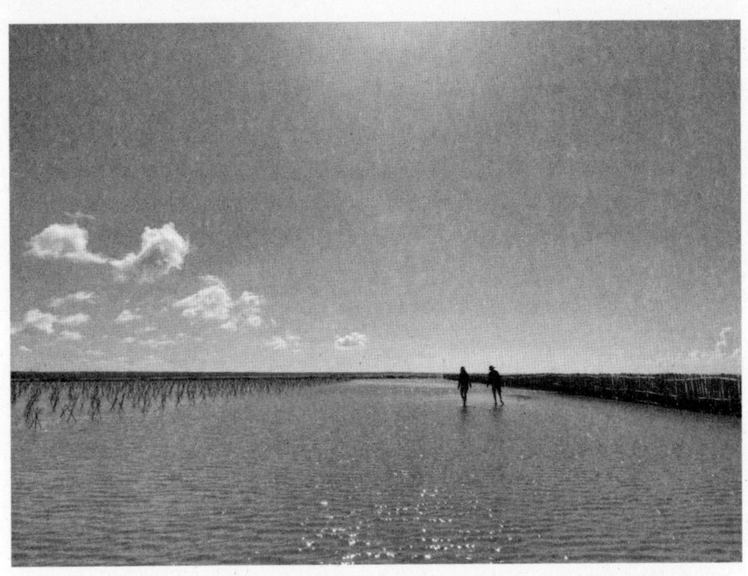

Picture taken at 8:48 AM on 23 May, 2023. As the tide reaches its peak, the men started their work while we check out the area near the bamboo fence which helps prevent incoming waves and wind from the nearby sea. As this area is closer to the sea, it is sandier and firmer to walk on. On the left of the image is the newly planted forest. Photo by the author.

history, the term's suggestion of stagnation remains relevant as the region is confronted with pressing geopolitical, socio-economic and environmental issues. The term is also the title of David Biggs' "Quagmire: Nation-Building and Nature in the Mekong Delta," a book that has shaped my curatorial and research interests in this part of Vietnam. Biggs' approach to historiography through environmental history offers an animated and comprehensive account of what constitutes the delta politically, culturally and economically today. His book effectively portrays the complexity and diversity of the region, suggesting that only interdisciplinary methods can adequately engage with it. After more than an hour, and with the help of the local workers, we finally reached the spot where the bus had dropped us off that morning. Covered in mud from head to toe and sitting on the side of the street to rest, a strong wave of gratitude flooded over me – I had finally experienced a part of the Mekong Delta that I had previously only known through books and movies.

Had it not been for Trần and the invitation to join his team at the Center for Art Patronage and Development on their field trip to Sóc Trăng a few months earlier,[5] I would never have set foot in this town, let alone experienced the mangrove-regrowing process and made several friends with whom I am still in contact today. Our journey did not end that morning; we continued roaming the town exploring its cultural diversity over the following two days. We were even

5. The group consisted of Ngụy Hải An, performance artist Flinh, and artist Lê Tú Anh who are currently working at the Center for Art Patronage and Development, as well as Ho Chi Minh City-based artist Nguyễn Khôi and myself.

invited into the house of Mr Kim Nạng, a Khmer farmer who has been monitoring the newly planted mangroves since 2020. It was in his house where, over steaming bowls of bún nước lèo prepared by his wife,[6] we learned about the impact Green Happiness has had on the town and its ecology. Mr Kim Nạng observed that even though the forest is still relatively young, its web-like roots have begun to retain the boggy alluvium brought in by sea waves. The arrival of Green Happiness in the village has also provided young local men, who juggle farming and odd jobs, with an extra source of income. By allowing us to go on this field trip, Trần hopes that we will see beyond our comfortable and convenient city life and begin to think about our social responsibilities as artists and cultural workers. At least for me, his plan worked well, as I have decided to dedicate myself to developing a research-based curatorial project for and with the region over the next two years.

6. A salted fish-based noodle dish that is popular among the Khmer community in the Mekong Delta.

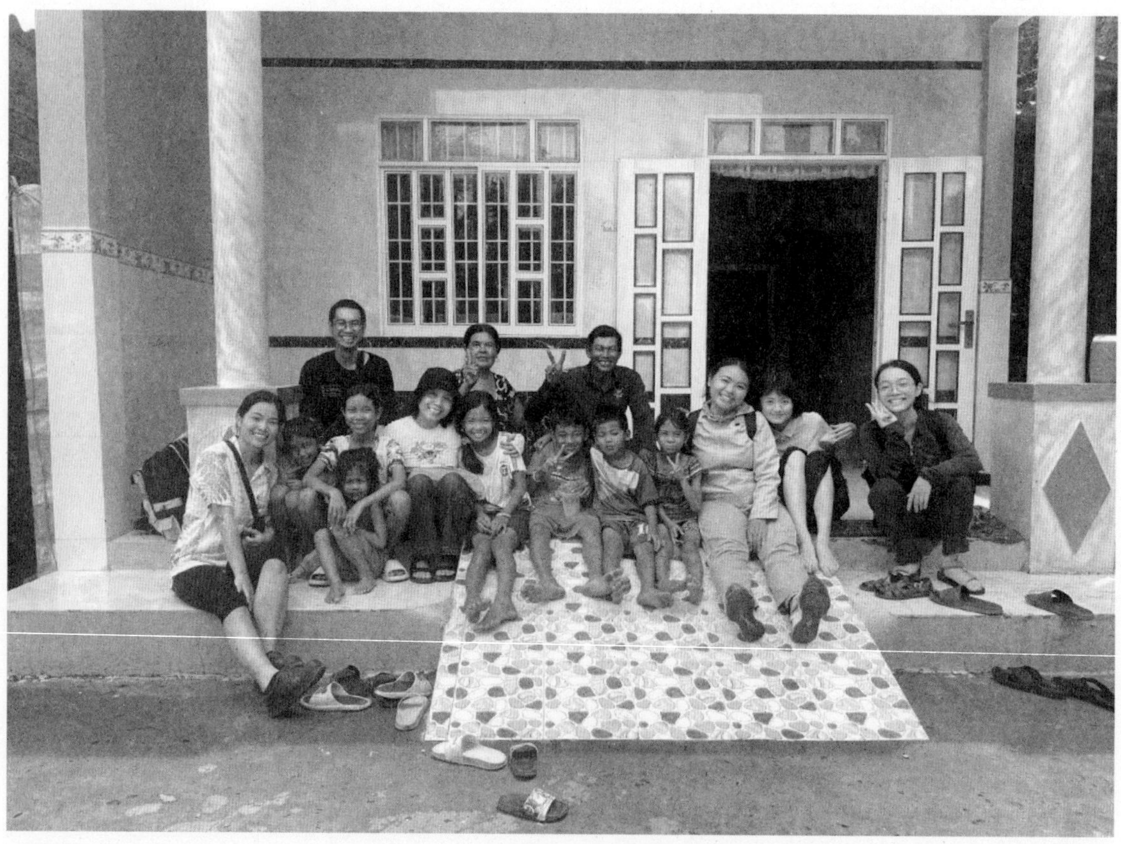

Picture taken at 10:59 AM, 25 May, 2023. The group visits Mr Kim Nạng's house before taking the bus back to Ho Chi Minh City. From left to right: performance artist Flinh, three of Mr Kim Nạng's grandchildren, artist Nguyễn Khôi (in black), the author (in black hat), four of Mr Kim Nạng's grandchildren, Mr Kim Nạng's wife, Mr Kim Nạng, Tú Em – Green Happiness's project coordinator, Ngụy Hải An and artist Lê Tú Anh. Photo by the author.

Trần Lương's strategic involvement with the Sống Foundation started in 2013 when its founder was looking for partners experienced in working closely with different communities in Vietnam, raising funds for charitable causes through art auctions, as well as navigating delicate relationships with local authorities. Although his position has never been publicly promoted due to concerns that his reputation as a vocal and critical artist might potentially affect the organisation's legal status, Trần Lương played a pivotal role in shaping Sống Foundation from its inception. The foundation's first and probably most widely recognised programme in Vietnam is *Resilient Houses*, which provides housing solutions for residents who have lost their homes during seasonal storms and floods along the coast from North to Central and South Vietnam. Similar to the Green Happiness project, it took many months, if not years, and countless field trips for Trần and Sống Foundation to advocate for authoritative approval and institutional support in each province where the project was implemented. After more than a decade, Resilient Houses has introduced nine housing models in response to each specific area's climate conditions, while providing technical and partial financial assistance for the construction of 1,203 houses in 11 provinces.[7]

Even before joining the Sống Foundation, Trần had already demonstrated a serious tendency towards community development through his artistic practice, particularly through the *Field Trips* (2001 – ongoing), a series of public space intervention projects. In these projects, artistic practice transcended the confines of the artist's studio and aesthetic conventions mandated by galleries and art spaces. Some notable projects include the seminal *Mạo Khê Coal Mine project* (2001), *On the Banks of the Red River* (2001), *Fairy Tale Soup* (2003), *Lim Dim* performance art festival in Hà Nội (2004), *Water Droplets* (2005), and *Hà Nội – Phnom Penh Art Exchange program* (2006). In retrospect, these projects, in which Trần acted as both curator and participating artist, not only provided a critical purview on the socio-political landscape of the post-Đổi Mới Vietnam, but also proposed a new approach to artmaking – one capable of bringing about change and disruption.

It is also worth unpacking the significance of these public space takeovers by Trần and his fellow artists within the context of official Vietnamese art historical discourse, which had been dominated by socialist realism for decades.

7. These housing models include; Isolated Floating House in Quảng Bình; Floating House attached to Normal House in Hà Tĩnh; Low Elevated House in Quảng Ninh; High Elevated House in Hà Tĩnh, Quảng Bình and Quảng Nam; Flexible Elevated House in Hậu Giang, Sóc Trăng and Bến Tre; Three-Shed House with a Loft in Hà Tĩnh, Quảng Bình, Quảng Nam and Khánh Hoà; Tube House with a Loft in Quảng Ninh, Hà Tĩnh, Quảng Bình, Quảng Nam, Khánh Hoà, Sóc Trăng and Hậu Giang; Double Loft House for Human Only in Hà Tĩnh, Quảng Bình and Quảng Nam; Double Loft House with Cattle Shelter in Hà Tĩnh. Read more about Resilient Houses project at: https://song.org.vn/en/nha-an-toan.html

Field trips were a compulsory part of university Fine Art programmes. Accompanied by their lecturers, students would travel to the countryside or mountainous areas and live with the locals in their houses for around a month. During these stays, students both helped their host families with daily chores and practiced their drawing and painting skills, focusing on the scenic landscape and its inhabitants as subjects. Artistic output from these field trips often resulted in an extensive collection of exotic and overly romanticised portrayals of faraway lands and ethnic peoples, thus perpetuating the aesthetic and thematic conventions of socialist realism. For a long time, artists going outside their home environment to search for inspiration has been a universal practice, however, in the context of Vietnamese art, where field trips primarily served as a means of ideological reproduction, Trần's Field Trips, with their audacious artistic experiments, can be seen as a form of collective institutional critique.

Even outside of the artistic realm, group field trips are subject to monitoring by local authorities, possibly for security purposes. From Trần Lương, I learned about the many logistical efforts required to make possible our visit to the Green Happiness project site in Lạc Hoà village. In a way, it seems that there are things that remain unchanged since his time. Participating in that trip and later learning about the behind-the-scenes work from both Trần and the Sống Foundation staff, greatly enriched my understanding of logistics and organisation; knowledge that will undoubtedly prove helpful when organising my own ventures in the future.

FROM ONE TRIP TO MANY MORE

As I wrote this piece, I was on a research trip for my upcoming project in Trà Vinh province, which is a three-hour drive from Sóc Trăng. I decided to make a detour to visit Mr Kim Nạng and his wife in Lạc Hoà village. They greeted me with such warmth that it almost felt as though I were family. Over dinner, Mr Kim Nạng told me he had just come back from the field where he had checked on saplings because the impending storm would cause strong wind and waves which can fell the saplings. As they had only been planted less than two years before, some saplings were still affected by strong wind and currents. In such instances, Mr Kim Nạng would gather several village youths who had previously been employed by the Green Happiness project, to go out to the field and replant the saplings. As he recounted the events, Mr Kim Nạng showed me pictures he had taken earlier that day of the affected area, a way for him to keep the experts at the Green Happiness project informed about the real-time conditions of the young forest. His face brightened as he swiped to photos of fully-grown patches of white mangroves, the first areas that were planted in 2020. I could tell he was proud of the healthy, exuberant forest and of his work. Coming back here after almost a year, this time on my own, I noticed minimal changes to the landscape aside from a few newly built houses. The village is still that quaint, tranquil village on the edge of the Mekong Delta where significant changes have been taking place. As I was about to leave, Mr Kim Nạng and I exchanged promises of more visits in the future: I to his home, and him to mine. On the way back, I could not help but get emotional. I was beyond grateful for this precious connection to Mr Kim Nạng, to this little village and to all the encounters I had experienced there. I knew I would return, and soon.

Linh Lê
 March, 2024

HƯỚNG DẪN – ON FACILITATING

One evening, as we were wrapping up our working day in APD Center, a group of three youngsters – two men and one woman – walked in holding a nicely wrapped flowerpot. They handed it to Trần Lương and he hugged them warmly, visibly touched. I initially thought it must have been Lương's birthday, but it turned out to be Vietnamese Teachers' Day (November 20th), and these young people were artists participating in the workshop that he facilitates.[1]

Trần Lương, in discussing his practice, dislikes and avoids using the term "education." In Vietnamese, education implies an understanding of learning through guidance. He prefers to describe his work using the Vietnamese term "Hướng Dẫn," which translates to "facilitating" rather than "educating."

In Lương's own words:

> In its literal sense, facilitating involves assisting a person or an idea to go in the direction that they want or have planned. Those who seek facilitation may lack clear practice methods, structure, information or the skills necessary to develop their goals. Facilitating entails providing support to individuals or ideas based on their existing foundation, without imposing the facilitator's own ideas or knowledge. Therefore, 'facilitating' does not impose exams, grade assignments, or rank students as in education. Nor does it prescribe a specific amount of time for facilitation; rather, the duration depends on changes in awareness, practice outcomes and life events affecting the person being facilitated.[2]

This facilitating process is impossible to archive. Instead, we tried to foster storytelling practices through text and image, encouraging contemplation of facilitating processes as embodied and ongoing.

Biljana Ciric

1. Biljana Ciric, unpublished curatorial notes, Hà Nội, 2023.

2. Email correspondence between Trần Lương and Biljana Ciric, April 2024.

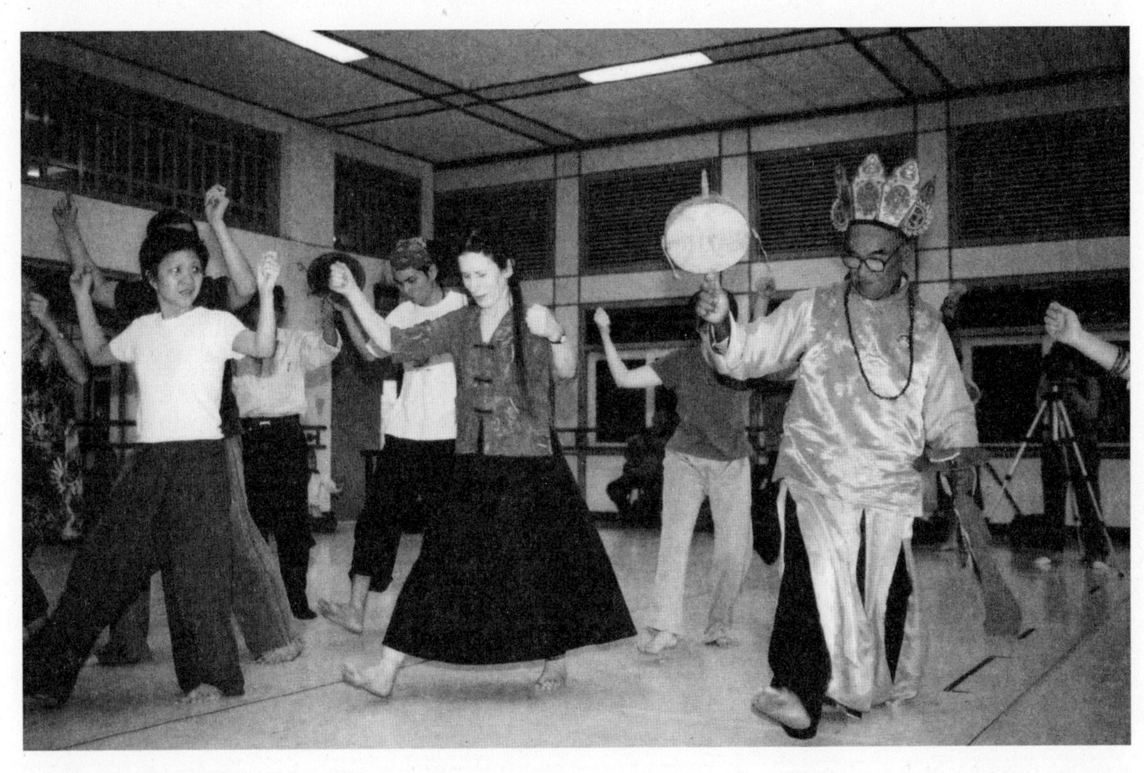

The Flying Circus Project, December 2000, conceived by T:>Works Artistic Director Ong Keng Sen. Photo: courtesy of TheatreWorks (S) Ltd.

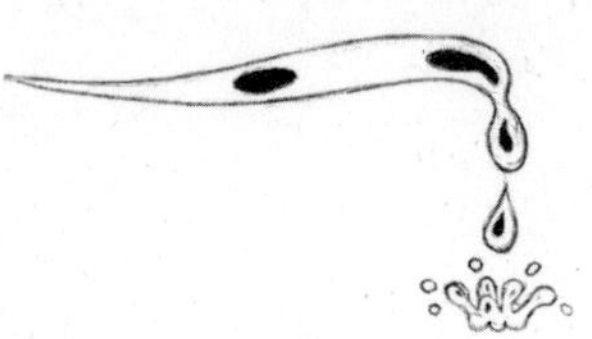

BC: When we talked about education, you expressed your dislike for the word "education." So, what terminology do you prefer to describe this kind of activity?

TL: In the Vietnamese context we are influenced by Chinese culture as we also belonged to China for a while. So, we use the term "Giáo Dục", which translates to education in English. "Giáo Dục" means leading young people and implies a level of control. "Giáo" is also used, for example, in reference to treating prisoners, signifying a person who exercises control. "Dục" conveys a desire and hope to learn. I'm against it because "Giáo Dục" is consistent with the dictatorship's policy of making people ignorant and is the root cause of low education levels in Vietnam. This term is very much a concrete outcome of conservative social structures.

BC: What term do you use in Vietnamese?

TL: I use "Hướng Dẫn," which means facilitating. Hướng Dẫn implies merely pointing out possible different directions, allowing young people to choose for themselves. No matter what direction they choose along the way, you accompany them with your knowledge, experience and your example, acting as a mirror and talking with them. You need to be there for open discussion. Whether they turn right or left, we try to discuss it together, before they turn either way. I share my experience with them, and my knowledge. Hướng dẫn is two words: "hướng" is the direction and "dẫn" suggests showing the way or holding their hand. So, I use the terms "facilitating" or "mentoring" much more than "teaching."

BC: When did you start engaging in these facilitating activities?

TL: I think it started at Nhà Sàn Studio towards the end of 1998. That's when I began to realise what Vietnam needed and what the main problems are here. Around 1998, it became clear to me that individual success, whether as an athlete or an artist, is lonely. You cannot do much to change your environment alone. So, I realised the importance of the environment not only for the community, but for oneself as well. I was hoping for an artmaking environment with more freedom, giving more energy to daily life. I thought deeply about how my reputation would grow by simply selling my artwork and exhibiting abroad often, but life around me would never change.

Sitting with the artist community, drinking and eating, I noticed that while I had changed, they still had the same fears, they still considered art as something beautiful and eye catching. So, the process of facilitating started with the question, *how to make change?* Working towards making a change doesn't mean that you are teaching and preaching that change. The first thing I did was to establish an alternative art space. The space was important because people could share their ideas with no fear. They felt free to say things, to have a chance to start any discussion without self-censorship. Not to be afraid of lacking knowledge or information, feeling free to ask even stupid questions or talk about stupid topics. After establishing the space, the second step was to gather together their voices, their hopes, their designs, their futures. When I look back at myself and the members of Gang of Five, we were successful modern painters for a while, for seven or eight years. So, curating come up at that moment. Curating and gathering the power of artists and their voices. The importance of curating started to appear in my mind in around 1995. I spent three years, from 1995 to the end of 1998, learning about curating before I began practising it when we opened Nhà Sàn Studio at the end of 1998. I realised that curation is a kind of way to raise power, raise voices. So, that's why I started to learn curating.

BC: Do you also understand curatorial work as a form of facilitation?

TL: Sure, sure. In the specific context of Vietnam and some neighbouring countries in the Mekong Delta region, curating is actually facilitating. We start with the practical work, you see. For example, practical tasks like the lighting arrangement for the work is important, it's crucial to understand how the lighting affects the language of the artwork.

It's quite basic, really. For example, if you install your work here, you will not have flow in the space. It's important to think about whether placing the artwork in a specific place will cause a blockage in the flow of the entire exhibition space. Many of these small skills I had to learn abroad. Through my own work, I learned all kinds of practical things. Then, we started to educate lighting engineers and sound engineers, but with a focus on the specific context. On the other hand, these knowledges had to be adapted to the local context. For example, Nhà Sàn was in an old wooden house, not a white cube space, so sound flows differently within a wooden structure compared to other kinds of spaces.

BC: When did you start organising workshops for facilitation?

TL: In the beginning it was hard. If you called them "workshops" people would not follow and participate as they don't believe in this format or its possible value. So, I always needed to connect it with a specific exhibition, field trip or specific project. I started more concrete workshop formats when I started working at Hà Nội Contemporary Art Center in 2000. As a government platform, HCAC had power, it was a name. I officially started organising many workshops by local and foreign artists, not only visual arts but also contemporary dance, performing music, noise, all kinds of experimental approaches.

BC: Who were your references for making workshops?

TL: You know, from the beginning, the need to make workshops was very natural. So, it started very simply, like, just make a small workshop as an action. Every time I travelled out of the country, I made it a point to document what I saw, knowing that people in Vietnam were very hungry for knowledge. Whenever I returned from a trip, I would do a lot of talks, sharing my own experiences and observations on how artists in different countries were practising and living. The talks started like a workshop because the talks were intended not only to tell people what I had seen, but also to prompt discussion about that situation, about different conditions and then returning to reflect on our own context and how we do things here.

During the same period, from 1998 to 2000, I also attended different workshops and conferences, but the most important was *The Flying Circus Project*. It was a project that started in 1996 in Singapore and, depending on the budget, it took place every few years. I was invited to participate in 2000 and 2007. It was a big international gathering, with senior artists from different fields and over seventy participants. The presentations were mixed with workshops and with spontaneous performance, film screenings, dance and movement. Through that gathering I learned a lot about how to do different kinds of mentoring and workshops, it's a different skill.

STORIES

by **Vũ Đức Toàn**

INTRODUCTION:

Due to historical circumstances, my generation had very few opportunities for thorough training in art-related writing. Because of academic limitations, I often hesitate to adopt an academic style in my writing. For this text, I chose the storytelling approach because I believe it offers a more accessible writing style. Having grown up and matured over 20 years in the field of contemporary art, our generation has many memories with Trần Lương to share. However, when I started writing, I realised it was more challenging than I had imagined. Recreating memories becomes truly effortless only when we sit together, telling stories in the intimate atmosphere of a gathering. When you have too many memories, choosing which ones to tell and which ones to leave out becomes difficult. Yet, this decision is crucial as it affects the fate of the text. I hope that the combination and openness of these nine stories will resonate with readers. These stories offer a different art history, a more intimate one, as if we were looking into each other's eyes.

The "hidden" and the "revealed" are central to how we perceive Trần Lương's image through these nine stories, which are defined by specific spaces, moments and contexts. Sometimes Trần Lương is the main character, while at other times, he is only alluded to indirectly. Through the character of Trần Lương, we embark on a vivid mental mapping, allowing us to explore and somewhat imagine the specificity of the local art scene in Hà Nội. We witness the "rituals" of artistic activities within a community of artists, at times narrow but always intimate. These stories also indirectly allow us to glimpse what lies in the environment and atmosphere of contemporary Vietnamese artworks and artists. Life and art intertwine in an interesting dualistic way. Perhaps that is why Trần Lương transcends mere descriptions of his works and career achievements. His intimacy and simplicity prompt us to recognise him not solely as a hero within contemporary Vietnamese art discourse, but as much more than that.

CHAPTER I: PEOPLE ON TV

Around late 2002 or early 2003, I was still a new student at art school. I often watched television programs about literature and art. At that time, there were few reports or events about contemporary art. I remember watching a program called "Contemporary Visual Art Appearing in Vietnam." Sitting next to me in the living room, watching TV, were my mother and sister. They had nothing to do with art, but they supported my art studies more than my father did. The TV program interviewed many people about their concepts and thoughts about visual art in Vietnam. I can't remember all the names of the people on TV that day. But Trần Lương was there, as was art critic and painter Nguyễn Quân, visual artist Nguyễn Minh Thành, composer and musician Vũ Nhật Tân, and a few more foreign artists who were working here, including perhaps, the videographer Brian Ring.

Apart from Mr. Nguyễn Quân, I hardly knew anything about these people. I noticed that among them, Trần Lương spoke and answered questions very well. I just had that feeling in my stomach and my mother and sister immediately asked, "who is that man in black?" (Trần Lương was wearing a black shirt that day.) "Is he a famous person in the local art world? He seems like the best speaker, right?" The questions were directed at me because I was studying art. I felt a bit embarrassed because I didn't know who was who. Honestly, at that time, I only knew that Trần Lương was an artist in the Gang of Five group and nothing more. In the Gang of Five, the paintings of Trần Lương and Phạm Quang Vinh seemed to be more challenging to appreciate than the work of the other three artists in the group. At that time, I was a fan of Hồng Việt Dũng's paintings of irresistible dreamy beauty.

Not long after that day, I saw Trần Lương in real life. I went to see the *Green Red & Yellow* exhibition in October 2003.[1] It was one of the exhibitions that I think was pivotal to the early days of Vietnamese contemporary art. It was also the first time I learned that there was a position called curator. I didn't understand what a curator was. At that time, I thought it was a bit like an MC (Master of Ceremonies) because I saw that Trần Lương had to talk a lot that day and was busy walking back and forth among the crowd of people at the exhibition.

CHAPTER II: DON'T TROUBLE THE TROUBLE UNTIL THE TROUBLE TROUBLES YOU.

This story happened in 2004, a period when I diligently went to see almost every contemporary art event. On this particular day, there was a talk related to contemporary art by Mr. Trần Lương and Mr. Nguyễn Quang Huy at the British Council. It was a somewhat quiet talk compared to previous talks I had

1. The *Green Red & Yellow* exhibition, held at the Goethe Institute in Hà Nội in 2003, was a contemporary art exhibition in Vietnam [see p.186–191 in this publication]. Unlike previous exhibitions that only focused on solo shows or small group exhibitions, this event was considered the first large-scale exhibition in the country. *Green Red & Yellow* showcased 16 works by 16 artists, featuring forms as various as performance, video, multi-channel video installations, photography, installations, and conceptual works, half of which were interactive. Importantly, this exhibition was also one of the first contemporary exhibitions in Vietnam to pioneer guerilla tactics and dialogue as a way to evade the strict censorship that was prevalent in Vietnam at the time.

attended. It became apparent that most people, including me, were very hesitant to engage in asking or answering questions. In the emerging field of contemporary art at the time, it seemed like we were encountering a form of art that was weird and difficult for people to comprehend.

After his presentation, Mr. Trần Lương enthusiastically encouraged everyone to ask questions or share. Yet not a single hand was raised. I still remember that I was sitting next to two young artists of the same age as me, Nguyễn Thế Hùng and Nguyễn Đức Lợi, both of whom were under the partial guidance of Mr. Trần Lương. I didn't dare ask a question, even though I really wanted to, and instead I looked over at them. Eventually, I mustered the courage to speak up. I remember that the first question I asked Lương was about the German artist Eberhard Havekost who made paintings of plane wings in cold, aluminum-silver metal tones using a challenging style. My next question was: "Why is contemporary art so troublesome? The work always has to be accompanied by a statement." I can't remember the exact wording of my question, but what I can't forget is that the spirit of my query reflected a growing skepticism about the trajectory of contemporary art in Vietnam. Trần Lương answered with patience, offering a somewhat tough rejoinder: "Don't trouble the trouble until the trouble troubles you." At that moment, I also vaguely understood that Trần Lương wanted me to understand the importance of contemporary art's continued existence and growth in Vietnam.

Within the art school at that time, most teachers and students were not sympathetic to contemporary art and were even somewhat disdainful of it. So, expressing my views on contemporary art felt very constrained by that environment. One of the very few people I could talk to was Mr. Trần Hậu Yên Thế, the most progressive teacher in the school. When I told him about the talk I had attended the day before at the British Council, Mr. Trần Hậu Yên Thế emphasised the importance of supporting contemporary art during that pivotal time, rather than only criticizing and questioning it.

CHAPTER III: AFTER A RATHER SAD ROUND OF ICED TEA

In the narrow circle of performance artists in Vietnam at the time, Phụ Lục was somewhat recognised and visible.[2] Objectively speaking, Vietnam has several good performance artists, but collective work in performance is rare. For that reason, Phụ Lục was favoured. However, our group's

2. The Appendix (Phụ Lục) is a group of 6 artists (Hoàng Minh Đức, Nguyễn Huy An, Vũ Đức Toàn, Ngô Thành Bắc, Nguyễn Song and Nguyễn Dương Hải Đăng) that formed in 2010. The artists are all of the same generation and all studied at the Hà Nội University of Fine Arts. The practices of the members are quite diverse but they are mostly recognised as a group practising performance art. Currently, only three members of Phụ Lục still practice together.

beginning was not easy.

It must be said that Trần Lương's influence as a guide and creator of spaces in Vietnam cannot be overstated. He has played a pivotal role in facilitating opportunities for performance art in Vietnam and diversifying every aspect of the field, from building connections to organising nationwide workshops for local artists. He also brought international colleagues and friends to Vietnam to conduct workshops, performances and talks. Additionally, he also introduced and facilitated the participation of domestic artists in events abroad, promoting exchange and learning. His practice is strong and distinct, sometimes displaying an uncompromising approach to performance. I have observed this trait in both his theoretical perspectives and practical demonstrations, particularly in his discernment between performing art and performance art, a position which is evident in both what he says and his performance practice. In any case, our group experienced significant growth every time we worked with him, especially in relation to performance.

At the beginning of 2010, we were using theatrical properties and were running on a theatrical platform; or at least it seemed that way. Of course, we also felt that Trần Lương favoured those of us who had always practised performance art. We had a meeting with Nguyễn Mạnh Hùng, who was temporarily managing the artistic direction of Nhà Sàn Studio at the time, to present our plan for a collaboration with Nhà Sàn Studio.[3] Our plan was not rejected, however, it's reception was rather cold, and they were not enthusiastic about our ideas. Nevertheless, they accepted our proposal. We gathered at the iced tea shop on Liễu Giai Street and told each other we had to do it no matter what. The next night we went to Trần Lương's house to share our idea for the performance piece. Trần Lương not only gave us great encouragement, he also shared his knowledge and expertise. Though it might be difficult for others to understand, at the time we strongly considered ourselves practitioners of performance art, even though many elements resembled experimental theatre. On the day of the performance in March 2010, Trần Lương was present (although Lương was no longer directly managing Nhà Sàn Studio, he continued to play an advisory role and influence its development) and he received the experience very openly and positively. I also recall that his eloquence when discussing his experience of the piece spared us from a lot of criticism.

Every beginning is difficult. Phụ Lục emerged with support from only a few individuals, but all were highly

3. Nhà Sàn Studio was founded in 1998 by Trần Lương and Nguyễn Mạnh Đức and was the first artist-run alternative art space in Vietnam after the "Open Door" period. Nguyễn Mạnh Đức is a painter and antiques collector who lives in Hà Nội.

reputable. Trần Lương, Nguyễn Mạnh Đức and the curatorial team brought Phụ Lục to *In:Act* for the first of the *Emerging Artists* programs.[4] Since then, Phụ Lục's practices have received a lot of recognition, leading to more opportunities for group endeavours. It's like inertia, people often refer to Phụ Lục's performances as carefully orchestrated and extreme. Our practice gradually evolved into something unique, and Trần Lương was the first person to critique us. Now, Phụ Lục has the opportunity to look back and reflect on the differences between our current practices and those of five years ago, when the group first began assembling individual performances into complex theatrical acts. Have there been changes in our approach, spatial processing skills, tempo and time? What do we need to leave behind from our current practice to mature further?

4. "Emerging Artists" has been one of Nhà Sàn Collective's prominent programmes for many years. This programme set the goal to promote a new, young generation of contemporary artists. Through introducing fresh faces in the art scene, the programme aims to reveal a greater variety of concerns and perspectives of life for the public and the art community. https://www.nhasan.org/program/emerging-artists-v

CHAPTER IV: DISSOLVING A STAR.

In 2010 the Goethe Institut held a series of workshops for young Vietnamese artists for which they invited a few performance experts from Germany. Perhaps the most famous of them was Marina Abramovic's disciple, Nezaket Ekici. Right before coming to Hà Nội, she had spent a few days conducting a workshop for students at Hue University. As to be expected of a disciple of Marina's, Nezaket is very strong and presentations of her work are similarly impactful, embodying a feminist ethos with the vigour to explore and question social norms. Consequently, her communication style in the workshop was often highly detailed and predominantly one-way, with directives like "Please follow my instructions." She followed us closely, editing and providing constant feedback and direct communication. However, at times this approach became suffocating as it demanded we assimilate her perspective. Not everyone can have such vision, such cultural habits, speed, sensitivity, intelligence and immense energy.

Every morning when I went to the Goethe Institut, Nezaket continued with her uncompromising method. Sometimes, we failed to respond or took a docile attitude, but this didn't lead to much understanding or real awareness. Instead, we rushed the actions and did them exactly as instructed. A few people decided to leave the workshop. I gave my own feedback to Nezaket. I only remember the part where I told her I was having a really hard time following the tone and tempo that she had set. After giving her my feedback, I saw Trần Lương lightly laugh. I think Trần Lương is always by the side of young artists. He was present in that room as an observer and was also there to help Nezaket if needed. I'm sure an experienced person like Trần Lương saw some problems earlier than us, but he remained quite patient and calm, simply observing the situation. Actually, given my experience of having worked with Trần Lương for nearly ten years by that point, I knew that sooner or later he would join in. It was just a matter of time.

During the break, I saw Trần Lương chatting with Nezaket in a private conversation. Right after that, Lương came back and told us something like: "We need to sympathise and understand Nezaket, who has come to Vietnam for the first time. She could not immediately understand the difference between Huế, Hà Nội or Sài Gòn. Wanting everyone to follow instructions is a difficult task here." From that session onwards, I saw Trần Lương become more involved in helping Nezaket connect with the students and young artists in the room. It was at this workshop, that I most clearly witnessed Trần Lương's calm and softness.

During the last days of the workshop, Nezaket needed Trần Lương's help even more. There was a class performance planned for the last day of the workshop. I think Nezaket was a bit nervous, she wanted everything to be perfect. We all worked like crazy on the last day. At the time, I don't know if many people realised it, but I observed Trần Lương's excellence while consulting for Nezaket on the show. His expertise, particularly in addressing spatial distribution and order issues, was evident, especially given the challenge of accommodating many artists in a room at the Goethe Institut that was not large enough to hold us all. Watching Trần Lương work with Nezaket taught me invaluable lessons. Especially now, as I find myself organising performance events with many performers, I can apply some of the knowledge I gained from that experience. Over time, this incident has evolved into a funny story that I tell my friends and young artists. Trần Lương truly shined during that period (Resolving a Star).

CHAPTER V: SHANGHAI WINTER.

On December 25, 2023, in cold Shanghai, there was a presentation of Vietnamese artists within the framework of a performance art festival. During the Q&A session, a question was posed to us concerning the issues of mortification and danger that artists often use in performance. The exchange brought to mind a memory from 2010, set in Trần Lương's old house on Hoàng Hoa Thám street. At that time, Phụ Lục had recently returned from a short stay at a residency program in Kunming, Yunnan, China, facilitated by Trần Lương's connection to the 943 Studio facility. That evening, we talked a lot about art, especially performance art. I vividly remember a poignant statement by Trần Lương: "Performance art is not about competing to see who can endure the most suffering or inflict the most pain on themselves. It's not about outdoing each other in enduring dirt or physical hardship or bleeding the most. Performance artists don't aim to impress others with acts of courage for mere spectacle."

I share this quote from Trần Lương in response to the concerns raised at the discussion in Shanghai, in an attempt to clarify our perspective.

CHAPTER VI: 20/11/2017

Sometime around August 2017, I was tasked by Nhà Sàn Collective to implement the 6th edition of the *Emerging Artists Program*.[5] My colleagues and I came up with another form of support, which was to organise a course for young artists. We invited leading artists in Vietnam to work with the young participants. The list included Trần Lương and Nguyễn Trinh Thi as the main participants,[6] along with many other supporting participants such as Nguyễn Phương Linh, Tuấn Mami, Nguyễn Quốc Thành and more.[7] Fortunately, Trần Lương was passionate about this field, so the young artists did not have to pay for his mentoring program.

November 20, 2017, was a busy and joyful day. It was Vietnamese Teachers' Day and by then, Trần Lương had already conducted several sessions of his mentoring program for *Emerging Artists 6*. Upon arriving home from the airport, I found all the participants of the program already there, waiting to go together to Trần Lương's house to celebrate this special day. Although I knew that Trần Lương didn't like being called a teacher, on this day he didn't have a choice because we "ambushed" him. It was truly a wonderful evening; Nguyễn Phương Linh, an artist from Nhà Sàn Collective, brought a very good bottle of wine. I remember she asked Trần Lương, "Which one of these students you have been working with has impressed you the most?" Trần Lương didn't hesitate for a second and immediately said, "Duy Mỡ" (who was one of the interesting young performance artists in Hà Nội at that time). Phương Linh then asked about another case, "and Quang Sinh Tồn, what about him?" The whole class burst into laughter, and Trần Lương also laughed

5. Nhà Sàn Collective is an independent artist collective in Hà Nội run by a group of young artists since 2013. The name Nhà Sàn inherited the spirit of Nhà Sàn Studio after its closure in 2011 due to pressure from authorities. https://www.nhasan.org/about

6. Video art artist living in Hà Nội.

7. Young artists run Nhà Sàn Collective.

brightly, saying it was a mystery (suggesting that he could be either impressive or a let-down). Shortly after, Duy Mỡ and Quang Sinh Tồn,[8] spontaneously joined in a playful jam session right in Trần Lương's living room to celebrate Teacher's Day. I remember Duy Mỡ's artistic nature, he requested all the lights be turned off to play the instrument in the dark. Those were such beautiful moments on November 20, 2017. That evening, I felt Trần Lương's happiness spreading to me and everyone else.

Now in 2024, I can point to some very successful artists who emerged from *Emerging Artists 6*, such as Đặng Thuỳ Anh, one of the best performance artists in Vietnam today; Lê Xuân Tiến, a unique video artist; Lê Đình Chung, an extremely promising artist; and notably, Flinh, who is also an important figure at Hayla (a platform for performance art in Vietnam). Meanwhile, Cấn Văn Ân has a very keen eye for paintings and of course, both the performers mentioned earlier, Duy Mỡ and Quang Sinh Tồn, who are still mysteries, even now. Another talented female artist is Linh Cam, who has now devoted herself to Buddhism.[9]

Trần Lương was dedicated to teaching, encouragement and transmitting knowledge. Upon completing his role in the course, he expressed an interest in curating the final show for the *Emerging Artists 6* in late 2018. However, I had already planned a program with staggered staging throughout the entire project. This may have left Trần Lương feeling somewhat disappointed and dissatisfied as he was unable to accompany this group of young artists to the project's final show. I don't know if I made a mistake by creating such a format for *Emerging Artists 6*, but I remain confident that many people continued to benefit from Trần Lương's mentorship during that final show and even for their artistic endeavours thereafter.

CHAPTER VII: UNSUCCESSFUL RESCUE

In 2012, a circus performance took place in my neighbourhood. A few days later, I discovered a monkey hiding on the roof and among the trees in my yard. Observing it, I suspected it might be the escaped monkey from the circus troupe. It moved around the area, sometimes disappearing and then reappearing. Its demeanour was tired, with eyes constantly vigilant and fearful. Despite my efforts to offer it food, it remained cautious and took a long time to approach the food. Eventually, it became accustomed to eating calmly and started coming to my house more frequently. Gradually,

8. Nickname of artists Nguyễn Hữu Hải Duy and Nguyễn Nhật Quang.

9. The above names are members of the Tầm Tã art practice course (in the Emerging Artist Programme), which was mentored by Trần Lương in 2017. Currently, they are visual artists, performers, video artists, musicians and composers.

it grew comfortable and openly regarded my place as its home, occasionally wandering off and then returning. When it ventured out, it would sometimes be surrounded and caught by people in the neighbourhood, prompting it to run back to my house, the safest place.

Over time, I became accustomed to the sight of the monkey at the top of the gate, with the two dogs below, eagerly waiting to greet me when I left for work and when I returned. One day, however, the monkey was nowhere to be found, even after I waited for a long time. I suspected it might have been caught again. Then, a few days later, the monkey returned. I was overjoyed. I noticed a new collar around its neck, confirming my suspicion that it had been recaptured and had managed to escape again. However, in that moment, I realised that this situation could not last forever. I discussed this with Trần Lương and he suggested relocating the monkey to a conservation area for its safety, which I agreed to.

Trần Lương managed to find a conservation area in Hòa Bình province that was willing to accept the monkey.[10] We discussed plans for how to facilitate the monkey's smooth transfer. He offered to help me with transportation to execute this plan. As the monkey had become more vigilant after being recaptured, we even considered the possibility of sedating it for the journey. Trần Lương emphasised the need to act quickly. Sadly, on that very day, when I returned home, the monkey was no longer there. Days passed without a trace...

I never saw that monkey again.

CHAPTER VIII: WE CAN'T FLY?

The title of this chapter comes from a talk by Trần Lương that I'll never forget. The context was a session within the *Skylines with Flying People II* project at Japan Foundation curated by Nguyễn Phương Linh. The first image presented during the talk was a photo of Trần Lương at the age of six or seven, wearing a straw hat from the wartime era.[11] That evening was quite special. Instead of speaking extensively about his works, Lương focused more on discussing generations, historical consequences, policies and social ideologies. He talked about his era and that of his predecessors, particularly emphasising the period of humanism. The intellectuals he talked about still hold significant positions in the history of Vietnamese literature and art in general.

One aspect that puzzled me was his repeated use of the

10. The province is 100km west of Hà Nội.

11. Hats were woven with straw to protect the head during the US bombing of the North (1965-1972). Trần Lương braided a hat himself, which is the hat he is wearing in the photo.

word "fly". "They couldn't fly, or more accurately, their era couldn't allow them to fly," he said. As I understood it, he wanted to convey the notion of limitations when we consider the most outstanding figures of an era, who potentially could have achieved much greater success. He also made a very artistic remark: "they had to fly aided by alcohol."

One month before this talk, Trần Lương and I participated in a performance festival in South Korea.[12] I created a piece inspired by a poem written by Phùng Cung, a prominent figure in the Nhân Văn Giai Phẩm group.[13] The poem reads as follows,

> Quất mãi nước sôi / Whipped with boiling water endlessly
> Trà đau nát bã / Tea dregs in pain, battered and torn,
> Chẳng đổi giọng Tân Cương[14] / Yet the flavour of Tân Cương remains unchanged

At that time, I needed Trần Lương's help translating the poem into English so that international audiences could understand its meaning. Trần Lương agreed with me that the use of the word "Chẳng" here is quite remarkable. It does not assert anything but rather leans towards an exclamation, through which one can perceive the sense of limitations and helplessness of human existence. He also noted the challenge in translating the word "Chẳng" (in the context of this sentence "chẳng" means "not willing"). Sadly, in contemporary publications of Phùng Cung's poetry collections, the word "Không" is exclusively utilised. ("Không" meaning "not", in this context, asserts an affirmative declaration that there is nothing that can change the flavour).

CHAPTER IX: THE REJECTION

The following is the most recent development, and for now, marks a temporary pause in the series of stories I can share related to Trần Lương. At the end of 2023, our group of young, local curators was determined to bring to fruition a plan that had long lingered on paper: a seminar on curatorial practices in Vietnam. Initially, we wanted to hold it on April 1st, April Fools' Day. There were several reasons for such a choice: to make it seem less serious, potentially circumventing the need to apply for a license from the state cultural management agency, and perhaps avoiding troubles with licensing and scrutiny. We started with a list of curators. It

12. PAN Asia, Performance Art Network Asia in Seoul.

13. Phùng Cung was a famous poet in the 1950s and 1960s, a member of a group of spirit reform writers, artists and intellectuals called Nhân Văn Giai Phẩm. They were leading intellectuals who supported the revolution, but very soon recognised the reality and raised questions about communism.

14. Tân Cương is the name of a commune in Thái Nguyên province in Northern Vietnam, where the famous and delicious green tea plant is grown.

was clear that Trần Lương would be one of the first people we would send an invitation to. He was arguably the first curator in Vietnam. With nearly 30 years of curatorial practice, we were aware that he had recently organised and conducted a training course on curating for young artists at the APD Centre.[15] After waiting some time, his response arrived; Trần Lương declined to participate.

15. Center for Art Patronage and Development is an art organisation co-founded and operated by Trần Lương in Hà Nội since 2020.

In his response, Trần Lương expressed very straightforward opinions about the program, such as that it focused solely on fragmented aspects and lacked an overarching vision regarding the role of curating at the present time, which he deemed crucial for determining next steps. He also mentioned that his presence in the workshop might disadvantage young curators, as it could make them hesitant to fully express their thoughts. He added, "my practices serve as material for you to dissect without hesitation, so I shouldn't be present." Although he declined to participate, he provided several direct comments, affirming that "this is my participation."

Initially, my reaction was one of acceptance; I acknowledged this rejection as simply an understanding of his perspective. It's hard to express how one understands a person's perspective thanks to the accumulated experience from a relationship spanning nearly 20 years. Trần Lương is more than just an elder, a teacher, a friend or a colleague. Ours is a relationship that extends from professional matters and artistic expertise to shared moments drinking or watching football together and even to stories like rescuing a monkey. I have more experience working with Trần Lương than with any other colleague or friend. Regret was inevitable, not just for me but for our whole group. I couldn't help but think, if only he could have participated and brought those critical viewpoints into the workshop.

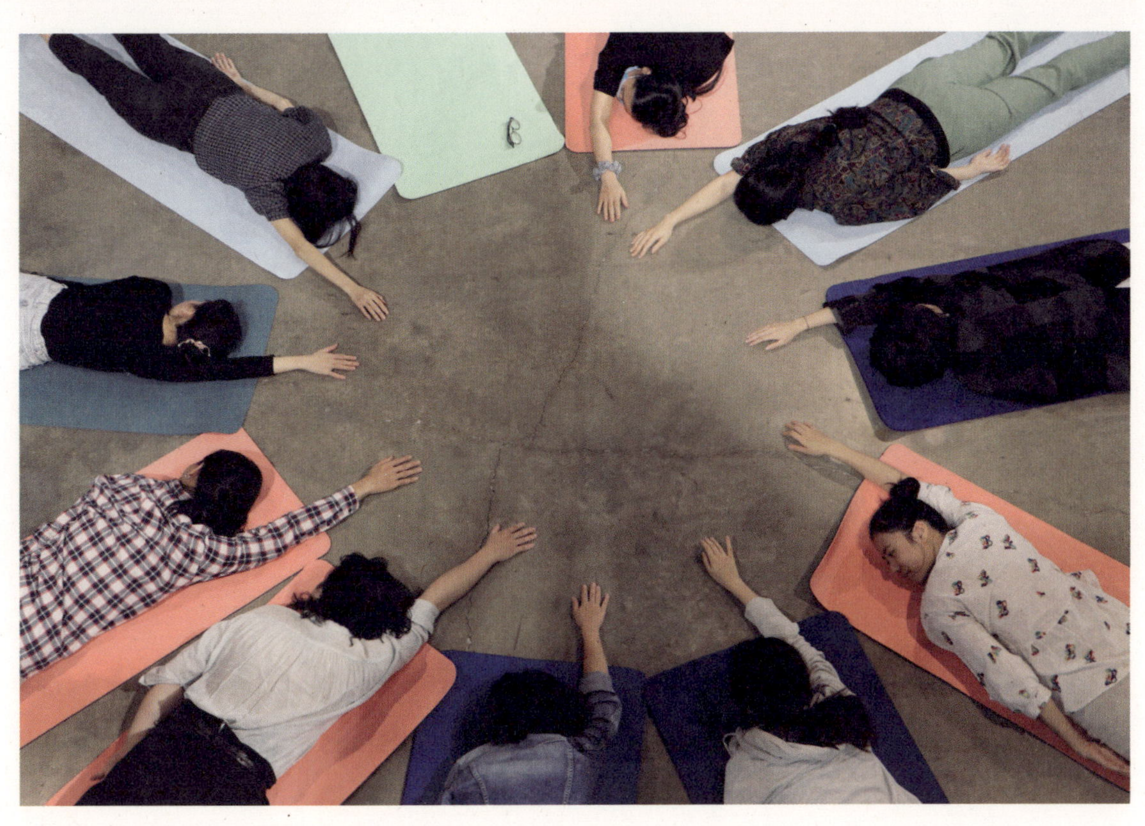

An exercise on body movement in the Tầm Tã Course held at APD Center in 2021. Photo: Flinh.

SOAKED IN THE LONG RAIN - A DRAWING SERIES ABOUT TẦM TÃ

1. The group consisted of Ngụy Hải An, Lê Tú Anh, Flinh, Trịnh Ngân Hạnh and Phạm Việt Hoàng who are all currently working at APD - Center for Art Patronage and Development.

2. "Industrial chicken" is Vietnamese slang commonly used, since the 2000s, to refer to urban children raised under excessive parental sheltering and overprotection and who often lack real-life experience. This phrase also critiques a lifestyle driven by rapid urbanisation and modernisation, prioritising fast career success and material wealth over traditional values.

3. The first person to encounter this course was Flinh, when Tầm Tã did not yet have a name and was a short-term course specifically for young artists at Nhà Sàn Collective. Flinh then became a teaching assistant at Tầm Tã at Erato School of Music & Performing Arts Hà Nội in 2020. In 2021, the Tầm Tã course was officially organised within the framework of APD's

educational programme and was open to a diverse audience, beyond the field of art. At that time, An was working at APD as an organiser and communications manager. The two became companions and continued as joint facilitators of the course. That was also when Tú Anh and Hạnh stepped in as participants, two young people who had just graduated from Visual Arts programs in Korea and France respectively. In 2023, the most recent course to date, Hoang, the youngest member of the five of us, with a background in graphic design, participated in the course and also became a collaborator of APD.

4. APD - Center for Art Patronage and Development is a Vietnam-based non-profit social enterprise that was established in October 2020, of which Trần Lương is the co-founder and director. Practising on the border between contemporary art and social development, APD has been the organiser of the Tầm Tã art course from 2021 until the present.

Soaked in the Long Rain is a collaborative effort by five individuals – children of the same generation, all born between the 1990s and 2000s, two decades after the Vietnam War, during a period of booming industrialisation and modernisation in Vietnam.[1] Despite noticeable economic and social development, the education system we experienced remained entrenched in tradition, emphasising theory and disconnected from reality. It required us to memorise mechanically rather than to develop critical thinking and creativity. Growing up in our shells, we were often compared to "industrial chickens," insensitive to our surroundings and to the realities of our upbringing.[2]

Tầm Tã is an art course led by Trần Lương since 2020. Each one of us engaged with the course at different times, assuming different roles. Thanks to Tầm Tã, we eventually got to know each other and became friends.[3] The course initially opened up in each one of us a more genuine sense of ourselves, our interconnectedness, and the role of art in social development. Shotly after attending the course, we also became members of APD, where we have been working side by side with Trần Lương ever since.[4]

The *Soaked in the Long Rain* drawing series for this publication is our way of sharing our observations, feelings and reflections on Tầm Tã, based on our own experiences. Through many discussions, we have incorporated each person's vision of what Tầm Tã is and our journeys of perception transformation during the course.

Given our differences in age, background and abilities, our first ever creative collaboration was initially a bit confusing. We started by developing ideas independently, then found many overlaps in terms of content, yet each person's way of expressing themself was distinct. We continued to work together on these materials to create an overall flow of content and images, during which process we also learned how to negotiate, compromise and make appropriate adjustments, while respecting our differences.

This drawing series is a reflection on Tầm Tã by five young art practitioners who find pleasure and joy being soaked in the long rain. We believe that this rain will reach other lands and other people, and that there will be more stories to be told.

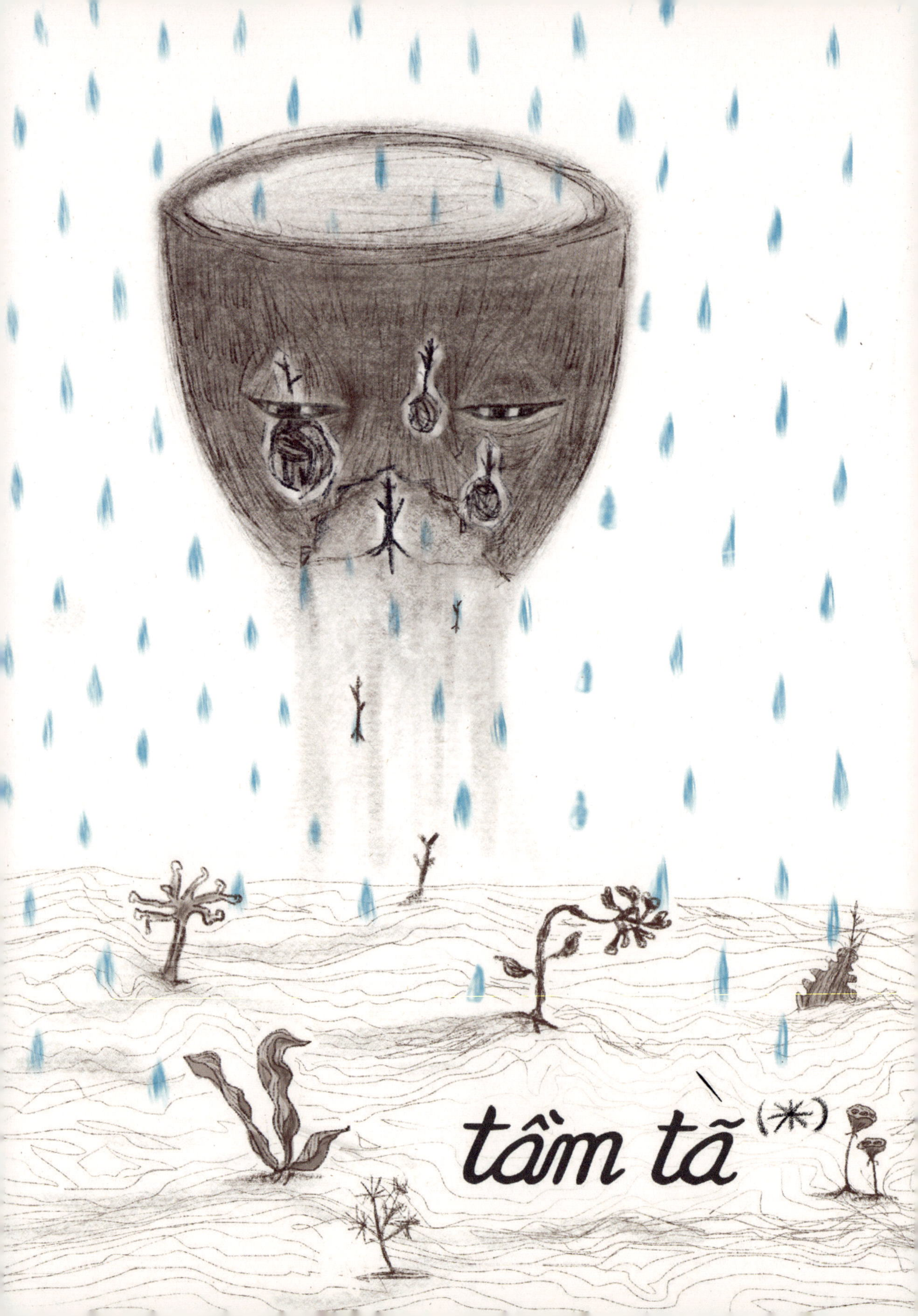
tầm tã(*)

... soak in a long rain ...

An art practice course in the spirit of present tense, present space, in the context of local background and on the edge of academic standards.

... waking up entities that are living on a "standby" admist the aridity

The journey of exploring and awakening the senses to reflect on oneself and understand the world, a long road full of boundaries that need to be broken down...

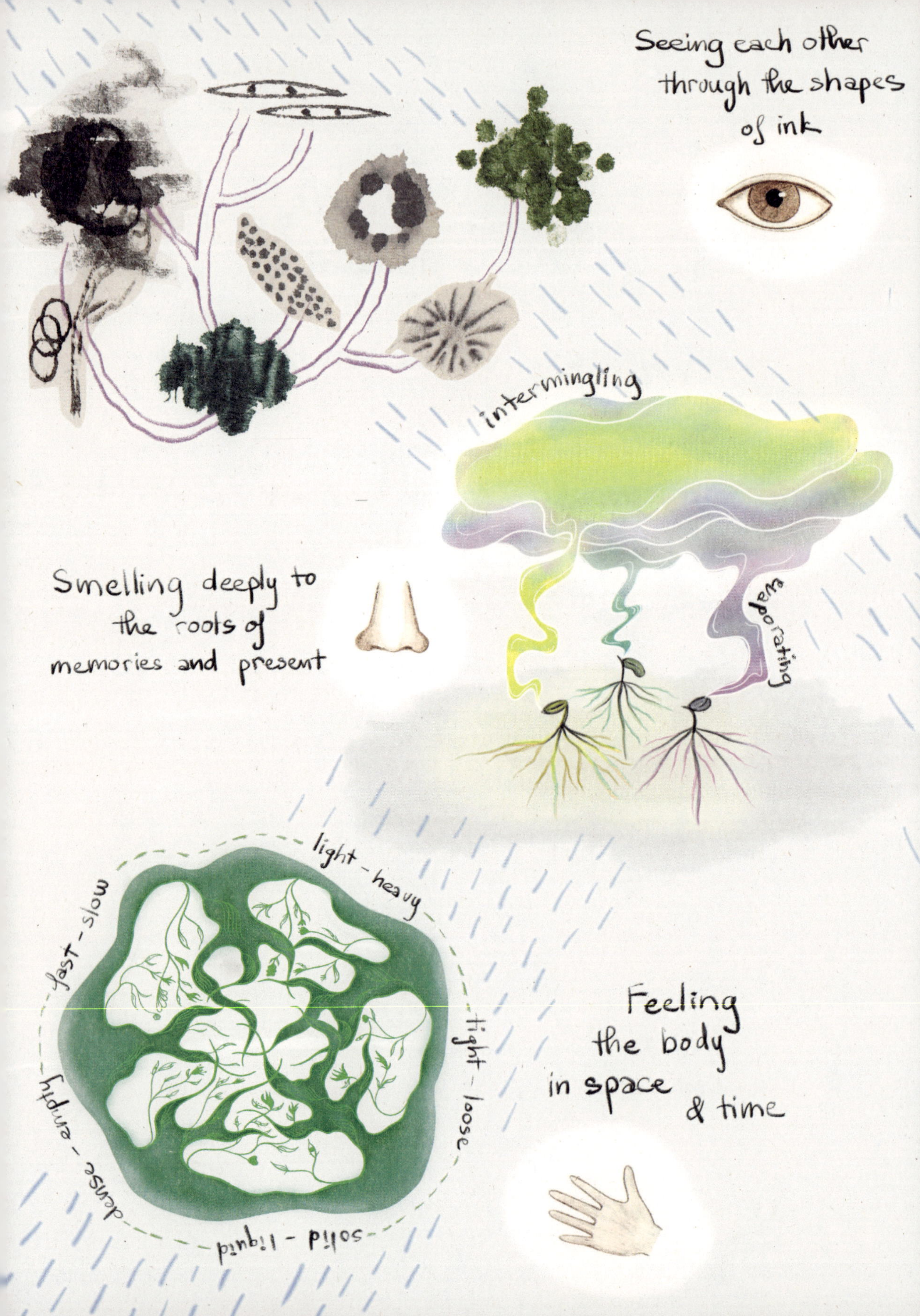
Seeing each other
through the shapes
of ink
intermingling
evaporating
Smelling deeply to
the roots of
memories and present
light - heavy
fast - slow
tight - loose
dense - empty
solid - liquid
Feeling
the body
in space
& time

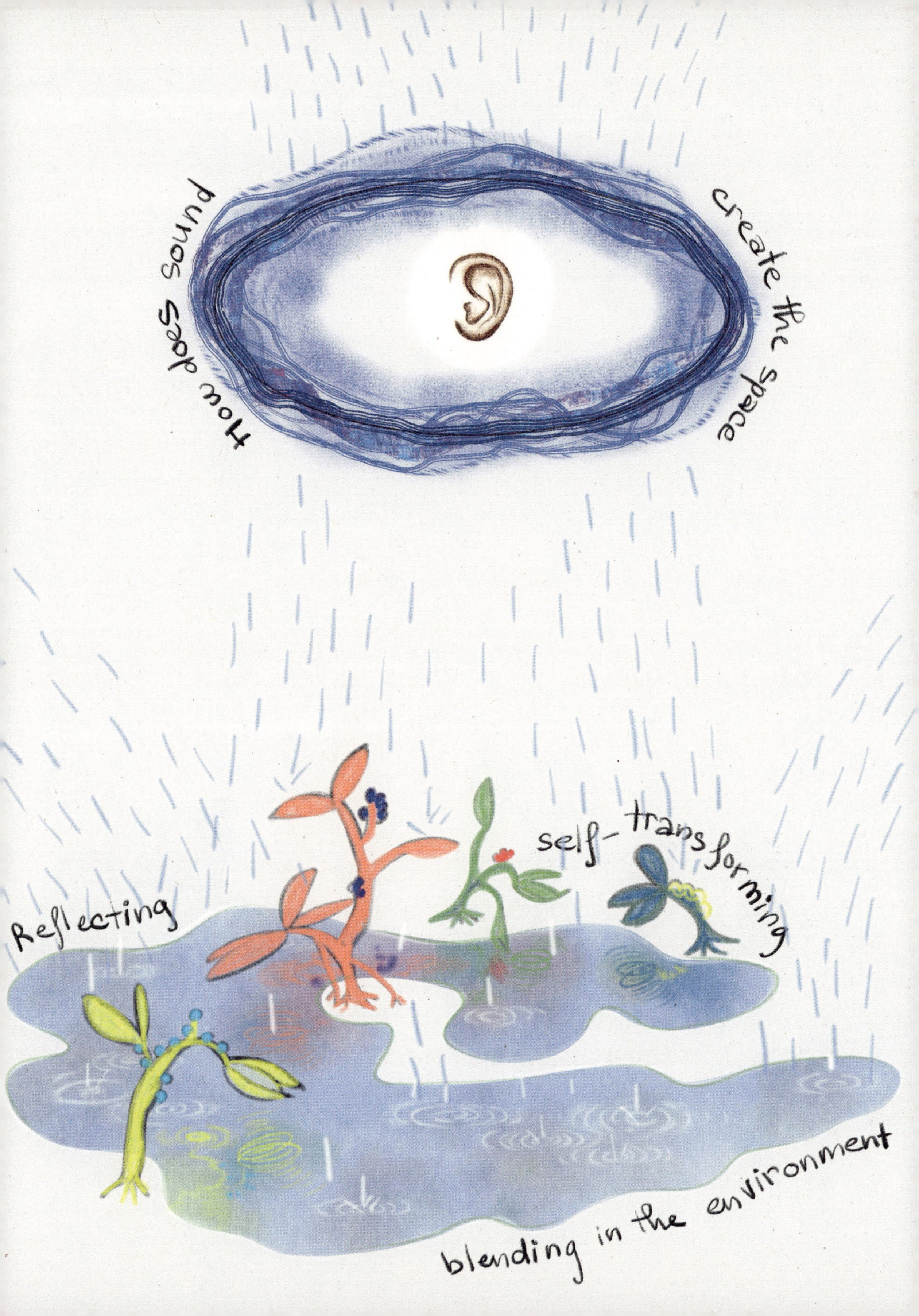

How does sound create the space

Reflecting

self-transforming

blending in the environment

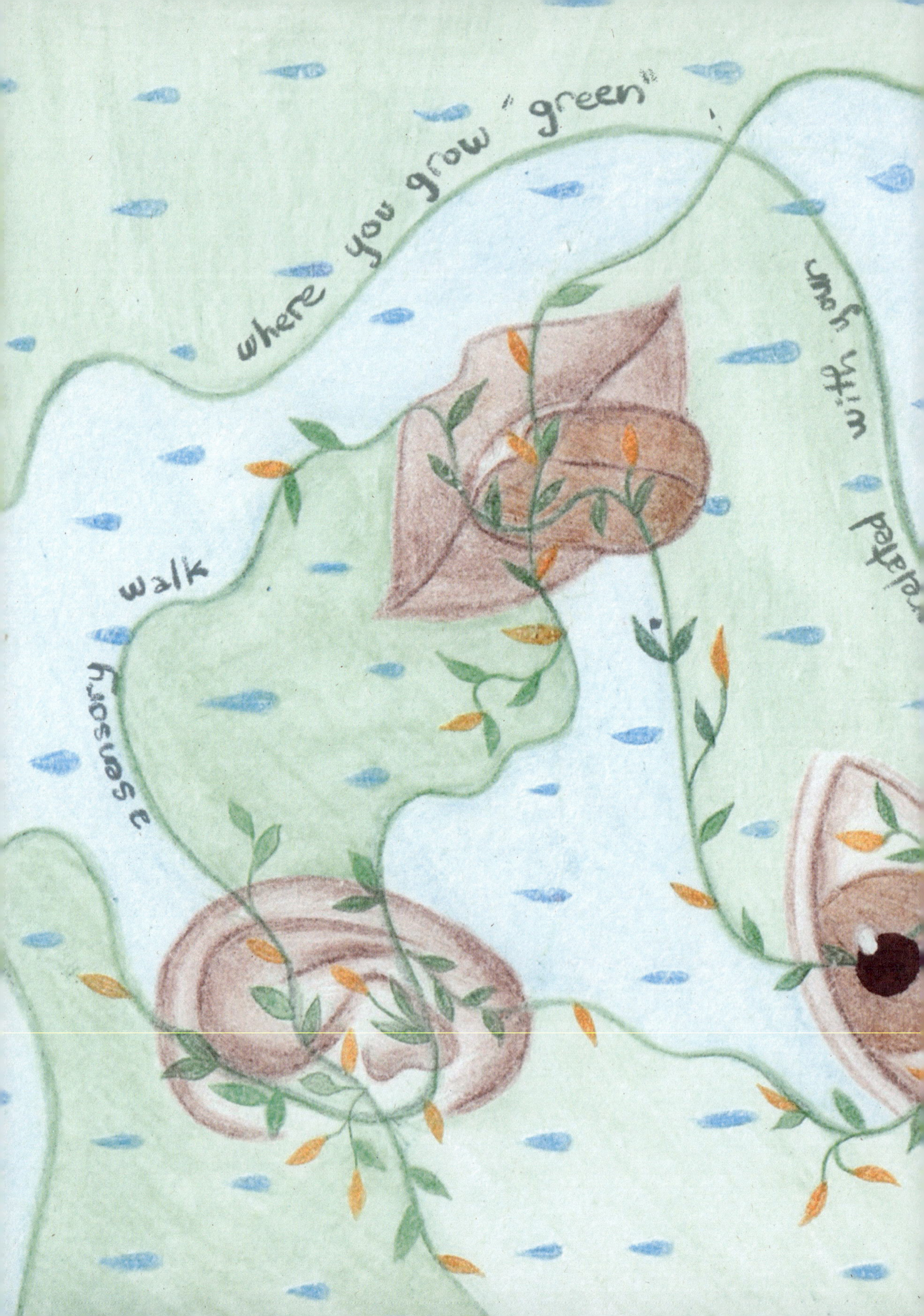
where you grow "green"
elated with your
walk
a sensory

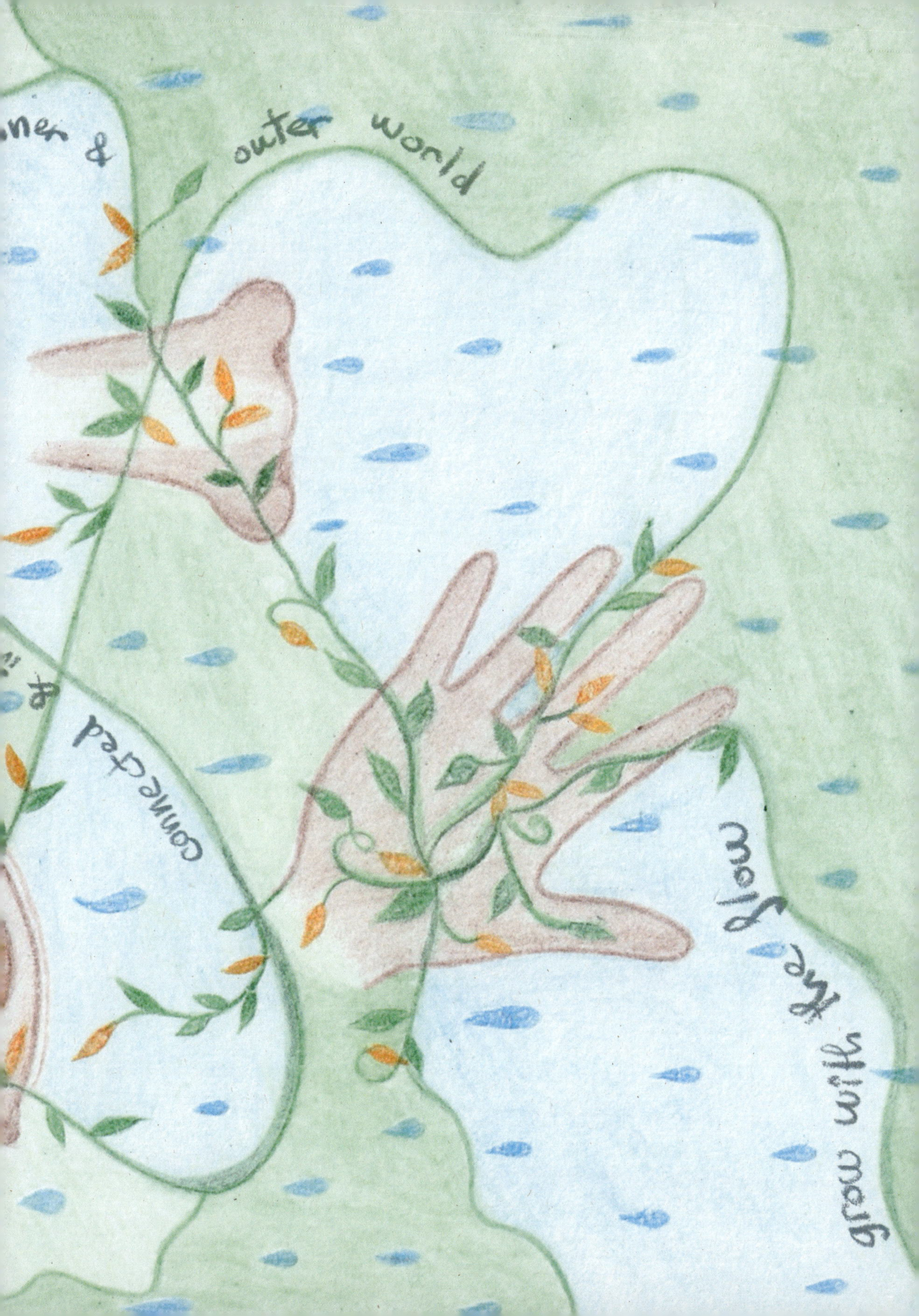

nner & outer world

connected &

grow with the flow

TẦM TÃ

THE SCALE OF THE EVERYDAY – SITUATING THE CURATORIAL

by **Biljana Ciric**

After working with Trần Lương remotely for months on the exhibition, I arrived in Hà Nội on the 14th of November 2023. Colleagues from APD Art Center who picked me up from the airport told me that Trần Lương was very happy with the apartment he had found for my stay in Hà Nội and was hoping that I would like it as much as he did. I arrived at the apartment and walked down the narrow lane and into the modest house, struggling to lift my suitcase up the stairs of the building. It was a studio apartment with basic facilities, and I was a bit puzzled as to why Trần Lương found it to be such a great place to stay. After meeting him I quickly understood. Across from the building where I was staying there was a small triangular park called Tây Sơn Garden, and it was facing a playground where Trần Lương played during his childhood. A hundred metres from the apartment was his maternal grandfather's house on Tràng Thi Street where Lương grew up. His school was in the lane next to the apartment. After understanding where I was, I felt grateful to Trần Lương for choosing this place for me to stay with such care, allowing me to physically experience and position myself in relation to a place that had formed him, both as a human and as an artist. One of the most important aspects of the curatorial is being close to the one who practises. Lương's gesture of choosing where I would stay with so much care, was an opening towards that space of proximity.

This exhibition and publication are an attempt to look at the life of Trần Lương and the complex role that he continues to play within contemporary art of Vietnam and the region that we usually call Southeast Asia. It is also an attempt to present the work of a practitioner whose engagement through contemporary art is shaped to a significant degree by drastic socio-political changes in the last three decades in Vietnam, and whose work and contribution on many different levels has thus far not received the care, support and international acknowledgment that it deserves. This research is also an attempt to recognise the complexities of practising, producing knowledge and sustaining communities on the margins of global capital; complexities that in our future filled with uncertainties, will serve as a relevant reference for art and culture of situated practices in times of scarcity.

As a research project, *Tầm Tã* privileges undervalued curatorial and artistic gestures, and proximity as a condition for knowledge production. At the same time, it brings into tension art world margins and centres and questions how knowledge is disseminated both locally and globally as facets of the curatorial. Through a wide collaborative network of partners in this project we hope to provide a modest contribution towards actively creating different citations on how artistic and curatorial histories are written, as a practice of creating citations from the margins.

Throughout this research and leading towards an exhibition and publication, we worked collaboratively. Trần Lương and I both refrained from framing this research project as a retrospective or a solo project, avoiding our very poor curatorial vocabularies when speaking about typologies of exhibitions. Lương felt uncomfortable with the word "retrospective", feeling that it implies a burden of history when he feels that he still has much work to do. "Solo" also felt inappropriate as many of the projects, works and ideas were the collective effort of many. We decided to borrow a term from the Vietnamese language: *Một chặng đường*, which means "A Journey", as a proposition to merge past, present and future, but also as an indicator that many things we talk about in this project are in process and dynamic.

Trần Lương's art and life are deeply entangled with the everyday. Both the exhibition and the publication look at the number of roles he embodies that are constantly merging into one another – from artist to curator, facilitator, mediator, activist, archivist and mentor. These positions were not given, they are active choices of taking on the responsibility to create spaces for the exchange of ideas within contexts in Vietnam where there is still no public infrastructure for contemporary art and where censorship continues.

SITUATING TRẦN LƯƠNG

Canadian Indigenous scholar Donald Dwayne notes that in order to understand what someone is saying you need to know their story, you need to situate the context.[1] In an attempt to situate Trần Lương, I offer here some fragments.

Trần Lương grew up in his mother's house, in a wealthy intellectual family in Hà Nội. His grandfather on his mother's side owned one of the first photography studios in Hà Nội.

1. "Dwayne Donald - Homo Economicus and Forgetful Curriculum: Remembering other ways to be a human being," YouTube video posted by the Sustainability Council (University of Alberta), Jan 23, 2020, 51:05, https://www.youtube.com/watch?v=VM1J3evcEyQ

At the age of five, Lương was forced to leave his family due to the American bombing of North Vietnam and was sent to the countryside on his own. Between 1965 and 1972, Trần Lương lived in the countryside by himself, much like many city kids at the time, returning occasionally to his family in Hà Nội when the bombing stopped. Lương talks about this period through his relation to water and the more-than-human world that he discovered in the water, which accompanied him in the village during those years.

In 1954, the Communist Party became the ruling party in North Vietnam, with the North and South of the country only re-uniting in 1975. For many people over this 20-year period, life changed from affluence to scarcity due to new regulations on abandoning private ownership, collectivisation and a planned economy. In the 1960s, newly implemented laws on living conditions changed the lives of many families, including Lương's. Family-owned houses were taken away and redistributed according to new regulations in which each family would be given eight square metres per adult to live.[2] Trần Lương's family lost their big house and the 12 family members started to live in only a few rooms. He remembers his grandfather selling their items from their home to survive, including bonsai trees from the courtyard. From 1954 to 1990 (a period that included the American bombing campaign that began in early 1965 until the end of the subsidy economy in 1986), the whole country experienced great international isolation caused by sanctions, inflation and natural disasters which profoundly affected basic food production and supply.

Trần Lương usually describes life during these few decades in very simple terms, "I was hungry most of the time until I was 32."[3] His early thirties were framed by experiments in economic reform that began in the early 1980s with the aim of transitioning the country from a central planned economy towards a market economy and culminated in the official implementation of the Đổi Mới reforms in 1986. Despite lifting many out of hunger, the process of opening up also brought with it corruption and greater inequality.

Trần Lương started out as a painter and along with the artist group he was a part of, known as the Gang of Five, he had viable prospects for having a successful artistic career. But in 1997 Lương quit painting. He understood that in a context such as Vietnam, where there is no infrastructure of support, being an artist and having an individual practice was not enough. He started to organise events and exhibitions and create local art infrastructures, while also creating the conditions for exchanges throughout the region; a practice

2. The whole house had eight main rooms and small auxiliary rooms, a garden, a front yard and back yard and a large shop opening onto the street. The communist state left his family four rooms and the rest were given to strangers to live in. The shop was taken over by the state.

3. from unpublished conversation between Biljana Ciric and Trần Lương, 2023.

that today we name as the curatorial. For Trần Lương, the curatorial is not just about making exhibitions, it is also a process of creating safe spaces where ideas can be experimented and shared. This practice of creating space as a curatorial gesture, has remained a constant in his work, through his continued attempts to co-fund art centres, such as Nhà Sàn Studio, Hà Nội Contemporary Art Center and currently, APD. Lương understood early that exhibition rituals offer a temporary reality, and that local practitioners need spaces that can provide continuous support. The curatorial and artistic position he has taken bears the responsibilities of encounter. For decades he has facilitated encounters with different communities on the margins through field trips that he self-initiated and organised, as well as encounters with official systems in Vietnam that constantly challenge the acceptance levels of contemporary art. He has also developed encounters and projects with Indigenous communities in Vietnam, artistic communities throughout Southeast Asia and global art communities. By bridging the existing gaps, Lương also challenges conventional notions of art production – where, with whom and for whom it is created.

The 30-year journey of Trần Lương's art practice is shaped by political and social transitions in Vietnam. Despite the opening up of the economy in the Đổi Mới period, today economic growth is still unevenly distributed, while a very repressive political regime allows little or no space for different ways of thinking and practising. Informed by these changes, Lương continues to work and discover possibilities for practising otherwise. In Lương's case, that otherwise is situated in a struggle for how to create space for artistic production within Vietnam and how to continue to support the local artistic community.

Although drastically changed today, Vietnam continues to be a complex space to navigate the voice of art and culture within the public realm. Art communities still work in semi-underground modes when speaking with more contemporary critical languages of art. Due to this position, many who know Trần Lương's work would describe his practice as political, and I would agree. Understanding the political within his practice is not only about responding to political tensions of today, but also fundamentally working on questions of inclusion within culture, working with marginal groups, working through long-term engagement with communities and creating structural changes. The political in his practice also encompasses his quest for equal rights to culture and the right to access to clean water.

Starting as a painter in the 1980s, Trần Lương's work from that period can only be accessed through a few photographs (Lương explains simply that he sold many works very cheaply in order to eat). These early works underline themes of figuration, semi-figuration, as well as the presence of the naked body, which was not a common topic in the public realm of art in Vietnam at that time. From the late 1980s he turned to Vietnamese myth, specifically the story of Chử Đồng Tử and Tiên Dung, as a symbol of freedom from social constraints. Through these series, the more-than-human world that inhabited the water from his childhood memories during the bombing of North Vietnam, started to interconnect with mythical storytelling. Water became an important element that is however, never directly depicted in the work. Water becomes an archive of life, of the human and more-than-human, where reality and myth cannot be separated. It is also an archive of hardship, the destruction of life and livelihood caused by bombing, along with its resilience and survival. The *Flowing* series shows the disturbance of life caused by the bombs, but also the return to life after destruction. In this series his repetitive metaphor of the amoeba or the eye, appears often. This abstract symbol opens many possibilities for readings, representing many things all at once – the human, the more-than-human, all floating.

Lương didn't create preliminary sketches for his paintings, as with his performance work later on. Preparatory work is reduced to a minimum, opening space for improvisation and a sensitivity to the material. In his painting process, only the material itself dictated the velocity of the process. Many of his paintings were created on sensitive Dó paper,[4] which requires patience during the drying process. To revise the paintings, he had to work on them at the precise time when the paper was neither too wet nor too dry, resulting in him usually working on several paintings at the same time.

In 1997 Lương quit painting, and soon after turned to institution making by co-establishing Nhà Sàn art studio in 1998, where he began explorations towards more performative work. His first performative gestures were in his solo exhibition, which was Nhà Sàn's opening exhibition, in which he interacted with an installation in the empty gallery in the absence of an audience. The performance was only captured in photographs. During the late 90s, Trần Lương intensively

4. A type of handmade paper using a herbaceous plant called *Dó* that grows in the Northern midland hills of Vietnam.

organised workshops, encounters and exhibitions, while also starting to travel abroad more often. I would suggest understanding the exhibitions that he organised during this period as pedagogical frameworks, where he would regularly practise and implement certain methodologies as both an artist and a curator. These methodologies were informed by his trips abroad and interactions with the international art scene, which he then aimed to apply locally.

As in his painting, repetition is also present within Lương's performance work. He often returns to one work, revisiting and re-performing it, continuing a relationship with it. Through repetition, his performance work escapes a static position of being seen and understood as a linear structure – the works continue to be dynamic and adaptive over several years. The materials for his performance work are basic and everyday. A red scarf, a bamboo whip, plastic bottles, clothes, a toothbrush and his own body. Many performances are re-performed in different places around the world and this revisiting, while incorporating situated contexts, becomes crucial to the work. In many of his performances, Lương repeats everyday gestures. For him, daily actions have their own power – they contain community memories as well as individual ones. When changing context they gain power: he washes clothes on a tree or instigates a collective tooth-brushing session in public space. He uses performance as a tool to allow people to release their own hidden pressures, allowing them to speak without words, opening a space for interaction through bodily gestures. In some work he creates complex structures to work with participants and institutions through workshops and long-term research processes, ending up with a final moment of action. Presence, participation and embodied experience are fundamental for his performance work. Living conditions define working conditions for Lương, highlighting the importance of the artist's body as material through the performative gesture. He understands the body as the only material that cannot be censored.

During our conversations Lương often reflected that Vietnam lacks the space and material conditions to support installation work, including inadequate resources to ship and install them properly. As a result, people interested in experiencing installation art need to travel to see it. Performance as a form provides much greater flexibility, allowing him to go to communities, to engage in the most direct way, to learn from that engagement but also to disappear fast if needed, in order to avoid censorship.

ARRIVING WITH A PURPOSE

The Australian Indigenous Wurujneri people, traditional owners of Aboriginal land, use the word *Wominjeka* to welcome someone's arrival. The Wominjeka could be translated as "coming with a purpose." *What is our purpose when arriving in a place?* is a question that we don't often ask or address. Trần Lương's work with communities usually existed parallel to his so-called artistic practice, only occasionally rubbing up against art systems, and until this project, was never articulated as part of his artistic practice. Through this exhibition and publication, for the first time within the art context, we are sharing and thinking with others about the importance of creating space for working with communities on the forefront of climate change, practising how to decentralise our work within the culture. The purpose of many of Trần Lương's travels to remote places in Vietnam were related to climate disasters or the lack of fundamental conditions for living, such as clean water, housing and the need for structural change. Many of these places receive very little public governmental support for improving living conditions, and sometimes even that modest support is rejected, as the communities see it as a danger to their culture and tradition. The artistic gesture doesn't end with documenting these struggles, but extends to working together with communities creating long-term structural changes such as building more resilient houses or growing mangrove forests.

These initiatives are complex and multilayered projects engaging local governments, indigenous elders, local communities and their needs, as well as young cultural workers. They are also complex in execution, involving architects, researchers, geologists, botanists, local farmers and many other different knowledge holders who know the land and the water. Many of the initiatives challenge knowledge structures, languages and vocabularies that Trần Lương himself as an artist is accustomed to. One of the great challenges of these projects is that they require not only the creation of hard infrastructure but, more importantly, the careful building of soft infrastructures and relationships that are needed in order to become part of a community. Trần Lương has engaged in this work through many different initiatives, but in the past decade most of the work has been done through the Sống Foundation, where he is vice president.

Repetition within these initiatives also becomes crucial. Trần Lương explained to me that the first mangrove planting started in September 2019, with 10,000 bần chua trees (Sonneratia caseolaris) on seven hectares in the Định An estuary, Cù Lao Dung, Sóc Trăng Province. After six months, the plants were fiercely attacked by barnacles, making them too weak to survive the strong waves and they eventually died. At the same time, when there is a lack of flood water due to the construction of dams upstream, the salinity in the sea water near the shore increases, causing oyster larvae to penetrate near the shore and cling to the roots of young Avicennia trees, which eventually kills them.

After this failure, different strategies were learnt and the following year the Sống Foundation successfully planted ten hectares of mangrove trees. To date, the Sống foundation has planted 28.5 hectares of mangroves in Lạc Hòa commune, Vĩnh Châu town, Sóc Trăng province. Repetition is a way of learning but also a way of creating deeper and more entangled connections to place through everyday struggle.

The working process towards this exhibition and publication uncovered how much Trần Lương is a man of making things happen – an initiator. He has done so many things that have been documented, and yet how much has gone undocumented, or documented but not edited, or created without name or titles? During this process of working together we realised that many works, especially performances, have no titles due to the fact that he was never asked to give them one. Many works have been process-based, starting with workshops (often interactive) and these moments are very hard to grasp through images. There have been many theatre plays for which he created the lighting design, books he illustrated, stories and poetry he has written, among much more. What we are sharing here is only a fragmented, partial perspective on his journey, but as Donna Haraway reminds us, only a partial perspective brings objective vision.[5]

5. Donna Haraway. 'Situated Knowledges: The Science Question in Feminism and the Privilege of Partial Perspective'. *Feminist Studies* 14, no. 3 (Autumn 1988).

ON TẦM TÃ

Trần Lương describes the act of art making writ large, as a gesture of farming. It is a very slow process that requires a number of different conditions to come together to allow a process of transformation to take place. It is constantly in a process of becoming; testing the ground for ways that becoming can be shared and fostered within the community, towards collective harvesting. Institution making, curatorial work, facilitating – these are all forms of making and they are informed by many elements, both internal and external, from the politics of the time to the inner dynamics of the scene and even the weather.

Our exhibition title is described by the Vietnamese term *Tầm Tã* (in English it is usually translated as "soaked in the long rain"). This term is also the name of the educational program that Trần Lương runs in Hà Nội, and it projects his way of doing things – his constant insistence and pushing towards something. *Tầm Tã* suggests an overwhelming feeling of encounter or experience, the way Lương continues along the journey of art and life; giving in full, but also insisting that people around him embrace that fullness in order to continue practising. Some people can embrace it, but some find it too overwhelming, like the feeling of being soaked in constant rain.

Going back to the gesture of art making as farming, it is important that rain falls at the right time, otherwise the harvest will be destroyed. Navigating needs and conditions defines the moments of *Tầm Tã*.

THE CAT

During my stay in Hà Nội, our working mornings would start like this: I would be picked up by Trần Lương on his motorbike and we would arrive at APD Center around 10am. After unlocking the door, the first thing Trần Lương would do is start the ritual of feeding the cat that lives in the centre. The cat lived in between the space of the first and second floors, in a narrow gap no more than 30cm high and very deep. For most visitors, the cat is invisible. During the day the cat would not come down to us. She would make herself visible to Lương in the morning and he would happily go to pick up the ladder to climb up and feed her. He didn't ask much from the cat, only to be there, and she didn't seem to mind. The bond was there although it is not an easy one to articulate. He needed the cat's presence and the cat probably needed food.

Having a cat in an art space seemed natural and nobody questioned it. In a post-pandemic context and with numerous writings around multispecies ecologies, I often wondered – but never asked – about the cat's presence as a proposal for human and more-than-human co-existence in art spaces; something that within the Western context of the white cube is impossible. The cat was simply there, and it was part of everyday life. Any theorizing about it would feel inappropriate. APD is the cat's home, as it is to many youngsters that I met while working on this project. As it is to Trần Lương.

BIOGRAPHIES

IOLA LENZI

Iola Lenzi is a Singapore-based art historian and curator of modern and contemporary Southeast Asian art. Holding a degree in law (LLB), and a PhD in Modern Asian Art History, she researches socially engaged contemporary Southeast Asian art analysed from multidisciplinary perspectives. Her doctoral project focused on emerging practices in 1990s Hà Nội, tracing the aesthetic-conceptual methods of a small avant-garde as these artists engaged social-cultural-economic shifts driven by 1986's Đổi Mới reforms and global integration, to pioneer contemporary Vietnamese art. Lenzi has curated numerous exhibitions of Southeast Asian art in Asia and Europe with institutional partners including Singapore Art Museum; ARTER Space for Art, Istanbul; BACC, Bangkok; Goethe Institut Hà Nội, HCM City, Yangon; Galeri Nasional, Jakarta; James H.W. Thompson Foundation, Bangkok; Samsung Corporation Art Projects; The Substation, Singapore; Grand Palais, Paris, among others. She has commissioned and authored several multilingual research anthologies on Southeast Asian contemporary art and its discourses and teaches Southeast Asian contemporary art history and curatorial methodologies at Nanyang Technological University, Singapore, and in the Asian Art Histories Masters programme at University of the Arts, Singapore. She is the is the author of *Museums of Southeast Asia* (2004).

PHOEBE SCOTT

Phoebe Scott is a Senior Curator and Curator of Research Publications at National Gallery Singapore. Her curatorial projects include *Between Declarations and Dreams: Art of Southeast Asia since the 19th Century* (2015 – ongoing), the inaugural exhibition of the National Gallery's Southeast Asia galleries; *Reframing Modernism: Painting from Southeast Asia, Europe and Beyond* (2016); and most recently, *Familiar Others: Emiria Sunassa, Eduardo Masferré and Yeh Chi Wei, 1940s-70s* (2022-23). She is also an Adjunct Lecturer in art history at the National University of Singapore. Prior to joining the Gallery, Phoebe completed her PhD on the subject of modern Vietnamese art.

LÊ THUẬN UYÊN

Lê Thuận Uyên is currently Curator and Artistic Director of The Outpost – a Hà Nội based private organisation committed to the collection, presentation, and discussion of contemporary art in Vietnam. Informed by her former training in political science, Uyen is interested in alternative histories – personal narratives that are rendered absent or undesirable by the official record. Her practice is also concerned with the investigation of forms and ideas within the social context and aesthetic traditions of Vietnam. Uyên is also a keen advocate for integrating art experiences into the universal educational system, as well as building capacity for the Vietnamese art landscape. Some of her past curatorial projects include, *Fractured Times* (The Outpost, Hà Nội, 2022); *And they die another death*

(Nguyen Trinh Thi for Documenta fifteen, 2022); *Domestic Bliss* (Ilham Gallery, KL, 2019); *Gang of Five Chancing Modern* (Hà Nội, 2017) and *Sindikat Campursari* (Jakarta, 2016).

LINH LÊ

Linh Lê is an independent curator, writer and researcher from Ho Chi Minh City (Vietnam), whose work explores the (im)possibilities of the archive. In 2021, Linh received a research grant from Dogma Collection (Ho Chi Minh City) to investigate the cult personality of Ho Chi Minh as observed in propaganda posters, public monuments and his namesake museum franchise. Linh also expands her curatorial scope to publishing, discussions, workshops and teaching. Some of her past projects include *CáRô – an* arts education programme for local youth (Ho Chi Minh City, 2020-21); *Măng Ta* – a self-initiated journal on Vietnamese arts and culture (2020-pending). Some of her past curatorial projects include *Chợt Mộng Tan* (2022, Á Space); *Dept. Of Speculation* (2022, Galerie Quynh); *All Aboard* (2023, Galerie Quynh) and *Soon The Time Will Come* (2023, Á Space). She is a member of the organising committee of *The First Conference on Curating in Vietnam* (Hà Nội, April 2024). Currently, she is a research fellow of ArtsEquator's Southeast Asian Arts Censorship Database project and a curatorial board member at Á Space, an independent art space founded in 2018 in Hà Nội.

VŨ ĐỨC TOÀN

Primarily working with performance and installation, Vũ Đức Toàn has consistently engaged with the correlation between the spectator and the performer and the social rituals, as well as historical lapses of time, that punctuate or bridge the past and the present. His works often begin with simple concepts and are then materialised through the repetition of performative gestures or visual motifs and through a laconic yet capacious selection of objects and materiality. Toàn has participated in many exhibitions and performance art events locally and internationally, such as *Returning to the island of South* Performance Art Festival (Taiwan, 2017), solo exhibition *Disorderly Departure* (Nhà Sàn Collective, Hà Nội, 2017), *MoT+++* Performance Residency and Exhibition (HCMC, 2017), *Guyu Action* (China – Hong Kong – Taiwan, 2016), *PAN Asia 5* (Seoul, Korea, 2012) and *Benign Tumor* (L'Espace, Hà Nội, 2011).

In 2010, Vũ Đức Toàn and Nguyễn Huy An founded The Appendix Group, a performance artist group then including six members: Vũ Đức Toàn, Nguyễn Huy An, Nguyễn Song, Ngô Thành Bắc, Nguyễn Dương Hải Đăng and Hoàng Minh Đức. The Appendix Group is recognised as an outstanding performance group in Vietnam that pioneered group performance with a signature aesthetics blending vernacular sensibility with composition, imbued with symbols rich in constant contemplation of bygone eras and anticipation of the future.

Since 2005, Toàn has also worked as an editor at the Association of Fine Art and its affiliated magazine. He has been a member of the Curatorial Board at Nhà Sàn Collective since 2013, where he has mentored several generations of younger artists, as well as curating *Skylines with Flying People 4* with the Appendix Group (King's Storage, Hà Nội, 2020). Most recently, he curated several performance art events including *Morning - Noon - Afternoon - Evening* (Á Space, Hà Nội, 2022), *IN:ACT 2022* (Nhà Sàn Collective & Á Space, Kassel & Hà Nội, 2022), and *Tái Nạm* (Mơ Art Space, Hà Nội, 2022).

The writers' collective comprises five members: Flinh, Ngụy Hải An, Lê Tú Anh, Trịnh Ngân Hạnh and Phạm Việt Hoàng. They currently work for the APD - Center for Art Patronage and Development, an art centre supporting artistic creation and promoting socio-cultural development based in Hà Nội, Vietnam, of which Trần Lương is the co-founder and director.

Flinh is a visual artist. She studied painting at the Vietnam University of Fine Art and began experimenting with contemporary art in 2016. She works primarily with performance art, drawings and moving image. Flinh was among the participants in Tran Luong's workshop in 2017 and later worked as a teaching assistant for the first *Tầm Tã* Course in 2020. Flinh currently works as registrar at APD and has also served as the assistant of the Tầm Tã course since 2021.

Ngụy Hải An is a public program coordinator and a communicator at APD. She graduated with a Bachelor and a Master of International Politics from the Diplomatic Academy of Vietnam. An was a reporter on international news before starting to work in the art field in 2018 and has been serving in different positions including educational curator, communicator, event coordinator, producer and project manager. She has served as the coordinator of the Tầm Tã course since 2021.

Lê Tú Anh graduated from the Department of Painting, Ewha Womans University, Korea (2019). She participated in the Tầm Tã art practice course in 2021 and Tầm Tã curating course in 2022. She has worked as an administrator at APD since 2022. She also teaches art to children (including autistic children and children with intellectual disabilities) at Tòhe Social Enterprise and is a member of the Chaap Collective.

Trịnh Ngân Hạnh graduated with a Bachelor of Visual Arts (Arts Plastiques) from Université de Rennes 2, France (2020). From 2021 to early 2023, she was the art director and curator at Ngã Art Space (TÁCH SPACES, Hà Nội). Ngân Hạnh is currently a graphic designer at APD, along with teaching art to autistic children at Tòhe Social Enterprise. She was a participant in the Tầm Tã art practice course in 2021 and Tầm Tã curating course in 2022.

Phạm Việt Hoàng graduated with a Bachelor of Contemporary Creative Practice in Photography from British University Vietnam (2019–2022). He works as a freelancer in design, art handling and tattoo. Hoàng currently serves as a collaborator at APD. He was also a participant in the Tầm Tã art practice course in 2023.

TRẦN LƯƠNG

Born in Hà Nội in 1960, Trần Lương is a performance and visual artist, independent curator and major figure in creating space for critical contemporary art in Vietnam. Among the first local artists to experiment with performance and video, his artwork is grounded in local experience. Active in creating opportunities for artists, Trần Lương co-founded the Gang of Five (1983-1996), which organised monthly exhibitions in alternative spaces. In 1998, he co-founded Nhà Sàn Studio, the country's first, artist-led, experimental art space, and curated the majority of its exhibitions in the initial four years. He was founding director of the Hà Nội Contemporary Art Centre in 2000, a post from which he resigned in 2003 in protest of government corruption. In 2020 he co-founded Center for Art Patronage and Development (APD), an organisation focusing on artistic development with the orientation of intersecting activities between artistic development and social development. He has continued to direct APD's programme since its founding. Among his collaborative projects that take art to the people to generate debate about ways of living are the *Mạo Khê Coal Mine Art Project*, involving workshops with a worker's community in a rural mine; and *On the Banks of the Red River*, which presented interactive performance in an impoverished area of Hà Nội.

A generous mentor of Vietnamese youth, Trần Lương goes beyond normal curatorship, encouraging performers to push the boundaries, negotiating censorship with the authorities, creating exchanges between North, Centre and South Vietnam, bringing diasporan artists back and hosting international artists. His artworks critique repression, emphasise human resilience and empower the individual through personal action and self-reflection. He is recognised for his dedicated energy in developing spaces, initiatives, networks and communities for performance and video arts in Vietnam; for questioning the dominant norms and supporting alternative visions in a context of censorship and conformity; and for his commitment to freedom of expression, community enrichment and nurturing younger generations. After 2000, he did not just play a role as an artist and curator, but also acted as a social developer. He has organised and operated several long-term social development projects in areas such as: changing public awareness in the new social interface, environmental issues and improving and developing the skills of expression for poor and isolated communities. He served as chairman of the advisory board, and later as vice chairman of the Sống Foundation, a non-profit social development organisation founded in 2013. He continues to live and work in Hà Nội.

BILJANA CIRIC is an interdependent curator.

Ciric was curator of the Pavilion of Republic of Serbia at 59th Venice Biennale in 2022 where she presented *Walking with Water*, a solo exhibition by Vladimir Nikolic. She conceived of the inquiry for the first Trans-Southeast Asian Triennial in Guang Zhou, *Repetition as a Gesture Towards Deep Listening* (2021/2022), which led to a collaboration with Trần Lương and a number of partner institutions, which made this book and exhibition possible. Ciric was the co-curator of the 3rd Ural Industrial Biennale for Contemporary Art (Yekaterinburg, 2015), curator in residence at Kadist Art Foundation (Paris, 2015) and a research fellow at Henie Onstad Kunstsenter (Høvikodden, 2016). Her recent exhibitions include *An Inquiry: Modes of Encounter* presented by Times Museum, Guang Zhou (2019); *When the Other Meets the Other Other* presented by Cultural Center Belgrade (2017); *Proposals for Surrender* presented by McAM in Shanghai (2016/2017); and *This exhibition Will Tell You Everything About FY Art Foundation* in FY Art Foundation space in Shen Zhen (2017).

In 2013, Ciric initiated the seminar platform *From a History of Exhibitions Towards a Future of Exhibition Making* with a focus on China and Southeast Asia. The assembly platform was hosted by St Paul St Gallery, AUT, New Zealand (2013); Rockbund Art Museum, Shanghai (2018); and Times Museum, Guang Zhou (2019). A book with the same name was published by Sternberg Press in 2019 and was awarded best art publication in China in 2020. Her research on artist organised exhibitions in Shanghai was published in the book "History in Making; Shanghai: 1979-2006" published by CFCCA; and "Life and Deaths of Institutional Critique" co-edited by Nikita Yingqian Cai and published by Black Dog Publishing, among others. She was nominated for the ICI Independent Vision Curatorial Award (2012).

In 2018 Ciric established the educational platform *What Could/Should Curating Do?* and in 2019 she initiated a long-term project reflecting on China's Belt and Road Initiative titled *As you go . . . the roads under your feet, towards a new future*. She is a PhD candidate in Curatorial Practice at Monash University, Melbourne.

THANK YOU

This book is dedicated to my parents and extended family. Family history is the earliest and most enduring "school" that has imparted to me countless "lessons" – experiences and materials closely linked to the contemporary history of the country.

I extend special thanks to Biljana Ciric, curator of this project; without her proposal and development, the book and the exhibition could not have come to fruition.

I also express gratitude to the museums and art spaces for their sharing of knowledge and resources for this project: Jameel Arts Centre, Govett Brewster Art Gallery, The Art Gallery of Western Australia and the Art Museum of Guang Zhou Academy of Fine Arts. Institutions are run by people and here I would like to extend gratitude to devoted individuals who made this possible. Chen Xiaoyang, director of the Art Museum of Guang Zhou Academy of Fine Arts; Nora Raizan, deputy director of Art Jameel; Zara Stanhope, director of Govett Brewster Art Gallery; Rachel Ciesla, curator at AGWA Perth; Giacomo Pietro Lamborizio, Simon Gennard and many others.

Sincere thanks to the following artistic organisations, archival repositories and museums: Asian Art Archive, Singapore Art Museum, Bildmuseet Art Museum and Twork.

Thanks to the experts, curators, researchers, art critics, designers, artists, collectors and friends who have assisted or provided information, photographic and video materials: Iola Lenzi, Phoebe Scott, Lê Thuận Uyên, Linh Lê, Vũ Đức Toàn, Nguyễn Trinh Thi, Natalia Kraevskaia, Ưu Đàm Trần Nguyễn, Nguyễn Mạnh Hùng, Nguyễn Minh Phước, Nguyễn Thế Sơn, Trương Công Tùng, Vũ Trâm, Brynjar Bjerkem, Nguyễn Huy An, Trần Yến Chi, Trần Hậu Tuấn. Bùi Tiến Phúc, Phạm Trần Việt Nam, Phạm Thị Hương Giang, Nguyễn Mỹ Linh, Đinh Bá Vinh, Thái Kế Toại, Vipash Purichanon, Mikael Lundgren and Điện Thu Lê.

A big hug to the entire APD staff, volunteers and dedicated assistants: Flinh, Ngụy Hải An, Trịnh Ngân Hạnh, Lê Tú Anh, Phạm Việt Hoàng, Nguyễn Bá Ngọc.

COLOPHON

TẦM TÃ
SOAKED IN THE LONG RAIN
– A TRẦN LƯƠNG JOURNEY

PUBLISHED BY
Art Jameel,
Govett Brewster Art Gallery,
The Art Gallery of Western Australia,
Art Museum of Guangzhou Academy of Fine Arts
and Mousse Publishing.

PUBLICATION CONCEIVED BY
Biljana Ciric

DESIGN:
Toby Tam

COORDINATOR:
Flinh

COPYEDITOR AND PROOFREADER:
Susie Quillinan

ARCHIVAL PROCESS SUPPORT:
APD Center

DOCUMENTATION AND PHOTOGRAPHS:
Phạm Việt Hoàng, Điện Thu Lê

This publication is produced on the occasion of the exhibition
Tầm Tã that will tour to all partner venues between 2024 and 2027.

Jameel Arts Centre:
December 2024 - May 2025

Govett Brewster Art Gallery:
November 2025 - March 2026

The Art Gallery of Western Australia:
July 2026 - December 2026

Art Museum of Guangzhou Academy of Fine Arts:
March 2027 - June 2027

PUBLISHED AND DISTRIBUTED BY
Mousse Publishing
Contrappunto s.r.l.
Via Pier Candido Decembrio 28,
20137, Milan–Italy

AVAILABLE THROUGH
Mousse Publishing, Milan
moussemagazine.it

PUBLISHING EDITOR
Ilaria Bombelli, Mousse

EDITED BY
Biljana Ciric

DESIGN BY
Toby Tam

First edition: 2024
Printed in Italy
ISBN 978-88-6749-663-1
€ 30 / $ 35

ART JAMEEL

Established in 2003, Art Jameel is an independent organisation that supports artists and creative communities. Art Jameel's two institutions - Jameel Arts Centre, an innovative contemporary institution in Dubai, UAE, and Hayy Jameel, a dedicated complex for the arts and creativity in Jeddah, Saudi Arabia, offer programmes across exhibitions, commissions, research, learning and community-building in order to promote contemporary art and creative entrepreneurship across the Middle East and beyond.

Jameel Arts Centre
Jaddaf Waterfront
Dubai, United Arab Emirates
artjameel.org
jameelartscentre.org

DIRECTOR: Antonia Carver
DEPUTY DIRECTORS: Uns Kattan (Head of Learning and Research), Nora Razian (Head of Exhibitions and Programmes)

EXHIBITIONS AND COLLECTION: Rhoda Azizoghly (Registrar), Qutouf Elobaid (Special Projects Coordinator), Naseef Ismail (Logistics Coordinator), Daniya Jawwad (Collections Research Assistant), Dina Khatib (Graphic Designer), Giacomo Pietro Lamborizio (Exhibitions Manager), Zahra Mansoor (Design and Production Coordinator), Lucas Morin (Curator)
LEARNING: Azim Al Ghussein (Senior Manager, Library and Research), Ebla Al Hawi (Learning Assistant), Hadeel Al Heeti (Learning Manager), Abhirami Suresh (Library and Youth Coordinator)
OPERATIONS, AV AND FACILITIES: Brent Galotera (Senior Manager, Operations and IT), Christopher Tiu (Facilities Manager), Alex Wachira King'ori (Technology Assistant)
COMMUNICATIONS, OUTREACH AND VISITOR EXPERIENCE: Neelham Abdullah (Visitor Experience Assistant), Lama Mosallem (Social Media Specialist), Rita Rutainurwa (Visitor Experience Coordinator), Ruba Alsweel (Senior Manager, Communications), Murad El Zagal (Senior Manager, Strategy and Outreach)
PARTNERSHIPS AND EVENTS, ENTERPRISES, ART JAMEEL SHOP: Mary Ann Gallardo (Retail Coordinator), Sobia Ghias (Senior Manager, Partnerships and Events), Jannah Hernandez (Events Assistant), Vladimir Kurumilian (Enterprises Manager), Francis Moulic (Retail Manager - Global), Julie Torres (Part-time retail assistant)
FINANCE AND PROCUREMENT, ADMIN, PEOPLE: Vanessa Adim (Accountant), Hassan Butt (Senior Accountant), Mohamed Eldesoky (Head of Finance), Jenny Estioko (Finance Manager), Naveen Meethale Veettil (Procurement Coordinator), Hisham Mosmar (Head of People), Monalisa Purcia (Administrative Coordinator), Siva Ramji (Finance Manager), Jawad Ullah Hussaini (PRO)

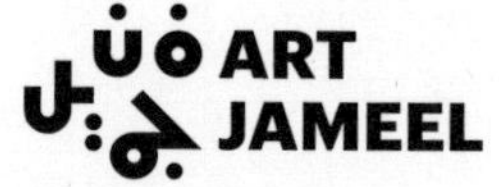

GOVETT-BREWSTER ART GALLERY | LEN LYE CENTRE

The Govett-Brewster Art Gallery | Len Lye Centre in Ngāmotu New Plymouth presents programs that fire the imagination, connect people and communities, and encourage critical dialogue about the world we live in.

Govett-Brewster Art Gallery
42 Queen St
Ngāmotu New Plymouth
Aotearoa New Zealand
info@govettbrewster.com
govettbrewster.com

The Govett-Brewster Art Gallery | Len Lye Centre is principally funded by New Plymouth District Council.

LEN LYE CENTRE GOVETT-BREWSTER ART GALLERY

THE ART GALLERY OF WESTERN AUSTRALIA
Kedela wer kalyakoorl ngalak Wadjak boodjak yaak.
Today and always, we stand on the traditional land of the Whadjuk Noongar people.
AGWA is the State's premier art museum. Situated in the heart of Perth's Cultural Centre, the Gallery houses the State Art Collection with works by renowned local and international artists from the 1800's to today.

The Art Gallery of Western Australia
Perth Cultural Centre
Boorloo/Perth
Australia
artgallery.wa.gov.au

DIRECTOR: Colin Walker
LEAD CREATIVE, SIMON LEE FOUNDATION INSTITUTE OF CONTEMPORARY ASIAN ART: Rachel Ciesla
REGISTRAR: Aston Gibbs
EXHIBITIONS MANAGER: Natalie Hewlett
EXHIBITIONS DISPLAY COORDINATOR: Ben Green
EXHIBITION DESIGNERS: Dani Lye and Todd Harrison
PUBLICATIONS MANAGER: Richelle Singh

AGWA acknowledges the support of our principal partner Wesfarmers Arts, The Art Gallery of Western Australia Foundation, Simon Lee Foundation and Singapore Airlines.

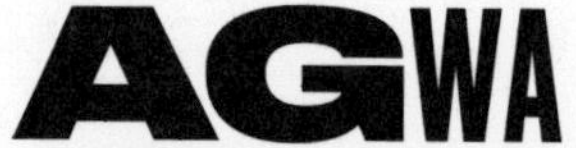

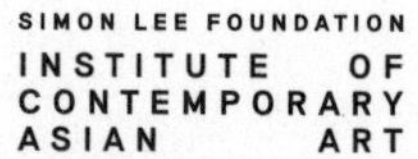

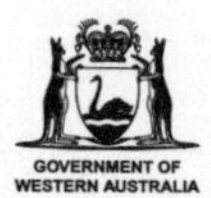

The research on Trần Lương's practice was initiated through the Trans-Southeast Asia Triennial exhibition *Repetition as a Gesture Towards Deep Listening*, as part of the *Trans Southeast Asia Art Research Forum Series* (6050520703) of Guangzhou Academy of Fine Arts.

ART MUSEUM OF GUANGZHOU ACADEMY OF FINE ARTS

GAFA Art Museum serves as a window into the Guangzhou Academy of Fine Arts (GAFA) and a stronghold for its internal and external academic exchanges. It is a professional art research institute with high academic rigour and is an integral part of the national system of public cultural services.

Art Museum of Guangzhou Academy of Fine Arts
168 Waihuanxi Road, Higher Education Mega Center
Panyu District, Guangzhou
Guangdong, China
https://artmuseum.gzarts.edu.cn/

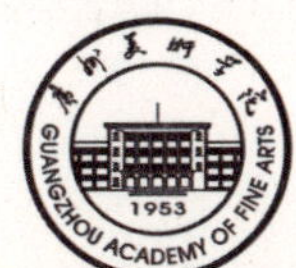

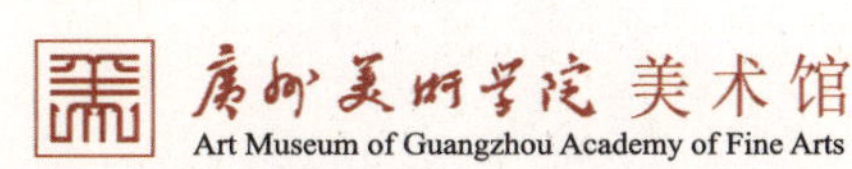

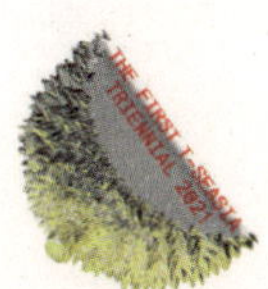

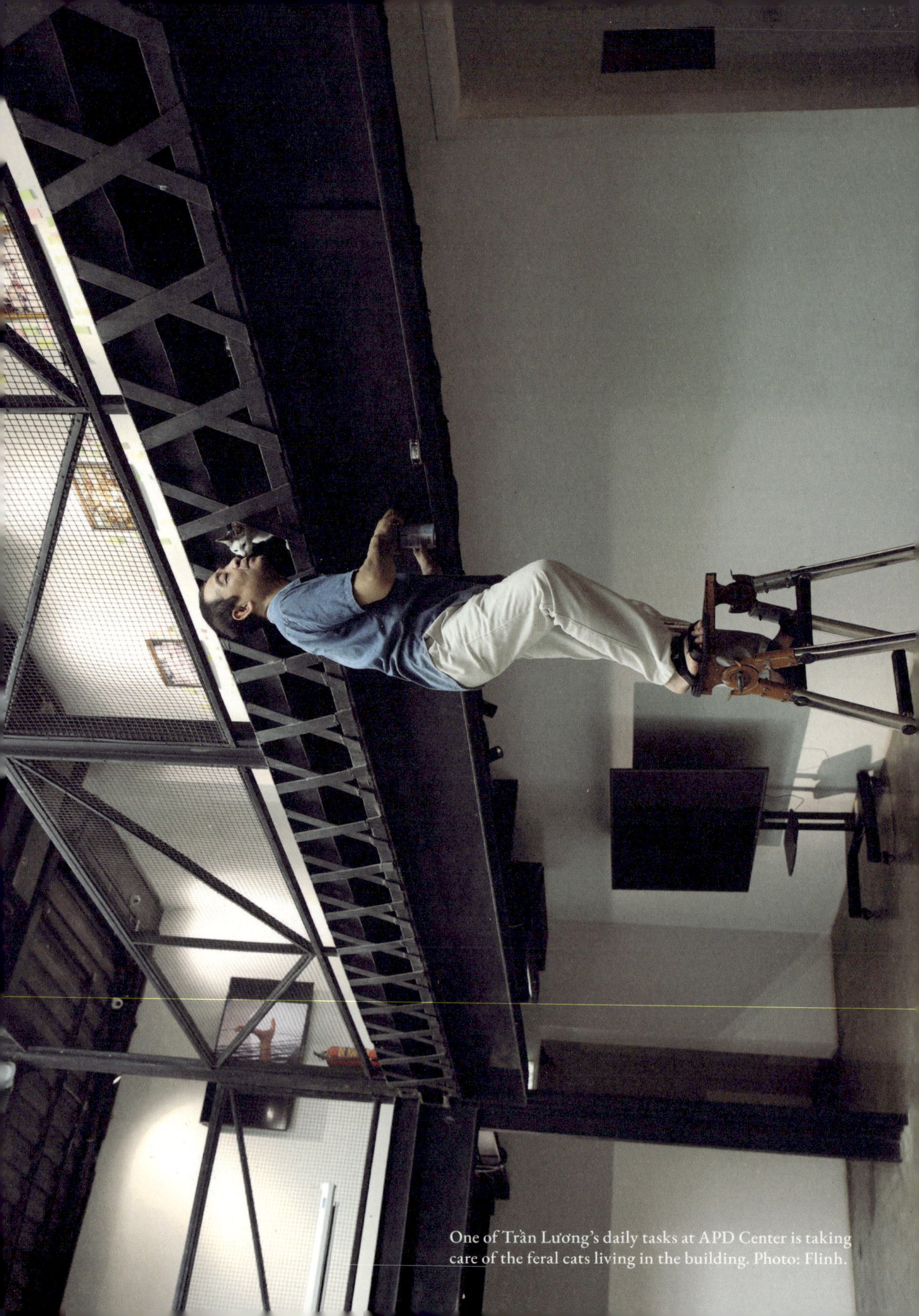

One of Trần Lương's daily tasks at APD Center is taking care of the feral cats living in the building. Photo: Flinh.